Connop Thirlwall

Remains Literary and Theological of Connop Thirlwall,

Late Lord Bishop of St. David's

Connop Thirlwall

Remains Literary and Theological of Connop Thirlwall,
Late Lord Bishop of St. David's

ISBN/EAN: 9783337018528

Printed in Europe, USA, Canada, Australia, Japan

Cover: Foto ©Lupo / pixelio.de

More available books at **www.hansebooks.com**

REMAINS
LITERARY AND THEOLOGICAL
OF
CONNOP THIRLWALL

LATE LORD BISHOP OF ST. DAVID'S

EDITED
By J. J. STEWART PEROWNE, D.D.

HONORARY CHAPLAIN TO THE QUEEN; CANON OF LLANDAFF; AND HULSEAN
PROFESSOR OF DIVINITY, CAMBRIDGE

VOL. II.—CHARGES
DELIVERED BETWEEN THE YEARS 1863 AND 1872

LONDON
DALDY, ISBISTER & CO.
56, LUDGATE HILL
1877

TABLE OF CONTENTS.

VOL. II.

                                                                               PAGE

EIGHTH CHARGE, 1863. ESSAYS AND REVIEWS.—WRITINGS OF THE BISHOP OF NATAL 1

NINTH CHARGE, 1866. STATE OF THE DIOCESE.—NATIONAL EDUCATION, THE REVISED CODE.—DIOCESAN SYNODS.—FINAL COURT OF APPEAL.—RITUALISM 91

TENTH CHARGE, 1869. DISESTABLISHMENT OF THE IRISH CHURCH.—RITUALISM.—THE EUCHARISTIC CONTROVERSY.—THE VATICAN COUNCIL . . 203

ELEVENTH CHARGE, 1872. THE VATICAN COUNCIL.—DISSENSIONS IN THE CHURCH OF ENGLAND.—THE ATHANASIAN CREED.—THE EDUCATION ACT OF 1870 290

VIII.

A CHARGE

DELIVERED OCTOBER, 1863.

ESSAYS AND REVIEWS.—WRITINGS OF THE BISHOP OF NATAL.

MY REVEREND BRETHREN,

In what might once be considered as ordinary times, passing events, of local or temporary interest, afforded but rare and scanty topics for a Bishop's charge: and it might often happen that it was entirely occupied with some general observations on the duties of the clergy, and with exhortations, which might be always edifying, but not more so at one time or place than another. The condition of the Church on the whole was apparently stationary; its mo\ ent, if any, too slow to be perceived by contemporary ҏ tors. It was much if the universal stillness w҃ w anɑ . ⋯ broken by an Act of Parliament, affecting soɪ. clesiɑ nterest, which might need explanation, or invite discussion, or by some abuse hurtful to the Church which appeared to call for the interposition of the Legislature. Very different has been the state of things since I was charged with the administration of this diocese. During the whole of this period the Church has been more or less threatened from without, and agitated within. I need hardly remind you of the controversies which arose in the last generation, and have been carried on uninterruptedly to the present day, with regard to the Sacraments, and the whole range of theological questions connected with them. The gravity and practical importance of these disputes may be estimated, not only from the extent of the literature which has grown out of them, or from the heat with which opposite views have been maintained, but, partly, from the number of secessions from the Church, which have taken place in opposite directions, of persons who carried their views on either side to an extreme inconsistent with her formularies, and partly from the various efforts which have been made to obtain such a modification of those formularies, as may enable such of her ministers as are dissatisfied with them to feel themselves more at their ease within her pale.

Fitness of the occasion for treating prominent questions. It always seemed to me that such questions claimed a prominent, indeed the foremost, place among those which might be fitly treated on such an occasion as the solemn periodical meeting between a Bishop and his clergy; and that a survey of them taken from the point of view best suited to the character of the episcopal office, and in a spirit befitting the occasion, might serve a practical purpose; one, perhaps, more important than any which only concerns the temporal prospects of the Church. If, as was pretty sure to be the case, the result of a calm examination, conducted with a single eye to truth and charity, was to show that the theological differences which parted the contending schools had been greatly exaggerated by party zeal, and that there was ample room for both within the common pale, it might tend to allay some bitter feelings, to revive mutual confidence and good will, and to combine energies which would have wasted themselves in barren strife, for united efforts in the cause of Christ. And this is an object which, however far beyond the power of any one man to attain, is certainly worthy of all the pains that can be spent upon it.

Questions affecting the Church externally. Of late years the position of the Church, as an institution connected with the State, has undergone a change which is certainly of no light significance, though its ultimate consequences lie beyond the range of our view. The aggression of the party which aims at dissolving that connexion has been more systematically organized, and carried on with more concert and vigour than in former times. A society has been formed for the purpose of urging and guiding its movements, on every point where the Church seems most open to attack. By way of preparation for greater things, this society has been striving more especially to effect the abolition of church-rates, and in the mean while, as far as possible, to prevent them from being levied, even where they have been willingly granted; and to deprive the Church of her hold even on schools endowed by members of her own communion, and most clearly designed by them to enjoy the benefit of her teaching. In these and other enterprises directed to the same object, the society has achieved but a very moderate degree of success, and has rather thwarted its own aims by a premature disclosure of its ulterior views. But this aggressive organization has called forth a counteractive movement of defence on the part of the Church, set on foot and conducted chiefly by laymen, which has already exerted a very wholesome influence, and promises to serve, not only for the protection of her legitimate interests, but for the extension and increased efficiency of her work.

But while on this side, though there are motives enough for constant watchfulness and redoubled activity, there has been no ground for alarm, it has befallen us to witness the Internally. upgrowth of questions within the Church, not only of a different kind, but of a different order, from those to which I was just now pointing, questions stretching very far toward the foundations of the Christian faith. How widely they are parted from those which had previously occupied the minds of churchmen may be gathered from several signs. While the interest roused by the previous controversies was confined to a comparatively narrow circle, and the points on which they turned were regarded by the bulk even of our own people rather as matters of ecclesiastical learning than of common practical concern,—except when they happened to be forced on public attention by some ill-judged introduction of ritual innovations,—the recently promulged opinions have found their way among all classes of the community, and have been felt by all to involve very grave consequences; and, within the circle in which the earlier controversies were waged, the contending parties have suspended the old conflict to unite their forces against a movement which seems to threaten all that each holds most dear. Nor can any of those who stand outside the Church, and are even most hostile to many of her distinguishing doctrines and institutions, if they only hold her fundamental creed, look on this new struggle as unconcerned spectators. They are aware that they are no less interested in the issue.

<small>Inquiry into the cause of the neology of the day.</small> When men have been startled by a new phenomenon, it is natural that they should inquire after its cause, and so attempts have not been wanting to trace the neology of our day to its source. Nor is this to be regarded as a question which can serve only to satisfy a vain curiosity. It has its practical use. For the nature of a thing can hardly be fully understood without some insight into its origin; and there can be no right judgment on its quality which is not grounded on a clear view of its nature. But the subject opens large room for conjectures, which it is equally hard to prove and to refute. One readily presented itself with much show of likelihood. It was natural to suppose that there was some connexion between the present and the immediate past; between the new opinions and the two great parties which had been so long striving for ascendancy in the Church. And to some it appeared that the newly raised sceptical spirit was no more than the inevitable effect of a recoil which was sure to come, sooner or later, from the excess to which one of them had pushed its distinguishing tenets. When the claims of human authority have been advanced beyond their due limits, it would not be surprising that they should provoke a reaction, which is carried over bounds on the opposite side. This explanation might not be altogether groundless, and yet quite inadequate; and there may be as good reason for ascribing the result to a sequence rather than to a reaction, and for regarding the New as the offspring of the Old. For where the witness, either of the Church or of the individual consciousness, has been allowed practically to supersede that of Holy Writ, and has been treated as the supreme authority, the value of the historical record must more or

less sink in comparison with both, and so may easily come to be positively disparaged. We know, in fact, that such was the effect of the opposite exaggerations of the Church of Rome on the one hand, and of the Reformation movement on the other. The Church of the Papacy has uniformly either forbidden or discouraged the reading of Scripture, as not only needless and useless, but dangerous for the mass of the laity. The place which she assigns to the Bible is subordinate to the living oracle of her visible Head. In her view the written Word borrows its whole title to belief from her sanction; and she would eagerly endorse the sentiment which has lately been expressed by a Bishop of our Church, that "if the whole Bible was removed," the Christian faith would still stand fast; that is, on that Rock on which she conceives it to have been founded by the Lord Himself, and which she sees in the succession of His earthly Vicegerents. Among the sects which sprang out of the Reformation, and marred and dishonoured it by their narrow and fierce fanaticism, there were several which, both in theory and practice, adopted the same sentiment, only in a widely different sense, subordinating the Record of Revelation to the manifestation of the light which shines in every man's breast, and bidding each seek truth from the dictates of his own inward oracle. Such a view is evidently no less adverse to the supremacy of Scripture than to the authority of the Church.

But yet, indisputable and worthy of note as is this ideal affinity between modes of thinking, which outwardly have so little in common, it would be unsafe to treat it as sufficient proof of a historical connexion; and I am unable to find any other. I am not aware of any more special grounds of a personal kind, which warrant such a supposition; and I do not believe that any discovery that could be made in this direction would repay the trouble of the search. The real state of the case seems to be disclosed plainly enough by the writings which have suggested the question. They exhibit opinions which had been long "Essays and floating in the public mind; some as old as the earliest Reviews." attacks on the Christian faith, revived in the last century by our own deistical writers, since then reproduced in various forms; in a few points perhaps of foreign origin, but on the whole of native growth. No one who has reflected on the character and tendencies of modern European society, especially of our own, can be at any loss to account for the fact that such opinions should find easy, ready, even eager acceptance among many in our day. It is a natural consequence of the increased stimulus which has been given to physical studies, not only by the progress of discovery, and the craving for knowledge thus continually sharpened by that which feeds it, but by the wants and desires of our animal nature, to which it ministers, and which in our fast-growing population are constantly multiplying their demands with more clamorous importunity. I am only pointing to an unquestionable fact, without the remotest intention of disparaging the value and dignity of physical science, or the slightest wish that it should be less actively cultivated, or that its well-ascertained results should be less widely diffused, least of all in the belief that they are or can be in themselves adverse to religious truth; they may, nevertheless, by the excitement of too absorbing an interest, tend to create a disposition of mind generally unfavourable to its influence.*

* Some remarkable words connected with this subject occur in a letter of Prince Metternich to A. v. Humboldt, which is printed in Humboldt's "Briefe an Varnhagen von Ense," p. 219 : "Le faux mène au faux, comme le vrai conduit au vrai. Aussi longtemps que l'esprit s'est maintenu dans le faux, dans la sphère la plus élevée que l'esprit de l'homme puisse atteindre, les conséquences de ce triste état ont dû réagir dans toutes les directions morales, intellectuelles, et sociales, et opposer à leur développement dans la droite voie, un obstacle insurmontable. *La bonne nouvelle* une fois annoncée, la position a dû changer. Ce n'est pas en *divinisant les effets*, que ceux-ci ont pu être suivis dans les voies de la vérité ; leur recherche est restée circonscrite dans la spéculation abstraite des philosophes et dans la verve des poètes. *La cause* une fois mise à couvert, les cœurs se sont mis en repos et les esprits se sont ouverts. Ceux-ci sont longtemps encore restés enveloppés dans les brouillards de la sceptique païenne, quand enfin la philosophie scolastique a été débordée par la science expérimentale. Trouvez-vous mon raisonnement juste? Si vous le trouvez, je ne suis pas en doute que vous ne partagiez ma crainte, que les progrès scientifiques véritables courent le risque d'être arrêtés par des esprits trop ambitieux, qui veulent remonter des effets à la cause, et qui trouvant la route coupée par les limites infranchissables que Dieu a posées à l'intelligence humaine, ne pouvant avancer, se replient sur eux-mêmes et retournent à la stupidité du paganisme en cherchant la cause dans les effets." The italics are Metternich's. Humboldt describes it as "einen sehr merkwürdigen Brief," "der halb theologisch endigt, voll Geist und Schwung der Rede, mit ein wenig Furcht

One thing is certain. It was not either the novelty of the opinions themselves, or the originality of the arguments by which they were maintained, that attracted public attention to the writings of which I am about to speak. The really new feature in the aspect which they were presented, was the character of the authors. It was just because the opinions were for the most part by no means new, but familiar to persons conversant with such subjects in the works of writers who, as holding such opinions, had deemed themselves, and been regarded by others, as hostile to Christianity, that they produced so startling an effect when they were announced by ministers of Christ. For the writers did not belong to a religious body which, while claiming the name of Christian, repudiates all theological formularies, and imposes no restriction on its ministers, unless it be that they must not preach any very positive doctrine. They were ministers of a Church which aims at a definite teaching, and exacts conformity to that teaching from those whom she admits into her ministry. Nor were they among the obscure members of their order, whose personal character could add no weight to their opinions. They were all men of literary eminence, some filling very important places in the rearing of the rising generation. And if it might be supposed that scholastic pursuits, however favourable to deep research and comprehensive views, might deaden their sympathy with the feelings and needs of ordinary Christians, and might thus lead them to overlook some very important elements even of their own learned speculations, yet this could only be the case with some. There were others of the number who were engaged in pastoral duties, which brought them into daily contact with the practical problems of the Christian life. Such a combination of talents and opportunities might have been expected to yield two great advantages. On the one hand, a very clear consciousness, not only of the precise import of their statements, but of the perhaps remote, yet logically inevitable consequences which flow from

Public attention attracted, not by the writings, but by the character of their authors.

---

vor dem Pantheismus." More exactly, it was a relapse into Paganism which Metternich thought he saw reason to apprehend, from a certain direction of scientific pursuits.

them, so that, when such consequences were not designed, the utmost care should be taken to guard the premises from the appearance of involving them. And on the other hand, it was to have been hoped that there would have been shown, in the handling of religious subjects, however free, a certain tenderness for beliefs which, in the minds of common Christians, are interwined with the holiest feelings of their hearts, and that, if it was necessary for the object in view to make a separation between them, it should be done so as to inflict the smallest possible amount of pain. One thing at least might have been thought to have been effectually secured, that no one in whom the characters of the academic teacher and the pastor of souls happened to meet, would, when treating such subjects, express himself so that an educated layman, called upon to give the closest attention to his words, should find it a difficult task to ascertain their meaning, and should be forced to " doubt whether, if the author had studied to express his sentiments with ambiguity, he could have been more successful:"* but above all, that no one, occupying that twofold position, would so far forget what was due to both, as to indulge in a tone of scornful bitterness against those of his brethren in the ministry who held a belief common to the vast majority of their own flocks, as well as of all Christians throughout the world, and in all ages of the Church.†

Form and conditions of publication. But even if these expectations had been fulfilled, there would have remained the very great fact, that opinions generally thought contradictory to the principles of the Christian faith, were proclaimed in a work proceeding from eminent divines, ministers of the Church of England. Here, however, we cannot avoid noticing the peculiar form of the

---

* Dr. Lushington's Judgment in the case of the Bishop of Salisbury *v.* Williams, p. 18.

† On this point the judgment of the Edinburgh Reviewer (No. CCXXX., p. 479) will not be suspected of partiality: "The flippant and contemptuous tone of the reviewer often amounts to a direct breach of the compact with which the volume opens, that the subjects therein touched should be handled 'in a becoming spirit.' Anything more 'unbecoming' than some of Dr. Williams's remarks we never have read in writings professing to be written seriously."

publication, as a collection of the independent contributions of different authors, writing wholly without concert with one another. It would indeed be unjust and absurd to represent them as having consciously co-operated with one another for any definite object, or as in any way antecedently pledged to one another's views; and the most entire credit was due to them, when they disclaimed such a joint responsibility and concert.* But at least this disclaimer, whether it was from the hand of one of their number, or from one who was authorised to speak in their name, must be considered as common to all. And what it clearly implied was, that, however each might reserve his private judgment as to any doctrine advanced by any of the rest, there was nothing in the whole that appeared to any of them inconsistent with that which, as clergymen of the Church of England, they were bound to maintain.† If the fact had been otherwise, there would have been a breach of "compact," of which those who dissented would have had a right to complain. Not only was no such complaint heard at the proper time, immediately after the publication, when it could not have been liable to misconstruction, but as far as silence was broken by any of them, it was in language signifying a more than contented acquiescence in every part of the whole teaching. And this was really the only point with which the Church had any concern. If the opinions, however questionable, did not go beyond the latitude allowed by her to her ministers, then their truth or falsehood was of little

<small>How far the Church was implicated.</small>

---

* This, however, may depend on the precise meaning of the word "concert." Mr. Kennard, who, writing the history of the book as a warm admirer and thorough-going advocate, is likely to have been well informed, states ("Essays and Reviews, their Origin, History, &c.," p. 26): "They determined to vindicate for the clergy practically the right of treating openly, in language addressed to the people generally, questions concerning prophecy, miracles, &c. They associated at the same time a layman with them in the undertaking." It is so far from unusual to speak of persons who are "associated in an undertaking" as acting in "concert," that if, while conscious of the "association," they were to deny the "concert," they would hardly be thought to be making a perfectly fair use of language. But whether such a concert may be properly termed a "conspiracy" must depend on the nature of the object.

† Here the authority of the Edinburgh Reviewer cannot be disputed: "Every one of them by lending his name to the book does beyond doubt assert that, however much he may differ from the views contained in any other Essay than his own, he yet vindicates the lawfulness of holding those views within the English Church." P. 489.

importance, except as it might affect the reputation of the authors. But the question, whether these opinions were or were not consistent with her doctrines, was one on which depended something far more important than the reputation of any individual, however eminent in station, learning, and ability; that is, the character and position of the Church itself, as a branch of the universal Church of Christ. This was a question which interested every one of her members, the more deeply in proportion to the breadth of the doctrines propounded, and the closeness of their connexion with the foundations of the Christian faith. And to this extent it does appear to me that each of the clerical contributors did incur a responsibility, which he could not shift from himself, for opinions which he did not expressly disavow.

<small>General unanimity among the writers.</small> There was yet another point of view in which, notwithstanding the divided authorship, the book might be not improperly treated as if it had been the production of a single mind. Though consisting of a number of distinct essays on various subjects, it might exhibit a close affinity of thought and feeling, and strong indications of general unanimity among the writers. The different parts might appear to fit into one another, as if they had come from the same hand. There might be everywhere signs of a common drift and tendency, just as if all had been arranged with a view to one object: and a total absence, not only of any express contradiction, but of anything to suggest the suspicion of a divergency of views, among the contributors. How far it presents the appearance of such harmony, must depend on the judgment we may form of its contents.* But before I proceed to consider what appears to me most important and characteristic in them, I think it may not be useless to make a few remarks on the public history of the book. Its private history will probably long remain a secret confined to a few.

<small>Public history of the book.</small> It was not until the work had passed through several editions, and had attained a celebrity which far exceeded

---

* If indeed Mr. Kennard's statement, cited in a previous note, is well founded, there would be no need of an appeal to internal evidence on this head.

the hopes of the authors, and perhaps even the wishes of some among them, and not until it had experienced a great amount of adverse criticism, which called forth neither defence nor explanation, that the attention of the episcopate was formally drawn to it by a memorial signed by a large body of the clergy. This step has been treated as a pitiable mistake on the part of the memorialists. But the conduct of the Bishops, who concurred in a general censure of the work, was visited with still severer condemnation. They were charged with abusing their position, to encourage a foolish and groundless outcry, and aggravate a senseless panic, and with attempting to stifle inquiry, and to restrain the rightful freedom of the clergy.* It was thought by some that they were not at liberty to express an opinion on the work, unless they at the same time entered into a discussion of its contents, and distinguished the various degrees in which their censure applied to the several contributors.† To some it appeared deplorable that they should censure the opinions of others, without at the same time avowing their own continued adherence to the doctrines of the Church.‡ But perhaps no complaint was more popular and oftener repeated, than that they had not refuted before they condemned.

Action of the Episcopate condemned.

It is evident that the justice of all these complaints must depend on the character of the work, and that each contains a tacit assumption which may be well or ill founded. It is on this account only that I now advert to them. If the questions raised in the work were of trifling moment, though through some unfortunate accident they had produced much temporary excitement, then it would have been the duty of the chief pastors of the Church to exert their influence for the purpose of allaying that excitement, and to enlighten those who had been blindly agitated by an imaginary danger. If again the opinions expressed in the work kept within the latitude which might be rightfully claimed by ministers of our Church, then,

Defence of that action.

---

* Edinburgh Review u. s. and Mr. Kennard *passim*.
† Edinburgh Review, p. 469.
‡ Tracts for Priests and people. "Religio Laici," p. 9.

however they might be opposed to those both of a great majority of the clergy, and of the whole episcopate, it would have been unfair to condemn them as repugnant to the doctrines of the Church, or inconsistent with the obligations of her ministers. But if such a repugnance did exist, then to require that, before any censure was pronounced, the opinions condemned should be disproved, would clearly involve consequences which can hardly have been generally contemplated by those who called for a previous refutation. By *refutation* they must have meant something more than an argument which, however strong in the judgment of the party which employs it, leaves the opponent unconvinced: and, if he is to be the judge of its cogency, it would follow that any minister of the Church may deny every one of her doctrines, and yet be allowed to remain in her ministry until he admits his error. It seems indeed as if there were persons who saw no absurdity in this extent of licence, or would only restrict it in the actual performance of sacred functions. But unless this be allowed, it is evident that in the case we are now considering, the question whether the doctrine propounded is true or false, though undoubtedly first in importance, is not that which has to be first discussed with a view to any practical result. For in general such a discussion would be only a renewal of an old and endless controversy. In the order of time the first question must be, whether the doctrine is in harmony with the teaching of the Church. This, which is the point of immediately practical concern, is also that which may in general be most easily ascertained.

Complaints against the Bishops' censure. This was the sum and substance of the censure pronounced on the book. It was a declaration that, in the opinion of the Bishops, its contents *were* repugnant to the doctrine of the Church. It has been made matter of complaint that this censure was expressed in terms which were likely to inflict needless pain on the authors; and it has been invidiously described as demanding the removal of five of the number from their positions in the Church.* It was even thought that, if the

* Edinburgh Review u. s., p. 469. Farther on, in the warmth of his peroration.

work had been less severely condemned, some of them might have felt themselves at liberty to declare their dissent from the extreme opinions avowed by others; but that, after so many voices had been raised against them, especially from the high places of the Church, a sense of honour prevented them from entering into any explanations, that might indicate a disapproval of any portion of the book. I have already pointed out, that there was an earlier occasion, when this might have been done without any risk of misconstruction. And highly as we may respect such a point of honour, we may doubt whether in this case it was consistent with a higher law of duty, and the dictates of Christian charity; and whether the more sacred obligation was that which they owed to a few persons with whom they had become accidentally associated in a literary undertaking, or that under which they lay toward the great body of their brethren and the Church at large. But as to the language of the censure, whatever pains might have been taken to soften it, it could not without dissimulation have left any uncertainty on the main point: that clergymen had published doctrines opposed to those of their Church, and this not on any nice and doubtful questions, in which much subtlety was needed to discern the line which separates orthodoxy from error,* but on such as lay at the root of all revealed religion.

the Reviewer does not scruple to charge the Bishops with the "design of terrifying or driving out of the Church those whom they themselves confess to be among its chief ornaments."

* The main drift of the apology in the Edinburgh Review is to show that the public had been entirely mistaken in its notion of the work, and that, with a possible immaterial exception or two, it had only freely handled questions on which a great latitude of opinion had always been allowed, and exercised by many eminent divines of our Church. This afforded the Reviewer the additional advantage of enabling him, while defending his friends, to retaliate on some of those who had joined in the censure, as having "published opinions exactly coinciding with those which they condemned;" and as thus aggravating the offence of an unjust persecution by a shameful inconsistency. The justice of this charge depended on the assumption, that the censure which they had pronounced on the book was levelled at those opinions. This however was a mere surmise, which would have been purely arbitrary, even if it had happened not to be, as it was, certainly unfounded; and it is not easy to reconcile it with the Reviewer's own complaint, that the censure "abstained from all distinct specifications of offence." He himself owns that, according to the sense in which it has been almost universally understood, one of the Essays appears to him

It is worthy of note, that the call for refutation was raised by those who also most strongly deprecated any resort to judicial proceedings against the persons who were charged with unsound doctrine. In this I think they were quite consistent. If a minister of the Church has a moral right, while he continues to exercise his ministry, to impugn her most fundamental doctrines, until he has been convinced of their truth, it would be unjust to invoke the aid of the law to convict him of that which would then be a mere technical offence. But it seems to me not quite so consistent, that the persons who called for refutation, should also have condemned the proceedings which were instituted in Convocation for the purpose of determining the theological character of the book. But those who were most strongly convinced that this character was essentially at variance with the fundamental teaching of the Church, might be most inclined to doubt whether that question could be fairly tried in a Court of Justice. And experience has shown how ill the forms of penal judicature are adapted to that end, and this just on account of what constitutes their highest excellence. In a criminal prosecution, it is the duty of the judge to require the most rigorous proof of the charge: to interpret ambiguous language in the sense most favourable to the writer: to refuse to listen to any accusation of merely constructive

<small>Refutation demanded by those most adverse to judicial proceedings.</small>

---

to have transcended the limits of devout belief." He does not indeed say, but much less does he deny, that what transcends those limits must also overstep the range of legitimate freedom within the pale of the English Church. Yet, on his own construction of the joint disclaimer, all the other Essayists meant to " vindicate the lawfulness of holding those views within the English Church;" or at least have contentedly allowed the world to believe that they do so. The other admitted exceptions are represented as trifling, because contained in "a few words." Yet four monosyllables have sufficed for an important proposition, which it would be difficult to bring within the limits of devout belief (Ps. liii. 1). In substance, the Reviewer perfectly agrees with the " Episcopal Manifesto," which he brands as " the counterpart of the Papal excommunication levelled against Italian freedom." The chief difference is, that the admissions of an advocate are the most conclusive evidence, and the censure of a friend the most likely to be fully deserved, though as mild in form as the nature of the case will permit.

It is only a noble and generous spirit that will ever make too great a sacrifice to friendship; yet that is too great which is made at the cost of justice. A moralist who enjoyed a high reputation even before he was thought to be inspired, laid down the rule: *nulla est excusatio peccati, si amici causa peccareris.*

heresy: to shut his eyes to the spirit and tendency of a work, however apparent, unless they are embodied in some distinct and tangible proposition. I can never lament that rules based on the first principles of right should have been strictly observed, though the effect might seem in some instances a failure of substantial justice. I cannot regard it as an unmitigated evil, that the decision of questions involving abstruse points of Divinity, should be committed to a layman, with no guide but his natural good sense for the interpretation of language, the full import and bearing of which could be correctly appreciated by none but an expert theologian. When civil rights are at stake, there can hardly be too great a jealousy of professional bias or learned refinements. It may happen that one man suffers a severe penalty through his incapacity clearly to express a right meaning, while another escapes through the studied ambiguity with which he insinuates a wrong one. The former may be the greater evil of the two; but neither could lead me to desire a change by which the trial of a criminal prosecution for matters of religious opinion, should be taken out of lay hands.

Happily, just on this account, the character of the Church as a religious communion can never be compromised by such a decision, and it is only through a vulgar error, or a disingenuous polemical artifice, that it can be treated as having that effect. No judgment pronounced The character of the Church cannot be compromised by judicial decisions. under such circumstances can afford a measure of the quality of a theological work, so as either to preclude the right, or to dispense with the need of examining it from a different point of view for the purpose of estimating its orthodoxy. The distinction between a judgment pronounced on a work in its purely theological aspect, and one delivered by a judge before whom the author is prosecuted for heresy, may appear somewhat subtle and difficult to grasp. But unless it be admitted, and in the sense, that the same person might consistently, when exercising the functions of a Judge, acquit that which he had condemned as a Divine, we should be driven to a conclusion revolting to common sense. For it would follow that, on the appearance of a work in which a clergyman broached unsound doctrine which might expose him to legal penalties, a Bishop, who lies under a special obligation to guard the purity of the Church's doctrine, would be the one person in his diocese who would have no right, even when consulted by those who are entitled to his advice and guidance, to express an unfavourable opinion of the work, because he might afterwards be called upon to sit in judgment on the author.

Writings of laymen and clergymen on miracles productive of different effects.

We may venture to believe that no very strong sensation would have been excited in the public mind by a layman who in our day should have revived the speculations of Spinoza and Hume on the absolute impossibility, or the incredibility of miracles. They would have been felt to belong to a metaphysical system, so wholly foreign to the principles of the Church, as to render it needless for Churchmen to protest against it, and quite allowable for them to decline a controversy where the disputants had scarcely any common ground to stand on. But just for this reason the reproduction of these opinions in the work of a clergyman, could hardly fail to excite general surprise; and it is only a little less surprising that the fact should appear to any one so natural, and so manifestly consistent with the author's profession, as to make it absurd to attach any importance to it, and wrong to treat it as, with respect to his ecclesiastical position, worthy of censure. When we think for a moment of the Evangelical History, and of the Creeds, to say nothing of the Liturgy, we rather find it difficult to argue the incongruity of such views with the teaching of our Church, for the opposite reason: because the proving of a point so evident, would be a waste of words. And this difficulty is increased when we find that the writer, in whose view the study of the "evidences of Christianity" must lead every duly cultivated mind to reject the belief in supernatural interposition, appears altogether to ignore the existence of any but secondary, or—as they are sometimes termed by an unfair assumption,—natural causes in the world. He admits indeed that the "broader views of physical truth, and universal order in nature," which are now increasingly prevalent, "point to the acknowledgment of an overruling and all-pervading supreme intelligence."* But this language would at least as aptly express the fundamental doctrine of Spinoza, as that of any theist; especially when coupled with the statements, that "creation is only another name for our ignorance of the means of production," † and that "the Divine Omnipotence is entirely an inference from the language of the Bible:"‡ and the argument employed to prove the impossibility of miraculous interposition moves wholly within the circle of a purely materialistic philosophy. It would however be unfair to overlook, that the author sometimes expresses himself as if his standing-place was still in some sense Christian ground, and as if in his own judgment he was only doing his best to carry out the common object of the Volume, by rescuing the subject which he handles from the danger of "suffering by the repetition of conventional language, and by traditional methods of treatment." He distinguishes between the provinces of reason or science and of faith, as if both had a real existence, though governed by different laws, and might flourish peacefully side by side, if only their respective limits had not been confounded by ill-judged attempts at mutual encroachment. It may thus have appeared to him, that he was filling the part of a peacemaker, and laying down the conditions of a lasting reconciliation, between parties which had been separated through an unhappy misunderstanding. We would fain believe that such was the aim with which he undertook his last work, and may hope that he himself derived comfort from the faith which he still recognized as surviving the evidences which it was the object of his argument to overthrow.

But our wishes and hopes cannot alter the nature of things, and charity does not require or even permit us to shut our eyes to the truth. The distinction between the dominion of physical science and of faith, which qualifies the merely negative and destructive character of the general conclusion, is indeed a question of the gravest moment, and of an interest quite independent of any temporary controversy. If it be true that faith may find all that she needs, to satisfy her

<small>Dominion of physical science distinct from that of faith.</small>

* P. 126. † P. 139. ‡ P. 113.

highest aspirations, within her own sphere, and that she is there secure and inaccessible to the inroads of physical science, which neither seeks nor is able to invade her sanctuary, why should she not be content with the undisturbed enjoyment of her proper and undisputed domain? That is the position on which the author takes his stand, and in which he may have won the sympathy of many who totally dissent from the negative side of his doctrine. That there is such a life of faith, conversant with purely spiritual truths, abstracted from all conditions of time and sense, could not be denied without rejecting the experience of the holiest men in all ages. We must go farther and say, that it is only with such truths that faith is ever properly conversant. Historical facts are the object of a historical belief, which Scripture itself teaches us to distinguish from that faith which it describes as the indispensable condition of salvation.* I am sure that there is no error against which you, my Reverend Brethren, would more earnestly warn your hearers, than the confounding of this distinction. And certainly such a faith has no injury to dread from the progress of physical science. The region in which it lives and moves is wholly spiritual and supramundane: one in which a science, which deals only with the laws of matter, can find no footing, and therefore must needs leave it in peace.

The condition on which faith is to be unmolested. But then we must consider what is the price which, on the author's terms, has to be paid for this security; the condition on which faith is permitted to remain thus unmolested. It is that she shall not attempt to cross the border of her own province, and claim a standing-ground in the world of nature; in other words, that she shall hold no doctrine which involves the supposition of a supernatural interruption in the predetermined sequence of physical phenomena. She must not only forego, but renounce the belief in any such event. "Miraculous narratives" may "become invested with the character of articles of faith;" but it is on condition that they be "accepted," not as records of historical facts, but "in a less positive and certain light, or perhaps as involving more or less of the parabolic or mythic

---

* James ii. 19.

character."* This restriction excludes, not only outward supernatural events, but also every fact of inward experience which cannot be explained, on psychological grounds, as a phase of a merely human development. A direct communication of Divine grace would be as much a breach of continuity in the order of causation as any visible miracle, and might as well be described as only "another name for our ignorance of the mode of production." It is indeed "confessed" "that, beyond the domain of physical causation and the possible conceptions of intellect or knowledge, there lies open the boundless region of spiritual things which is the sole dominion of faith."† But this description seems to show that there are two insurmountable obstacles to any communication between this region and the material universe in which we live. The things which belong to this spiritual region "lie beyond the possible conceptions of intellect or knowledge," and even if they could be grasped by our faculties in our present state of being, as they are extrinsic to the domain of physical causation, there is no mode by which they could be conveyed to our minds, but a supernatural intervention, which is rejected by "intellect and philosophy," as "inconsistent with the universal order and indissoluble unity of physical causes." It would be at once a miraculous enlargement of human capacity, and the introduction of a new element into the series of historical events, not linked by a natural dependence with those which preceded it. We readily admit, or rather, as Christians, we earnestly maintain the possibility of a direct communication between the Father of spirits and the soul of man. But whatever is so imparted to man is an object, not of simple faith, but of knowledge; and since the recipient of such a communication is not a disembodied spirit, but one dwelling in a human frame, and so united with it, that every successive idea and emotion involves a corresponding change in the bodily organization, it is clear that a Divine inward revelation is as much a miracle, and therefore, according to the Essayist's view, as truly impossible as any related in the Bible.

And so it appears in what sense we are to understand the admis-

* P. 142. † P. 127.

sion, which is held out as a compensation for so much that is denied. The "dominion" assigned to faith may be filled with the most sublime and satisfying spiritual realities. But since for man in his present state there is no avenue through which he can receive any certain information concerning it, it must for him remain, as long as that state lasts, a region unknown and unknowable. Its realities are not such to him. To him it is either a mere void, or peopled only with phantoms, the creatures of his imagination, the reflex it may be of his earthly experience, indefinitely enlarged and beautified. It may be the object of a deep yearning, as a better country, a future home; but in no other sense can it properly be called the "dominion" of faith.

The dominion assigned to faith.

There may, however, be danger of misunderstanding in the use of such figurative expressions. And it is to be regretted that the language employed by the author in his positive statements is much less clear and precise than that of his negative propositions. His reasoning against the possibility of miracles, if indeed it consists of any thing more than naked assertions, will be more or less convincing according to the state of mind to which it is addressed; but it leaves no room for doubt as to its meaning.* On the other hand, his description of the proper province and objects of faith is so vague and ambiguous, that it is hard to believe he can himself have formed any distinct notion of the sense in which it is to be understood. "An alleged miracle can only be regarded in one of two ways: either abstractedly, as a physical event,—and therefore to be investigated by reason and physical evidence, and referred to physical causes,—or as connected with religious doctrine, regarded in a sacred light, asserted on the authority of inspiration." In the latter case, "it ceases to be capable of investigation by reason, or to own its dominion. It is accepted on religious grounds, and can appeal only to the principle and influence of faith." † "The

The writer's positive propositions more ambiguous.

---

* As this has been questioned, and the question involves some points of great importance, I have considered it in a note, which will be found at the end of the Charge.

† P. 142.

miracles are merged in the *doctrines* with which they are connected, and associated with the declarations of spiritual things, which are, as such, exempt from those criticisms to which physical statements would be necessarily amenable." * But an " alleged miracle " is not the less a physical event because connected with religious doctrine. It cannot on that account be less capable of investigation by reason. If it is "accepted on religious grounds," it is accepted *as* a physical event, and only by those who do not admit that as such it is incredible. It is not the more exempt from the criticisms of those who have adopted that principle, though it may have a stronger claim on their forbearance. So long, indeed, as we confine ourselves to abstractions, such language may not appear to involve any contradiction or absurdity. It assumes that there is no real, but only an imaginary connection, between the miracle and the doctrine; so that the doctrine may be retained, while the miracle is rejected. But the religion to which the whole argument is meant to apply, is one in which the fundamental article of faith, according to the belief of the Church of England, is itself a physical event, a historical fact, and, if true, is supernatural. The fact and the doctrine are inseparably blended together. To deny the fact is to reject the doctrine. It is indeed possible to make away with the doctrine, and in its room to substitute one which should not involve a departure from the order of nature. What that doctrine should be, would indeed have to be left to every one's private judgment. It might be some moral truth; it might be some philosophical speculation. It might be " exempt from the criticisms to which physical statements are amenable." But it would not be a mystery; it would not be a point of faith; it would have no need to be held " sacred from examination," and " shielded within the pale of the sanctuary." Making no pretension to sanctity, it would claim neither reverence nor indulgence, but would simply assert its right as a matter of private opinion.

A different question arises as to the miracles which were simply manifestations of the divine character of the Founder of our

* P. 143.

religion. They are not indeed, when considered each by itself, so intimately connected with its fundamental truths; there is no one of them, except the Resurrection, so identified with any article of faith, that if it had never been wrought, or had never been recorded, it would have made any difference in our creed. But it could only be through a strange thoughtlessness that any one could maintain, that the Christian faith would be no way affected, though all should be rejected as matters of fact, and received only as "parables or myths." When the miraculous portions of the Gospel history are expunged, there will remain only a meagre outline of our Lord's life, ending with His death. Discourses indeed, attributed to Him, will be left, full of wisdom and holiness. But of the speaker Himself, His character and work, it will be impossible, from sources so utterly corrupt as, on this supposition, those to which alone we have access, would be, to gain any distinct image. All that would be known of Him with any approach to certainty, would be, that having appeared as a teacher, and gathered disciples around Him, He had provoked the enmity of the Jewish rulers, and been put to death. All beyond this would be involved in obscurity, and would only afford occasion for doubtful conjectures. When the most original and trustworthy accounts of His life had been so disfigured by fiction, no reliance could be placed on reports contained in them, of any declarations which He had made concerning Himself.

Consequence which would follow the rejection of the miracles. But the loss of all information which would enable us to set Him before our eyes, not as a mere abstraction, but as a real living person, would be far from the most painful consequence which would flow from this rejection of all that purports to be miraculous in the history of His life. For even as fiction, it must have had some adequate cause or occasion; and it would be hard to believe, that such a mass of miraculous legends should have gathered round one who had never made any pretence to supernatural powers; and that works which He never attempted or professed to perform, should have been represented as one main part of the business of His ministry, and as that to which He constantly appealed as evidence of His divine mission.* I need not observe how dark a shade the alternative supposition must cast even on the purity of His human character, to which, nevertheless, those who would divest Him of all titles to any higher ground of reverence, are used to point, as a compensation for the divine attributes which they withhold from Him. †

But here I feel myself bound to observe,—and it is a point which in the heat of controversy we are all too apt to overlook,—that although these inferences appear to me to follow unavoidably from the author's premisses; though in my judgment he has entirely failed to reconcile his scientific theory with the elementary truths of the Christian faith; still, that which has been pointed out is no more than an inference: one which the author himself has not expressly drawn, but on the contrary has earnestly striven to avoid: one therefore with which personally he could not be fairly charged. We may not only fain hope, but reasonably believe, that many at this day who are perplexed with like intellectual difficulties, are nevertheless enabled to hold fast the foundation of a true and living faith, perhaps more firmly than some who have never undergone the like trial. However unintelligible to us may be the process by which they are enabled to combine views, which we can only regard as radically inconsistent with one another, this is no reason for denying its existence, as a fact of the individual's consciousness, which may be to him not the less satisfactory because he is unable to explain it clearly to others, or even, it may be, distinctly to understand it himself. The student of nature, who, without surrendering one particle of physical truth, or admitting any restriction on the freedom of scientific investigation, is yet able to withstand the most dangerous temptation which besets his favourite pursuits—the tendency to a mechanical philosophy, or the resting in second causes—and who, resigning himself to

<small>These inferences not absolutely antagonistic to the possession of true faith.</small>

---

* Matt. xi. 4 foll. and 20 foll. John xiv. 11. This is of course quite independent of the question as to the value of the element of power in the miracles.

† As even M. Renan has not been prevented by his admiration for his "noble initiateur," from reviving Woolston's worst outrage, and representing our Lord as abetting Lazarus and his family in a deliberate imposture.

the consciousness of his limited faculties and imperfect knowledge, clings to the centre of his spiritual being, and finds a secure anchorage in the love of his heavenly Father, as revealed in the Gospel of Jesus Christ,—such a one exhibits one of the noblest examples of Christian humility, wisdom, and self-control, that in these days it is possible to witness.

But useful as these considerations may be to guard us against rash judgments with regard to persons, they cannot alter the plain sense of words, or the character of propositions, or empty them of the inferences logically involved in them. Every one is at liberty to disown conclusions which flow unavoidably from his premisses; and we may often rejoice in this inconsistency, where we believe it to be sincere; but it can neither break the tie which knits the premisses to the conclusion, nor prevent others from perceiving that connexion, and so feeling themselves constrained either to adopt or to reject both. What must become of Christianity after its supernatural groundwork has been withdrawn from under it, I do not now inquire. But to maintain that the fundamental doctrines of the Church of England can survive that displacement, is a paradox which no ingenuity can reconcile with common sense.

Object of the writers of the Essays. It has been said,* and, as I am quite willing to believe, with justice, that "the object of the writers was not to create, but to remove difficulties in the way of the reception of the truth as it is in Jesus;" "to place Christianity beyond the reach of accidents whether of science or criticism." But the excellence of the end could not relieve them from all responsibility in the choice of means; and the whole question is whether the means adopted are such as can be reconciled with their relations to the Church. No doubt, when the supernatural origin of Christianity is abandoned, it will be effectually secured from many assaults; for as against the larger part of its adversaries there will remain nothing to defend. When that point is once conceded to them, they in their turn will be liberal enough on every other. As they do not deny the existence of the Christian religion, or of a body calling itself the Church of Christ, they will mostly be very

* By Mr. Kennard, u. s. p. 134.

tolerant of any other mode of accounting for the historical fact. They will not be averse from the theory, that it entered into the designs of Providence, as an instrument for the education of the world. Viewing it in that light, they may not even scruple to speak of it as divine; for they will admit that it has as much right to that epithet as any other event in the history of mankind. They will not begrudge the praise due to its beneficent influence on the progress of civilisation; and there are hardly any terms which some of them would find too strong to express their respect and admiration for the character, whether real or ideal, of its Founder. Rousseau and Strauss have been eloquent on this theme. But, on the other hand, they whose "difficulties" are to be "removed" by this concession, will be satisfied with nothing short of it. Of all the other questions discussed in this volume, there is not one in which they would feel the slightest interest, unless so far as the way in which it is treated may seem to lead to that conclusion. Any rejection of particular miracles, any depreciation of the authority of Scripture, any attempt to do away with all specific difference between Christianity and other religions, or to reduce it to the smallest amount, they would welcome, as a promising indication, as a step in the right direction, as an instalment of the full truth. But they would remain parted as much as ever by an impassable gulf from every view of Christianity which included a supernatural element. And so it has happened that those of the Essayists who have most startled ordinary readers by the boldness of their language, have in some quarters incurred the reproach of timidity, of a want of openness and sincerity. When so much was said, and by persons in their positions, it seemed incredible that more should not be meant. Where there was so near an approach, it was thought that only outward and temporary causes could have prevented a complete concurrence. Such censure might indeed have been regarded as a proof that those on whom it fell had observed the right mean, but only on condition that they had taken some pains to guard themselves against misapprehension by positive statements.

I have not thought myself precluded from bringing out the

real character of the Essay which strikes most directly at the root of revealed religion, by the author's removal out of the sphere of personal controversy. He indeed has passed beyond the reach, not only of ecclesiastical censure, but of literary criticism. But this is by no means the case with his writings; though to some it has appeared a reason for refraining from pronouncing a decided judgment on his Essay. It can never cease to occupy the foremost place in every general survey of the volume. And he himself would probably have strongly deprecated such forbearance. As a sincere lover of truth, a clear-headed thinker, and a practised writer, he would hardly have been thankful for an indulgence which assumes that his writings were not able to answer for themselves.

<small>Reasons for exhibiting the true character of the Essay on Miracles.</small>

It might, however, well have been,—all things considered it was, perhaps, rather to have been expected than otherwise,—that among the other contributions to the volume, there should have been some one which might have served to counteract the impression likely to be made by his Essay, and that this might have induced the Editor to admit one which, if left to stand by itself, neither refuted nor balanced by an opposite view, seemed to be fraught with such alarming consequences. If such a corrective was to be found, there is perhaps none of the Essays in which it would more naturally have been sought than the opening one on the Education of the World. But the relation in which this stands to the other is one, I will not say of an opposite, but certainly of a very different kind. This indeed is no fault of the author, who only happened not to have provided for a want which he could not foresee; but it is a fact worthy of remark, as illustrating the general character of the volume. His Essay stands apart from the rest, as well in its subject as in the occasion which gave rise to it, having been originally delivered as a Sermon before the University of Oxford. It is in fact a Lecture on the Philosophy of History from the Christian point of view, and with special reference to Christianity. It was perhaps not altogether a happy thought to ground a theory on the analogy,—due it may be to Pascal, who, however, employed

<small>Essay on the Education of the World.</small>

<small>Scheme of the writer.</small>

it simply to illustrate the progress of knowledge,*—between the development of the race and that of the individual. But the scheme is that the period preceding the coming of Christ answers to childhood, the age of law; the "whole period from the closing of the Old Testament to the close of the New," or that of the Early Church, to youth, the age of example. The latest, whenever it may have begun, is that of manhood, in its mature, still unabated vigour; and this it is in which we of this day have the happiness, a privilege indeed coupled with grave responsibility, to live. The distinctive character of the present period is, that the restraint of a merely outward law, and the influence of example, have been superseded by the supremacy of the "spirit," which is identified with the "conscience," and which has now "come to full strength, and assumed the throne intended for him in the soul," where he is "invested" with plenary and absolute judicial and legislative "powers."† This scheme includes a vindication or elucidation of the Divine wisdom in the arrangement by which the appearance of the great Example, in which character alone our Lord is viewed, was ordained to coincide with the world's youth. The peculiar fitness of this economy is thus explained:—"Had His revelation been delayed till now, assuredly it would have been hard for us to recognize His Divinity: for the faculty of faith has turned inwards, and cannot now accept any outer manifestations of the truth of God. Our vision of the Son of God is now aided by the eyes of the Apostles, and by that aid we can recognize the express image of the Father." "Had

---

* "Pensées, Fragments et Lettres, ed. Prosper Faugère. Préface sur le Traité du Vide," p. 98. After having pointed out the advantage derived by each successive generation from the accumulation of knowledge previously acquired, he proceeds: "De sorte que toute la suite des hommes, pendant le cours de tant de siècles, doit être considérée comme un même homme qui subsiste toujours et qui apprend continuellement: d'où l'on voit avec combien d'injustice nous respectons l'antiquité dans ses philosophes; car comme la vieillesse est l'âge le plus distant de l'enfance, qui ne voit que la vieillesse dans cet homme universel ne doit pas être cherchée dans les temps proches de sa naissance, mais dans ceux qui en sont les plus éloignés? Ceux qui nous appelons anciens étaient véritablement nouveaux en toutes choses, et formaient l'enfance des hommes proprement: et commes nous avons joint à leurs connoissances l'expérience des siècles qui les ont suivis, c'est en nous que l'on peut trouver cette antiquité que nous révérons dans les autres."

† P. 31.

He come later, the truth of His Divine Nature would not have been recognized."*

<small>His arguments calculated to increase rather than remove doubts.</small> All this was no doubt written with a view to edification; but language more directly suggestive of the most perplexing doubts, could hardly have been employed.

It is not easy to understand on what ground a man of mature intellect can be required or expected to view an object in the same light in which it appeared to him in his youth; or why he should be better satisfied, if he was reminded that youth is the age most susceptible of lively impressions. That, to his riper judgment, might be exactly the reason why he should be no longer governed by them. And so those who have been taught that the age in which they live is one of independent thought, in which conscience is invested with supreme authority, and which is distinguished from former periods in the history of the world, not only by larger knowledge, but by superior clearness of view, must find it hard to reconcile this advantage with the requirement that they should look at a phenomenon of the past with the eyes of its contemporaries, whose "vision" had not attained to the same degree of keenness as their own. They must think it strange that they should be asked to recognize our Lord's <small>How our Lord's Divinity is to be recognized.</small> Divinity, not upon any evidence directly offered to themselves, but on the ground of an impression made by His example on witnesses who, through the general imperfection of their development, were much less capable of accurately discerning the things presented to them, and above all of drawing correct inferences from the seen to the unseen. And this would appear to them the more unreasonable when they found it laid down that, whenever "conscience and the Bible appear to differ," the inference is, not that conscience is not sufficiently enlightened, but that "the Bible, if rightly understood, would be found to confirm that which it seems to contradict." †— "Conscience is the supreme interpreter;" ‡—and its system of interpretation is grounded on the postulate, that the true sense of Scripture is always conformable to its decisions. These at all

* Pp. 24, 25. † P. 44. ‡ P. 45.

events are to be obeyed, and the sanction of the Bible, when not evident, is to be presumed. And yet one and not the least authentic or important part of the Bible consists of the record left by the Apostles of that "vision," by which they were led to recognize their Lord's Divinity. But conscience would be abdicating its prerogative, if it accepted the "aid of eyes," which were illumined with a light so much less full than its own. This would be a retrograde step, an example of that "tendency to go back to the childhood and youth of the world," which "has retarded the acquisition of that toleration which is the chief philosophical and moral lesson of modern days." This lesson has not yet been perfectly learnt; though "we are now men," we have still to grow riper in knowledge, and steadier in practice. We shall not have reached absolute maturity, until we have entirely ceased to rely on "the impulses of youth or the discipline of childhood," and submit to no government but that of our own principles. Those whose education has been so completed, will of course cast aside the aids which they no longer need to sustain their weakness. They will put away the childish and youthful things which they will have then outgrown. These general propositions are safe, but barren. The interesting question is, What are the things which fall under this description? Do they include that belief which it is the object of the third Essay to root up? On this the author is silent, nor, under the circumstances in which he first produced his discourse, could he have been expected to speak. But he has reason to complain of a juxtaposition, by which a question which he had innocently suggested, has been brought into outward connection with an answer which he would no doubt earnestly repudiate.

If of this Essay nothing more can be fairly said, than that it opens the broadest room for an assault on the foundations of historical Christianity, without setting up any defence against it, this would not be enough to describe the bearing of some of the others on the same question. A much more positive impression on the same side is left by the second Essay, Character of the second Essay. though it is on other accounts that it has given more general offence than any other in the volume, and not least to those who most revere the honoured name which it bears on its title. It purports, indeed, to be only a sketch of the most important results of the researches of another author, which therefore could throw no direct light on the opinions of the reviewer. The difficulty of collecting these with certainty is much increased by the writer's characteristic manner; and might well seem almost insurmountable to one who was called upon, under judicial responsibility, to extract any definite propositions from such a series of epigrams and enigmas. But to any one who only desires to form a judgment on their main drift for his own satisfaction, there can be no doubt as to their general tendency, though it may not be quite clear to what extent they follow it out. It is manifest that the review is designed, not simply as a report, but as a vindication of the views described. There is an occasional expression of dissent, but mostly on points in which the author, in the opinion of his critic, has erred on the side of credulity, and so in contradiction to the spirit of his own system. That any difference exists between them on any fundamental principles, which was not thought worthy of the slightest notice, would be hardly credible, as it would imply a want of candour and openness, where reserve would have been alike improper and unnatural.

The question of supernatural agency. The opening remarks, at least, are entirely the Essayist's own, and they bear mainly on the question of supernatural agency. Even here, indeed, the ambiguity which marks his style in the treatment of theological subjects, and which may perhaps be traced as much to the vagueness of his views as to the character of his mind, obliges us to be very cautious when we undertake to interpret his language, and somewhat distrustful of the result. But the passages which are most salient and pregnant, and which seem least likely altogether to conceal the thought which they may fail distinctly to express, all point unmistakably in the same general direction. It is only just to admit that they contain no express denial of the possibility of miraculous interference. They merely indicate the various grounds on which it has been questioned. It may even seem as if its reality was recognized; for it is said that there are "cases in which we accept the miracle for the sake of the moral lesson."* But as it is certain that in fact no one ever believed in a miracle for the sake of a moral lesson, which indeed the miracle, as such, could not convey; so the context indicates the meaning to be, that we *accept* the miracle for the sake of the moral lesson, only as we accept a fruit for the sake of the kernel, in its shell, which we break and throw away: and this is in perfect conformity with the sense in which we have already heard from another of the authors, that "an alleged miracle is *accepted* on religious grounds." The writer is strongly impressed with the importance of the question; only, according to his wont, he states it in such a manner as to exclude the possibility of more than one answer; for when our choice is limited between the alternatives, "whether God's Holy Spirit has acted through the channels which His Providence ordained, or whether it has departed from these so signally, that comparative mistrust of them ever after becomes a duty," there can be no room for rational hesitation: and he himself anticipates an approaching unanimity on this head, among all whose minds are not either narrowed by priestcraft and formalism, or darkened by moral corruption.† Whether the question, thus stated, can be correctly termed a question at all, and is not simply a form of controversial argument which begs the real question, I need not ask. But certainly there is a far *greater* question, one on which minds are at this day divided, and on which, as we have seen, one of the contributors to this volume has pronounced a very decided opinion; namely, the question whether there has ever been in the history of mankind any interposition of a supernatural agency, or simply a course of events, ordained indeed by Divine Providence, but linked together in an unbroken sequence of purely natural causes and effects. This is indeed a great question, one of momentous bearing on the truth of Christianity; and it is also a real question, not involving the only possible answer, but one on which men may and do take opposite sides. This writer

Has there ever been any supernatural interposition?

* P. 51. † P. 52.

not only substitutes a fictitious and misleading question for the real issue, but passes over the single important point in a silence which, considering the occasion for speech, we can hardly help regarding as emphatic. It is not he who will pronounce supernatural interference impossible; all that he maintains is, that if possible, it would be useless, and that the whole result of the most mature observation on the education of the world is in favour of the opposite alternative. Yet his language might lead an incautious reader to believe that he had incidentally conceded the whole matter in dispute; for in a note he speaks of an "irrational supernaturalism." It may seem to follow that he admits a supernaturalism which he regards as rational. And so indeed he does; but no one who studies the context can fail to see what kind of supernaturalism this is.* It is simply the order of Divine Providence, which so far may be said to be above nature, though strictly limited to natural "channels." The actings of the Holy Ghost through these channels are supernatural, inasmuch as they are in their origin Divine, though not at all confined to the Christian revelation. That is a revelation, but only in the same sense, in which every religion which contains any "elements of good" is a Divine, and therefore supernatural revelation also.

The Essayist, whose opinions in this volume it is sometimes difficult to distinguish from those of the author whom he reviews, had previously written much on kindred topics. And the conclusion to which I was led, as to the impression likely to be made by a work in which he spoke throughout in his own person, was that "its ultimate tendency was to efface the distinction between

* M. E. Renan, in his "Etudes d'histoire religieuse," p. 137, has a note on the use of the term *surnaturel*, which may help to throw light on the sense in which it is employed by the Essayist. Having observed in the text, "l'essence de la critique est la négation du surnaturel," he subjoins in the note: "Une explication est devenue nécessaire sur ce mot, depuis que des écrivains ont pris l'habitude de désigner par le mot *surnaturel* l'élément idéaliste et moral de la vie, en opposition avec l'élément matérialiste et positif. En ce sens, on ne pourrait nier le surnaturel sans tomber dans un grossier sensualisme qui est aussi loin que possible de ma pensée; car je crois au contraire que seule la vie intellectuelle et morale a quelque prix, et une pleine réalité. J'entends ici par surnaturel le *miracle*, c'est-à-dire, un acte particulier de la Divinité, venant s'insérer dans la série des événements du monde physique et psychologique et dérangeant le cours des faits en vue d'un gouvernement spécial de l'humanité."

natural and revealed religion." His reply to that remark was in the form of a question, raising a doubt as "to the reality of the distinction between Natural and Revealed, and whether it does not diminish, if not vanish, upon a view of the comprehensiveness of the Divine dealings," or "upon examination of St. Paul's argument to the Romans and Galatians." In perfect accordance with this intimation, he observes in the Essay: "It is not a fatal objection (to what he thinks the 'reasonable' interpretation of St. Paul's words) to say that St. Paul would thus teach Natural Religion, unless we were sure that he was bound to contradict it;" and that it would be a great "relief to some minds, to find the antagonism between Nature and Revelation vanishing in a wider grasp and deeper perception of the one, or in a better balanced statement of the other." * I need hardly observe that there never has been, or could be, a question as to a contradiction or antagonism between Natural and Revealed Religion—truth can never contradict truth—and therefore the supposed objection which is brought forward to be so refuted is purely imaginary; but it diverts the reader's attention from the real point at issue, which is not, whether there is "antagonism" between Natural and Revealed Religion, but whether there is any essential distinction between them, or they are only different names for the same thing. This question must hinge on that of supernatural agency; on which, as I have said, I am quite aware that men may and do take opposite sides. But that a clergyman of the Church of England is at liberty to take which he will, I cannot so easily understand or so readily admit.

Distinction between Natural and Revealed Religion.

The Essayist adverts to a doubt which some may feel as to his author's claim to the name of Christian, notwithstanding the orthodoxy of his language: for he exposes himself, it is said, to the charge of "using Evangelical language in a philosophical sense." But in the critic's own opinion, the philosophical sense is simply the "reasonable" sense. He himself thinks it "possible to defend our traditional theology, if stated

Philosophy of the Essay.

* P. 81.

reasonably." That his author was an adherent of any more special philosophy than that of reason or good sense, the reader would never, by any word of his, be led to suspect. Indeed, if it were not almost incredible, it might be supposed that he was not aware of it himself. For when he has occasion to allude to the sources from which his author's speculations on the Trinity may seem to have been drawn, he admits that they have a Sabellian or almost a Brahmanical sound (and again, p. 90, a Brahmanical rather than a Christian sound). That they have any affinity to those of a School of much more recent date, and much nearer home,—not of Ptolemais or Benares, but of Berlin,—he entirely ignores. He is indeed partly aware of one wide difference between his author's position and his own. His author was "a philosopher sitting loose to our Articles," in plainer words, bound by no obligations, save that of his diffusive Christian charity, to the Church of England: in that respect at full liberty, either absolutely to reject any of her doctrines, or to adopt them in any sense or with any modification he might prefer. But how far such liberty may be rightfully claimed, or such laxity as to the Articles consistently exercised, by a Clergyman of the Church of England, is certainly a different question; one in which the example of the illustrious foreigner can afford no guidance to persons placed in entirely different relations. That which was possible for him "without any paltering with his conscience," may not be so for them. He indeed could reconcile his philosophical system with a faith which in him yielded the richest fruits of the Christian life. But in the judgment of his critic, this was rather an amiable weakness, than a model for imitation, for, as he thinks, "the philosopher's theology could hardly bear to be prayed."* It was better adapted to the School, than to the Church or the closet. The prayers of the Christian were "not brought into entire harmony" with the "criticisms" of the philosophical (Hegelian) theologian. This discordance is represented as indicating an imperfection, not in the quality of the theology, but in that of the religious consciousness. "It may be," it is said,

* P. 91.

"that a discrepancy is likely to remain between our feelings and our logical necessities:" but it is one "which we should constantly diminish;" not of course by a vain attempt to elude a logical necessity, but by reconciling our feelings, as well as we may, to a theology which will not bear to be prayed.

The most remarkable Essay in the volume is one which might have been entitled "a plea for National Churches established on comprehensive principles." We must all sympathize with the writer's object, so far as it is to vindicate the national character of our own Church, among others, against those who deny the lawfulness of any established Church, and we may fully assent to his general position, that the Apostolical Churches, though differing from it as to their relation to the State, were not more exclusive in principle, and were constantly tending toward that outward form into which they were finally brought by the recognition which they received from the Civil Power: though we may hesitate to adopt his opinion as to the extent to which the Apostles tolerated both the rejection of fundamental truths, and viciousness of life, among those who called themselves by the name of Christ. It seems to rest on a doubtful interpretation of some obscure texts, and on an assumption as to the nature of the Apostolical discipline, not warranted by our very scanty knowledge of the internal condition of the primitive Churches in the earliest stage of their history. But the question with which we are now concerned is not one of antiquarian erudition. It is one of the highest practical moment, which may and must be decided on general principles; and the Essay is chiefly occupied with a statement—which indeed includes a discussion of a great variety of very important though subordinate questions—of the conditions on which a National Church, such as our own, may hope to endure and prosper. It cannot do so unless it realizes, if not in its absolute fulness, yet in a sufficient measure, the idea implied in the title which it bears, unless it is, as nearly as possible, not merely in name but in deed, the Church of the whole nation. But this, according to the author's view, it can never be, unless it be freed "from dogmatical tests and other

Mr. Wilson's Essay.

Condition of the prosperity of National Churches.

intellectual bondage." It was, he thinks, the unhappy, though perhaps unavoidable mistake of Constantine, that together with his "inauguration of multitudinism," (that is, of a system including members in various stages of spiritual life, and not limited by Calvinistic terms of communion,) "by the sanction which he gives to the decisions of Nicea," he inaugurated the essentially incongruous "principle of doctrinal limitation." "Sufficiently liberated from the traditional symbols," a National Church like our own might comprehend all but Calvinistic Nonconformists (an exception indeed which would probably exclude four-fifths of our Dissenters). It will be untrue to its essential character, and will provoke separation, "if it submits to define itself otherwise than by its own nationality," or if it lays any restraint on freedom of thought and speech among its ministers, from which other classes are exempt.*

Adjustment of old things to new conditions. Such being the general object in view, the question arises, how is it to be attained; or "what is the best method of adjusting old things to new conditions;" in other words, what changes are needed in the existing state of things? The result of this inquiry is, in the author's view, cheering and hopeful, to a degree which must startle many, who suppose the actual obstacles greater than they are. It turns out that they are more apparent than real, and that even now there is in fact next to no doctrinal limitation at all. In the first place it is observed, that "as far as opinion privately entertained is concerned, the liberty of the English clergyman appears already to be complete."† *Liberty of Clergymen.* Many persons have been startled by this observation, just on account of its unquestionable truth. For a man hardly likes to be reminded that, as a free citizen, he is at liberty to harbour the foulest thoughts, and the most nefarious intentions, as long as he does not let them appear in word or deed; and the suggestion would certainly sound like the most shameless Jesuitical sophistry, if an English clergyman was really bound to any opinions, either by virtue of his office, or by subscription, or the use of certain formularies. But the writer

* Pp. 173, 174. † P. 180.

proceeds to show that this is not really the case; that subscription to the Articles may mean any thing, and therefore means nothing; that to *allow* signifies only an acquiescence, totally distinct from approval, and consistent with the deepest abhorrence of the thing *allowed;* that nothing more definite is implied in the *acknowledgment* of them "to be agreeable to the Word of God;" partly because *acknowledge* may mean simply not to gainsay, and partly because it is impossible to fix the import of that to which the Articles are declared to be *agreeable.* For "when once the freedom of interpretation of Scripture is admitted," it will be "happily found" that "the Articles make no effectual provision for an absolute uniformity." The only question indeed will be, whether, with that freedom of interpretation which is advocated and illustrated in the Essay itself, they make any provision for any kind or degree of uniformity.

But since it turns out that a clergyman of the Church of England, if he only knew his own happiness, already enjoys almost absolute freedom, not only of thought, but of speech, unfettered by Bible, Articles, or Liturgy, what more can be needed to fulfil the idea of a National Church exempt from doctrinal limitation? All that remains to be done is to remove the appearance of a restraint by which some are perplexed and deterred either from the communion or the ministry of the Church; and for this purpose in the first place to abolish the bugbear of an unmeaning subscription, and let the Articles remain as a regulative symbol, not to be impugned. So treated, they will, it is supposed, be at once safe and harmless; secured from contradiction by the protecting statute, and incapable of provoking separation, because they will have only a negative value; a venerable relic, kept out of the reach, both of rude desecration, and of superstitious use. The only remaining obstacle would arise from the Liturgical formularies, which "present a fair and substantial representation of the Biblical records, incorporating their letter and presupposing their historical element." "If they embodied only an ethical result, addressed to the individual and to society, the

<small>Subscription to the Articles.</small>

<small>Liturgical formularies.</small>

speculative difficulty would not arise." But unhappily they seem, and are commonly thought, to do something more; and hence arises a fresh problem. But with this the author does not deal quite so satisfactorily as with that of the Articles. He does not propose to empty the Liturgy of doctrine, but merely points out that it can have no more definite meaning than the Biblical records themselves. But as it was not the real, but the apparent stringency of subscription that calls for its abolition, and for consigning the Articles to an honourable seclusion, so it would seem that the like appearance of a doctrinal character of the Liturgy requires a similar treatment, and that it cannot be safe to leave it in its present form, without any guarantee that it shall be effectually explained away, so as to evacuate it of all doctrinal substance. That which is so liable, so likely, if not certain, to create misunderstanding which may provoke separation, ought clearly, on the author's principles, to be either entirely abolished, or reduced to a form, in which it could not be suspected of embodying more than ethical results.

This however leads us to observe another defect in the scheme, which the author seems to have overlooked. Even after all doctrinal limitation, hitherto either really or apparently presented by Bible, Articles, and Liturgy, shall have been cleared away, whether by legislative enactment or by an enlightened interpretation, still there is the clergyman himself who may provoke separation by his doctrine. He will indeed have been released from all restraints which were intended to secure what was called the soundness of his teaching; but no security is suggested to guard society and the Church against the mischief which he may cause if he should happen to have doctrinal opinions of his own; if, for instance, he should believe that the Articles are agreeable to the Word of God, in a certain definite sense, and that the Liturgy embodies something more than ethical results. Surely the National Church would have a right to be protected against the danger of schism, which would arise from the indiscreet disclosure of such views. It is not enough that a clergyman should be forbidden to impugn the Articles for the sake of those

No provision made against schism.

who assent to them. It would be equally necessary that he should also be restrained from giving offence to those who reject them, by preaching in accordance with his own view of their import. The proper use of the Articles and other doctrinal formularies, on the author's principles, would seem to be that they should serve as a table of subjects, from which the clergyman should be strictly enjoined to abstain in the pulpit. This, of course, would only affect the freedom of his public ministrations, and he would have no right to complain; for, "as far as opinion privately entertained is concerned," he would still be at liberty to hold what are now called orthodox views.

But after the obligations of a minister of the National Church have been thus determined on the negative side, it is still necessary that some functions of a positive kind should be assigned to him, and he cannot be entirely divested of the character of a teacher. It is true this description does not exhaust all that may be properly considered as belonging to his office. His position may afford peculiar opportunities for beneficent action, which it will be a part of his duty to turn to the best account. But still the functions of a public teacher are at least among those which must always be most characteristic of his ministerial calling, and, indeed, will be rather likely to supersede every other. We must therefore see how these will have to be performed in that Church of the future which is foreshadowed in this Essay. If its language is to be understood in its most obvious sense, there can be no doubt as to the author's views on this head. It is clearly laid down * that "the service of the National Church is as properly an organ of the national life as a magistracy, or a legislative estate;" and that "to set barriers before the entrance upon its functions, by limitations not absolutely required by public policy, is to infringe upon the birthright of the citizens." If we wish to know what these needless limitations are, we find that they are the doctrinal limitations which have been before described as the bane of all Multitudinist Churches, and at variance with their essential character. "When the office of the Church is properly

marginal note: The positive functions of clergymen.

* P. 190.

understood," * it will be found that its objects nearly coincide with those of the State. In fact, Church and State are only the Nation considered under different aspects. The immediate object of the State is the maintenance of public security and order. But the Nation, if it is conscious of its highest objects, "will not content itself with the rough adjustments and rude lessons of law and police." The State itself will desire that all its people should be brought under a moral influence, which will supply motives of conduct, operating toward the same end, but at once nobler, stronger, and purer than those which only impose an outward restraint. For the fulfilment of this desire, the nation "will throw the best of its elements into another mould," and out of them "constitute a spiritual society," to exercise that "improving influence," under which the State would have "all its people to be brought." This society is the Church. But the purposes both of Church and State would be defeated alike by "errors and mistakes in defining Church membership, and by a repulsive mode of Church teaching." The preservative against this danger, even if it was not distinctly pointed out, would be obvious enough from the nature of the case. It is to confine the Church's teaching to matters in which Church and State have a common interest. But the State can have no "concern in a system of relations founded on the possession of speculative truth." And therefore this is and should be treated as alien to the object of the Church. "Speculative doctrines should be left to philosophical schools. A National Church must be concerned with the ethical development of its members, and the wrong of supposing it to be otherwise, is participated by those of the clericalty who consider the Church to be founded, as a society, on the possession of an abstractedly true and supernaturally communicated speculation concerning God, rather than upon the manifestation of a divine life in man."

<small>Limitation of the Church's teaching.</small>

It is impossible to listen to such a reflection without asking how far it is well founded. And this concerns us the more nearly, the more fully we assent to the author's general view of the proper object of a National Church. That this is to act

* Pp. 194 foll.

on the spiritual nature of its members, with a view to their ethical development, we shall all, I trust, readily admit, however conscious we may be of our individual shortcomings, in our several contributions toward the progress of the work. But while we may be surprised to hear any one—above all, one of our brethren in the ministry—speak of any thing which we regard as *supernaturally communicated truth*, as a *speculation*, so long as we believe ourselves to be in possession of such truth, we could not without both great dishonour to it, and I hope no little injustice to ourselves, as a body, admit that absence of all real connexion between such truth and the manifestation of a divine life in man, as both this reproach of "the clericalty," and the whole tenor of the author's statements, assumes. We cannot be more thoroughly convinced of the truth itself, than we are that, if supernaturally communicated at all, it was so with a view to that manifestation. We may indeed have reason to reproach ourselves with the imperfection of our mode of teaching in this respect, however we may question the right of any one of our number to rebuke the rest on this score: but we are very sure that, if our best endeavours are inadequate to the object, it is not because we are mistaken in supposing a connexion between the truth and the life, but because we are not ourselves sufficiently impressed, and therefore fail to impress others, with its reality.

It is not essential to my immediate object to inquire how far the proposed solution of the problem, "the best method of adjusting old things to new conditions," is practicable. *Practicability of the scheme.* We are now concerned rather with the principles on which it is founded, than with the measure of success which may be likely to attend it. But yet the practical inquiry is not only interesting in itself, but may help to throw light on the theory. The author himself indeed warns us against extravagant expectations. "It is not to be expected," he says, "that terms of communion could be made so large as by any possibility to comprehend in the National Church the whole of such a free nation as our own. There will always be those who from a conscientious scruple, or from a desire to define, or from peculiarities of temper, will hold aloof from the religion and the worship of the majority." It is not easy to understand how either conscientious scruples or peculiarities of temper should keep any aloof from a religion and worship, which had been duly weeded of all "speculative doctrines:" but "a desire to define" would no doubt be in direct contradiction to the whole spirit of a scheme, which aims at the utmost possible levelling of all doctrinal barriers. It is only a little surprising, that the author should pass so lightly over this obstruction, and should appear to be so little aware of the extent to which it is likely to interfere with the comprehensiveness of a National Church, such as would realize his idea. He considers Calvinistic opinions as fundamentally adverse to the very notion of a Multitudinist or National Church. How widely such opinions prevail among our Nonconformists, he seems hardly to have taken into account. Still less does he notice the great number of persons who—however inconsistently, according to his view—do in fact reconcile Calvinistic tenets with membership in the Established Church, and with the functions of its ministry. But those who do not hold these tenets may hold others to which they are not less decidedly attached, and if so, "the desire to define" will in them be very likely to take the shape of a strong repugnance to terms of communion, which in their judgment are not sufficiently definite. The one class would say: "If we tolerate a National Church, which we admit is not quite in harmony with our principles, it is only on condition that it teaches sound doctrine." The others would say: "Much as we value a National Church, we must abandon it, if it renounces its office of teaching that which we believe to be the truth." Even in point of numbers, those who would "hold aloof" or separate themselves from the new National Church, just on account of its breadth and freedom, would constitute a very formidable secession. But, what is a still graver consideration, these dissenters would include almost all the earnest religious feeling of the nation. The author alludes to the masses both of the educated and the uneducated class, who—as appeared from the census of 1851—neglect to attend any means of public worship. He supposes these persons

[margin: Calvinistic opinions adverse to a National Church.]

to be "alienated from the Christianity which is ordinarily presented in our churches and chapels," solely "because either their reason or their common sense is shocked by what they hear there." This is indeed a somewhat bold assumption, and it might have seemed possible to assign a different cause for the absence of some at least of them from all public worship. But if we give all of them credit for higher intelligence and a finer moral sense than belong to the rest of their countrymen, we can hardly believe their religious cravings to be very strong. Unhappily, it is a notorious fact with regard to very many of them, that they have been alienated from all Christian communion, not by "conscientious scruples," nor by "peculiarities of temper," least of all by "the desire to define," but by the total absence of any kind of religious belief which could express itself in worship. They are practical, if not speculative, atheists, not acknowledging a God in the world, and living as if there was none. Beside those who have reached this extreme, there are, it is to be feared, many, both educated and uneducated, who are not less opposed to every form of revealed religion. *Why the masses are alienated from churches and chapels.*

It may seem that this is the class most likely to be won to a National Church in which they would not be offended by any speculative doctrines, and the only business of the minister would be to promote their ethical development. The author deals in some detail with the case of persons, who hold aloof from the Church of England, because they are unable to reconcile its real or supposed dogmatism with the advanced state of their scientific or literary knowledge. For their benefit, or that of his brethren who may be called upon to recover them to the Church, he expounds the principle of "ideology." Even though for some time to come the formularies of the Church should continue to "present a fair and substantial representation of the Biblical records," their effect may be neutralized by the application of this principle. As the ancient philosophers could extract metaphysical or moral truth from the fables of the heathen mythology, without either pledging themselves, or requiring the *Ideology expounded.*

assent of their hearers, to a single point of the mythical narrative as matter of fact, the like treatment may be applied to the Biblical records; and, however they may be emptied of the historical element, its place will be abundantly supplied by the "ideas" which they will not cease to "awaken." The author thinks, indeed, that this method of interpretation has been "carried to excess" by Strauss,* whom he represents with some exaggeration as "resolving into an ideal the whole of the historical and doctrinal person of Jesus." But not only has he omitted to draw any line which might have precluded this excess, but he seems not to be aware that on Strauss's principle no such line can be drawn, and that Strauss has only followed out his principle to its legitimate conclusion. The fundamental assumption, the groundwork of the whole system, is the absolute rejection of supernatural interference. When that principle is once laid down, there can be no exception or selection among miraculous narratives. All must pass out of the domain of history into that of fiction. When, therefore, the author says that "liberty must be left to all as to the extent in which they apply the principle," this does not correctly express the state of the case. On the one hand there is, instead of liberty, a logical necessity, by which the application must be carried to the denial of every supernatural fact of revealed religion. On the other hand it may be thought that the Church, when she teaches truths involving such facts, does fix certain "limits," beyond which such "liberty" cannot be "exercised," whether "reasonably" or not, consistently with the confession of her fundamental doctrines. But, at all events, nothing short of the extent which the principle requires will satisfy the scientific and literary sceptics, whose views are represented in the third Essay, and whom the author of the fourth wishes to conciliate by the substitution of the ideal for the real "in the scriptural person of Jesus."

It only remains to consider what will be gained when this has been done, and what is the prospect of winning the irreligious class for whose sake we are to run so great a risk of losing all who

* P. 200.

sincerely profess the faith of Christ. They will not be offended by the announcement of any "supernaturally communicated truth." In the teaching of the National Church, when its office is properly understood, theology will make way for "ethical results." It is assumed—with what seems to me a strange neglect of patent facts—that as to ethical results no speculative difficulty would arise; as if a perfect unanimity prevailed among the professors of moral philosophy, or their various systems all led to the same practical results. But since the National Church is still to be, in name at least, a Christian Church, its ministers will probably teach Christian ethics. But can they, indeed, reckon on a general acceptance of this system among those who reject the supernatural origin of Christianity? Will it not be necessary that they should allow equal latitude in ethical as in theological speculation? If not, on what ground can they claim a hearing from those who take an entirely different view of the nature of happiness, of the obligations of duty, of the value and purpose of life? If they preach active, self-denying charity and heavenly-mindedness to men whose maxim—the common, if not inevitable result of a materialistic philosophy—is, "Let us eat and drink, for to-morrow we die," what authority can they plead for their message? In what character are they to present themselves, that can give any weight to their exhortations? They may indeed say, "We do not pretend to guide your speculative opinions. You are at perfect liberty to think as you will as to the origin and the doctrines of Christianity. We do not even absolutely require you to admit the historical existence of its Founder." And so far they may find willing listeners. But if they proceed to say, "All we ask is, that you should adopt the moral principles which Christ is supposed to have taught, and should regulate your conduct in conformity to them,"—the answer which they would have reason to expect would be, "We think ourselves the best judges of that which concerns our manner of life; and it is quite consistent with the religious opinions which you allow us to retain. We can understand those who, themselves believing in the divine authority

Prospect of winning the irreligious class.

of Jesus, come to us in His name. Though we cannot share their faith, we respect their sincerity and earnestness; we admit that they are acting in accordance with their own professions. But we do not know what right you have to call upon us to regulate our lives by your opinions, rather than by our own inclinations." And if such minds are prevented by unbelief from receiving moral instruction, it can hardly be expected that they should be brought to join in public worship, for which some common basis of belief is still more requisite.* The more highly educated may, indeed, be able to apply the ideological principle, so as to reduce the formularies, which appear to involve dogmas which they reject, to a mere embodiment of ethical results. But they might justly complain of being required to go through such a process, for the sake of a result which they might attain as well without it. They may think that the parables and myths, which might once have been useful vehicles of truth, are no longer suited to that maturity of intellect and conscience, which distinguishes the present period in the education of the world. They may say, "For theologians these exegetical feats may be a pleasant exercise; for us they are neither needful nor profitable; and we cannot repress a misgiving that this tampering with the natural meaning of words is something worse than laborious trifling. It seems to us hard to reconcile with perfect openness and truthfulness; and we cannot help fearing that, however it may sharpen the intellect, it is not likely to produce a wholesome effect on the ethical development of those who practise it."

<small>Attitude of the more highly educated.</small>

The drift of the whole scheme is to bring the Church down to

---

* M. Jules Simon, in the concluding part of his work, "La Religion Naturelle," discusses the question: "Si l'on peut et si l'on doit se mêler aux exercices d'un culte positif, quand on n'a pas d'autre croyance que la religion naturelle?" He feels a difficulty (un embarras) which he states thus: "D'un côté, la religion naturelle nous enseigne l'utilité et la nécessité d'un culte extérieur; de l'autre, il est évident qu'elle nous laisse bien peu de moyens de rendre témoignage de notre foi, et qu'elle nous met dans une impossibilité presque absolue de nous associer pour prier." Nevertheless, he answers the question, though with evident reluctance, in the negative. This is very noteworthy, because his system of natural religion is really nothing more or less than a philosophical abstraction from the positive doctrines of Christianity, and appears to correspond as closely as possible to that which would be left in the National Church, when freed, according to Mr. Wilson's scheme, from "doctrinal limitations."

the religious level of those who hold least of Christian doctrine; or—as this class is assumed to include the most en- lightened minds in the nation—to lift the Church up to their intellectual level. And, unless the clergy are to lose all influence over this class, this is the level on which they must take their stand. The opponents of National Churches, who object to them on religious grounds, would think their cause gained, when it is admitted that a National Church can subsist only on such conditions. But the graver question is, how far such a society has any right to the name of a Church. It is not generally understood that this name would be properly applied to an association formed for the purpose of mutual "improvement," among persons of the most discordant views on all religious matters, even if it was possible that such persons might be unanimous as to the nature of the "improvement" which is the common object. A Church, without any basis of a common faith, is not only an experiment new in practice and of doubtful success, but an idea new in theory, and not easy to conceive. And when we remember the quarter from which this proposal comes, it may well seem hardly credible that it can have been designed with so great a latitude. I have had this difficulty fully in view throughout my examination of this Essay; but, after not only the most attentive observation but the most careful search in my power, I have been unable to discover so much as a hint to qualify the apparently indefinite terms of the proposal. We have seen that no such limitation is implied in the admission, that there will after all remain some who cannot be gathered into the bosom of the National Church. For they will be excluded mainly, not by the nullity or vagueness, but by the definiteness of their belief. And then it must be owned that there is some force in the remark, —When a clergyman puts forth opinions, which he is aware must startle and offend great numbers both of the clerical and lay members of his own communion, it may be expected that, as well for their sake as his own, he will not express himself in language stronger or broader than is required for the full exposition of his views; that charity, no less than prudence, will lead him care-

Drift of the scheme.

fully to guard his statements from the risk of being misunderstood in a sense which would be commonly thought inconsistent with his profession. Otherwise he must be prepared to find that he is generally suspected of meaning, not less but rather more than he says; and that the ambiguity, which in a layman might be attributed to indistinctness of ideas, will in him be imputed to a calculated reserve.

<small>The relation of this Essay to the one on Miracles.</small> This Essay is the practical complement of that which, by the absolute rejection of all supernatural interposition, subverts the historical basis of Christianity. The one prepares us for a loss which it represents as inevitable, the other offers the compensation of an ideal to be substituted for the historical reality. That it retains any thing which would be inconsistent with the principle by which all that, in our traditional belief, is derived from such interposition, is referred to the evolution of merely natural causes, is nowhere intimated by a single word, and is a supposition at variance with the whole tenor of the Essay. It begins and ends with a speculation on the future state. The mystery of God's dealings with that large part of mankind which has not yet received the Gospel, is represented as one chief cause of modern scepticism; and it must have surprised some readers to hear, that it is only through an enlargement of geographical knowledge which has taken place "since our own boyhood," that we have become aware of the existence of populous empires in the far East, pagan, or even atheistic, which flourished <small>Scepticism attributed to recent geographical discoveries.</small> many ages before the Christian era. Within the sphere of the author's observation, it is this recent discovery which has given the chief impulse to the sceptical movements of our generation; and, at all events he himself uses it to show that, "without a denial of the broad and equal justice of the Supreme Being," we cannot hold that "to know and believe in Jesus Christ is in any sense necessary to salvation," though such knowledge and belief may confer an advantage on its possessors, involving an "unequal distribution of the divine benefits," of which "no account can be given." The solution of the difficulty is found in the uselessness of creeds; and the Essay, as we have

seen, is chiefly occupied with the exposure of their worthlessness and noxiousness, and with practical suggestions for getting rid of them. It turns out, indeed, that even within the pale of Christianity the like difficulty arises as with regard to the unconverted heathen, and that we cannot be content with believing that the Judge of all the earth will do right, unless we determine— whether in contradiction or not to our Lord's words—what it is right for Him to do. I am here only concerned to point out how perfectly all this agrees with that appreciation of the author's views, to which I have been led from every other point in the Essay.

It seems needless for my present purpose to enter into any farther details on the contents of this volume. Of the three remaining Essays one is the work of a layman, and therefore, even if it had been distinguished from the rest by the boldness of its speculations, it would not have been liable to the censure which they have incurred. It might, indeed, have helped to mark more distinctly the character of the miscellany. But in fact it does not even so much as this. The author has used his privilege with great moderation. If he had been a clergyman, he would have had the same right to criticize the speculations of other authors, on what he calls the Mosaic Cosmogony; and the conclusion to which he is led does not differ essentially from one which has been since proposed by a clergyman of unimpeached orthodoxy.* Still less would any one question the right of a clergyman to take a survey of the "tendencies of religious thought in England" in the last century, or, as the writer of the Essay on this subject likewise describes his work, of the Theory of Belief in the Church of England. It may be his own misfortune, as well as the reader's, that his researches should have led him to no more positive result than a suggestion, that it is very difficult to "make out on what basis Revelation is supposed, by the religious literature of the present day, to rest," while the general tendency of the investigation is to raise a doubt whether any of those on

Essay on the Mosaic Cosmogony.

Essay on the Theory of Belief in the Church of England.

* "Replies to Essays and Reviews. The Creative Week."

which it has been supposed to rest is sufficiently firm; and any one who should look for a hint to supply the defect would be utterly disappointed. This indeed is quite in accordance with the principles laid down in the previous Essays, but is not sufficient to charge the author with the responsibility of maintaining them.

The same remark will apply to the last Essay in the volume. The subject of which it treats, "the Interpretation of Scripture," is indeed of vast range, and in itself of all but the very highest importance: but, by the side of those which are discussed in other parts of the volume, it sinks into comparative insignificance. There may be, and are, wide differences of opinion as to the inspiration of Scripture, among those who believe in a supernatural revelation: but for those who reject the possibility of such a revelation, an inquiry as to the nature of inspiration can have neither interest nor meaning. The view of the question taken in the Essay may be that which those who reject supernatural revelation are forced to take: but it does not follow that the author is by his theory of inspiration at all committed to their denial of revelation. I have the less occasion to enter into this question, as I could add nothing to what I stated in a former Charge, as to its ecclesiastical aspect, and I have seen no reason to alter any opinion which I there expressed on the subject. We may well believe that the truth lies somewhere between the position of those who either altogether reject the existence of a human element in the Bible, or seek to reduce it to a minimum, and that of those who deal in the same way with the divine element. Whether indeed it is possible to draw a line between these extremes, in which the truth may be found, will depend on the farther question, whether the two elements are not so inextricably blended together as to forbid the attempt. But so much is certain, that there is no visible organ of our Church competent to define that which hitherto has been left undetermined on this point. I cannot profess to desire that such an organ should be called into action for such a purpose, or that a new article should be framed to bind the opinions of the Clergy on this subject, even

Essay on the Interpretation of Scripture.

if it should only serve—as we have seen proposed with regard to the rest—to mark a limit which must be kept sacred from direct impugnment. But I earnestly deprecate all attempts to effect the same object by means of any authority, legislative or judicial, short of that which would be universally recognized as rightfully supreme, because fully representing the mind and will of the whole Church.

Looking at the volume as a whole, I do not understand how any one reading it with common attention can fail to observe, notwithstanding the variety of topics and of treatment, that all is the product of one school. I am not aware, indeed, that this has ever been disputed, and it would probably be admitted with complacency by all the contributors. The only question is as to the character of the school to which it belongs; and that this, so far as it may be inferred from the work, is mainly negative, is acknowledged by its warmest and ablest apologist.* All that can seem doubtful is, how far the negation extends; whether that which is rejected is any thing essential to the Christian faith, or only some things which have been erroneously deemed such, but are really no more than excrescences, once perhaps harmless, but now burdensome and hurtful. Such, no doubt, is the light in which it is viewed by the authors themselves. I have already stated the grounds on which I have been led to a very different conclusion; that the negation does reach to the very essence and foundation of Christian faith; that after the principles laid down in this work have been carried to their logical result, that which is left will be something to which the name of Christianity cannot be applied without a straining and abuse of language. It will be no longer a religion, and will not yet have become a philosophy. No longer a religion, because it will contain nothing which is not supposed to have been originally derived from the processes of unassisted human reason. Not yet a philosophy, because it will retain many traditional elements, and will still appeal to authority in matters on which reason claims a supremacy, which, at the present stage of the education of the world, can no longer be

[margin note: The school to which the work belongs.]

* Edinburgh Review, p. 472.

questioned. It will have no right to exist, and will only be enabled to drag on a precarious, feeble, and barren existence by the force of custom and other external aids. How long it may so linger it is impossible to say; but its final doom, as that of all that belongs to a mere state of transition, will have been irrevocably fixed by the nature of things.

<small>The relation of the Church to its Founder.</small> The character of a Church must depend on the view which it takes of its Founder. But the very name of a Church, in its received acceptation, implies that it regards its Founder as distinguished from the rest of mankind in some peculiar way, by His connexion with the Deity; as having in some special sense come forth from God. Otherwise there would be no distinction between a Church and a School of philosophy. No amount of admiration and reverence which the disciples of a philosophical school may feel for their Master, not even if exhibited in periodical commemorative meetings, could entitle it to the name of a Church, so long as they acknowledge him to have been nothing more than an extraordinary man. This being distinctly understood, the case would not be altered, though in the fervour of their affectionate veneration they should sometimes style him divine. It might well be that in the National Church of the future foreshadowed in this volume, Jesus might continue to receive like homage from those who reject the possibility of a supernatural revelation, or admit it only in a sense in which the term would be equally applicable to any doctrine taught in a philosophical school. His human person might be invested with ideal attributes, independent of its historical reality, but equally suited to the purpose of an example; if indeed a mode of influence which was adapted to the nonage of the world, was any longer needed or useful in the present period of its education. But that which, in such a system, He cannot be, is a Teacher of superhuman authority. His sayings may retain their value, so far as they commend themselves to the reason and conscience of the readers; but that they are His, cannot exempt them from contradiction, or give them any decisive weight in controversy. Least of all could He be an object of personal faith. A man of strong though coarse

and narrow mind, an avowed unbeliever, whose only pretence to the name of Christian, which it was convenient to him not to renounce, was, as his biographer states, an impertinent assent to some of Christ's moral precepts,* writing to one who sought his guidance in his religious inquiries, said, "If you find reason to believe that Jesus was a God, you will be comforted with the belief of His aid and His love." † Such comfort of course can never be enjoyed by those who reject the possibility of supernatural revelation. Nor can they consistently join in the worship of one who differs from themselves only as a rare sample of their common nature. The language in which He is addressed by our Church would be rank idolatry. In a word their Christology is one which, to borrow a significant phrase of one of our authors, *will not bear to be prayed.*

But though I cannot but regard this book as the production of a school to which all the contributors belong, I would not be understood to mean that all of them have followed out its principles to that degree of development which is disclosed in two or three of the Essays. I have endeavoured to mark as clearly as I could the position in which each appears to me to stand with regard to it. Most of them probably would recoil from this extreme as utterly repugnant to their feelings and convictions. It is possible that hardly one of them has placed it distinctly before his mind, even while making statements which involve it by the most direct and necessary implication. These, however, are merely personal considerations, with which I am not concerned, and to which I advert only to guard against misunderstanding. The unity of the general tendency is, I think, too manifest to be fairly denied; and in two, at least, of the Essays this tendency has been carried very near indeed to its

<small>How far the writers have carried out the principles of their school.</small>

---

* Thomas Jefferson : par Cornelis de Witt, p. 347. "Son prétendu Christianisme n'allait pas au delà d'une adhésion impertinente à quelques-uns des préceptes moraux du Christ." At p. 4 he quotes from Jefferson's Works a passage which illustrates the looseness of this adhesion : "It is not to be understood that I am with Him (Christ) in all His doctrines. I am a Materialist; He takes the side of spiritualism."

† Jefferson's Memoirs and Correspondence, by Thomas Jefferson Randolph. Vol. ii. p. 217. Letter to Peter Carr.

ultimate point both in theory and practice. The theory is perfectly intelligible in itself, and only not familiar to us in the quarter from which it has been recently announced. But its practical application, in the proposed "adjustment of old things to new conditions," is not only startling from its novelty, but one of which happily it is not easy for us at present to form a clear conception. This, however, does not prevent it from being highly worthy of our most serious attention. And we may be in some danger of undervaluing its significance.

<small>The ideal National Church.</small> The ideal sketched in this volume of a National Church, without a theology, without a confession, without a creed, with no other basis of united worship than a system of universal equivocation, has probably struck many with surprise at its extravagance. The scheme by which it is to be realized seems to exhibit an incongruity, almost amounting to direct opposition, between the means and the end. It aims at the cementing of religious unity, by a process apparently tending to the most complete disintegration of all religious communion. It proposes to attract larger congregations to our services, by extinguishing as much as possible the devotional element in them, and turning our churches into lecture-rooms, for the inculcation of ethical commonplace, as to which there is supposed to be no room for any difference of opinion in the audience. To many it must be a satisfaction to feel sure that if, in some paroxysm of public delirium, such a thing was to be set up under the name of a National Church, it would, even without any outward shock, through its intrinsic incoherence, very speedily crumble into dust. And so it may be thought almost a waste of time to dwell upon it. But whatever may be the merits of the scheme, here is the fact, that it has been put forth by a clergyman of no mean ability and of considerable Academical reputation. And then, though among ourselves it is still only in the state of a crude project, it is not a mere dream. It has been realized elsewhere. There are Protestant Churches on the Continent, in which the preachers are not prevented by their open rejection of the supernatural basis of Christianity, from solemnizing the Christian festivals by discourses, in which the

idealizing principle fills the place of the historical reality.* It would, perhaps, be not impossible that a brilliant eloquence might render such rhetorical exercises attractive to some hearers among ourselves. For a time, at least, the contrast between the traditional occasion and the views of the preacher might give a certain zest to the entertainment; though few can imagine that, on the whole and in the long run, such a substitute for the Gospel of Christ would be found to satisfy either the educated or the uneducated classes in this country; still less that it could ever exert any beneficial influence on their minds and hearts. But we are not yet generally prepared to entertain such a question. Most of us think it rather too much, that such a scheme should have appeared in print under a respectable name. Any proceeding which looked like the beginning of a movement for carrying it into effect, would be regarded by the great body of English Churchmen with suspicion and alarm.

I am therefore not surprised that a proposed amendment of the Act of Uniformity which, though I believe framed with a very different view, might be considered as a first step in this direction, was rejected last session in the House of Lords by a great majority. I am not aware that any argument was adduced in behalf of the declaration which it sought to abolish, considered in itself. Those who wished to preserve it, did not profess that it was one which they would have adopted, if it had been then for the first time submitted to deliberation.

Proposed amendment of the Act of Uniformity.

---

* "Predigten aus der Gegenwart." Von D. Carl Schwarz. It is however due to the author to observe, that the anti-supernaturalistic views, which are so distinctly avowed in the Preface, are so little obtruded on the hearer in the sermons themselves, that several of them might easily be mistaken for an expression of the ordinary Christian belief. In an excellent Essay by Dr. J. J. Prins of Leiden, on "The Reality of Our Lord's Resurrection from the Dead," I find the interesting statement (p. 3), that in the General Synod of the Reformed Church of the Netherlands in 1860, the question was raised, "whether a candidate who denies the resurrection of Jesus Christ as a historical fact, is admissible into the ministry." To this question no answer was given by the Synod as a body; but those of its members who were charged with the consideration of the question did not hesitate to declare, each for himself, "that they should not deem themselves competent or able (dat zij zich niet bevoegd noch in staat zonden achten) to exercise the ministry of the Gospel in the Reformed Church if they did not believe with all their heart, that Jesus Christ rose from the dead on the third day."

Probably every one felt that it was indefensible on its own merits. It was too notoriously a characteristic monument of evil days, on which Churchmen can look back only with sorrow; the offspring of a vindictive spirit, which so far overshot its mark, as to ensure the defeat of its own object. For, interpreted literally, it would bind every one who makes it to the opinion that the Prayer Book is, what no uninspired composition can be, absolutely faultless; and in the construction of such a document, the passions of those who framed it, however notorious, cannot be allowed to determine its meaning, which, as the mind of the Legislature, must be supposed to be reasonable and just, at least not to involve any thing manifestly absurd and impracticable. And therefore, though I should be glad to see it abolished, I believe that the mischief it has caused, apart from the discredit it has cast on the Church, has been greatly exaggerated. But, viewed in the light reflected on it by the proposal we have been considering, it not unnaturally lost its true colours, and instead of an odious display of sectarian animosity, and a dark blot on our ecclesiastical legislation, presented the aspect of a precious safeguard against a danger which threatens the life of the Church. I can fully understand this illusion, though I should be loth to share it. For I can never believe in a necessary connexion between that which is bad and wrong in itself, and any thing really valuable or sacred, however long they may have stood side by side. The parasitical bygrowth does not really support, but, on the contrary, compresses and weakens the stem to which it clings. In the present case—as was observed in the debate—there is the less need to retain an indefensible form, as its place might be supplied by another, which would answer every useful purpose, while free from all reasonable objection.

The failure of this attempt may serve as a sample of the difficulty which may be expected to attend the introduction of any larger measure of a like nature. Those indeed who are most fully convinced of the importance and necessity of subscription as a condition of office in the Church, might, notwithstanding, if not on that very account, most earnestly desire the abolition of a particular form which seems to them useless and mischievous. And therefore the proposal which has been recently made,* to remedy the evils which are supposed to arise from the present state of subscription, by doing away with all subscription to the Articles and Prayer Book, and substituting a general declaration and promise of approbation and conformity, with regard to doctrine, worship, and government, or discipline of the Church of England,—is not merely one of much broader scope, but of an essentially different kind, resting upon altogether distinct grounds. But if it was to be presented for legislative action, it would most probably have to encounter a still more determined and general opposition. This however is no reason why it should not be carefully weighed and calmly discussed; though even this is rendered difficult by its apparent affinity to the suggestions of the writer whose views on this subject I have set before you. It must, I think, be admitted that subscription to formularies, if it does not answer the purpose for which it is exacted, is likely to be worse than useless. It is in that case an unjustifiable restriction of personal freedom, which cannot fail to be attended with pernicious consequences. It may be discovered that it never did answer its purpose, or that it does so no longer. In either case, when the fact is well ascertained, the requirement ought to cease. Perhaps it may be added, that, in a country where institutions of every kind are open to unlimited freedom of discussion, it will inevitably do so sooner or later. The argument which has been urged in behalf of the declaration which many wish to see expunged from the Statute Book, that, although it would have been better if it had never been imposed, yet, having once been enacted, it must be retained, because its abolition might be misconstrued into a legislative sanction of unconscientious conformity, is one which at the utmost can only have weight so far as to suggest some easy precaution against such misapprehension. But, on the other hand, the right and fitness of calling upon those

Proposal to remedy the evils of the present mode of subscription.

---

* "A Letter to the Lord Bishop of London on the State of Subscription in the Church of England, and in the University of Oxford." By Arthur Penrhyn Stanley, D.D.

who are to minister in the Church, to express in some form or other their assent to the doctrine which is to be the matter of their teaching, can hardly be denied; and even the largest measure of relaxation which has yet been proposed, does not dispense with the obligation altogether, but only imposes it in a more simple or less definite form. This very much narrows the question, but not I think in favour of the proposed innovation. At present I do not believe that we are sufficiently in possession of the most material facts of the case. It seems to me open to great doubt, whether the existing state of subscription is fairly chargeable with the evils which have been imputed to it, and whether its alleged "inefficacy" has been clearly proved. As to the first of these points I will only remark that it must always be extremely difficult, without an intimate acquaintance with the persons concerned, to ascertain whether those who are said to have been repelled from Holy Orders by the terms of subscription, would have been able to undertake or to retain the ministerial office, if no subscription had been required. And with regard to the second point, it must be observed that although subscription has failed, and must always fail to secure complete unanimity in all particulars, it does not follow that it has been inefficacious toward maintaining a general substantial agreement in matters of doctrine among the clergy. It also deserves to be considered whether that which it has been proposed to substitute for the present form of subscription is not liable to the same objection. It is assumed that persons, who would scruple to subscribe or declare their assent to the Articles and Prayer Book, would be willing to declare their approbation of the doctrine of the Church. But surely this can only be if they forget to inquire where that doctrine is to be found. Unless they are satisfied that it is not either in the Articles or the Prayer Book, the omission of these names from the form of subscription will afford no relief to their scruples, as they would implicitly bind themselves to the contents of those formularies just as much as if they were expressly designated. Reference has been made, as to an example in point, to some Nonconformist bodies in which, though no subscription is required, there is said to be "a marked uniformity of opinion on all important points, though with some diversity in minor matters." No doubt, a congregation which can any moment at its pleasure dissolve its connexion with its minister, can care little about his previous professions of orthodoxy; as all know that his teaching will be sure to conform to their opinions, not only "on all important points," but even in "minor matters" which happen to interest them. I hardly need observe how inapplicable this is to the case of a clergyman who has no motive, but either a sense of duty, or a wish to avoid giving offence, for adapting his teaching to the sentiments of his hearers. To them, in proportion to the soundness of their own churchmanship, it must be a matter of no little interest to know that their pastor acknowledges a rule of faith in accordance with their own belief. If we were to look abroad to the condition of the Churches in which subscription has been either abolished, or retained in a merely nugatory form, which leaves a boundless latitude of opinion to the subscriber, we shall not, I believe, if we set any value on Christianity, be much tempted to imitate their example. If there are some from which we might gain a lesson, there are far more which can only serve as a warning. It is true, where the licence has been carried to the utmost excess, the relaxation of subscription has been not so much the cause as the sign or the effect. But the farther we are actually removed from such a state of things, the more loth should we be either to hasten its approach, or to anticipate any of its results.

I am aware that I have already trenched on the ordinary limits of a Charge; and yet I have not touched on the subject which has occupied the attention of the Church during the last twelve months more than any other: the publications of the Bishop of Natal. In the absence of any special motive for addressing you earlier on this subject, I thought it best to wait for the present opportunity; and I now gladly avail myself of it to state the reasons which, on more than one occasion, prevented me from concurring in the course which the greater part of my Right Reverend brethren thought fit to

Publications of the Bishop of Natal.

adopt in this matter. On one of these occasions, the ground of difference was a question, not of principle, but of personal feeling, which may therefore be dismissed in a very few words. It was thought that, in the first Part of his work, the author had made admissions, showing that he was conscious of an inconsistency between his avowed opinions, and his office in the Church, which warranted an appeal to his sense of duty, as requiring him to resign his functions. I was myself under the same impression as to the meaning of his language. But just on this account I could not reconcile it with my sense of fitness to join in a remonstrance, which seemed to imply, that the person to whom it was addressed was deficient either in intelligence or in moral feeling, and which otherwise must, as it appeared to me, be either superfluous or unavailing. All the facts of the case were before him, more fully indeed than they could be before any one else. It was also evident that the practical question arising out of them was distinctly present to his mind, and had occupied his most serious attention. Under such circumstances, I thought that the decision might be more properly left entirely to himself. It turned out, however, that the ground on which the appeal was made, was an erroneous interpretation of his words. He does not admit the alleged inconsistency, but regards his position as both legally and morally tenable. I cannot reconcile this with his previous language: but as to the fact, that is, the view he takes of his own case, there can be no farther dispute. Whether that view is the right one, is of course a totally different question, but one which no private judgment is competent to determine. And although the legal aspect of the case is distinct from its moral aspect, there is so close a connexion between them, that the legal right, if ascertained, would involve a moral right. Only that right might or might not be exercised rightly. And in this respect, while I cannot but lament the tone of bitterness in which some have expressed their disapprobation of the author, if on no other account, because I believe it can only tend to strengthen his influence among a large class of readers, I must say that, after every allowance for the peculiar circumstances of the case, and with all the respect due to his sincerity and earnestness, he appears to me to have laid himself open to just censure.

It is true the Church of England not only permits but enjoins her ministers to search the Scriptures. It is not merely their right, but a duty, to which each of them is bound by his Ordination vows. The purpose indeed for which they are exhorted to the assiduous cultivation of this study, is entirely practical. It is partly their own growth in godliness, and partly the enlargement of their capacity for the discharge of their pastoral duties; "that by daily reading and weighing of the Scriptures, they may wax riper and stronger in their ministry." A searching of the Scriptures, undertaken with any other ultimate aim, would be one of those "worldly cares and studies," which they are charged "as much as they may, to forsake and set aside." But, apart from the general spirit of this admonition, the Church has not attempted to fence the study of Scripture, either for Clergy or laity, with any restrictions as to the subjects of inquiry, but has rather taught them to consider every kind of information which throws light on any part of the Sacred volume, as precious, either for present or possible use. It was therefore in perfect harmony with the mind of the Church, that the Committee of the Lower House of Convocation appointed to examine the Bishop of Natal's book, "desired not to be understood as expressing any opinion opposed to the free exercise of patient thought and reverent inquiry in the study of the Word of God." But if the inquiry is to be free, it is impossible consistently to prescribe its results: especially with regard to matters which in themselves have no more immediate connexion with Christian doctrine, than any contents of what is commonly called profane history. It is indeed possible that the investigation of such matters may be found to have a bearing on very important points of doctrine, and may lead the inquirer to conclusions apparently at variance with the position of a minister of the Church. That may be his misfortune, but, if truth was his only object, would not be his fault. Nor, considering the endless variety of minds, can we be sure that wherever this is the case, it proves that the inquiry

Free inquiry in the study of Scripture.

was begun with a wrong aim, or conducted in an irreverent spirit.

But after these admissions have been carried to the utmost extent, there remain grounds on which, as it seems to me, the Church has reason to complain of the course taken by the Bishop of Natal in the publication of his researches. He was himself fully aware that it could not fail to be attended with consequences which he deplored. Perhaps he hardly appreciated the full extent of the evil, as well as enormously overrated the benefit which he expected to arise from it. But undoubtedly that which, above all things beside, gave currency to the work, was the apparent contrast between its contents and the author's official position. From the nature of the subject, not one reader in a hundred could be qualified to form a really independent conclusion on the reasoning itself. But there was one palpable fact manifest to all: that a Bishop was announcing opinions contrary to those which were generally received in the Church, and likely to subject him to much obloquy and ill-will. It would therefore be taken for granted by many who had no other means of judging, that he had not only been urged by the love of truth, but that opinions which nothing but a love of truth could have led him to promulge, must be well founded. This was in some degree an unavoidable evil. He could not limit the circulation of his work to those who were able to appreciate the force of his arguments, and not in danger of being misled by his authority. In his own judgment, indeed, this inevitable mischief will be more than counterbalanced by the benefit which he anticipates from the publication, and when he assures us that his own reverence for Holy Writ is not abated by the discovery that it is full of pious frauds and forgeries, we are bound to believe an assertion relating to something which can be known only to himself. But when he would persuade us that Scripture will gain in general estimation, in proportion as such a view of it is commonly received,* this is a paradox as to which

<small>*Part I., p. xxxiv. The object of the book is " to secure for the Bible its due honour and authority ;" and Part II., p. 381.</small>

we may well remain incredulous. But at least this conviction could not exempt him from the duty of doing all in his power to lessen the evil which he foresaw, and of guarding, as far as he could, against hasty judgments, which with many might shake the foundation of their faith, and of their whole moral being. The course which he has actually taken seems to me that which tended most to aggravate this danger.

There may be cases in which it is not only perfectly allowable, but expedient to publish the results of a literary or scientific investigation in successive parts. The criticism which they undergo in the intervals of the publication may modify the author's views and contribute to the improvement of the work. But in the present case such a mode of proceeding could only lessen its value, and increase the mischief it might cause. *Effects of his mode of publication.* One effect was to bring it into the hands of a larger number of such readers as were most likely to suffer injury from it. Another was to deprive it of the advantage it might have derived from a more mature study of the whole subject. This the author himself perceived; but unhappily was so feebly impressed by this consideration, that he allowed it to be outweighed by a motive of temporary convenience, which, in a matter of such importance, was hardly worth a serious thought.* Another effect still more to be deplored was that the premature publication of his first views entirely altered and almost reversed his own position with regard to them. The controversy which it could not fail to stir, as it imposed on him the part of a disputant, rendered it hardly possible for him to retain the character of a perfectly impartial and disinterested inquirer after truth. If he had committed himself to statements which maturer reflection might have induced him to modify, he could no longer do so without a sacrifice of self-love, of which few men are capable, and was thus exposed to a temptation, which those who have the best reason to trust themselves would perhaps most anxiously avoid. Still more *The tone of his language.* open to censure is, as I think, the tone in which he has announced his conclusions; one which could hardly

* Part I. Preface, p. xxxii.

have been more confident if he had been favoured with a Divine revelation,* and which too often seems to indicate a mind so pre-occupied with a foregone conclusion, as to be incapable of viewing the subject from more than one side, and that unhappily the side directly opposed to his earlier and more natural prepossessions. The impression left on the unlearned or half-learned reader is, that these conclusions not only express the decided conviction of one whose station lends extraordinary weight to such opinions, but that they do not admit of fair or reasonable doubt, and may safely be taken for granted as " self-evident truth," † which can only be questioned through ignorance or bad faith. Unhappily a very large class of his readers were sure to be satisfied with this result, and would not care, even if they had the means, to know what might be said on the other side, and whether alleged " absolute impossibilities" might not turn out to be merely very difficult historical problems, capable of diverse conjectural solutions, though, for want of sufficient data, of none which leave no room for doubt. The author had been reminded by a judicious friend,‡ that " we should be very scrupulous about assuming that it is impossible to explain satisfactorily this or that apparent inconsistency, contradiction, or other anomaly." But he has neither been himself sufficiently on his guard against this error, nor taken due care to inculcate the requisite caution on those of his readers who most needed it. They are not warned of the obscurity of the subject, of the relative scantiness of the historical data, of the constant danger of confounding the accuracy of arithmetical calculations with that of the premisses on which they are based. Difficulties are magnified into "plain impossibilities;" seeming discrepancies into direct contradictions. Whatever is narrated so as to raise such difficulties, is pronounced " unhistorical." This term, indeed, is explained so as not to involve a charge of " conscious dishonesty " against the writer,

---

* Part II., p. 371. "It is not I who require you to abandon the ordinary notion of the Mosaic authorship and antiquity of the Pentateuch. It is the TRUTH itself which does so." And again p. 380, "Whatever is done, it is not *I*, but the TRUTH itself, which does it."

† Part I., p. xxxiii. ‡ Part I., p. xvii.

but the qualification loses much of its value, when it turns out that the absence of " conscious dishonesty " only means the obtuseness of his moral sense, which prevented him from feeling that there was any thing dishonest in a pious fraud.*

These, however, are questions which only affect the responsibility of an individual; and whatever harm may have been done by his indiscretion, if there was nothing more in the case, it could not be a subject of permanent public interest. That which alone concerns the Church in this matter is the character of that which has been published by one of her chief pastors, in its relation to her doctrine. Whether, and in what degree or proportion, the book contains truth or error, is, except so far as her doctrine is involved, a purely literary question, which may and must be left to the tribunal of literary criticism. The author regards his own ecclesiastical position as impregnable. That is a point on which I am quite incompetent to pronounce, and am not called upon to express an opinion. But his position might be legally secure, and yet be one which subjected him to the charge of inconsistency and unfaithfulness. And this is a question so intimately connected with the character of the Church itself, as fully to deserve all the attention that has been paid to it. Perhaps I might have said that it deserves a great deal more. For when I compare the amount of discussion which has been bestowed on the book in the historical or critical point of view, with that which has been applied to its theological quality, without saying that there has been too much

The Bishop's writings in relation to the doctrines of the Church.

---

* Part I., p. xvii. The comparison with Homer and the "early Roman annalists" misses just the most material point of the case. If the poet or the annalists had invented a story with the deliberate intention of introducing or recommending a religious innovation, however the end may be thought to sanctify the means, they could not be acquitted of an "*intention* to deceive." But with regard to them there is no reason to believe that they " practised " such a " deception ;" while the Bishop's hypothesis distinctly attributes it to Samuel (II., p. 263). His act would be none the better though a heathen had done the like. It might be very much the worse, inasmuch as it was not a heathen who did it. But it is difficult to believe that, if the Bishop's work had not been published in successive parts, we could have read in Part I., p. xvii, that, "the writer of the story did not *mean* it to be received as historically true," and afterwards (II., p. 263) that he wrote "the account of the revelation to Moses in E. iii.," "with the view of accounting for the origin of the Name."

VOL. II.   F

of the one, I must think that there has been far too little of the other. Strictly speaking I can hardly say that, of the theological kind, there has been any at all. Its place has been filled, as far as I am aware, by nothing but unverified statements and arbitrary assumptions. It was expected that Convocation, which met when the excitement caused by the publication of the first part of the work was at its height, would address itself to this subject, and in both Houses it was generally regarded as the most important to which their attention could be called. It was thought, indeed, by some that the reason which had led the Upper House to suspend its proceedings in the case of the *Essays and Reviews*, applied to this, and that it was not desirable to forestall the decision of a question in which personal interests were involved, when it was likely to be brought ere long before another tribunal. It was, however, decided that a Committee of the Lower House should be appointed to examine and report on the contents of the work; and thus its theological character was submitted to the scrutiny of a select number of eminent Divines.

<small>The action of Convocation on the subject.</small>   This is the second occasion, since the revival of Convocation, on which it has undertaken to express an opinion on books. It is an exercise of its functions which had probably not entered into any one's mind at the time of that revival, and was certainly never expressly included among the objects for the sake of which the revival was sought, still less contemplated by those from whom, notwithstanding much opposition, it was obtained. There were strong reasons, suggested partly by the past history of Convocation, partly by the spirit of modern times, which rendered it more than ever desirable that the newly-recovered liberty should be both sparingly and cautiously used; never without urgent occasion, and always within the measure marked by the nature of the end proposed. The urgency of the occasion must depend, partly on the character of the book, and partly on the special circumstances of the case. It will probably be generally admitted, that Convocation would be lowering its dignity, if it were to assume the office of a literary critic, and to pronounce censure on defects of taste, or judgment,

or reasoning, or of any thing extrinsic to the proper domain of theology. But, even within that domain, there is much that does not properly come within the province of Convocation. There may be a great deal of very bad, unsound divinity, crude theories, rash speculations, erroneous opinions, such as, if developed into their ultimate issues, might even be found at variance with fundamental truths, which, nevertheless, Convocation neither need nor ought to notice. It appears to me that whatever error it does undertake to deal with, should be such as at once touches the foundation, and lies very near to the surface; in other words, that its action in the censure of books should be confined to cases in which clergymen have either directly, or by plain implication, impugned the doctrine of the Church as universally admitted to be laid down in her Formularies. No mistake which Convocation could commit, could be more disastrous to its credit and usefulness, or more imperil its very existence, than if it should attempt to circumscribe the freedom of opinion sanctioned by the Church by any new determination of its own, or should identify itself with any religious party, and endeavour to make its views the standard of orthodoxy. On the other hand it may seem superfluous to observe, that the judgments of such a body should be delivered in precise and unequivocal terms.

The Judgment of Convocation, founded on the Report of the Committee of the Lower House, is memorable as the first which it has pronounced since its revival. The doubt which was felt whether it was advisable to take any action at all in the matter, though it was not allowed to prevent the passing of a censure, was permitted to determine the form in which the censure was expressed. I rejoice that it did so. Though I think that, if nothing more was to be said, it would have been better to have been silent, I am thankful that nothing more was said. But the form of the censure seems to betray the influence of a persuasion, which I fear has but very slight foundation in fact. It is natural that the members of Convocation, who take a lively interest and an active part in its proceedings, should be apt to overrate the importance attached to them out of doors, and the impression

First judgment since its revival.

which they make on public opinion. There may have been a time when its authority in religious controversies was generally acknowledged, and the simple declaration of its judgment, unaccompanied by any statement of the grounds on which it rested, was sufficient to ensure universal acquiescence. But such a state of things, if it ever existed, belongs to the remote past. We live in a generation which has but lately become familiar with the name of Convocation, and in which it is not always associated with feelings of submissive veneration and unquestioning confidence. There are some who regard it with distrust and aversion. Others watch it as an institution on its trial. Many, no doubt, look to it with respect, sympathy, and hope. But I believe that its warmest friends are aware that its credit and influence must depend, not on a time-honoured name, or conventional epithets, but on the character of its proceedings, and that these will be submitted to the same free examination, to which among us all matters of public interest are subject. Nor would they wish it to be otherwise. The Resolution by which the Bishop of Natal's book was condemned, assumes a paternal authority which rather suits an earlier period in the education of the world; and it presupposes a childlike docility and obedience in those over whom it is exercised, which are now very rarely to be found. It also suggests the question, what practical purpose it was designed to answer. Two were indicated in the Committee's Report,—"the effectual vindication of the truth of God's Word before men," and "the warning and comfort of Christ's people."* But it is not clear how either of these objects could be attained by a declaration, that the book "involves errors of the gravest and most dangerous character." Both seem to require that the censure should have pointed out the errors involved, or have stated the doctrines which the book had at least indirectly impugned, so as to make it clear

* How widely different an impression it has made on some minds, may be gathered from a paper in Macmillan's Magazine for July, 1863, where the writer, who describes himself as a " Lay Churchman," speaking of the Report of the Lower House, observes: " No friend of the Church of England can read it without shame and sorrow:" not without assigning reasons for his assertion. What is saddest in this is: " talia nobis et dici potuisse, et non potuisse refelli."

that the alleged errors affected, not merely prevalent opinions, but truths universally recognized as part of the Church's creed.

To me, indeed, it appears that whenever Convocation undertakes to pronounce on a theological work, its judgment should be dogmatical, containing some definite theological proposition. Otherwise, it may convey an expression of feeling which is not required, and perhaps in such a case would better be suppressed, while it withholds the one thing really wanted, a declaration of distinct opinion on the teaching which it condemns. In the present case the vagueness of the judgment was the more remarkable, because the attention of Convocation had been specially drawn to certain propositions, extracted from the substance of the book, which appeared to the Committee to "involve errors of the gravest and most dangerous character;" and the Judgment, taking no notice of these propositions, applies the same description to the whole book, and was thus the more likely to disappoint and perplex those who might look to it for some kind of guidance, or means of discriminating between truth and error. I cannot consider this as an auspicious inauguration of the revived judicial action of Convocation. But still, as I have said, it seems to me to afford matter for deep thankfulness, so far as the Upper House abstained from pronouncing on the propositions to which its attention had been drawn. It was infinitely better that it should confine itself to generalities, of doubtful meaning and little practical worth, than that it should have undertaken to dogmatize on those propositions. According to the view which I have ventured to take of the proper limits of synodical action in the cognizance of books, the Committee overstept those limits. They were appointed to examine the parts which had then appeared of the Bishop's work, and to report "whether any, and, if any, what opinions heretical or erroneous in doctrine were contained in it." They extracted three propositions which they characterized as we have seen. All that they say beside might, indeed, have entered into a controversial discussion of the work. But this was something foreign to the business with which they were charged. It was, not to

The Judgment of Convocation on theological works should be dogmatical.

refute any errors which they might find in the book—a task which probably no one would have thought of assigning to such a number of persons, however well qualified each of them might be for it individually—but to mark the character of the opinions contained in it with reference to the standards of the Church's doctrine. To inquire whether they were tenable or not in themselves, was here wholly beside the purpose.) Yet this is really all that is done in the Report.

How the Committee dealt with the Bishop's first proposition. It may seem indeed as if the Committee, in their mode of dealing with the first of the propositions which they cite or extract for censure, had shown that they were aware of the precise nature of the function they had to perform, and meant to confine themselves to it. That proposition is—(" the Bible is not itself God's Word." The author himself immediately adds, " But assuredly ' God's Word ' will be heard in the Bible, by all who will humbly and devoutly listen for it.") Of this qualification the Committee, in their remarks on the proposition, take no notice whatever. But they first observe that the proposition, as they cite it, "is contrary to the faith of the universal Church, which has always taught that Holy Scripture is given by inspiration of the Holy Ghost." They seem to have overlooked that this statement, however true, was irrelevant; but they then proceed to refer to the Articles and Formularies of our own Church, which are, indeed, the only authority binding on her ministers. But unfortunately not one of the passages to which they refer applies to the proposition condemned. Many, indeed, among them do clearly describe the Bible as the Word of God. But not one affirms that "the Bible is *itself* God's Word." Before the negative of this statement could be shown to be contrary to the language of our Articles and Formularies, it was necessary either to prove or take for granted that the addition *itself* in no way affected the sense of the proposition. This, however, being a matter depending entirely on the author's intention, did not admit of proof. But, for the same reason, it could not safely or justly (for the purpose of a solemn censure) be taken for granted. No doubt the expression indicated that the author made a distinction between the Bible and the Word of God, and considered the two terms as not precisely equivalent or absolutely interchangeable. But if he affixed a meaning to the term *Word of God*, according to which it might be truly said, that the Bible was not *itself* that Word, this—even if the proposition had stood by itself without any qualification—would not imply a denial, that there may be another sense in which the Bible is truly described as the Word of God. And there is certainly high authority for the distinction. Among the numerous passages of the New Testament in which the phrase, *the Word of God*, occurs, there is not one in which it signifies the Bible, or in which that word could be substituted for it without manifest absurdity. *_{Meaning of the phrase "the Word of God."}* But even in our Articles and Formularies there are several in which the two terms do not appear to be treated as synonymous. The expressions, "God's Word written" (Art. XX.), "ministering God's Word" (Art. XXXVII.), "dispenser of God's Word" (Ordinal for Priests), "hinderer or slanderer of God's Word" (Office of Holy Communion), seem to point to the New Testament use rather than to the Biblical record; and, at least, there can be no doubt as to the meaning in the Collect for St. Bartholomew's Day, where the prayer is, that God, who " gave the Apostle grace truly to believe and preach his Word," " would grant unto His Church to love that Word which he believed, and both to preach and receive the same." When you, my brethren, preach the Word of God, it may happen that your text is the only portion of the Bible which you quote: and though even your text should not be taken from one of the Gospels, you might not feel the less sure that it is the Gospel which you preach. That which you preach would not, indeed, be the Gospel or the Word of God, unless it was agreeable to God's Word written. But there may be substantial agreement without literal identity, which would confound the offices of reading and of preaching. If the Word of God is to be found nowhere but in Holy Writ, not only could no other Christian literature be properly called sacred, but the Bible itself would be degraded to a dead and barren letter, and would not be a living spring of Divine truth. On the whole, the Report first attaches an arbitrary meaning to an ambiguous expression, and then charges it with contradicting authorities, which are either wholly silent upon it, or seem to countenance and warrant it. The appeal to the faith and constant teaching of the universal Church is not only, as I observed, irrelevant to a question of Anglican orthodoxy, but introduces a topic which is by no means necessarily involved in the proposition—the inspiration of Holy Scripture; and a reader who did not verify the references, might easily be led to imagine that they contain some declaration of our own Church on that subject. Yet all they do contain that bears upon it, is the frequent application of the description *Word of God* to the Bible. Our Church has never attempted to determine the nature of the inspiration of Holy Scripture; and whether such a determination is desirable or not, no friend to Convocation would wish to see it undertake a task of such perilous moment, and so far beyond its legitimate province.

<small>Treatment of the second proposition.</small> But in their treatment of the next proposition, the Committee seem almost entirely to have lost sight of the principle which, although misapplied, appeared to guide them in their examination of the first. For, with a single insignificant exception, they confront it, not with our Articles and Formularies, but with passages of Scripture. Quotations from Scripture may add great weight to a theological argument; they are essential for the establishment of any doctrine of a Church which professes to ground its teaching on Scripture; but they are entirely out of place where the question is, not whether a doctrine is true or false, but whether it is the doctrine of the Church of England. Some years ago the Venerable Person who was Chairman of this Committee, and is believed to have had the chief share in the framing of its Report, was charged with the publica-
<small>Arguments grounded on texts of Scripture inadmissible in law.</small> tion of unsound doctrine with regard to the Sacrament of the Lord's Supper. In those proceedings, though they affected his civil rights, and but for a technical defect might have subjected him to penal consequences, the Court refused to listen to a plea set up in his defence,

grounded on texts of Scripture. The principle of that refusal has since been repeatedly affirmed by the highest judicial authority. It was briefly, but clearly, laid down by the Judicial Committee of the Privy Council in the following terms :—" In investigating the justice of such a charge we are bound to look solely to the Statute and the Articles. It would be a departure from our duty if we were to admit any discussion as to the conformity or nonconformity of the Articles of Religion, or any of them, with the Holy Scriptures." And in the more recent case of the " Essays and Reviews," the Judge, commenting on that opinion, observed, " Were I once to be tempted from the Articles and other parts of the Formularies, the Court could assign no limit to its investigations; it would inevitably be compelled to consider theological questions, not for the purpose of deciding whether they were conformable to a prescribed standard, but whether the positions maintained were reconcilable with Scripture or not. Against pursuing such a course as this, the reasons are many, and in my judgment overwhelmingly strong." And after stating them he says, " I will not be tempted, in the trial of any accusation against a clergyman, to resort to Scripture as the standard by which the doctrine shall be measured." This is no legal refinement, but a plain dictate of common sense; and it does not at all depend on the composition of the tribunal before which such questions are tried; so as to be less applicable if the Court consisted entirely of ecclesiastics. On one supposition only would such a plea be admissible, that is, if the Judge was acknowledged to possess the authority of an infallible oracle in the interpretation of Scripture. Otherwise there could be no security, that an argument from Scripture which to some minds appeared perfectly convincing, might not seem to others miserably weak, or utterly worthless. I should think it a great misfortune to the Church if Convocation, sitting in judgment on the orthodoxy of a theological work, though without any view to proceedings against the author, should ignore and practically reject that principle. And if in this respect the Report betrays the influence of a personal prepossession, which, however natural, ought not to be allowed to

<small>Soundness of the rule.</small>

sway the decisions of a grave assembly, above all, so as to bring them into conflict with the highest legal authorities of the realm, we have the more reason to rejoice, that it did not obtain the sanction of the Upper House.

When I look at the Scriptural arguments adduced in the Report against the second proposition extracted for condemnation, they do not seem to me of such a quality as to deserve to form an exception, if any could be admitted, to the rule which would exclude them from such an investigation. The proposition is, "that not Moses but Samuel, and other persons of a later age, composed the Pentateuch." It would perhaps have been better not to have brought the negative and positive substance of the book thus together, as the hypothesis about Samuel is, for the purpose of the inquiry, quite immaterial, except as denying the Mosaic authorship; and the argument of the Report is entirely confined to that denial. But upon this the Committee observe, "that Moses is spoken of, by our Blessed Lord in the Gospel, as the writer of the Pentateuch." I suspect that even a layman, little acquainted with the manifold aspects of the question, and the almost infinite number of surmises which have been or may be formed concerning it, would be somewhat disappointed, when he found that the proof of this statement consists of three passages, in which our Lord speaks of Moses and the prophets, of the Law of Moses, and of writings of Moses. It is true that it would not be a fatal objection to the argument, that the word Pentateuch does not occur in the Bible. It might have been so described as to connect every part of its contents with the hand of Moses, as distinctly as if the observation of the Committee had been literally true. But in fact this is not the case; and still less is any such distinct appropriation to be found in any of the passages cited by the Committee in support of their assertion, that "Moses is recognized as the writer of the Pentateuch in other passages of Holy Scripture." They are neither more nor less conclusive than the language of the seventh Article, to which the Committee confine all the reference they have made to the judgment of the Church on this question, though this was the only

The authorship of the Pentateuch.

matter into which it was their proper business to inquire. The Article alludes to "the law given from God by Moses;" a slender foundation for any inference as to the record of that law, much more as to the authorship of other parts of the Pentateuch; especially as the name of Moses does not occur in the enumeration of the Canonical Books in the sixth Article. If the question had been as to the authorship of the book of Psalms, few persons probably would think that it had been dogmatically decided by the Church, because in the Prayer Book the Psalter is described as "the Psalms of David." Similarly and equally inconclusive appear to me the passages cited in proof of the observation, "that there are portions of the Pentateuch to which our Blessed Lord refers as being parts of the books of Moses, the Mosaic authorship of which is expressly denied in the Bishop's book."

The third proposition, "variously stated in the book," relates to the historical truth of the Pentateuch, which the author denies; not in the sense that every thing in it is pure fiction, but that all is not historically true.* Of the fact with which he is charged there can be no doubt; and it was superfluous to give instances of that which he has expressly stated in general terms. But it is to be regretted that the Committee should again have lost sight of the object for which they were appointed, and have omitted to refer to any doctrine of the Church which the author has contradicted. This was the more incumbent on them, since a recent Judgment has formally sanctioned a very wide latitude in this respect. It is clear that in such things there cannot be two weights and two measures for different persons, and also that it does not belong to any but legal authority to draw the line by which the freedom, absolutely granted in theory, is to be limited in practice. The author's scepticism appears to me, as to many others, very rash and wild. But that was not the question before Convocation. It was

Third proposition, on the historical truth of the Pentateuch.

---

* Part II., p. 372. The value, however, of the admission is not very great, since it is supposed that Samuel's materials consisted entirely of "legendary recollections," which were so dim and vague as to leave even the existence of Moses open to doubt. P. 376 (where Ewald's credulous dogmatism is gently rebuked by a note of interrogation) and p. 185.

whether, or how far, such scepticism had been forbidden by the Church. And on this, the only point which required their attention, the Committee are totally silent.

These are the propositions which they extract as "the main propositions of the book," which, though not pretending to "pronounce definitively whether they are or are not heretical," they denounce as "involving errors of the gravest and most dangerous character." But they proceed to cite a further proposition, which the author states in the form of a question, to meet an objection which had been raised against his main conclusion, as virtually rejecting our Lord's authority, by which, as the Committee state, "the genuineness and the authenticity of the Pentateuch have been guaranteed to all men." Whether the passages in which our Lord quotes or alludes to the Pentateuch, amount to such a guarantee, is a point which they do not discuss. They only observe that the proposition "questions our Blessed Lord's Divine Knowledge," and with that remark they drop the subject.

<small>Fourth proposition.</small>

Considering that this proposition is incomparably the most important of all that they cite, and that whatever importance the others possess depends ultimately on the connexion into which they may be brought with it, one is surprised that it should have been dismissed with so very cursory and imperfect a notice. For it is not even clear that it correctly expresses the author's meaning. The question which he raises does not properly concern our Lord's Divine Knowledge, that is, the knowledge belonging to His Divine nature. It is, whether His human knowledge was co-extensive with the Divine Omniscience. It is obvious at the first glance, what a vast field of speculation, theological and metaphysical, is opened by this suggestion. And perhaps a little reflection would satisfy every one capable of appreciating the difficulties which beset the inquiry, that the subject is not only one of the most abstruse with which the human mind can be engaged, but that it lies beyond the reach of our faculties, and is one of those mysteries which are to be embraced by faith, not to be investigated by reason. If any

<small>Its relation to the others.</small>

<small>Definition and extent of the question raised.</small>

one thinks that he is able to explain the mode in which the operations of our Lord's human nature were affected by His Godhead, or to distinguish between that which belonged to the integrity of His manhood, to the extraordinary gifts with which He was furnished for His work, and again to the proper attributes of Deity, he is of course at liberty to make the experiment, but should not be surprised if his solution satisfies none but himself. Bishop Jeremy Taylor observes: "They that love to serve God in hard questions, use to dispute whether Christ did truly or in appearance only increase in wisdom. For being personally united to the Word, and being the eternal wisdom of the Father, it seemed to them that a plenitude of wisdom was as natural to the whole person as to the Divine nature. But others, fixing their belief upon the words of the story, which equally affirms Christ as properly to have increased in favour with God as with man, in wisdom as in stature, they apprehend no inconvenience in affirming it to belong to the verity of human nature, to have degrees of understanding as well as of other perfections: and although the humanity of Christ made up the same person with the Divinity, yet they think the Divinity still to be free, even in those communications, which were imparted to his inferior nature; and the Godhead might as well suspend the emanation of all the treasures of wisdom upon the humanity for a time, as he did the beatific vision, which most certainly was not imparted in the interval of his sad and dolorous passion."* It is clear to which side Taylor inclines. But I must own that I should be sorry to see these "hard questions" revived, as I am persuaded that there could not be a less acceptable "service to God," or a less profitable exercise of learning and acuteness. Still more should I deprecate any attempt of the Church of England to promulge a new dogma for the settlement of this controversy. And I lament that the Committee of the Lower House should have expressed themselves as if either there was no "dispute" on the subject, or it belonged to them to end it by a word. But at least, as their remark indicated, that the Bishop had, in their judgment, fallen into

* Life of Christ. Works, ed. Heber, ii. p. 142.

some grave error, it was due, not only to him, but to the readers of their Report, and to the Church at large, that they should have pointed out what the error was, by a comparison with the doctrine of the Church which it was supposed to contradict.

Omissions of the Report. Little as I am satisfied with the contents of the Report, I think there is no less ground for surprise at its omissions. Since the Committee felt themselves at liberty to animadvert, not only on the propositions extracted from the book, but on its general spirit and tendency, it might have been expected that they would omit nothing worthy of special notice, as serving to mark its peculiar character. Yet, while they hold up to reprobation the results of purely historical investigations, because in their opinion at variance with doctrines of the Church, which however it is left to the reader's sagacity to discover, they pass over in silence passages which, however they may admit of a different explanation, appear in their most obvious sense irreconcilable with the admission of a supernatural revelation. An eminent writer of the last century, who may be called the father of German rationalism, startled his contemporaries by the assertion, that as religion was before the Bible, so it might continue to subsist though the Bible should be lost.* It has been questioned whether in this proposition the religion meant was Christianity or Natural Religion. In the former sense the proposition was an idle surmise, which it was impossible to verify. But in the latter sense, it was admitted that it could be only understood as treating Christianity as no more than a form of natural religion. † The

---

* So the proposition is stated by Gurlitt in the Theologische Studien und Kritiken, 1863, p. 763. Mr. Farrar, in his Bampton Lectures on the History of Free Thought, p. 319, states a different proposition to the like effect: "that, as Christianity existed before the New Testament, so it could exist after it." There may be here, either a misprint, of *after* instead of *without*, or an omission of the words *was lost* at the end. Each of these statements no doubt expresses Lessing's meaning, though neither accurately reports his words. His fifth axiom is: "Religion existed before the Bible." The sixth: "Christianity existed before Evangelists and Apostles had written." The eighth: "If there was a period in which the Christian religion was widely spread, though not a letter of all that has come down to us on the subject had yet been written, it must be possible that all the writings of the Evangelists and Apostles should be lost, and the religion which they taught still subsist."

† Gurlitt, u. s.

Bishop of Natal consoles himself for the "serious consequences" which he "painfully forebodes" as likely to ensue in many cases from the publication of his book, by this reflection:—"Our belief in the living God remains as sure as ever, though not the Pentateuch only, but the whole Bible, were removed." "The light of God's love did not shine less truly on pious minds, when Enoch walked with God of old, though there was then no Bible in existence, than it does now."* What kind of religion it is that would thus survive the loss of the Bible, seems, as far as the words go, hardly to admit of a doubt. It may be called Christianity; but hardly in any other sense than that in which a deistical writer of the last century entitled one of his works, "Christianity as old as the Creation." Religion without the Bible.

It is indeed, in the author's view, a revealed religion; but so was that which he finds expounded in a passage of Cicero, in the confession of the Sikh-Gooroos, and in the ejaculations of an Indian mystic. Their pure deism was, he doubts not, "revealed to them by the same Divine Teacher," who spake by prophets and apostles. † If there was no special revelation in Christianity, such statements would be not only conformable to the Apostle's teaching, that "every good gift comes down from the Father of lights," but also relevant to the case, and of great practical importance, as either showing the needlessness of Christian missions, or at least preventing them from assuming a character to which they are not entitled. But if there was such a special Christian revelation, it is difficult to see either the appropriateness or the practical use of the remark. The author indeed intimates his "entire and sincere belief in our Lord's divinity;" ‡ and this must silence all doubt as to his orthodoxy on that head; but as he does not profess to view any of the founders of other religions in the same light, it might have been expected that he would have explained how that belief is to be reconciled with language which seems to place all religions, which acknowledge the being and unity of God, with regard to their divine origin, on the same level. The apparent sense of that language is In what sense revealed.

* Part I., p. 12.   † Part I., p. 155.   ‡ Part I., p. xxxi.

also the only one that is clearly consistent with his anticipations of a coming happier time, when " missionaries of the Jewish race," as soon as they have " given up the story of the Pentateuch as a record of historical fact," shall go forth, to co-operate with our own as " heralds of salvation, proclaiming with free utterance the name of the living God."* It is in perfect harmony with this sense, but not with any other which the words readily suggest, that he looks forward to changes at home, by which " the system of our Church is to be reformed," and her boundaries at the same time enlarged, so as " to make her what a National Church should be, the mother of spiritual life to all within the realm, embracing, as far as possible, all the piety, and learning, and earnestness, and goodness, of the nation." † This hint indeed is so vague, that it would have been difficult to gather its precise import, if the Essay, of which I have already spoken, in which a like view of the National Church is more fully developed, and the conditions of the proposed reform more distinctly explained, did not furnish a commentary, and relieve me from the necessity of making any further observation upon it.

Remarks on the study of the work.   I do not know how many of you, my brethren, may have found leisure for the study or even for the reading of the work I have been considering. Possibly if you happened to have learnt that its results are almost entirely negative, and that as to those of a more positive kind the author appears to have convinced no one but himself, not even foreign critics who willingly accept his arguments on the destructive side ; ‡ some of you might think, not unreasonably, that their time might be more profitably spent than in following the course of such a barren inquiry, and that it was better to wait until it should have yielded some amount of generally-recognized positive truth. If, however, you chose to judge of the book for yourselves, and did not allow yourselves to be deterred from the examination of its contents by the opinion that the Church had forbidden an investigation which presupposed that there was room for doubt on the subject, though

---

* Part II., p. 384.   † Part I., p. xxxv.
‡ Among the latest see Kamphausen in Theol. Stud. u. Krit. 1863, p. 795.

you might soon see ground to suspect that the author must, from the peculiar turn of his mind, be a very unsafe guide wherever there was need of the higher faculties required for the study of obscure periods of ancient history, you would nevertheless find proofs of no mean sceptical acuteness, and much specious reasoning, to which you might not be able readily to devise even a possible answer. This with you might not be enough to extort an absolute assent to that which you felt yourselves unable to refute; but it would probably induce you to read some of the replies, in which, as is stated in the Report of the Committee of the Lower House of Convocation, "the difficulties propounded by the author have been fairly discussed." From several of these replies you could not fail to gain much valuable information. You would find many things placed in an entirely different light from that in which they had been first set before you. In most cases the conditions on which the author's objections are founded, would appear to be by no means so simple or so clear as he had represented them. Relatively to his position of absolute assurance, you might think the replies on the whole perfectly successful. But if you had expected that they would remove all difficulty, and satisfy every doubt, you would find yourselves disappointed, as in fact you would have looked for more than, according to the present state of our knowledge, any amount of learning and ability can achieve. But, should this be so, what follows? There will be nothing in such a discovery, by which any one need be saddened or perplexed; but it may suggest some reflections which it will be well for every one to lay to heart.

There are many things in which our highest wisdom is to resign ourselves to the consciousness of our ignorance, and to the certainty that, on this side the grave, we shall never know more of them than we do. This is the case with many subjects of abstract speculation; and perhaps even more so with the history of the remote past, where our knowledge entirely depends on evidence which, however scanty and imperfect, admits of no enlargement or further corroboration. So it is with regard to the two ancient nations which, next to the chosen people of

Limitation of our knowledge.

God, have left the deepest traces of their presence in the existing state of the world, and continue to exercise the most powerful influence on modern society. The longest period in the annals of each is shrouded in darkness, which is broken only at intervals by some faint gleams of light, not sufficient to afford a distinct view of the few objects on which they fall. And even in later ages a like bar is frequently opposed to our curiosity. We reconcile ourselves to this insurmountable limitation of our knowledge because, after all, that which we possess is sufficient for the most important purpose of our inquiries, as it enables us to understand the character and general progress of each people, and its place in the history of the world. If the same thing has occurred in the early history of the chosen race, have we any reason to be surprised, or any right to complain? It is true the particulars of this history are more interesting to us than those of any other, just as the geography of the Holy Land is more interesting to a Christian pilgrim than that of Italy or Greece. But our wishes, however natural and reasonable, cannot prescribe or control the course of the Divine government; and we may be sure that whatever knowledge God's Providence has thought fit to withhold from us, cannot be necessary with regard to any of the higher interests of our being. If the process by which the Pentateuch was brought into its present state has not been revealed to us, but affords room for manifold conjecture and endless controversy, however we may wish it had been otherwise, our part is humbly to submit to the Divine will. We see that, in fact, all the information that has been vouchsafed to us as to the earlier period of the Sacred History is very scanty and fragmentary. A few pages, sometimes a few lines, are the only remaining record of the lapse of centuries. In the Pentateuch itself, as in other parts of the Old Testament, we meet with frequent reference to works, which would probably have shed much light on persons and events, now but dimly perceptible, and presenting an ambiguous aspect; but it was not the Divine pleasure that they should be preserved to us. But that which we have is not only sufficient, but more than sufficient, for the main end, the exhibition of the Divinely appointed preparation for the coming of Christ. Every line of this record is precious to us; but there is much as to which it seems to us that our view of the whole would have been no more affected by its absence, than it has been by the loss of those works to which the Sacred Writers refer for information which we can no longer find in them.

Another thought which may well be brought home to our minds by the controversies of the day, is that we have greater need than ever to distinguish between things which do and things which do not concern our Christian faith and hope. A great part of the events related in the Old Testament has no more apparent connexion with our religion than those of Greek or Roman history. It is true that even the minutest and seemingly most insignificant facts may have entered into the scheme of Divine Providence, as part of the process through which a way was prepared for the introduction of the Gospel. But this is no more than may be said of every thing that has happened every where upon earth from the beginning of the world. The adaptation of the means to the end is one of the secrets of the Divine counsels; and we cannot presume to say that the same end might not have been attained by some other means. This therefore is not sufficient to invest the means with any share in the sanctity of the end. The history, so far as it is a narrative of civil and political transactions, has no essential connexion with any religious truth, and, if it had been lost, though we should have been left in ignorance of much that we should have desired to know, our treasure of Christian doctrine would have remained whole and unimpaired. The numbers, migrations, wars, battles, conquests, and reverses of Israel, have nothing in common with the teaching of Christ, with the way of salvation, with the fruits of the Spirit. They belong to a totally different order of subjects. They are not to be confounded with the spiritual revelation contained in the Old Testament, much less with that fulness of grace and truth which came by Jesus Christ. Whatever knowledge we may obtain of them is, in a religious point of view, a matter of absolute indifference to us; and if they were placed on a level with the saving truths of the Gospel, they

Need of distinguishing between things which do, and things which do not, concern our faith and hope.

would gain nothing in intrinsic dignity, but would only degrade that with which they are thus associated. Such an association may indeed exist in the minds of pious and even learned men; but it is only by means of an artificial chain of reasoning, which does not carry conviction to all beside. Such questions must be left to every one's private judgment and feeling, which have the fullest right to decide for each, but not to impose their decisions, as the dictate of an infallible authority, on the consciences of others. Any attempt to erect such facts into articles of faith, would be fraught with danger of irreparable evil to the Church, as well as with immediate hurt to numberless souls.

<small>Concluding remarks.</small> A single word more. That which now unhappily disquiets many will turn to your profit, if it should lead you to take a firmer hold on the centre of your faith and hope; to draw closer to Christ Himself, and to seek in a more intimate and practical communion with Him, that light and life, which He alone can impart. If the historical and critical questions which have lately been brought anew under discussion, were capable of a solution which should leave no room for doubt, it would not bring you one step the nearer, or at all help you to find your way to Him. At the best it could yield only an intellectual satisfaction, perhaps at the risk of diverting your attention from that which is alone needful. But if you take your stand, and make good your footing, on that Rock which is the sole foundation that is laid for the Church, and therefore the only one on which any of us can find a sure resting-place, you will enjoy more than one great advantage in looking abroad on the field of controversy which is spread before you. One will be the sense of a happy security, not to be shaken by any fluctuations of public opinion, or any strife of doubtful disputations. And in proportion to the calmness of that assurance which you derive from your personal experience, will be your attainment of the still greater blessing of a meek, charitable, and peaceable spirit, which will guard you from harsh judgments and inward bitterness toward those from whom you may differ, while it leads you forward in the way of truth. And then—though your aim is not the knowledge which

puffeth up, but the charity which edifieth—this shall be added unto you, that you will also see farther and more clearly than those who are standing and striving on the lower and debatable ground. It is not that you are to expect any supernatural illumination which will supply the place of patient study, and enable you to solve questions which have eluded the grasp of the most learned and sagacious inquirers. But you will gain something which is far better; a faculty of spiritual discernment, which will guide you safely where others, with perhaps superior natural advantages and ampler opportunities of knowledge, may have gone astray. In the ripening of your inner life, and, above all, in the assiduous discharge of your pastoral duties, you will be constantly acquiring a deeper insight into the nature of the things which belong to your own peace, and to that of those who are committed to your care; and you will thus possess an unfailing test by which you may try the character, and measure the worth, of whatever is proposed for your assent: and, having learned more and more clearly to distinguish between that which rests on the sure Word of God, and that which floats on the shifting current of human speculation, you will so " prove all things" as to " hold fast that which is good."

APPENDIX.

NOTE ON PAGE 20.

WHETHER all but two or three readers have misunderstood the main drift of Professor Powell's Essay, is a question which does not much concern those, who, sharing the general opinion, expressed themselves in accordance with it, unless they themselves had felt a doubt on the subject; and, for my own part, I can say that none has ever for an instant crossed my mind. But it does very deeply concern the character of Professor Powell; and in my opinion no greater wrong could have been done to his memory, than the attempt to vindicate him from the charge of "denying miracles." Unless he meant to do that, he would have been guilty of an ambiguity of language, which, in one so capable of expressing himself clearly, could hardly be unintentional, though its motive would be difficult to explain. What ground the Edinburgh Reviewer saw for the doubt which he intimates, p. 475, he has not stated. Mr. Maurice (Tracts for Priests and People, p. 13), though anxiously seeking for points in which he could agree with the writer, could not shut his eyes to so glaring a fact. "Mr. Baden Powell," he says, "was an English man of science. The miracles, regarded as departures from order, contradicted, in his judgment, the very idea of physical science; he could not reconcile them. He believed that no one could." Mr. Kennard alone, as far as I know, has ventured positively to assert that Professor Powell "does not deny miracles;" but he has fairly stated his ground for that assertion (p. 76). He first quotes some words of Professor Powell—"The question, then, of miracles stands quite apart from any consideration of *testimony*; the question would remain the same if we had the evidence of our own senses to an alleged miracle, that is, to an extraordinary or inexplicable fact. It is not the mere fact, but the *cause* or *explanation* of it, which is the point at issue." On this Mr. Kennard remarks: "He does not, the reader will be careful to observe, 'deny miracles,' but, feeling the increasing difficulty which scientific and historical criticism places in the way of the old unreasoning reception of them as mere wonders, he seeks to explain and account for them consistently with the requirements of science, and the demands of an enlightened Christian faith."

What Professor Powell admitted, and what he denied, in this matter, is perfectly clear. He fully admitted that, among "alleged miracles," many have been real facts; what he denied was, that any of these facts were real miracles. He believed that they only appeared to be such to persons ignorant of the laws of nature. On the other hand, he never meant to deny that many alleged miracles, if they had taken place, would have been works of superhuman power; what he denied as to these was, that they were real facts. "An alleged miracle," he concludes, "can only be regarded in one of two ways:—either (1) abstractedly, as a physical event, and therefore to be investigated by reason and physical evidence, and referred to physical causes, possibly to *known* causes, but at all events to some higher cause or law, if at present unknown; it then ceases to be supernatural, yet still might be appealed to in support of religious truth, especially as referring to the state of knowledge and apprehensions of the parties addressed in past ages; or (2) as connected with religious doctrine, regarded in a sacred light, asserted on the authority of inspiration. In this case it ceases to be capable of investigation by reason, or to own its dominion; it is accepted on religious grounds, and can appeal only to the principle and influence of faith.' In the Charge I have pointed out the fallacy of this alternative. Here I have only to observe that nothing can be plainer than the negative proposition. Unless the "alleged miracle" may be "referred to physical causes, known or unknown," and so "ceases to be supernatural," and to have a right to the name of miracle, it was not a "physical event," or real fact. According to Mr. Kennard's representation, Professor Powell would have admitted the reality of the facts related in the Gospels, which are commonly regarded as miraculous, and only denied that they were supernatural. Mr. Kennard would vindicate the Professor from the charge of excessive scepticism, by convicting him of the most extravagant credulity; which, without raising his character as a divine, would have ruined his reputation, not only as a man of science, but of common sense. It would indeed be too much to affirm that a time may not come, when acts such as the most marvellous of those attributed to our Lord, shall have been brought within the ordinary operations of the human will, even acting directly, without the intervention of the bodily organs. But this hypothesis would not in the least affect the character of our Lord's miracles, unless it could be shown that, when they were wrought, the human will possessed such a direct power over outward nature. Probably no supposition could be more foreign to Professor Powell's habits of thought.

Mr. Wilson, in his *Speech before the Judicial Committee of the Privy Council* (p. 47), gives an extract from Professor Babbage's *Ninth Bridgwater Treatise,* containing "a solution which," he says, "to a great extent, is satisfactory to many minds." It is headed, "*Argument from*

Laws intermitting on the Nature of Miracles." "The object," as the author states, is to show that miracles are not deviations from the laws assigned by the Almighty for the government of matter and of mind; but that they are the exact fulfilment of much more extensive laws than those we suppose to exist." The argument is ingeniously illustrated by the analogy of the calculating engine. But there is an unfortunate ambiguity in the statement of the object, which might well withhold Mr. Wilson from "adopting it as an undoubted or complete solution of all questions connected with the subject of the miraculous." For it may mean either that all "alleged miracles" fulfil the conditions described, or that no events which do not fulfil those conditions are real miracles. The former would be a bold assumption, if the universe is to be considered as a "mechanism," like the calculating engine, and it is one not to be hastily ascribed to Professor Babbage. In the second sense the proposition seems to leave "the subject of the miraculous" just where it was. For all theologians would agree in referring miracles, no less than all other events, to the Divine Will. None would consider them as exceptions to the universality of the Divine foreknowledge, or as thoughts which had suddenly entered the Divine mind. But it would not follow that they should be regarded as parts of a system of machinery, set in motion once for all, and working by a blind necessity.

Much as there is that is both true and valuable in Mr. Llewelyn Davies's Essay on this subject (Tracts for Priests and People, *The Signs of the Kingdom of Heaven*), I fear that there are parts of it which are likely to leave a misleading impression on the minds of many readers. In his anxiety to correct the error of those who, as he thinks, lay undue stress on the element of power in our Lord's miracles, he reasons so as to suggest a grave doubt, whether whatever benefit resulted from them was not much more than counterbalanced by the apparent countenance which they gave, both at the time and in all succeeding ages, to what he calls "wonder" or "miracle worship." For, apart from the effect on the persons on whom the miracles were wrought, which cannot be properly taken into the account, the benefit, according to the author, consisted in the illustration of certain spiritual truths. That they were suited to that purpose none will deny. But those truths did not, as Mr. Davies would probably be the first to admit, absolutely need such illustration; and a mode of illustration which tended to divert attention from the thing illustrated, and to fix it on something quite foreign to our Lord's intention, might seem hardly worthy of His wisdom; and Mr. Davies acknowledges that such an effect was in general inevitable. He says very truly (p. 40), "It is difficult to imagine the mind upon which the element of power would not tell with some force." I cannot so fully assent to the exception which he subjoins: "but we are at liberty, I think, to assume that the cultivated mind might be impervious to such an argument." It is easy for a man of science at his desk to say: " Even if I was to witness any of the ' miracles ' related in the New Testament, I would not believe that they were the effect of any superhuman power possessed by the person who appeared to perform them." When I know an instance of such incredulity, I shall believe it possible. At present I suspect that the sight would make a deeper impression on a cultivated, than on an uncultivated mind. But Mr. Davies seems to overlook the distinction between that part of our Lord's teaching which would have been equally true and impressive in the mouth of a merely human teacher, and that which related to His own superhuman character. His ethical teaching could neither need nor admit of confirmation from miracles, as acts of power. But, as such, they were eminently fitted to gain credence for His declarations with regard to His own person in His relation to the Father. Indeed, for those who did not enjoy the privilege of His intimate society, or a special gift of the Holy Spirit, they might be absolutely indispensable, though not in all cases sufficient. The comparison (p. 41) with missionaries, who would, no less earnestly than the Apostles at Lystra, deprecate the being " taken for superhuman personages," seems to me to miss the point.

I cannot help thinking that the general tendency of the Essay is to depreciate the importance of the question as to the reality of our Lord's miracles. It is therefore the more satisfactory to observe, that Mr. Davies is aware that " they are so bound up with all else that is told us regarding Him, that the history must be torn in fragments, if we attempt to sever the signs and wonders from the other acts and discourses of Jesus " (p. 35), and that "an attempt to cut out from the Gospel narratives the ' supernatural element,' would make such havoc in them, that we should no longer know what to make of them, or how to trust them " (p. 37): that " we cannot shut our eyes to the fundamental nature of modern unbelief or doubt " (p. 30): that he does not share Mr. Kennard's mistake as to the purport of Professor Powell's Essay (p. 31), and sees that " the sanguine divines who wish to make the acquiescent philosophy (that which would dispense with ' the thought of God as really present in nature and society ') compatible with something of the old religion, by keeping the actual course of things in one sphere, and ' faith ' in another, will satisfy neither the cravings of the believing soul, nor the rational instincts of the philosopher " (p. 44).

The differences of opinion as to the proper significance of miracles, which exist among those who admit their reality, may be very wide and important : but they are quite insignificant in comparison with the gulf which separates Christian faith from the views of Jefferson, or Comte, or Strauss, or E. Renan. On whichever side the Church of England is to stand in future, it is at least desirable that her position should be clearly understood. That she should have to contend against Deism and Pantheism, may be unavoidable; but she has reason to complain when attempts are made to palm either system upon her, as her genuine doctrine.

IX.

A CHARGE

Delivered October, 1866.

STATE OF THE DIOCESE.—NATIONAL EDUCATION, THE REVISED CODE.—DIOCESAN SYNODS.—FINAL COURT OF APPEAL.—RITUALISM.

My Reverend Brethren,

On this occasion of my ninth Visitation my thoughts are almost necessarily carried back to the beginning of the period, now more than a quarter of a century, during which I have been permitted to fill this chair, and to the view which I then took of the state of things around me, and the feelings with which I looked forward to the future which now lies behind us. In this retrospect I find one ground of satisfaction, on which I may dwell without the slightest temptation to self-complacency. Though I am sure that the estimate I then formed, and which I indicated in my first Charge, of the difficulties which beset the Church's work in the Diocese, was not at all exaggerated, it was certainly far from cheering; and the very moderate expectations which it seemed to warrant, were hardly liable to much disappointment. Much brighter hopes might, as the event has shown, have been safely indulged by one of more sanguine temperament or larger foresight. I was able, indeed, to point to many gladdening signs of growing vigour and expansive energy in the Church at large; but I could not discover any clear evidence that this spirit had penetrated into our corner of the field, or any sure ground of confidence as to the degree in which it would overcome the manifold obstacles it had to encounter there. I should be still more loth to fall under any illusion of an opposite kind, however agreeable; but I do find much cause for thankfulness when I compare the present state of the Diocese, in many important aspects, with my recollections of the past. I need not scruple to express this feeling, whether the progress which has been made be great or small, because in the efforts by which it has been brought about, I can claim no share but that of a sympathizing and encouraging spectator. It is, under Providence, to the clergy and the faithful laity, though not without large help from without, that the whole is due.

I look in the first place to the condition of our sacred buildings, as the most important of all outward aids to religion, and the surest sign of the interest it excites. The records of the Church Building Society furnish a measure of the activity with which the work of church restoration has been carried on among us within the last half century. Between 1818 and 1865 it has made grants to this Diocese in 183 cases. Of this number two-thirds belong to the latter half of the period. This list, indeed, is far from representing all that has been done in our time. It omits many of the undertakings which have been accomplished by private, unaided, unostentatious munificence, to which we owe some of the goodliest of our churches, among them seven due to the munificence of the late and the present Earl Cawdor. And, I may add, that there are at this moment more than thirty parishes in which new or restored churches, are in various stages of progress, from the first step, to immediate readiness for consecration or re-opening. I do not expect to see all of them completed. They must more or less interfere with one another. But this simultaneous movement in all quarters of the Diocese is a gratifying sign of healthy life.* I may also observe, that this increase in the number of our churches has been accompanied by a great improvement in their architectural character. The contrast between the earlier and the later buildings in their style, would in general be sufficient to mark the date to which they belong. This indeed is a benefit which, in common with the

Condition of churches in the Diocese.

* See Appendix A.

whole Church, we derive from the awakening of a better feeling, and the diffusion of more accurate knowledge and more enlightened taste in these matters. And much as we have reason to congratulate ourselves on this happy change with regard to our new churches, it is still more important with regard to some of those which had fallen into decay. A new church in the style which would have satisfied those who saw it fifty years ago, would now offend all who try it by a higher and more correct standard. But this evil is very slight, when compared with that which we have to deplore, when a venerable monument is irreparably defaced by a misnamed restoration. It must therefore be deemed a happy coincidence, that in the case of some of the most precious remains of ecclesiastical architecture which have been handed down to us, the work has been reserved for our day, and for skilful and tender hands, by which they will be not only preserved from further decay, but renewed in their original freshness.

Among these our Cathedral unquestionably occupies the foremost place, as well for its historical associations, as for its architectural beauties, still surviving all the injury it has undergone through the violence and neglect of ages. *Restoration of the Cathedral.* I cannot lament that the imminent and growing danger of total ruin with which it was threatened, rendered it absolutely necessary to devote a large sum to the single purpose of warding off that disaster, without any change in the outward appearance of the building. For it followed, almost of course, that this occasion should not be allowed to pass by, without an effort, both to preserve whatever else was ready to perish, and to restore the mutilated features of the original design. I was aware, indeed, in common with all who engaged in this undertaking, that the peculiar disadvantages with which it had to contend in the raising of the requisite funds, precluded all hope that it would be brought to an early completion. The obscurity of its position—known by actual inspection only to a few occasional visitors, while out of Wales its very existence, as any thing more than a mere ruin, is by no means generally received as an unquestionable fact—not only debars it from the sympathy which it seldom fails to excite in those who see it, but with some passes for an argument against the undertaking itself. We have, therefore, cause to be thankful, that, by an extraordinary exertion of mechanical skill and ingenuity, which has reflected some additional lustre on the name of Mr. Gilbert Scott, the most important and difficult part of the work, that by which the stability of the fabric was to be secured, has been achieved.

Tardy response to the appeal for assistance. Still, after every allowance for unfavourable circumstances, I must own that I have been somewhat surprised and disappointed by the tardiness of the response which has been made to the appeal of the Dean and Chapter. I had hoped—not I think unreasonably—that the object would have roused a more general and lively interest throughout the Principality, as well as among lovers of art and students of archæology elsewhere. At a time when archæology is so zealously cultivated —in Wales by a special Association—it might have been fairly expected that, even if the Cathedral had no claim on the public but as an ancient monument, this would have sufficed to secure a much larger amount of support to the undertaking. On churchmen it has the further claim of being at once the Cathedral of the Diocese, and the only church of the large parish in which it stands. I have therefore been grieved to hear murmurs, calling *Propriety of the undertaking questioned.* in question the usefulness of the undertaking; suggesting a doubt, whether it would not have been better to let the building sink into utter ruin, and to make some less costly provision for the spiritual wants of the congregation. I cannot deny that there is a disproportion between the scale of the building, and the want which it actually supplies. It is a disproportion of superfluity, not of deficiency, and may, it is to be hoped, hereafter become less sensible, while the room remains the same. But is any one prepared, either in theory or in practice, to accept the principle, of exactly adapting the provision for the worship of God to the need of the worshippers, and to condemn all further outlay as waste? I will not ask whether the earliest example of such parsimony among Christ's disciples is one which we should wish to follow. But if the principle was consistently applied, how many of us must stand convicted of waste, like that which excited the indignation of Judas? How many costly churches have we built, when four walls, roofed over, with a few holes to let in the light, would have served the purpose of public worship? Even if, in ordinary cases, we had acted on such a principle, there would have been one which would have had a right to be treated as an exception—the Cathedral of the Diocese. Surely this ought not to be the exception, where the cheerful sacrifice of worldly things for God's honour is the rule. I rejoice that it is no longer a question, whether we shall abandon or preserve a sacred and precious deposit, bequeathed to us by the pious munificence of former ages, and that I may before long be permitted to see the work carried to within a few stages of its final completion. For this happy change in its prospects we are indebted to the arrangement into which the Dean and Chapter have just entered with the Ecclesiastical Commissioners. I must, however, observe, that their grant, together with the fund previously raised, will not cover more than about two-thirds of the estimated cost, and that it will still be to private liberality that we must look for the remainder. Let me add that, even if we should descend to lower ground than I think we are at liberty to take, I am persuaded that the outlay is likely to yield a large return, in the impulse which this great work may be expected to give to the progress of church restoration throughout the Diocese.

To return for a few moments to the general subject. By far the larger part of the funds with which the work of church building has been carried on in the Diocese within my own experience, has been supplied by voluntary contributions. In one point of view this is a cheering fact, as it shows that the movement has not been checked by the difficulty which besets the collecting of Church Rates, and therefore is likely to advance, even if they should be entirely abolished. But I am far from thinking that therefore we can be indifferent to the state of the law on the subject, either as regards others or ourselves. It is true that, even where the rate appears to be hopelessly lost, active exertions on the part of the clergyman have

Church building mainly carried on by voluntary contributions.

almost invariably succeeded in accomplishing the restoration of his church. But in many of these cases a light rate, made in time, would have prevented the building from falling to decay, and have spared the congregation the inconvenience of assembling in it, while in a condition painful to devout feeling, if not perilous to health, or of transferring their attendance to some private room, of scanty dimensions, rudely fitted up for the temporary purpose. No doubt the privation often purchases a much greater benefit: the exchange of a very unsightly building for a new one of more becoming character. But frequently the only difference is, that what has been done at last with great difficulty, cost, and inconvenience, would have been done earlier, more easily, and cheaply.

The Church Rate question has been left on its old footing. The clergy were almost universally opposed to the measure by State of the Church Rate question. which an attempt was made in the last Session of Parliament to provide a substitute for the compulsory Rate. It appeared, I believe, to most of them, that, if they were to be thrown entirely on the voluntary principle, they might as well, if not much better, act upon their own judgment as to the mode in which they availed themselves of it, without any legislative regulations, which might as often fetter and weaken, as promote its operation. The loss to the Church was clear and certain: the gain confined to one class of society, which has no more right to it than any other. And if there were any who had ever imagined that the loss would be compensated by the removal of a constant cause of strife and bitterness, these had been long undeceived by the candid avowal of the Liberation Society, that they set no value on the abolition, except as a step which would give them vantage ground or leverage for further assaults on the Established Church. The general object of the Bill was one which most Churchmen would have agreed in regarding as highly desirable. They were quite willing that Nonconformists should be exempted from the Rate. It was by the Dissenters themselves that Mr. Hubbard's Bill, brought in for that purpose, was rejected, on the singular ground,—which throws a very instructive light on the character of their conscientious scruples,—that they did not like to be *ticketed*, or recognized as Dissenters, though on other occasions they glory in the profession of their principles, and of their hostility to the Established Church. It almost looked as if they did not like to part with a grievance which they had found to be not only harmless, but useful. The Government Bill of last Session met this objection, so as to satisfy the representatives of the Dissenting body, who required nothing more than the abolition of the compulsory Rate. But as the compulsion of which they complained was that which was exercised on themselves, while Churchmen, as far as they themselves were concerned, did not object to it, but desired its continuance, it would have seemed enough if those who complained of it had been relieved from it, all things in other respects remaining as they were.

But the Bill went much further than this. It swept away the whole system, both with regard to Dissenters and to Churchmen, and only permitted voluntary contributions to be levied in the form of a Rate, but without any power of enforcing payment. It might be open to question, whether such a power should exist: but the right of entering into a voluntary engagement, with the liberty of eluding it, could hardly be considered as a very valuable boon by those for whose benefit it was designed. Abolition of the Rate.

I will take this occasion to remark, that a wish has been expressed in some quarters for the establishment of a Diocesan Church Building Society. There are, no doubt, Dioceses in which this institution has produced very beneficial results. My only objection to trying the experiment in ours, is my fear that the only certain appreciable effect would be to add to the burdens of the clergy. It can hardly be expected that the laity would take even so lively an interest in the promotion of church building as in the diffusion of education; and the state of the funds which they contribute to that object does not encourage reliance on their aid toward one in which they would not feel themselves so nearly concerned. Still, if it should appear that the clergy are generally desirous of making such an effort I should be Desire for a Diocesan Church Building Society.

quite ready to comply with their wishes, and to second it to the best of my ability.

<small>The Augmentation Fund.</small> Before I pass to a different subject, I must say a word on another point of purely Diocesan interest. The Augmentation Fund, which I founded in 1851, has now yielded 24,000*l*., of which very nearly 17,000*l*. has been already expended, almost entirely in the building of parsonage houses. As no part of this sum has been granted unconditionally, and the larger part has been met with grants of equal amount by the Ecclesiastical Commissioners, it may be considered as representing a sum exceeding 30,000*l*. already applied to this object, which, when the remainder of the 24,000*l*. shall have been dispensed in like manner, will be increased to upwards of 40,000*l*. The number of the livings which have hitherto shared the benefit of the Fund is thirty-four. I still intend to apply the remainder now at my disposal and whatever may hereafter accrue to the Fund, in the same way. But though it will be equally beneficial to the livings augmented, I am sorry to have to inform you that it will not be so to the present incumbents who receive the benefaction; for the Ecclesiastical Commissioners have found themselves compelled, in order to provide for the still more important object of putting an end to the renewal of leases on payment of fines, to substitute permanent annuities for capital sums; and the only way in which their grants can be made available for the purpose of building is by loan from Queen Anne's Bounty, entailing a charge of interest on the living. Future applicants must bear this in mind. I hope indeed, though with no great confidence, that means may be found to enable the Ecclesiastical Commissioners to revert to their original practice. But I must also express an earnest wish that they would modify their requirements as to the scale of building, which is too often in excess, not only of the wants, but of the means of the clergy in this Diocese, and would, if it had been lower, have rendered my Fund somewhat less inadequate to the object; and there are still more than two hundred benefices destitute of glebe houses.

I am sure that I shall be borne out by the experience and observation of my reverend brethren in this and in every Archdeaconry of the Diocese, when I say that the progress made in the work of popular education has been not less steady than that of church building and church restoration during the same period. Many of you can witness to that which is mainly your own work,—the fruit of heavy pecuniary sacrifices, as well as of much labour and anxiety,—the founding of new schools, the erection of new school-buildings, or the adaptation of the old to the requirements of a higher standard. I may also point to the foundation of our Training College, as having marked a great epoch in the history of education in the Diocese, and as the origin of an impulse which has never slackened, but has been strengthened by the institution of our Archidiaconal Boards, which has, I hope, ensured its permanently progressive action. But we must not disguise from ourselves, that this progress is apparent only in places which may be considered as centres of a more or less considerable population. The Returns which I have received from you continue to exhibit a sad blank with regard to day schools in the more thinly inhabited rural districts. I find no less than 120 parishes in which it does not appear that any provision has yet been made, through the instrumentality of the Church, for the education of the poor. I cannot, of course, undertake to pronounce with regard to all these cases, that more might not have been done to cover this grievous blot. But knowing what I do of the general character of these rural districts, on the one hand, and, on the other hand, of the difficulties which beset the founding and support of schools, even in more favoured neighbourhoods, I may venture to say that the fact of the absence of a day school is by no means in itself conclusive proof of culpable remissness, indifference, or want of energy in the clergyman, and also to express my conviction that, under the present system, and without more effectual public aid, there is no prospect that this state of things will ever be materially amended.

Progress of education in the Diocese.

Sharing, as we have done, in the benefits derived from the distribution of the Parliamentary Grant for Education, we have also suffered, in common with others, from the changes which have taken place in the principles or maxims on which it has been administered, and which, however reasonable they may have been in themselves, have certainly been far from purely beneficial in their consequences. We have no right indeed to complain, because the dispensation of the grant is regulated by a more rigid economy than when it was comparatively small. The more firmly we are convinced that there is no worthier object to which the wealth of the country can be applied than the intellectual and moral training of the great mass of the people, the more we must desire that no part of the funds destined to this purpose should be wasted, and that, if there had been any superfluous, though it may be not absolutely useless expenditure, this should be retrenched, and the saving reserved for the supply of real needs. Such retrenchment was one object of the Revised Code. But it is much to be feared that it has been carried too near to the quick, has increased the difficulties of the promoters of schools, and has tended to discourage all who have engaged or were ready to engage in the work of education. Such a result, though no doubt wholly undesigned and unforeseen, must be deeply deplored by all who believe that the present system, in which private undertakings are seconded by the State, and animated by the prospect of that assistance, is on the whole best suited to the circumstances of our mixed society; because in the same degree in which it impairs the efficacy and shakes the credit of that system, it favours the views of those who wish to see that system superseded by one more comprehensive and more nearly adequate to the wants of the nation: though with the inevitable, at least partial, sacrifice of much which the promoters of schools mostly consider as of supreme importance. It cannot be denied that the present system needs, not contraction, but expansion; that it does not reach all for whom it was designed; that this country is still, with regard to the diffusion of elementary education, in a position of humiliating inferiority to other States, to which it is far superior in wealth. The Revised Code has certainly gained no step in this direction. It has not only been attended with serious losses to the managers of schools through

Effects of the Revised Code.

causes beyond their control, for which, therefore, they could not justly be made answerable; but it has driven some, and those among the ablest teachers, from their profession into other walks of life, and it has so reduced the average amount of reward for their services, and rendered it so precarious and uncertain, as to lower the value and credit of the profession, and to deter the rising generation from entering it. We have thus the prospect that many schools depending on the Parliamentary Grant will be closed, and that in those which are able to maintain a struggling existence, at the cost of hard sacrifices and painful anxiety to their managers, the work will be continually passing into less and less competent hands.* Thus one of the most precious fruits of the old system—the training a great body of well-educated teachers—will have been lost. And I cannot help thinking that this unhappy result is due, not only to an excessive and mis-directed parsimony, but in part to a mistake, which can never be quite harmless, and may become a serious evil—I mean the committing the administration of a system to persons who are notoriously and avowedly hostile to it, as was very conspicuously the case with one at least who for five years held a high office in the Committee of Council on Education. † To the same cause may be still more distinctly traced the offensive and no less absurd and unjust imputation on school managers, with which the Revised Code was introduced. Men who had made the greatest personal sacrifices for the promotion of education, found themselves charged with selfish motives, because they opposed a change, which in their view threatened the very existence of their schools, and which has been attended with effects which few who do not desire the aboli-

margin: Evil of committing the administration of a system to persons hostile to it.

---

* See an article on the Revised Code in the Fortnightly Review, May 15, 1866, p. 75. The last Report of the Committee of Council on Education states (p. xiii.): "The introduction of the Revised Code has been followed by a great diminution in the number of pupil-teachers, especially of male pupil-teachers; the total number of pupil-teachers in 1862 (December 31) was 15,752, against 11,221 in 1865, showing a diminution of 28.7 per cent."

† See the evidence of Mr. Lowe before the Select Committee on Education, pp. 38, 39, and Professor Plumptre on the Conscience Clause, in the Contemporary Review, April, 1866, p. 580.

tion of the Denominational System, can view without sorrow and uneasiness.

<small>The Revised Code in relation to Training Colleges.</small> It was to be expected that the Training Colleges should feel the effects of the revised system, and that to many of them it should have proved fatal, while as to the remainder, it is impossible to foresee how long they may survive. Our own has hitherto endured the crisis, but has not passed through it. Perhaps we have more reason to be surprised that any of them should have been allowed to subsist. I always indeed thought that there was an enormous and almost absurd disproportion between the variety and difficulty of the branches of knowledge cultivated in these establishments, and the extent of proficiency required, on the one hand; and, on the other hand, the character of the schools and the capacity of the scholars for whose instruction this multifarious and profound learning was supposed to be acquired. While complaints were heard on every side of the early age at which most of the children were taken away from school, and which rendered it almost hopeless that they should retain even the first rudiments of knowledge, the training of their teachers was carried nearer and nearer to a point not far below the average conditions of a University degree. Still, under the previous system there were opportunities, though comparatively rare, of imparting this knowledge to some of the elder scholars. It was found, indeed, in many cases, that an undue share of the master's time and attention was bestowed on the favoured few, while the many were abandoned to the care of his young assistants, without any effectual security for their instruction in the first rudiments of the most necessary knowledge. That was the ground alleged, I cannot help suspecting with some exaggeration, for the revolution effected by the Revised Code. But now that all motive supplied by the dispensation of the Parliamentary grant for any instruction beyond the arts of reading and writing and a few rules of arithmetic has been withdrawn,* it seems clear that such

---

* "The Revised Code has tended, at least temporarily, to discourage attention to the higher branches of elementary instruction—geography, grammar, and history." (Report u. s.) This is the concurrent testimony of thirteen School Inspectors. On the authority of three others it is added: "There are however signs of recovery;

elaborate culture of minds to be employed in this very simple task, is altogether superfluous and out of place. The Training Colleges do not really belong to the system of the Revised Code, and if it was to be considered as the final phase in the history of the subject, might almost as well cease to exist.

But it appears to me that such a state of things would be a very lamentable and humiliating issue of all the thought and work that have been spent on the subject. I think there ought to be, in schools for the labouring classes, a large demand for that higher training which the Normal Colleges were intended to give, though perhaps with some modifications, calculated to increase their practical usefulness. To the principle, indeed, on which the Revised Code was based, we cannot but give a most hearty assent. No one can deny the right and duty of the State to demand results, where they may be obtained, as the only sure test of real and honest service, and the indispensable condition of remuneration granted out of a public fund. Nor can it be doubted that the elementary knowledge required by the present regulations is equally needful and profitable for all, and for a very large, perhaps the largest part, of the labouring class, both sufficient for their wants, and as much as, under the narrow limitation of their school years, they are capable of receiving. But there remain in the upper and more important division of the labouring class, a very great number whose existence is ignored in the Revised Code, which makes no provision for their wants, but leaves and almost forces them to seek the education which they need to fit them for their probable future occupations, from private adventurers, utterly destitute of all real qualifications for the duty they undertake, and who look to it only as a gainful speculation by which they exchange empty professions for solid if not perfectly clean lucre. The question has been asked, "Do our National Schools provide education for all whom they ought to train?" * and it has been proved beyond a doubt, and those schools do best in the elementary subjects where the higher are not neglected."

Its operation on the labouring classes.

---

* By the Rev. Robert Gregory, in a pamphlet with this title, addressed to the Archbishop of Canterbury.

both that they do not make such provision, and that the tendency of the Revised Code is to prevent them from so doing. The National Society has shown itself awake to the importance of the question, and has announced its intention of the taking steps with a view to the supply of this great deficiency. I can only commend the subject to the attention of those of my reverend brethren whose position may afford them the opportunity of practically dealing with it. On the whole, I can only consider both systems, the present and the past, as experiments, each of which has been but partially successful, though neither has entirely failed. It is to be hoped that the experience which has been gained through both, at no light cost, both to individuals and to the public, may serve to prepare the way for a happier state of things.

In the meanwhile, the attention of the Church has been much occupied by another question connected with this subject, which has been discussed with great warmth, and has caused an interruption in the relations which had for many years happily subsisted between the National Society and the Committee of Council on Education. It is most earnestly to be desired that those friendly relations and that harmonious co-operation should be restored, and I observe signs which lead me to hope that this event is not very far distant, and that a change has already taken place in many minds favourable to the prospect of a better understanding between the parties. You will readily perceive that I am speaking of the Conscience Clause, which the Committee of Council have felt it their duty in certain cases to require to be inserted in the trust deeds of Church schools, as the condition of aid from the Parliamentary grant. I feel it incumbent on me to say a few words in explanation of my present views of the subject, because they may appear not quite in accordance with those which I expressed, not indeed on this precise question, but on one connected with it, some years ago. It may be in your recollection that I had then occasion to contend against a proposal which had been made to supersede Church schools in Wales by others on the model of the British and Foreign Schools.

The Conscience Clause.

I opposed this innovation, as proceeding on a partial and erroneous view of the facts of the case, as needless for its avowed purpose, and as tending to substitute a worse for a better kind of school. That opinion I retain entirely unaltered, or rather strengthened by subsequent inquiry. But it might seem as if in that controversy I was taking common ground with those who resisted the imposition of a Conscience Clause. The agreement, however, was merely apparent and accidental. My own opportunities of observation led me to believe that the clause was unnecessary, and ought not to be imposed until its necessity was proved. It also appeared questionable whether the Committee of Council were not exceeding the limits of their lawful authority, when they introduced such an innovation without the express sanction of Parliament. This last objection has been continually urged by the opponents of the Clause, though it is evidently quite foreign to the merits of the Clause itself. But it seems now very doubtful whether this is an argument which can be used without taking an ungenerous advantage of a forbearance for which the Church has cause to be thankful. It is now certain that the motive which withheld the Committee of Council from applying to Parliament for its express approval of the Conscience Clause, was the very reverse of an apprehension lest it should not obtain the assent of the House of Commons. It was a fear lest they should be thought not to have gone far enough and should be forced to take steps which would drive many of the clergy to forego all benefit from the Parliamentary grant.* This, however, as I have said, is a formal and technical rather than a substantial and practical objection. It may not be an unfit argument for a political debate, but it is not one which much concerns or raises a scruple in the minds of the clergy or the managers of Church schools. If they decline to accept a grant on the condition of a Conscience Clause it is because they dislike the clause in itself, on grounds which would be just as strong if it had been imposed by the Legislature. It has indeed been so vehe- [Vehement denunciation of it.]

---

* See the evidence of Earl Granville before the Select Committee on Education, p. 109.

mently denounced by persons who exercise no inconsiderable influence on public opinion in Church questions, that it is not easy for it to gain a calm and fair hearing. It requires a certain amount of moral courage in a clergyman, whatever may be his private opinion, to take a step which he has been told by persons whom he highly respects is inconsistent with his duty to the Church, and tends to the most dangerous consequences; above all, when he finds this proposition affirmed by a vote of the Lower House of Convocation.

Nature of the discussions on it. I venture to say with the deepest conviction, that never has the truth on any subject been more obscured by passionate declamation, sophistical reasoning, high-sounding but utterly hollow phrases, and by violent distortion of notorious facts, than on this: all, no doubt, completely unintentional on the part of the excellent persons who were betrayed into these errors, who were the first dupes of their own fallacies, and are perhaps of all men living the least capable of anything bordering on disingenuous artifice or wilful misrepresentation. It was the natural effect of the panic into which they were thrown by the suggestion of a danger threatening interests most justly dear and sacred to them, which prevented them from exercising a right judgment on this question, or seeing any object connected with it in its true light. But this deep earnestness, while it does honour to their feelings, renders their aberrations the more deplorable and mischievous. I have good hope, however, that the mist which they have raised is beginning to break and clear away. I am glad to see that the weakness of their "reasons," and the groundlessness of their position, have been exposed, both in and outside of Convocation, by clergymen at least their equals in ability and attachment to the Church, though lower in official station.* I feel too much

* Though the argumentative force of Archdeacon Denison's "Seventeen Reasons" has evaporated under Mr. Oakley's analyis ("The Conscience Clause, a Reply to Archdeacon Denison, by John Oakley, M.A.") they will always retain a certain value, as examples of a great variety of fallacies, which once actually deceived well-educated men. Perhaps I might have been content with referring to Professor Plumptre's very able article on the subject in the Contemporary Review, if readers were more in the habit of consulting books to which they are referred. But I strongly recommend it to the perusal of every one who takes an interest in the question.

confidence in the moderation and practical good sense of the great body of the clergy, to believe that they will be long misled by any authority which will not bear the test of sober judgment, and I am sure that they will sooner or later be found on the side of truth and justice.

The general ground of the opposition which has been made to the Conscience Clause cannot be more strongly expressed than when it is said to "undermine the foundation of religion." *[margin: Ground of opposition to it.]* But if there is any force at all in the arguments which have been brought against it, the expression is not too strong, for in whatever terms they may have been couched this is what they really amount to and imply, though the vagueness of the phrase is better fitted to excite a blind bewildering alarm than to raise any clear and definite issue. In fact, until it has been explained and limited it can only act upon the feelings and the imagination, and presents no hold for any rational opinion. But when it is translated into plainer language, it appears that the mode in which the foundation of religion is thought to be undermined by the Conscience Clause, consists in the *interference* which through it the State is alleged to exercise in the religious teaching of Church schools. This is an allegation which we can immediately compare with the Clause itself, so as to ascertain in what sense it is to be understood, and how far it is warranted by the meaning of the Clause.

Here, however, I must remark a peculiar and very significant feature in this controversy: that, though it relates to a practical subject, those who describe the Clause as fraught with such dreadful consequences, have never appealed to experience, but rely entirely on their own sagacity for discerning the effects of a contingency which it is their object to avert. * And they do so, not because the question is beyond the range of experience, and confined to the region of theological speculation. There *is* experience to consult, and such as would, I *[margin: Its opponents have never appealed to experience.]*

---

* Evidence of Archdeacon Denison before the Select Committee on Education. 3727: "It is then an opinion unsupported by any actual experience?—Yes, I cannot say that I have had any actual experience of the adoption of the Clause."

believe, in most cases be considered a sufficient guide. In the present case it has been rejected or ignored by those who condemn the Clause, but only for a reason which does not in the least lessen its intrinsic value, namely, that so far as it goes, it happens to run counter to their views. The Conscience Clause is not an experiment which has yet to be made: it has been already tried in a great number of schools. First, in all those in which the principle was voluntarily adopted by the managers of Church schools. I have yet to learn that this has ever been attended with the slightest perceptible ill-effect. It may however be said, that this is immaterial, and that the relaxation of the principle—the right and duty of the Church to inculcate every article of her doctrine on all children who are admitted into her schools—is, independently of consequences, the worst of evils, a virtual "undermining of the foundation of religion." I do not expect that the excellent persons who hold this opinion, would ever consent to submit it to the test of experience. It is for them one of those transcendental verities, belonging to a higher sphere, which are degraded and profaned when they are brought down to earth, and tried by their application to the actual condition of things, and the real affairs of human life. I am quite content that they should be spared such contact with the world of reality. All that I wish is, that the world of reality should not be subjected to their influence, but should be regulated by the results of practical experience.

View taken of it by the Committee of the National Society. But it has been contended, that the experience gained by such voluntary trials of the principle of the Conscience Clause, is not a satisfactory test: that the school which has flourished while governed by the principle, would begin to go to ruin, as soon as it became a matter of legal right. That is the ground taken by the Committee of the National Society in their last Report. And the way in which the subject is there treated, seems to me highly worthy of note in more respects than one. They state that they have always felt it their duty to object to the Conscience Clause as a condition of assistance from the Parliamentary grant. The fact indeed is unquestionable. And when we consider that this opposition, carried on to a rupture between the National Society and the Committee of Council, has actually—which ever party may be responsible for it—caused a great amount of serious inconvenience, not to say positive evil; perplexity in the minds of school managers, and obstruction to the work of education; it was certainly to be expected that the Committee, when they stated the fact, would assign a reason sufficient to show that the course they had pursued had indeed been prescribed to them by an inflexible law of duty.

But the ground which they assign is one which, to those who take the higher view of the inalienable prerogative and indispensable duty of the Church, must appear pitiably weak, and, when put forward alone, and therefore as the strongest, as amounting to little less than a treacherous abandonment of the cause, at least to a pusillanimous suppression of the truth. They say, "No such provision is practically required for the protection of Nonconformists, for Nonconformist parents and guardians scarcely ever object to the religious instruction given in National Schools; and when they do, the clergy and school managers almost invariably consent to some arrangement by which the objection is removed" (in other words they act on the principle of the Conscience Clause). "If, however," the Report proceeds, "an arrangement of this kind were made a matter of legal right, it may be feared that the peace and harmony which now prevail in parishes with regard to education would be broken —that parents and guardians might frequently be influenced to demand as a right what they seldom care to ask for as a favour." No doubt, the Committee had very good reason for taking this low ground, however it might dissatisfy and displease one section of their friends, who were most strenuous in opposition to the Clause. They were no doubt aware that the transcendental argument might do good service in its proper place; that it was well adapted for rhetorical effect, and when wielded by an able speaker, might kindle a useful enthusiasm in a mixed assembly. But they probably felt that it was one which would not bear to be produced

Weakness of their argument.

in a Report dealing with real facts, and could not be supposed to have influenced the minds of a Committee, composed in a great part of laymen, who, while warm friends of the Church, were also clear-headed men of business. The reason assigned therefore was such as they need not be ashamed to avow. But it laboured under the disadvantage and defect of being drawn, not from experience, but from conjecture: and experience, as far as it has gone, has proved the conjecture to be mistaken. The Clause has been accepted without the consequences which it was feared would ensue, when that which was conceded as an indulgence should become a matter of legal right. I have been assured by a clergyman who has had practical experience of the working of the Clause in large schools in the neighbourhood of London,* that there are "no practical difficulties whatever in carrying it out." And one well authenticated case in which the Clause has not only been accepted, but acted upon, and the right which it gives has been actually claimed on behalf of some of the children, seems decisive. But even without such testimony, I own that I should think meanly of the administrative ability of a clergyman who, having the will, was unequal to the task of overcoming such a difficulty. For it must be remembered that the question can only arise in parishes where Dissenters are in a minority, and commonly a small one. But I readily admit that the more or less of difficulty that may be found in adjusting the work of a Church school to the operation of the Conscience Clause, is quite a secondary consideration, and that what has the foremost claim on our attention are the principles which are said to be at stake in this dispute.

[sidenote: The Clause presents no practical difficulties.]

There are two which lie at the root of the Conscience Clause. One is, that every child in a parish has an equal right to a share in the benefits of education, for which a provision is made out of public money. The other is, that every parent—not labouring under legal disability—has a right to regulate the religious education of his children according to his own views. I am not aware that either of these propositions has

[sidenote: Principles at stake in the dispute.]

* The Rev. T. W. Fowle. See Mr. Oakley's pamphlet, p. 33.

been disputed, as a general principle, even by the most thorough-going opponents of the Conscience Clause; but it has been denied that they can be properly brought to bear upon it. It is contended that there are other principles, irreconcilable with the Clause, which have a prior claim to rule the decision of the question, and so prevent the first from ever coming into play. The right of the child, we are told, cannot justly be allowed to override one previously acquired by the Church; especially as it is always in the power of the State to make a separate provision for the Dissenting minority, however small. Even if there be only half a dozen, a school may be built, and a master paid for their instruction. The opponents of the Clause are liberal of the public money, and would not grudge an expense which it is to defray. But as outside of their circle it would be universally regarded as a scandalous waste, it is morally and practically impossible. This therefore is not a real alternative. The choice lies between the exclusion of some children from all the benefits of the school, and their admission, on terms which are said to be a *violation of compact between Church and State; to interfere with the religious instruction of Church schools, to introduce a system of secular education,* and thus to *undermine the foundation of religion.* How far the Clause is open to these charges, is the point on which, in the eyes of clergymen, and of all faithful Churchmen, the question must ultimately turn, and on which it must depend whether they can justly or safely accept the Clause.

It is to me satisfactory to find that little more is needed for the refutation of these statements, than to translate them into more exact terms, and to supply that which is wanted to make them fully intelligible. As soon as the light of truth and common sense is turned upon them, they seem to melt into air. The question as to *breach of compact,* is, as I observed, irrelevant to the merits of the clause. But yet the complaint suggests the idea of a wrong done to the clergyman, whose application for aid is refused, because he will not admit children of Dissenters into his school without teaching them every doctrine of the Church. But it has not, I think, ever been

Breach of contract.

asserted, that there was ever any compact which bound the Committee of Council to forego the exercise of their own discretion in giving or withholding their aid. It may be a question whether they have exercised it rightly or not, but this must depend, not on the supposed *compact*, but on the circumstances of the case. We may imagine a correspondence running in some such form as this. The clergyman writes: "I ask for a grant toward the education of the poor of my parish. It contains a few Dissenters, Baptists, and others, who probably will not send their children to school, because my conscience does not permit me to receive any children whom I am not to instruct in all the doctrines of the Church." The answer might be, "We are sorry that such should be the dictate of your conscience; but, as stewards of the public purse, we have a conscience too. And we should think it a misapplication of the fund committed to our disposal, if we were to build either two schools for so small a population, or one school only, from which a part of the population was to be excluded. We offer no violence to your conscientious scruples; we trust that you will respect ours. If you are resolved to admit Dissenting children on no other terms, we must reserve our grant until you shall have brought over all your parishioners to your own way of thinking." I must own that I do not see how this can be properly described as a compulsory imposition of the Conscience Clause; language which suggests an idea of violence which has not and could not be used. It would be quite as correct to say, that the clergyman compelled the Committee of Council to withhold the grant, as that, in the opposite event, they compelled him to accept it on their conditions. But all that is important is, that it should be distinctly understood in what sense the terms are used, and that, as between the clergyman and the Committee of Council, there is no breach of compact whatever. It is true that many suffer from the disagreement. The children of the parish may lose the benefit of education. But it cannot be fairly assumed that the fault lies on one side more than on the other. The principle on which the grant was refused, may have been quite as sincerely held, as that on which it was declined. In every point of view it is entitled to equal respect. Which of the two is the most just and reasonable, is a question on which every one must be left to form his own opinion.

So again, if we inquire in what sense it is asserted that the Clause *interferes with the religious instruction of Church schools*, it turns out that it is a sense so remote from that which the expression naturally suggests, and which it has probably conveyed to most minds, that any argument founded on its apparent meaning must be utterly delusive. It is not denied, that a clergyman who has accepted the Clause, not only remains at perfect liberty, but is as much as ever required to instruct all the children of his own communion in all the doctrines of his Church. So far the Clause does not in the slightest degree interfere with this branch of his pastoral office. But there is a sense in which it certainly may be said to *interfere* with his teaching. It interferes to prevent him from forcing that teaching on children whose parents wish that they should not receive it. This may be right or wrong; but certainly it is something of a very different kind; something to which the term *interference* is not usually applied. We do not commonly speak of *interference* as an intermeddling, when any one is prevented from doing a wrong to his neighbour. The clergy are used to such interference in other parts of their office, and never complain of it. It is both their right and their duty to instruct their parishioners in the doctrines of the Church. But in the exercise of this right, and the discharge of this duty, they are subject to a Conscience Clause, which does not even depend on their acceptance of it, but is enforced by the law. They may teach all who are willing to learn from them; but they are not allowed to force themselves into the pulpit of the Dissenting minister, for the purpose of instructing his congregation, nor to drag that congregation into the parish church. They submit most cheerfully to this interference. I should be surprised if there was one who desired more liberty in this respect, or did not abhor the thought of the dragonades of Louis XIV. Where then lies the hardship of a like interference—if it is to be so called—when

Interference with religious instruction in Church schools.

it limits their right of teaching the children of their schools, who, in case of danger, have still greater need of protection? Some distinction must be drawn, to show that what is so imperatively demanded by justice in the one case, becomes a wrong in the other. The distinction which has been drawn for this purpose rests on the assertion, that, although the religious instruction of the school may be precisely what it would have been, if there had been none but children of Churchmen in it, the presence of one who is withdrawn from this instruction, as the child of a Dissenter, vitiates and counteracts the effects of the whole. The Church children are deprived of all the benefit they would otherwise have gained from their religious teaching, while the knowledge imparted to the Dissenting child, being, as it is assumed, divorced from religion, is worse than useless.

<small>Groundless assumptions.</small> I say, *as it is assumed*, because the argument rests on the wholly arbitrary and groundless assumption, that unless the child receives religious instruction in the school, he will receive none at all; whereas the far more probable presumption is, that the parent who withdraws his child from the religious teaching of the school on conscientious grounds, will be the least likely to neglect his religious education. The supreme importance of moral and religious training, as distinguished from mere intellectual cultivation, may be fully admitted, but must be laid aside as a truth wholly foreign to this question; while the general proposition, that it is better for a child to receive no instruction of any kind than to attend a school in which it learns nothing but reading, writing, and arithmetic,* and that the moral discipline of the school, however excellent in itself, is utterly worthless, is one of that class which it is sufficient to state. For those who are capable of maintaining it, it admits of no refutation; for the rest of mankind it needs none. No doubt most Churchmen, and probably every clergyman, would greatly prefer a school, however inferior in other respects, in which religious instruction according

---

* "As to reading, writing, and arithmetic, I think that without religion (*subaudi*, such as I would teach them) they are better without it." Archdeacon Denison's evidence before the Select Committee on Education, 3764.

to the doctrine of the Church occupies the foremost place, to the public schools of the United States. But that these are worse than useless, nurseries of diabolical wickedness, armed with intellectual power, and that it would have been better for those who have been trained in them if they had grown up in utter ignorance of all that they learned there, is an opinion held probably by few. I do not attempt to refute it. I only wish to observe that it is an indispensable link in the chain of reasoning by which the Conscience Clause is made out to be an *interference* with the religious instruction of Church schools. But when we hear that the benefit of this instruction is neutralized by the presence of a child who has been withdrawn from it at the desire of his parents, and so the religion of the place damaged, we cannot help asking, If the religious principles of the Church children are "poisoned" when they find that some of their schoolfellows belong to the meeting-house, how are those principles to survive the inevitable discovery that this is the case with some of their young neighbours, though not admitted into the school? And as this would imply incredible ignorance and more than childish simplicity, so, when it is intimated that they will infer from the fact that their own teachers are indifferent to religion,* this is really to charge them with an excess of intellectual perversity, and of calumnious misconstruction, of which childhood is happily incapable, and which is reserved for riper years, and for minds that have undergone the baneful influence of long habits of political or religious controversy.

After this, we shall not find it difficult to do justice to the assertion, that the Conscience Clause virtually *insinuates the poisonous and deadly principle of secular education into the heart of the Denominational System*. We must observe that, independently of any Conscience Clause, this evil principle must be found in every Church school. In all, the education consists of three parts: the moral discipline—which the Clause does not in any way affect—the secular instruction, and the religious instruction. All the children may be said to be

Insinuation of secular education into the Denominational system.

* See "reason" four of Archdeacon Denison's seventeen.

receiving secular education during one, and that the longest period of their school work. The effect of the Conscience Clause is, that some receive in the school secular instruction only. But the character of a school must depend on that which it professes and offers to give, not on the number of those who receive all that it offers. A grammar school does not lose its character as such because all the scholars do not learn Latin and Greek, but at the wish of their parents are allowed to devote their time to a different course of study. But I am aware how this view of the case has been met by the opponents of the Conscience Clause; and it appears to me that a simple statement of their argument is sufficient to establish the truth of that which they controvert. It is argued that there ought to be no such thing as purely secular instruction in a Church school; that all manner of knowledge should be "interpenetrated with a definite objective and dogmatic faith;" and that "the thread of religion should run through the whole, from one end to the other."* It may appear, at first sight, as if these phrases were utterly unmeaning, and could only have been used by persons who had never reflected whether they are capable of any application to the real work of a school. How, it may be asked, is a sum in the Rule of Three to be "interpenetrated" with a definite, objective and dogmatic faith? That may seem hard; but I am afraid that it has been thought possible, and that excellent persons have believed they had accomplished it, by selecting examples of the rules of arithmetic out of Scripture. I leave it to others to judge how far this is likely to cherish reverence for Holy Scripture, or to imbue young minds with dogmatic faith. I only say this is the nearest approach I have yet heard of toward reducing the maxim into practice. I am not aware whether there are yet Church schools where all the copies in the writing-books are enunciations of dogma, and all the reading lessons extracted from treatises on dogmatic theology. But this appears to be absolutely necessary for the completeness of the system, as the completeness

sidenote: Purely secular instruction.

---

* Archdeacon Denison's speech in Convocation on the Conscience Clause, pp. 16, 23.

of the system is essential to the force of the argument. It must be presumed that the persons who insist on this argument enjoy a privilege which falls to the lot of very few clergymen, that of leisure, enabling them constantly to superintend the whole course of instruction in their parish schools, so as to make sure that every part, however nominally secular, is thoroughly "interpenetrated with a definite, objective and dogmatic faith." It cannot be supposed that they would feel themselves at liberty to commit so very difficult and delicate an operation to the schoolmaster, who can hardly ever be capable of conducting it. Even in their own hands, it must always require infinite caution, and be attended with extreme danger of a most fearful evil. The practice of *improving*, as it is called, all subjects of study by the importation of religious, particularly dogmatic, reflections, apparently quite irrelevant to their nature, seems much less likely to form habits of genuine piety than either to corrupt the simplicity of the child's character, or to disgust him with that which is so obtruded on his thoughts, and to lead him to suspect the earnestness and sincerity of his teachers. And one can hardly help indulging a hope that, if we were admitted to see the ordinary work of the schools, which must be supposed to exhibit the most perfect models of such religious education, we should find that they do not materially differ in this respect from others of humbler pretensions, and that the practice falls very far short of the theory; each being, in fact, applied to a distinct use; the one serving as an instrument of rational and wholesome instruction, the other as a weapon for battling against the Conscience Clause. *Improvement of studies by religious reflections.*

There is another aspect of the subject, which I cannot pass by in silence, because it is perhaps the most important of all, though I advert to it with some hesitation and reluctance. Unhappily there can be no doubt that a clergyman may be convinced that it is his duty to close the doors of his parish school against every child whom he is not at liberty to instruct in all the doctrines of the Church. He may firmly believe that, apart from this instruction, every thing *The admission of children to Church schools who are not to be instructed in her doctrines.*

else that is taught in the school is not only worthless, but positively pernicious, "not a blessing, but a curse,"* and therefore that kindness toward the child—if there were no other motive—demands that it should be guarded from this evil. To others, who quite as fully admit the supreme importance of religious education, it may appear that this is straining the principle to a length which shocks the common sense of mankind. That, however, is no reason whatever for questioning the perfect sincerity of those by whom the opinion is professed. But it is not credible that any clergyman should not be aware that this is not the view commonly taken of the subject by fathers of families in the labouring classes. He cannot help knowing that, probably without exception, they regard the secular instruction—whether accompanied with religious teaching or not—as a great benefit to their children, one on which their prospects in life mainly depend, one therefore for which an intelligent and affectionate parent is willing to make great sacrifices. A Dissenter who knows that he can obtain these advantages at the parish school, together with a superintendence which may be urgently needed for the child's safety, though clogged with the condition of its being brought up with the view of making it a proselyte to the Church, and severed from the religious connection in which he wishes it to remain, will be strongly tempted to purchase an advantage which he believes to be great, at a risk which he may hope will prove to be small. He may know that the religious impressions which are commonly left on the mind of the child by the school teaching—especially that which relates to abstruse theological dogmas—are seldom very deep, and that unless they are renewed after it has left school, they will vanish of themselves, and will be easily counteracted by parental authority. He may therefore consent to expose his child to the danger, though it will be with reluctance, in proportion to the sincerity of his own convictions. Few, I think, will be disposed to condemn him very severely, if he yields to such a temptation. But in the eyes of a clergyman, who attaches supreme value to a "definite, objective, and dogmatic faith," he

* Archdeacon Denison, u. s.

must appear to be guilty of a breach of a most sacred duty ; to be bartering his child's eternal welfare for temporal benefits ; to be acting a double part, allowing his child to be taught that which he intends it to unlearn, and to profess that which he hopes it will never believe. Can it be right for a clergyman holding such views, to take advantage of the poor man's necessity and weakness, for the sake of making a proselyte of the child ? Is he not really bribing the father to do wrong, and holding out a strong temptation to duplicity and hypocrisy, when he admits the child into his school on such terms ? And when he enforces them by instruction which is intended to alienate the child from the father in their religious belief, is he not oppressing the poor and needy ? I can understand, though I cannot sympathise with it, the rigidity of conscience which closes the school against Dissenters : but I cannot reconcile it with the laxity of conscience which admits them on such terms.

I must own that I have been sorry to observe the frequent reference which has been made, in the discussion of this question, to what is called, "the missionary office of the Church in educating the children of the sects." * I do not much like to see the word *missionary* used with reference to the "sects." I do not think it will tend to produce a happier state of feeling between the Church and the Dissenters, if they find that we speak of them as if they were heathen. It has indeed always been the policy of the Church of Rome to deny the right of all Protestants, Anglicans among the rest, to the name of Christians. † But this is one of the points in which I do not desire to see a nearer approximation to the Romish spirit or practice. But if the Church is to discharge her "missionary office in educating the children of the sects," this can only be

<small>Missionary office of the Church in educating Dissenters' children.</small>

---

* Archdeacon Denison, u. s.

† "The Catholics," writes the Spanish ambassador, "your Highness is aware, are also against her marriage with the Duke of Norfolk, not being assured that he is a Christian. The Earl of Arundel and Lord Lumley undertake however that the Duke will submit to the Holy See." (Froude, Elizabeth, iv. p. 105.) Most persons who know something of Roman Catholic countries, would probably testify, from their own experience, that this is still the language which expresses at least the popular view of the subject.

done by placing them under the instruction of missionaries, who will bring them over to the belief, that the religion of their parents—whether better than heathenism or not—is a false religion.* To do this against the will of the parents—and as long as they remain Dissenters it must be against their will, though they may have been induced by worldly motives to suffer the experiment to be made—appears to me a shameful abuse of an opportunity, which it was wrong to give, but far more culpable to take.

<small>Comparison between it and the Mortara case.</small> We have been seasonably reminded † of an occurrence with which Europe was ringing a few years ago—the foul deed by which, under colour of a sacrilegious abuse of the Sacrament of Baptism, a Jewish child was torn from its parents, to be brought up in the tenets of the Church of Rome. This outrage was sanctioned by the highest authorities of that Church. Much as it shocks our moral sense, we have no reason to doubt, that all who were parties to it acted according to the dictates of their conscience, and from motives of kindness toward the child. As much may be said for those who entice Dissenters into their schools, by opening the door to them, and then exercise the missionary office of the Church upon them. ‡ There is indeed a difference between the two cases, but I am not sure that it is in favour of the Anglican mode of proceeding. The Mortara case was one of sheer brute violence. There was no attempt to corrupt or tamper with the conscience of the parents. They protested against the abduction with all the energy of grief. It would have been far worse for them, if their consent had been bought: and the transaction, on the part of the purchaser, would have been not less unjust, but more dishonourable. We are indignant, but not surprised, when we hear of such acts in the Church of Rome. We are too familiar with numberless examples in which

---

* "No religion is true, except the religion of the Church of England." Archdeacon Denison, evidence, 3881. It is the old maxim, which had not been thought over-lax, with a special restriction: Nulla salus extra Ecclesiam—Anglicanam.

† Professor Plumptre, u. s. p. 593.

‡ So Archdeacon Denison, u. s. 3823. "We may be obliged to do things sometimes which may appear to trench upon other people's rights, but I do not think that there is necessarily unkindness connected with it."

she appears to have acted on the maxim, "Let us do evil, that good may come." But, that conduct which can only be justified by that maxim, should be avowed by clergymen of high position in our Church at this day, is both humiliating and alarming. There ought to be no need of such a provision as a Conscience Clause in this country. I at one time believed that it was not, and never would be needed. But when I find that some of the most honourable and high minded men among the clergy, may be betrayed by their professional studies and associations into a breach of morality, from which, if it had not seemed to them to be sanctified by the end, they would have instinctively recoiled, I am forced to the conclusion, that the protection afforded by the Conscience Clause can not be either justly or safely withheld. Even if it was not needed as a safeguard against a practical wrong, it would be valuable as a protest against a false principle.

I do not myself think that the language of the Clause can be fairly taxed with ambiguity; though both it and some explanations which have been given of it by the highest authority, have been strangely misunderstood. If, however, it be possible to make it less liable to unintentional misconstruction, it would no doubt be most desirable that this should be done. But that, as long as the circumstances of the parish remain the same, that is, such that no second school can be founded there, *On the perpetuation of the Clause.* succeeding managers should be enabled to release themselves from the clause, on refunding the Building Grant, and renouncing the aid of the State for the future, is a proposal to which the State could not consent, without giving up the whole matter in dispute, and admitting that it had no right to fetter the discretion of the managers. This indeed has been treated as a distinct grievance. Even, it is said, if a clergyman may accept such a restraint for himself, he can have no right to impose it on his successors. But those who most strenuously protest against such a right of perpetuating the Conscience Clause, are the very persons who, a few years ago, applauded the Committee of the National Society when it deliberately sanctioned a clause in a trust deed, which enforced the teaching of the Catechism to every child in a school, though in patent contradiction to its own repeated professions, of giving the largest liberty to the clergyman in dealing with exceptional cases of Dissenting children. * I now pass to another subject.

<small>Decision of Judicial Committee on two contributors to "Essays and Reviews."</small> Not long after our last meeting an event occurred which caused very deep and wide spread agitation in the Church, an agitation which has by no means yet subsided, and of which perhaps the final consequences still remain to be seen. I allude to the decision of the Judicial Committee of the Privy Council in the case of two of the contributors to the volume of "Essays and Reviews." The Judgment given in their favour was thought to sanction a new and excessive latitude of opinion with regard to the inspiration of Holy Scripture, and the awful mystery of future retribution. To counteract this effect some clergymen of high reputation and influence framed <small>Declaration of the Clergy.</small> a Declaration, expressing the belief that the doctrines which the Judgment seemed to leave open to question were doctrines maintained by the Church of England, and for this document they procured the signatures of a majority of the whole body of the English clergy. The value of this Declaration was indeed very much impaired by the ambiguity of its language, and it appeared to me consistent with the utmost respect for all who had signed it, to doubt whether it could serve any useful purpose, and was not more likely to create misunderstanding and confusion. It might be considered as a statement of the private belief of each of the subscribers in the doctrines which were supposed to have been unsettled. In this point of view it was indeed perfectly harmless, but as it was then only the exercise of a right which had never been disputed, it was not easy to see its practical drift. On the other hand, if it was taken as affecting to decide what was the doctrine of the Church on certain controverted points, and in opposition to the decision of the Supreme Court of Appeal, it seemed to invest a fortuitous, self-constituted aggregate of persons possessing no legislative or judicial authority, with functions for which, apart from all regard to their personal qualifications, they were manifestly utterly incompetent.

* See the evidence of the Rev. J. G. Lonsdale before the Select Committee on Education, 1853 and 1844.

If the promoters of this movement had any ground for congratulating themselves on its success, as indicated by the number of signatures attached to the Declaration, it could only be with a view to some ulterior object for which it might prepare the way, and though no such aim was openly avowed, subsequent proceedings appeared to show that it either was or might have been. Such was the chief, if not the sole motive, of the wish which was expressed in both Houses of Convocation and elsewhere, for the renewal of Diocesan Synods. It was hoped that these assemblies might be made available for the promulgation of "some declaration of faith as to matters which were thought then to be in danger."* They might serve other purposes, but this was evidently that which was foremost in the minds of those who conceived the project, and I think I shall not be wasting your time if I make a few remarks on this subject. *Its ulterior object.*

There seems to be no room to doubt that the convening of such Synods is perfectly within the power of the Bishop, and not subject to any of the restrictions which make the assembling and the action of Provincial Synods to depend on the authority of the Crown. No Royal licence is needed for it, any more than for our present gathering. And it has been observed by a writer of high authority in these matters, that "Diocesan Synods are represented among us at this day by episcopal visitations." † There is certainly some degree of resemblance between the two institutions. But there is also one material difference: that, with one or two exceptions, there is no Diocese in which the whole body of the clergy are assembled at the same place to meet the Bishop on his Visitation, and the assembly which is held on that occasion in each Archdeaconry could not easily be converted into a Diocesan Synod. The proper character and special value of this Synod depend on the attendance of the clergy from all parts of the Diocese. In early times, when every part of the Diocese was commonly within an easy distance from the chief town where the Bishop resided, there would be no difficulty in the bringing of all the presbyters *The revival of Diocesan Synods.* *Practice in primitive times.*

* See Chronicle of Convocation, April, 1864, pp. 1467, 1486.
† Joyce, "England's Sacred Synods," p. 30.

together, and they would seldom form a very numerous assemblage. In the present state of things the difficulty or inconvenience would in most Dioceses be considerable, and the numbers assembled, even of the clergy alone, would be so large as to be ill fitted to the purpose of united deliberation. Such, at least, was the opinion of some who advocated the measure. It was therefore proposed to guard against this inconvenience, as in our Provincial Synods, by a system of representation, which, however, has yet not only to be tried in practice but to be constructed in theory. Whether any such existed in the primitive Churches, though it has been asserted,* seems very doubtful, and hardly capable of proof.† In the *Reformatio Legum* the attendance of all the clergy is most strictly enjoined.‡ With regard to the clergy, indeed, it would no doubt be easy enough to devise a mode by which as many of them as chose to forego the right or the privilege of personal attendance might be fairly represented. If there is to be a restoration of Diocesan Synods, that right could not well be taken away from any of the presbyters, and the exercise of it, though it might be onerous to those who lived far away from the place of meeting, might not be disagreeable to those who lived near at hand. In either case the whole proceeding would be purely voluntary. No part of it could be enforced by any legal authority.

But another new and prominent feature in the constitution of the restored Synod, and that to which the highest value was justly attached, was the admission of the laity to a share in its functions. To awaken in lay Churchmen a livelier interest in the affairs of the Church, to bring them into regular and friendly intercourse with the clergy, to draw forth the expression of their views on Church questions, was described as the chief permanent advantage contemplated in the proposal; one which would give these assemblies an importance superior to that of the Provincial Convocations themselves, from which the laity are excluded, as

<small>Admission of laymen to them.</small>

---

* Kennett on Synods, p. 198. Lathbury, History of Convocation, p. 6.

† Joyce, p. 44.

‡ Cap. 20. "A Synodo nulli ex clericis abesse licebit, nisi ejus excusationem episcopus ipse approbaverit."

more faithfully or more surely representing the mind of the Church. This, though as it seems an innovation on ancient usage,* is quite in accordance with the directions of the *Reformatio Legum*, by which laymen selected by the Bishop are allowed to be present at his private conference with the clergy, though whether in any other capacity than that of listeners does not appear.† This is no doubt the most attractive side of the scheme. We all set the highest value on the presence and counsel of our lay brethren on every occasion which brings us together for the carrying on of our common work. We are glad to learn their opinions, feelings, and wishes on all questions concerning the welfare of our common Church. An excellent person very lately taken from us (Mr. Henry Hoare) earned a title to the gratitude of the Church, which has been publicly acknowledged in Convocation, by the efforts which he made to promote such intercourse between the clergy and laity. The course prescribed in the *Reformatio Legum* would perhaps have been sufficient for this purpose. But that which is contemplated in the proposed revival of the Diocesan Synod is much more than this, and something very different. It is a system of representation similar to that which is proposed for the clergy. I believe that to organize such a system would in every Diocese be found very difficult, in most quite impracticable. It has been suggested that the election of the lay members might be entrusted to the churchwardens. I will only say that, until the churchwardens themselves are elected with a view to the discharge of this function, I can hardly conceive that such a representation would either be satisfactory to the whole body of the laity, or be regarded as an adequate exponent of their mind and will. These, however, are only practical difficulties which may be found capable of some solution which I do not now perceive. The more important question is that of the functions to be assigned to the new Synod. It seems to be admitted that the deliberations of the old Diocesan Synods were confined—as indeed

<small>Functions of the new Synod.</small>

---

* See Chronicle of Convocation, April 20, 1864, p. 1505.

† The impression it leaves is decidedly for the negative. Cap. 22: "Ibi de quæstionibus rerum controversarum interrogabuntur singuli presbyteri. Episcopus vero doctiorum sententias patienter colliget."

might have been expected—to the affairs of the Diocese. And in the *Reformatio Legum* there is not only no intimation that they were intended to be occupied by any other kind of business, but the enumeration there given of the subjects of discussion seems clearly to imply the same limitation. They relate indeed mainly to the state of religion, with respect to soundness of doctrine and legal uniformity of ritual, but to both evidently no farther than as they came under observation within the Diocese. But the consultations of the Synod now proposed are intended to take a far wider range; one, in fact, co-extensive with those of the Provincial Synods, and, like them, embracing every kind of question affecting the interest of the Church at large. This is obviously implied in the peculiar advantage which is expected to arise from the presence of the laity, whose views, transmitted to Convocation, are to inform its mind, to guide its judgment, and, where action has to be taken, to strengthen its hands.

I must own that I could not look forward without alarm to such a multiplication of Synods, if one is to be held every year in every Diocese. And, on the other hand, if only two or three Bishops were to adopt the plan, I should not feel a perfect confidence that the conclusions arrived at might not rather represent their private opinions than the general sense of the whole body.

<small>Relation of the Bishop to it.</small> The presence of the presiding Bishop is, on every supposition, a most important element in the calculation of consequences. His official station must always give great weight to his opinion, which, even if not expressed, is sure to be known. It may happen that his influence is so strengthened by his personal qualities as to be practically irresistible, and that every measure which he recommends is sure to be carried with blind confidence, or with silent though reluctant acquiescence. But the opposite case is also conceivable. It may happen that questions arise, on which the opinion and convictions of the Bishop are opposed to those of the majority of his clergy. I am afraid I may speak of this from my own experience. Such opposition is no doubt always to be lamented; but where it exists, it neither can nor ought to be kept secret. A frank

avowal of opinion on both sides is most desirable for the interests of truth. But it would not, as I think, be desirable, but, on the contrary, a serious misfortune, if this divergency of views was to manifest itself in the vote of a Diocesan Synod on a practical question, so that either the opinion of the majority must overrule that of the Bishop, or the action of the Bishop contradict the express wish of the majority.

I may illustrate this possibility by reference to a controversy which has been recently stirred. There is a party in the Church which holds that a Bishop is bound, morally if not legally, to confirm every child who is brought to him at the earliest age consistent with the direction at the end of the Office for Baptism of Infants, and without reference to that which is implied in the language of the Preface to the Confirmation Office, which supposes the candidates to have "come to years of discretion." On the other hand, there are Bishops who—having respect to the terms of the Baptismal Office itself, which requires instruction in the Catechism as a previous condition, to the highly mysterious nature of the doctrines set forth in the Catechism, more particularly in the concluding part, to the ordinary development of our moral and intellectual nature, and to the testimony of their own experience and observation,—I say there are Bishops who, considering these things, have felt themselves bound to lay down a general rule, limiting the admission of candidates to a later period, when the rite may be expected to leave a deeper impression, and who believe that to rely on the grace which may no doubt attend the ministration at every age, to make up for the deficiency of ordinary capacity, is no proof of faith, but a presumptuous and profane abuse of the rite. By acting on this view of the subject, they have incurred much acrimonious censure, which however has not in the least shaken their conviction. But if the party to which I alluded was to gain the ascendancy in a Diocesan Synod, where the presiding Bishop took that view of his duty, and the question was raised, it would be decided in a way which, though the language used might be milder and more decorous, must in

Illustration of a divergency of views between a Bishop and his Clergy.

substance amount to a vote of censure on him, which the dictates of his conscience would compel him to disregard. I do not see how such an exhibition of discordant views would be likely to serve any useful purpose, or could be attended with any but very injurious consequences.

<small>Ruridecanal Conferences superior to Diocesan Synods.</small> For all purely Diocesan purposes, the conferences which I have always desired to see established in every Rural Deanery, appear to me to possess a great advantage over the Diocesan Synod, however constituted. They afford the means of a freer, more intimate, and confidential intercourse and interchange of ideas, than is possible in a large assembly of persons who are mostly strangers to one another. The benefit which they yield is unalloyed, and free from all danger; and I must take this occasion to observe, that they seem peculiarly well adapted for the discussion of some of the questions which have recently occupied a large share of the attention of the Church, relating as they do to matters of practice with which the clergy have constantly to deal, and in which they are to a very great extent at liberty to act on their own judgment. Let me assure my reverend brethren—though many of them, no doubt, are fully aware of the fact—that many of these questions, though of great practical importance, are by no means so simple as they may appear to any one who has looked at them only from one side, or under the influence of traditional associations. But, apart from any such special object, it is certain that a clergyman who lives in constant spiritual isolation from his brethren, meeting them only on secular or merely formal occasions, but, in the things which most deeply concern the work of his calling, stands wholly aloof from them, shut up within the narrow round of his own thoughts, reading, and experience, must lose what might be a most precious aid, both to his personal edification and his ministerial usefulness. If he was imprisoned in this solitude, as may happen to a missionary at a lonely station, by causes beyond his control, he would be worthy of pity. If the seclusion is voluntary and self-imposed, when the benefits of intellectual and spiritual communion with his brethren are within his reach, it can hardly

be reconciled with a right sense of duty, or a real interest in his Master's service.

For such purposes no Diocesan Synod can supersede the Ruridecanal Meeting, while, for the purpose of ascertaining the mind of the laity on Church questions, and bringing it to bear both on Convocation and the Legislature, another kind of machinery has been not only devised, but actually framed and set in motion, which, though its organization may be susceptible of great improvement, seems to me in its general idea far more appropriate, as well as much more easily applicable to the object, than a multitude of Diocesan Synods, subject to perpetual variation in their number, and depending on contingencies which cannot be foreseen, for their very existence, and still more for their capacity of furnishing an adequate or faithful representation of the whole body of lay Churchmen; I allude to the association founded by the late Mr. Hoare under the name of the Church Institution. It is now six years since I drew your attention to this subject in a Charge, expressing my sympathy with the general aim and spirit of the association, but at the same time stating some objections which had been made to its organization, as laying it open to the suspicion of reflecting a particular shade of opinion rather than the common feeling of the Church. Three years ago the subject was brought before the Upper House of Convocation, when the usefulness of the Church Institution was fully recognized, and its fundamental principle unanimously admitted, but with the same qualification as to the precise form of its organization, which however has not, as far as I am aware, been yet altered; perhaps because experience has shown that the danger apprehended from it is not very serious, and does not practically affect the working of the Institution. *The Church Institution.*

But there is a purpose for which the Diocesan Synod, in its primitive form, as a full assembly of all the clergy of the Diocese, with the addition of as many of the lay members of the Church as may be willing to meet them, is eminently well fitted, and just in the same degree as it is ill fitted for any decision which requires calm discussion and orderly *Purpose for which Diocesan Synods are adapted.*

deliberation. This is the purpose of proclaiming any foregone conclusion, and of passing resolutions by acclamation, without a dissentient voice. This function of the Diocesan Synod is recognized by a highly esteemed writer on the subject, whose work appeared when the Church was deeply agitated by the Judgment of the Judicial Committee of the Privy Council in the Gorham Case, as one main ground for recommending the revival of these Synods, with a "close adherence to the primitive model."* It would serve "for the plain assertion of any article of the faith which may have been notoriously impugned." And in the Diocese in which an article of faith was supposed to have been impugned by the decision of the Judicial Committee in the Gorham Case, such a Diocesan Synod was assembled, and did make "a plain assertion" of the article. This example has not been forgotten. Soon after the publication of the Judgment in the more recent trials for false doctrine, by which other articles of faith were supposed to be impugned, a resolution was passed at a meeting of Rural Deans and Archdeacons in the Diocese of Oxford, declaring "that the meeting would rejoice to see the action of Diocesan Synods restored in the Church of England," and "that the circumstances of the present times peculiarly call for such a gathering for the guardianship of the faith."† Such language inevitably raises the question, What is the precise object contem-

Objects contemplated by their restoration. plated by those who desire to see Diocesan Synods restored for this purpose? We see at once that it is something more than the personal satisfaction which each member of the Synod might derive from the expression of an opinion which he holds in common with a large body of his brethren. The avowed object is far more practical and more important. It is nothing less than "the guardianship of the faith;" which, if "the circumstances of the present times peculiarly call for such a gathering" for that end, must be supposed to be in danger. And the nature of the danger thus signified is too clear to be mistaken: it is that now again, as in the Gorham

---

* Joyce, England's Sacred Synods, p. 36,
† Chronicle of Convocation, April 19, 1864.

Judgment, articles of the faith are believed by many to have been "impugned;" and hence "the plain assertion" of them is again considered as the most pressing business of a Diocesan Synod. Now let us remember how the doctrines which are alleged to be articles of the faith have been impugned. They have been impugned in two ways: first, by the writers who disputed or questioned them, and who on that account were brought to trial; and, secondly, by the solemn Judgment of the highest Court of Appeal, which, after the amplest discussion and the maturest deliberation, decided that those writers had not, in the matters alleged against them, impugned any article of the faith, and were not liable to the penalties which they would have incurred if they had done so.

It would have been possible, and quite as easy, to have taken the step now proposed when the writings in which the doctrines in question were assailed first appeared. Diocesan Synods might have been assembled, and have "plainly asserted" that the propositions which the authors impugned were not only true, but articles of the faith. None can say what might not have been the effect of such a proceeding. It is not impossible that the writers might have yielded to such a weight of authority, and have retracted and abandoned opinions which they found to be opposed to those of an overwhelming majority of their brethren. On the other hand, as they have the reputation, and perhaps would not disclaim the name of rationalists, it is equally possible, and on the whole perhaps rather more probable, that they would have pleaded at the outset to the jurisdiction; would have denied that the question ought or could be decided by a show of hands; and that even the assertions of thirty Synods would have been as powerless as thirty legions, to produce the slightest change in their convictions. The question would then have remained exactly where it was before the Synods met. And not only would their decrees have made no change whatever in the ecclesiastical position of the writers whom they condemned; but it is clear that they would not have been admitted as evidence in any Court which had to try the question.

Their probable influence on the case of the "Essays and Reviews."

They could add nothing to the force of any proof which might be required to invest the controverted doctrines with the character of articles of faith; much less could they cause any thing which would not otherwise have been an article of faith to become such.

<small>Their efficacy when opposed to the Judicial Committee.</small> But if such would have been their impotence before the Judgment of the supreme tribunal had been pronounced, and therefore while it was possible that it might confirm their assertions, what efficacy can the decrees of such Synods, whether few or many, possess, when they contradict that Judgment? How are they to "guard the faith" against any danger with which it is threatened by the Judgment? The danger is supposed to arise from the latitude of opinion allowed to the clergy on certain points. But as long as the law under which we live remains unchanged, no number of voices, either of individuals or of clerical assemblies, can contract that latitude by a hair's breadth.

All this is too evident not to be thoroughly understood by the highly intelligent, sagacious, and well-informed persons who are promoting the restoration of Diocesan Synods. It cannot be supposed that they deceive themselves as to the intrinsic value or the immediate practical effect, either of Declarations endorsed by any number of signatures, or of Synodical resolutions proclaimed by any number of voices. If they attach any importance to such documents and proceedings, it must be with a view to some ulterior object. And I think there can be little doubt what that object is. It is, I believe, the same which has been only a little more fully disclosed by the efforts which have been made to bring <small>Constitution of the Court of Appeal.</small> about a radical change in the constitution of the Court of Appeal in ecclesiastical questions. It would probably be generally admitted that this Court is capable of some improvements, both in its composition and in the form of its proceedings. But those who are dissatisfied with the Judgment which gave occasion to this movement, would certainly care little about any change which did not hold out a prospect of reversing that Judgment, and of guarding against any like occurrence for the future. Various plans have been proposed for this purpose; but it will be sufficient to notice two of them, which may be considered as including all the rest, inasmuch as the others differ from them rather in details than in principle. One is, to abolish the present Court of Appeal, and to transfer its jurisdiction to Convocation, or to some purely ecclesiastical body; the other would retain the present Court, but without any ecclesiastical assessors, and would require it, whenever the case before it involved any question of faith and doctrine, to send an issue on these matters to the spiritual body, which should be constituted for that purpose, and to let its Judgment be governed by the answer it receives.

There is one advantage which the first of these proposals must be admitted to possess over the second : that it more distinctly and completely embodies a principle which lies at the root of both ; the exclusion of the laity from all share in the decision of questions touching the doctrines of the Church. There are not a few estimable persons—perhaps I might say a not inconsiderable party in the Church—who hold that the present constitution of the highest Court of Appeal is utterly vitiated by the admixture of the lay element : that this is in itself, irrespectively of its practical consequences, an intolerable grievance, a badge of an "ignominious bondage." It has been represented as a violation of the law of Christ, and as "a breach of compact between Church and State," by which functions, now exercised by laymen, were reserved to the Clergy.* The divine origin of the prerogative thus claimed for the Spiritualty, depends on an interpretation of a few passages of Scripture, which to many appear no more conclusive than that which is alleged in proof of the Papal supremacy. The history of the ages and countries in which the claim was most generally and submissively accepted by the laity, would hardly recommend it to any one who does not regard the Reformation as at best a lamentable error; but it sufficiently explains the language which continued to be used after our separation from Rome, while the Spiritualty was still identified with the Church,† and the tenacity with which the

marginal note: Exclusion of laity from doctrinal decisions.

* Joyce, Ecclesia Vindicata, pp. 11, 13.
† 24 Hen. VIII. 12, Preamble: "The Spiritualty, now being commonly called the English Church."

tradition kept its hold on men's minds. And, independently of the notion of a Divine right, and of the peculiar illumination which may be supposed to wait upon its exercise, there is a very solid and palpable ground of fact, which may at first sight appear to furnish an irresistible argument for assigning this function to the clergy. It is one for which they may seem to be pre-eminently, if not exclusively, fitted, though not by their calling itself, yet at least by the studies and habits of their calling. Whenever a question arises in any branch of human knowledge, those who are usually consulted upon it are the masters and professors of the art or science to which it relates. When a point is in dispute in the interpretation or application of the law, the only opinion which is ever thought to have any weight, is that of experienced jurists. Why should the maxim, "cuique in suâ arte credendum," be less applicable to theology, or render it less fitting and necessary to submit spiritual questions to the exclusive cognizance of learned divines?

Difference between law and theology. This question is treated by many as unanswerable. Yet there is in one respect a wide difference between the two cases, which at first sight appear most exactly similar, and it deeply affects the validity of the practical conclusion. We know of no such thing as schools of law, by which lawyers are divided into parties, holding the most widely diverging views on many of the most important principles of legal learning, and thus led to directly opposite conclusions in all causes in which these principles are involved. When we consult our legal advisers, we feel perfect confidence, that they will approach the subject without the slightest bias from preconceived notions, and that, if they do not agree in their opinion, the disagreement will be the result, not of any conflicting doctrines, to which on one side or other they were previously pledged, but simply to a natural, unavoidable disparity in the capacity or conformation of their minds. I hardly need observe how far otherwise the case stands with regard to theology and its teachers; how exceedingly rare and difficult it is for any of them to keep aloof from the schools and parties into which the Church is parcelled, and not to be, whether consciously or unconsciously, swayed by their influence in his views of Church questions, and the more in proportion to his earnestness and his sense of the sacredness of the subject. Probably there were few clergymen whose opinion on the Gorham Case might not have been safely predicted by any one who knew the school to which he belonged; and the bishops who sat on the appeal, were certainly not an exception to this remark. The importance and interest of the case turned upon the fact, that the individual defendant was the representative of a strong party, whose position in the Church would have been shaken and imperilled, if his doctrine had been condemned.

Hence the composition of a purely ecclesiastical tribunal, to be substituted for the present Court of Appeal in causes of heresy, is a problem beset with such complicated difficulties, as to render it almost hopeless that any scheme will ever be devised for its solution, which would give general satisfaction; even if there were not so many who would reject it for the very reason, that it appears to recognise a principle—the mystical prerogative of the clergy—which they reject as groundless and mischievous. If the Spiritualty is to have the final and exclusive cognizance of such causes, it becomes necessary to inquire, Who are the Spiritualty? And the answer to this question will be found to involve most perplexing difficulties both in theory and practice. By the proper meaning of the word, the Spiritualty would include all spiritual persons of every Holy Order. But as, according to the high sacerdotal view, the laity is for all purposes concerning the declaration of doctrine merged in the Spiritualty, so by some who most zealously maintain that view, the lower orders of the Spiritualty are for the like purposes held to be merged in the Episcopate, as invested with the fulness of Apostolical authority. It cannot be denied that this opinion may claim the sanction of antiquity, and of the whole history of Councils from the earliest to the latest times. But our own Church presents an exception to the general rule in the constitution of its Synods, in which the clergy of the second Order form an essential element. They, however, are only elect representatives of the body to which they

Difficulties involved in the establishment of a purely ecclesiastical tribunal.

belong, and by a fiction, which, however convenient, seems to be purely arbitrary, the third Order of the Ministry is for this purpose regarded as merged in the second. But though our two Convocations do legally, however imperfectly, represent our own branch of the Church, it does not appear on what principle either the Irish or any other branches of the Church can be rightly excluded from a share in deliberations which affect the common faith. At present there are no means of assembling even a National Synod. A Synod of the whole English Communion, which has been recently proposed, would require machinery which it would be still more difficult to frame and to work, and it would be still more doubtful whether, as long as the relations of our Church to the State subsist, such a Synod could answer the purpose for which it appears to be designed.

Synods unfitted for discussions on doctrine. But in this matter we are forced at every turn to choose between equal and irreconcilable difficulties. The larger and more comprehensive the Synod which may be brought together, at whatever cost, the more adequately will it represent, if not the Church, at least the Spiritualty. But in proportion as its numbers adapt it to this object, and so give the greater weight to its decisions, do they tend to unfit it for the discussion of controverted points of doctrine, and so detract from its authority. On the other hand, the smaller the body which meets for deliberation, so much the better, no doubt, will it be suited for the full ventilation of the matters in dispute; but in the same degree it will be liable to suspicions of partizanship and prepossession, and will appear incapable of becoming the organ of the whole Church for the declaration of its faith. Even so small a body as the whole English Episcopate, has been thought too unwieldy for a theological discussion, while every selection from it has been generally condemned, as inconsistent with public confidence in its impartiality. It will also have to be considered whether, when the faith of the Church is at stake, it is possible to dispense with absolute unanimity among those by whom it is to be determined; or, if the vote of the majority is to prevail, whether the minority must not be held to stand self-convicted of heresy, and if they refuse to recant, be excommunicated. This indeed would raise no difficulty in a Church unconnected with the State; but under the present mutual relations of Church and State, such a proceeding would be as ineffectual, as for one Bishop to excommunicate another of a different school, and, as a means of checking the growth of heresy, would be merely futile, and expose itself to derision.

These objections are equally applicable to the second of the two proposals we are considering, that of retaining the present Court of Appeal, under the condition of referring all questions of doctrine which come before it, to an ecclesiastical council, which remains to be constituted. For the issue sent by the Judicial Committee would be just as grave, as if the cause had been originally brought under the cognizance of the Spirituality. Yet it seems pretty clear that of the two this is the plan which has most voices on its side, and is commonly thought to look most like a practicable measure. But if I am not mistaken, there is another difficulty on which this project also must split. Either the lay judges must be governed by the decision of their spiritual referees, or, after receiving the answer to their question, they will be still at liberty to exercise their own judgment on the whole case. That the members of the Judicial Committee would ever consent, or be permitted, to renounce their supreme jurisdiction, and exchange their judicial functions in this behalf for a purely ministerial agency, by which they will have passively to accept, and simply to carry into effect, the decisions of a Clerical Council—this is something which I believe is no longer imagined to be possible, even by the most ardent and sanguine advocate of what he calls the inalienable rights of the clergy, so long as the Church remains in union with the State on the present terms of the alliance. But if they do not take up this subordinate position, the principle of the ecclesiastical prerogative in matters of doctrine, which to those who maintain it is probably more precious than any particular application of it, is abandoned and lost. The Church will, in their language, continue to groan in "galling fetters," and "an ignominious bondage." *

Margin note: Proposal to refer Doctrinal questions to an ecclesiastical council.

* Joyce, u. s. p. 220.

On the other hand, if the Judicial Committee retains its independence, and is not bound to adopt the opinion of its clerical advisers, it is quite certain that it will continue to act on the same principles and maxims of interpretation by which it has been hitherto guided, and will in every case test the answer it receives by these principles, and not the principles by the answer.

The Court of Appeal a blessing to the Church. For my own part, I heartily rejoice that this is so. I consider it as a ground for the deepest thankfulness, as one of the most precious privileges of the Church of England, that principles which I believe to be grounded in justice, equity, and common sense, are still the rule of judgment in ecclesiastical causes. I earnestly hope that she may not be deprived of this blessing by the misguided zeal of some of her friends, from whom, I believe, she has at present more to fear than from the bitterest of her enemies. The present constitution of the Court of Appeal is essentially conservative in its operation. Every radical change, such as those we have been considering, would be revolutionary and disruptive in its tendency, if not in its immediate result. A wrong decision of the Court, as it is now constituted, can only affect the positions of individuals in the Church, but leaves the doctrine of the Church just where it was; for it only determines that certain writings which have been impeached for heresy are or are not consistent with that doctrine, as laid down in the standards of the Church. But the very object of the proposed reconstruction or reform of the Court, is to enable an ecclesiastical council to pronounce a Declaration of faith, which, if it is to be of any use toward deciding the question in dispute, must be something more than a mere repetition of the formularies alleged to have been impugned, and will therefore be a new, more or less authoritative, definition of doctrine; in other words, a new article of faith. It will be this really, though, of course, its framers will disclaim all intention of innovation, and will assert that the doctrine which they declare is that which the Church has held from the beginning: just as the Pope maintains that his dogma of the Immaculate Conception was a part of the original Christian revelation, though its definition, as an article of faith, was reserved for the nineteenth century. I observe that the definition of doctrine which might be put forth by our divines would be more or less authoritative, and in this respect it differs widely from that of the Papal dogma. No member of the Roman Communion is at liberty to question either the truth or the antiquity of the newly-defined article of faith. But an Anglican definition could not pretend to any such authority, grounded on the attribute of infallibility. Its authority would entirely depend on the reputation of its authors for learning, ability, and impartiality, and according to the degree in which they might be believed to possess these qualities, might be great, little, or null.

Another subject closely connected with the foregoing, and which on that account claims a brief notice, is the reform of Convocation, which has been lately proposed and advocated with much earnestness. No doubt, in one point of view, this is a question of the gravest importance. If the Convocation of the Province of Canterbury is, either by itself, or in conjunction with other bodies, to be invested with that judicial and legislative authority in matters of doctrine which some contend for as the inherent, inalienable, and exclusive right of the Spiritualty, it is most important that it should be so organized as to afford as full and fair a representation of the clergy as possible, and the remedying of any defect in its constitution would be an object on which no amount of thought or pains would be ill-bestowed. But for any purposes which lie within the present range of its powers and duties, it appears to be perfectly adequate, and not to need any change. It is now, I believe, as much as it could be made by any new arrangement, a trustworthy organ for giving utterance to the views of the clergy of the province on Church questions. There is, probably, no shade of opinion among them which it does not reflect. And I think no one would say that, if it were differently constituted, it would be likely to contain a greater proportion of learned and able men, the ornaments and strength of our Church. And I must take this occasion to own that I cannot at all concur with those who, either with friendly or unfriendly motives, speak

Reform of Convocation.

Vindication of its proceedings.

of Convocation, some with bitter sarcasm, others in a milder tone of contempt, because its proceedings are almost entirely confined to discussion, and so rarely terminate in any kind of action. I am not at all sure that this is an evil or a loss. It does not in the least prove that the discussion is useless; and if it is in any way profitable, the profit is clear, and not counterbalanced by any disadvantage. Not only have both the Debates, and many of the Reports of Committees appointed from time to time on questions generally interesting to Churchmen, a permanent value as exponents of opinion and results of laborious inquiry, but I cannot doubt that they exert a powerful and generally beneficial influence on the mind of the Church. And this is a purely spiritual influence, without the slightest intermixture of physical force or secular authority, working solely in the way of argument and persuasion on free judgments. It is, therefore, that which eminently befits a spiritual body, and it seems strange to hear this very spirituality of its operations treated as a mark of impotence, which deprives it of all title to respect even in the eyes of spiritual persons. While, therefore, I can easily understand that an extension of the ecclesiastical franchise may be desired by many, simply on account of the value they set on it, without any ulterior object, and can so far sympathize with their wishes, I cannot regard this as an object in which the Church has any practical interest, and am quite content with the existing state of the representation. But so far as the demand for a reform of Convocation proceeds upon the supposition that, by some change in its constitution, it may be fitted for some enlargement of its powers, and for some kind of work, which it is not now permitted to undertake, I consider the efforts made for this object as futile and mischievous: futile, because they can only issue in disappointment; mischievous, because, however undesignedly on the part of those who are engaged in them, they contribute to spread and to heighten an agitation which seems to me fraught with serious and growing danger. I feel myself bound to speak out plainly on this subject, though I know that the warning, in proportion as it is needed, is the more likely to be neglected.

The various projects we have been reviewing—Diocesan Synods, General Councils, change in the Court of Appeal, Reform of Convocation—however independent of one another they may appear in their origin, are really parts of one movement, and are directed toward a common object; and, when we bring them together, so that they may throw light on each other, it seems impossible to doubt what that object is. It is evidently to recover the position in which the Church, as identified with the Spiritualty, stood before the Reformation, in the period to which so many of our clergy are looking back with fond regret, as to a golden age which, if it were permitted to man to roll back the stream of time, and to reverse the course of nature and the order of Providence, they would gladly restore. It matters nothing how many or how few of those who are furthering this movement are conscious of its tendency; if wholly unsuspicious, they would not be the less efficient instruments in the hands of those who see further, and with a more definite purpose. But the present union between Church and State, a union in which, happily, the Church is not identified with the Spiritualty, opposes an insurmountable obstacle to the attainment of this object. Few, probably, even among the leaders of this movement, desire to see this obstacle removed by a rupture and separation between the two parties. But there may be some who indulge a hope that, by continued agitation, they will be able to bring about a modification of the terms of the union according to their wishes, so as to free the clergy from the control of the State in ecclesiastical matters, while they retain all the advantages which they derive from its protection and support. Buoyed up with this hope, they may use very strong language, and urge their followers into very rash counsels, in the belief that, even if they fail in their attempt something may be gained, and no harm be done. But, as I just now observed, such agitation is not harmless because it is impotent and useless. It is not a light evil that men should be taught to consider themselves as living in "galling fetters" and an "ignominious bondage," if this is not a true description of their real condition. But those

Object of the various projects reviewed.

Effects of continued agitation.

who have been so taught, if they are conscientious and honourable men, will not be content to sit down and weep, but will strive with all their might to break their fetters and to regain their freedom. And it will be impossible for them, even with the example of their guides before them, long to forget that, after all, these fetters are self-imposed, and this bondage a state of their own choice: that they have only to will, and their chains will drop off, and their prison doors fly open. And while their old friends and fellow-sufferers are painting the misery and degradation of their house of bondage, and urging them to efforts for deliverance which experience proves to be utterly hopeless, there are voices enough on the outside, appealing to their sense of duty and of honour, bidding them to come forth, and inviting them to take refuge in that happy country where, among other blessings, the Church is not confounded with the people, and her freedom is well understood to mean the rule of the clergy, culminating in the absolute power of the Pope. This, however, is not the only alternative. If old associations, or strong convictions should prevent them from going forth in that direction, they may find room nearer at hand for a new Church, in which they may enjoy the shelter without the control of the State, and may both prescribe any terms of communion they may think fit, and enforce the observance of them by any course of proceeding which may seem best suited to the purpose of suppressing all variations of private opinion as to the sense in which they are to be interpreted.

There are persons who may be attracted by the spectacle now exhibited by one of our Colonial Churches, which has found itself on a sudden, without any effort of its own, severed from the State, and in full enjoyment of that independence which is so much coveted by some among ourselves. I think that its example holds out a very precious and seasonable warning. The unexpected release from the "galling fetters," and "ignominious bondage" of the Royal Supremacy, was unhappily accompanied by a no less complete emancipation from the rules and principles of English law and justice. The result showed how dangerous it would be to entrust a purely ecclesiastical

Example of sacerdotal independence.

tribunal with the administration of justice in ecclesiastical causes: how surely the divine would get the better of the judge: how easily the most upright and conscientious men might be betrayed by their zeal for truth, into the most violent and arbitrary proceedings; exercising an usurped jurisdiction by the mockery of a trial, in which the party accused was assumed to acknowledge the jurisdiction* against which he protested, and was condemned in his absence, not for contumacy, but upon charges and speeches which had the advantage of being heard without a reply, though it was admitted by the presiding judge that they referred to passages which "he had often felt to be obscure," and which exposed him to the "risk of misunderstanding, and consequently misrepresenting the defendant's views." † This, though instructive, is melancholy enough: but it is still more saddening to

---

* Trial of the Bishop of Natal for erroneous teaching, p. 340. The Bishop of Capetown founds his claim to spiritual jurisdiction on the alleged fact, of which he thinks "there can be no doubt," that "the Church, after long and careful deliberation, resolved upon the appointment of Metropolitans over Colonial Churches, and sent him out in that capacity:" the body dignified with the name of *the Church* being a private company of Bishops, who recommended the appointment to the ministers of the Crown.

† P. 343: "A letter written two years ago, and the preface to which he refers me, very inadequately represent the kind of reply which doubtless he would have made to the charges which have been brought against him, and to the speeches of the presenting clergy." One of these, the Dean of Capetown, had observed, that the letter read had been put in by the Bishop of Natal, "*in some degree* as his defence." And it was the whole that accompanied the protest. The real nature of the proceeding is candidly stated in the *Guardian* of July 4, 1866: "If the resolution (of the Upper House of Convocation) were to be construed as declaring that Bishop Colenso has been regularly deposed or deprived by any tribunal or proceeding known to Church law, it would assert more probably than could be proved—more certainly than has been proved, either in Convocation or out of it. But that Bishop Colenso's teaching is, as a matter of fact, dangerous and unsound to the extent of heresy—that he is a person clearly unfit to have the spiritual oversight of Churchmen in Natal, and that some one else ought to have that oversight; that the South African Church, there being apparently no regular jurisdiction anywhere competent to try and to depose him, has, regularly or irregularly, condemned and rejected him in such a way as it could; and that we ought for the sake of the faith to stand by the South African Church in this matter, though we may not approve all the grounds of the decision—these are propositions in which the great mass of English Churchmen would certainly agree." These last words may be too true. But such a view of duty involves the principle that the end sanctifies the means, and may be pleaded for every *coup d'état*. Violence openly avowed is less pernicious than when it puts on the mask of justice, and claims the sanction of religion.

think that such proceedings should have been defended by some among ourselves as a fair trial : though I am persuaded that this could not have happened, if the party in whose case justice was so outraged, had been less generally obnoxious, and I have no doubt that if the offence with which he was charged, had been one of a different kind—such, for instance, as the holding all Roman doctrine—the same proceedings would have appeared to the same persons in their true light, as an intolerable wrong. But I believe there are many who will learn from this example of the fruits of sacerdotal independence, among which might be numbered the danger of a permanent schism, better to appreciate the blessings we enjoy in the institutions under which we live, notwithstanding the opprobrious names cast upon them by some who rest and ruminate under their shade. One thing at least appears to me absolutely certain : that, if there had been previously any prospect of obtaining such a reconstruction of the Court of Appeal as would, either formally or virtually, transfer its jurisdiction to the clergy, that prospect would now be closed for ever.

There is indeed an unmistakable indication that the general tendency of our time does not set in that direction, but in quite another, in the Clerical Subscription Act of last year. That the Report on which that measure was founded, should have obtained the unanimous concurrence of so large a number of persons as composed the Royal Commission, representing every party in the Church, is one of the most remarkable and the most auspicious events of our day. It marks the crowning result of a reaction, that of Christian wisdom and charity against the spirit and the policy which dictated the Act of Uniformity, passed amidst the narrow views and evil passions of the Restoration. The declared object of the new Act was to relieve tender consciences, by the alteration of forms which were designed to be as exclusive as possible, and which have no doubt excluded many from the ministry of the Church, and have perplexed and distressed many more within it. The principle of subscription is preserved, but its terms are so modified as to allow a much larger range to the freedom of private opinion. This

[margin: Clerical Subscription Act.]

[margin: Its object.]

range indeed, is not, and, consistently with the general intention of the Act, could not be exactly defined. The stress is laid not so much on the subscription itself, as on the character of the formularies, to which the subscription is required, and which the subscriber is to use in his public ministrations. It was thought that, from conscientious men, this was sufficient security; while with others more explicit language would be of no avail. I consider this as not only a generous, but a just and wise confidence, and one certainly not more likely to be abused than the old jealousy to defeat its own purpose. But I think that it does tend to increase the difficulty of prosecutions for heresy, and to lessen their chances of success. Whether this is a consequence to be dreaded, or may not be the happiest settlement of the question about the Court of Appeal, I will not now stay to inquire. But I believe that, whether good or evil, it was not unforeseen or undesigned.*

It now only remains for me to state my views on the subject which for the last twelve months has occupied more of the attention of the Church than any other, and has been discussed with an earnestness and warmth which, while they show the deep interest it has excited in many minds, and so at least its relative importance, should admonish all who have to deal with it, of the great need of approaching it calmly and soberly, and as much as possible free from prejudice and passion. And to this end it is not enough that we should weigh arguments which may be opposed to our own preconceived opinions, with an even mind, unless we also try to place ourselves as far as we can in the point of view from which they proceed, and in some measure to enter into the feelings with which they are urged. You will have understood me to be speaking of that which for shortness I may call the Ritual question: and I trust that in the observations I am about to make on it, I shall not lose sight of the rule I have just laid down, and that whatever I shall say may tend to promote the common interests of truth, peace, and charity. And first a word as to the importance of the question. A relative importance,

The Ritual question.

---

* See the debate in the House of Commons on June 9, 1863, upon Clerical Subscription.

as I have observed, cannot be denied to a controversy by which the minds of Churchmen have been largely and deeply stirred. But I entirely differ from those who regard the dispute as in itself of little moment, and unworthy of serious attention, because it relates immediately to things so trifling as the form and colour of garments to be worn, and ceremonies to be observed, in Divine service. No doubt these are things indifferent in themselves, always subject to the authority of the Church, and deriving all their importance from the degree in which they minister to the use of edifying. But they would not be decreed by the Church, if they were supposed to be utterly unmeaning: and the meaning which they are intended to convey may be of the gravest moment. And whether they do or do not serve the end of edification, is surely a question in which the well being, not to say the life of the Church, is deeply concerned. At the very lowest estimate, no man of practical sense can deem it a light matter, if a change is made in the externals of public worship, such as to give a new aspect to the whole. Such a transformation must needs be the effect of some powerful cause, and the cause of some important effect. Nothing less than the future character and destiny of the Church of England may be involved in the issue of the movement now in progress.

Its past history. I must also say a word on its past history, as this has been strangely misunderstood. It has been suggested, in the way of apology for those who might be thought to be advancing too far in this direction, that the recent development of Ritualism is intended as a pious protest against recent innovations in doctrine, which are injurious to our Lord's Divine dignity. But this explanation, while it implies an unmerited imputation on the orthodoxy of the great body of the clergy who have declined to take part in this *protest*, also involves a very gross anachronism. Nearly five and twenty years ago, Mr. Robertson opened his very useful treatise, "How shall we conform to the Liturgy?" with these words: "Among the consequences of the late theological movement (meaning that which had been some years before inaugurated at Oxford, and was then in full swing) has been the manifestation of a feeling more energetic at least, if not stronger, than any that had before been general, as to the obligations of the clergy in matters of ritual observance. We hear daily of the revival of practices, which from long disuse have come now to be regarded as novelties." This revival continued to make its way; and in 1851 had gone so far that twenty-four Archbishops and Bishops of the two Provinces concurred in an Address to the clergy of their respective Dioceses, which began with the statement:—" We have viewed with the deepest anxiety the troubles, suspicions, and discontents which have of late in some parishes accompanied the introduction of ritual observances exceeding those in common use amongst us." Whether this Address produced any effect on those whom it was intended to restrain, I am not able to say. There were causes enough in the troubles and discontents of which it speaks, though not to stop, to retard the progress of the movement, and keep it within bounds: and it is not at all surprising that it should not sooner have reached the point at which it has now arrived. Its present phase does not in the least require or justify the conjecture of any new motives peculiar to our day; nor is that conjecture warranted by the professions of the Ritualists themselves, who are too conscious of their own history to advance such a plea, and too well satisfied with the grounds which they have alleged for their proceedings to feel that they need it.

Among these grounds that which used to be most strongly insisted on, was the lawfulness of the observances introduced. It was contended that though, in consequence of their long disuse, they presented the appearance of novelty, they were really part and parcel of the law of the land and of the Church, which had never been repealed, though, either through the fault of men or the misfortune of evil times, it had been neglected and disobeyed. It followed that those who revived these confessedly obsolete observances show themselves to be the true, loyal, and dutiful sons of the Church, and that those of their brethren who adhere to the long prevailing usage, though their conduct may admit of some charitable excuse, cannot be altogether free from blame. This is a position in which the

The lawfulness of Ritualistic observances.

great body of the clergy can hardly be prepared contentedly to acquiesce, and so the legal side of the question interests the character and the conscience of every parish priest in the country. It cannot be sufficient for him to be treated with indulgence by those who regard him as really guilty of a breach of duty. But though I do not expect that those who have taken this high ground will ever retract their language, I do not think it will continue to be repeated with the same inward confidence; as it must be felt that, to say the least, the assumption on which it rests has within the last half year suffered a somewhat rude shock and lost much of its credit. Several of the Bishops, a majority of the English Bench, thought that the state of things rendered it desirable to obtain a legal opinion on the lawfulness of some of the restored observances, and by their direction a Case very carefully prepared was submitted to four lawyers of the highest reputation, including one who was then Attorney-General. The joint Opinion of these eminent persons pronounced the practices in question to be unlawful.

Legal opinion on them.

How received by Ritualists. It was to have been expected that those who would have rejoiced if the answer had been in the opposite sense, should have been displeased and dissatisfied with this result. But I was not prepared to find that any one not pledged to their views would permit himself to decry the value of the opinion, on the ground that the Case was "of an *ex-parte* character," and that the counsel consulted fell into a "trap" which had been laid for them.* I refrain from all comment on the good taste of this language and on the reflection it implies on the character of the consulting Bishops, and on the learning and ability of their legal advisers. I will only observe that the infatuation thus indirectly but unmistakably imputed to the Bishops, is even greater than the disingenuousness with which they are charged. For if any one had a deep personal interest in ascertaining the real state of the law on the subject, it must have been those who might find themselves compelled to bring the question into Court at their

---

* See the speech of the Dean of Ely, in the debate on Ritual, in the Lower House of Convocation.

own charge and risk. They are supposed to have craftily contrived the defeat of their own object, by laying a "trap" into which their guides, whom they had carefully blinded, innocently but inevitably fell. In the meanwhile, however successful one who is not a member of the legal profession, may believe himself to have been, in convicting four lawyers of the first eminence, and acting under the gravest responsibility, of ignorance or carelessness, without the possibility of knowing the steps by which they were brought to their conclusion, it is satisfactory to reflect that, as far as I am aware, no one has ventured to throw out a suspicion that they were under the influence of any bias arising from personal feelings; as it is notorious that if any such had existed it would have been likely to operate rather against their conclusion than in its favour; nor do I know that any one has yet attempted to show that the case submitted to them either omitted or misstated any material fact or element of a judicial decision.

It has indeed been suggested that the persons whom it would have been proper to consult were those who are profoundly versed in what is called the science of Liturgiology. This would no doubt have been the right course if the object had been that which has been attributed to the Bishops, to procure a sanction for foregone conclusions. But if it was to obtain a thoroughly unprejudiced as well as enlightened opinion, no course could have been less judicious. Some of the most distinguished professors of the new science have made it clear that, even if they possessed the requisite impartiality in which they are so glaringly deficient, they would be very unsafe guides, not only in questions of law, but even in such as are immediately connected with their own special study, the tendency of which appears to be to develop the imagination at the expense of the judgment.*

Judiciousness of the Bishops' proceedings.

One advantage, not as it appears to me inconsiderable, will

---

* On Dr. Littledale's notable discovery, unhappily endorsed by Archdeacon Freeman, about the north side of the altar, see a pamphlet, "The North Side of the Table," by Henry Richmond Droop, M.A., Barrister, and one with the same title by the Rev. Charles John Elliott. On Archdeacon Freeman's own not less notable discovery as to weekly celebrations, see a Letter to the Archdeacon by the Rev. R. H. Fortescue. The extravagant licence of arbitrary conjecture and assumption in which Ritualist writers indulge when they have a point to make out, is a very evil have been gained by the Opinion, whatever else may be its result. Until it shall have been overruled by the Judgment of a competent tribunal, it may be hoped that no Ritualist will again reproach any of his brethren with unfaithfulness or wilfulness, because they abstain from observances which eminent lawyers believe to be unlawful. But I am quite aware that the opinion by no means sets the question at rest, and though I should be surprised if it was to be judicially contradicted, I am fully sensible of the possibility that the more thorough sifting of a trial may lead to an opposite conclusion. That the question in its legal aspect is one of very great difficulty will not be denied by any one who is at all acquainted with the voluminous discussion it has undergone. I will only venture to make one observation, which seems to lie fairly within my province, on the peculiar character of the difficulty. It is one of a kind which we have constantly to encounter in the highest regions of theology, when we find two truths—such as God's sovereignty and man's free agency—both undeniable, yet apparently irreconcilable with one another. In the present case we

Advantage accruing from the legal opinion.

---

sign, whether as indicating weakness of judgment or violence of party spirit: or, as is most probable, both at once. With its help, St. Paul's φιλόνη (2 Tim. iv. 13) becomes a "sacrificial vestment." The lights in the upper chamber (Acts xx. 8) which were burning while he preached, were manifestly designed to pay honour to the Holy Eucharist. The direction ascribed to St. James, in the forged Apostolical Constitution (viii. 12), for the ἀρχιερεὺς to officiate λαμπρὰν ἐσθῆτα μετενδὺς, is deemed conclusive as to the sacerdotal character of the vestment; though the real Apostle speaks (ii. 2) of a rich man coming into the Christian assembly ἐν ἐσθῆτι λαμπρᾷ, apparently not for the purpose of "celebrating." Still more seriously shocking is the abuse made of the Old Testament and of the Book of Revelation. Cardinal Baronius was not guilty of a worse outrage on truth and common sense, when he pretended to discover that our Lord robed Himself for the celebration of the Last Supper (*Annales*, tom. i. p. 154). Casaubon's rebuke (Exercitationes, p. 439) is, as to the abuse of Scripture, equally applicable to the Cardinal's modern imitators: "Quis ferat Baronii licentiam, hic quoque fingentis Dominum nostrum ad instituendam Sacrosanctam Eucharistiam pretiosam aliam vestem induisse, et pro actionibus vestimenta subinde mutasse! Hoccine est divina oracula cum timore et tremore tractare, humana figmenta sacris narrationibus ex suo semper immiscere?" The next remark shows that Baronius was more excusable than those who tread in his steps: "Enimvero non poterat continere se Cardinalis Baronius, vel Cardinalitios certe jam tum animos gerens, aulæ Romanæ splendori et regiæ Pontificum pompæ assuetus, quin aliquid de moribus hodiernis Domino affingeret."—To the above cited pamphlets may now be added an excellent article on the North Side of the Lord's Table, in the Contemporary Review, Oct. 1866.

have, on the one side, a Rubric still in force, which prescribes the use of certain ornaments in the Church by the authority of Parliament. On the other side, we have the uniform practice of three centuries, during which these ornaments have never been in use. Both facts are unquestionable, the difficulty is to find an explanation by which they may be reconciled. Such an explanation has been thought to be furnished by subsequent acts of Royal authority which, if valid, would qualify the Rubric, and even, if not, would sufficiently account for the practice. But why the Rubric was allowed to remain at the last revision of the Prayer Book in 1662, without either modification or explanation, is another difficulty which has been bequeathed to us by the Bishops of that day. I am afraid that it admits of a but too easy solution. When at the Savoy Conference the Ministers excepted to the Rubric on the ground that "it seemed to bring back" the vestments forbidden by the Second Prayer Book of Edward VI., the Bishops might either have admitted that they desired to see these ornaments restored, or have shown that the Rubric under the law as it then stood would not have that effect. They did neither the one nor the other, but simply declared that they "thought it fit that the Rubric continue as it is," for reasons which they had already given in answer to a more general remonstrance of the ministers on the subject of ceremonies. But when we refer to these reasons, we find that they relate to no other kind of vestment than the surplice.

Reconciliation of Rubrics with Church practice.

The Bishops of the Restoration may deserve censure for some parts of their conduct in that controversy. Not that they were more intolerant than their adversaries, but it was their misfortune to have gained the power, where the others only retained the will to persecute. But without wishing at all to extenuate their faults, I think we have no right, morally or historically, to put the worst construction on their words or actions, when they may be at least equally well explained on a milder supposition. If, when they gave that answer to the exception of the ministers, they believed that the Rubric did really authorize the use of the vestments which "it

Conduct of Bishops of the Restoration respecting vestments.

seemed to bring back," they would have been guilty of the most odious duplicity. But if, knowing or believing that it had been so limited as only to cover the use of the surplice, they nevertheless retained it unaltered, just because their opponents " desired that it might be wholly left out," this I am afraid would be too much in keeping with the general course and spirit of their proceedings to be thought at all improbable. It must, however, be observed that though on this supposition they were witnessing, as some of them did still more plainly by their subsequent acts, to the general understanding as to the state of the law on this head, it would not follow with absolute certainty that they were not under a mistake, and that the apprehension professed by the Puritans was not better grounded than they themselves believed.

Independently of whatever weight may be due to the recent Opinion, I think there was at least enough of obscurity and perplexity in the question, to restrain a cautious and modest man who had studied its history, even from making up his mind upon it with absolute confidence,* much more from acting upon his private opinion by the revival of obsolete observances. The use of three centuries may not be sufficient to prove the state of the law, but it can hardly be denied that it affords a strong indication of the mind of the Church, which it seems hardly consistent with either humility or charity for any of her ministers openly to disregard. But maxims of conduct which would govern ordinary cases may not be applicable to this. We are bound to judge men by the view they take of their own position and duties, however erroneous it may appear to us. And it is clear that the clergymen who are engaged in the Ritualistic movement do not consider themselves

Necessity of caution in forming an opinion on the subject.

---

* I venture to express this opinion, notwithstanding the high authority cited by Mr. Stephens (Book of Common Prayer with Notes, vol. i. p. 378), because I find that in that quotation a most material part of the history of the question was entirely ignored; as it is, most surprisingly, by Archdeacon Law, in his lecture on Extreme Ritualism, where, through this singular oversight, he finds himself driven (p. 124) to a conclusion most repugnant to his wishes. Mr. Stephens himself seems to me to beg the whole question, in his answer to the observations which he quotes from Bishop Mant, on the limitation effected in the Rubric of Elizabeth by the Advertisements and Articles of 1571 (p. 368).

simply as ministers of the Church of England, but as providentially charged with a missionary work of restoration and renewal, which they conceive to be urgently needed for her welfare.* The changes which have been introduced into the forms of public worship are a part only, though the most conspicuous, and perhaps the most important part of that work. In their eyes that usage of three centuries, to which they are called upon to conform, whether legal or not, has no claim to respect, but, on the contrary, is a corruption and an abuse. When they look back to its origin, they can feel no sympathy with the spirit from which it sprang. When they follow the stream of its history, they observe signs of progressive deterioration. And when they test it by its final results, they find on the whole failure and not success. The present state of things appears to them such as to warrant all lawful endeavours to try the effect of a different system. If the tendency of that which they advocate is to lessen the amount of difference in externals, which separates the English Church from the greater part of Christendom, they do not regard that as a ground of objection, but as an argument in its favour; and more especially with respect to our Missions to the heathen, as an incalculable advantage, supplying a defect which would be alone sufficient to account for their comparative barrenness. Missionary aspect of Ritualism.

Whatever we may think of the past, I am afraid that no one who does not shut his eyes to facts of the most glaring notoriety, can deny that this view of the present is but too well founded, and that the state of the Church with regard to the influence which she exercises on the people of this country is far from satisfactory. This indeed would be abundantly evident if it were only from the proposals and attempts which have been so rife of late years for supplying the acknowledged want. They show indeed that the Church is awake to the consciousness of her need, and bestirring herself to provide for it; but also that the means of so doing have not yet been found, at least in any degree adequate to the end. And I think this ought Present state of the Church's influence over the people.

* See Dr. Littledale on "The Missionary Aspect of Ritualism," in "The Church and the World."

to make us very cautious about rejecting any help which may be offered to us for this object, unless it be quite clear that it is offered on terms which we cannot lawfully accept. I do not mean now to speak of the difficulty of reaching vast masses of our population on whom the Church has at present no hold at all, and who have to be recovered from a state often much worse than most forms of heathenism. That would only divert our attention from the subject immediately before us. Those who never enter our churches because they are strangers to all religion, can have no concern in a question about modes of worship. But confining ourselves to this point, we can hardly fail to see clear signs of a *Ordinary Church services not sufficiently attractive.* wide-spread feeling that something is wanting in the ordinary services of the Church to make them generally attractive or impressive. Otherwise we should not hear so many complaints of their length and tediousness. And we cannot overlook the fact, that the outward posture and most probably the inward frame of perhaps the great bulk of our congregations, is not that of worshippers who are joining in common prayer, but that of persons listening, respectfully or otherwise, to some devotional utterances which pass between the minister and the clerk, while waiting for the sermon, as the only part of the service from which they expect any benefit. It is natural that many should wish to have this time of waiting abridged. But, on the other hand, we hear not less loud complaints of the length and tediousness of sermons, and wishes that they should be either reserved for special occasions, or kept within a much narrower compass.

It is not enough, by way of answer, to point to the crowds which frequent the special service of our cathedrals, as a proof that we may well be content with the present attractiveness of our form of worship. No doubt as often as it combines the attractions of a majestic building, a well-trained choir, and an eloquent *Remedies suggested.* preacher, it will never lack the attendance of large congregations. But it is very rarely that any of these are to be found, much more rarely that all are to be found together, in our parish churches. The example, however, shows what are the elements which contribute to the result : and experience appears to prove that they may be sufficiently efficacious even when present in only a moderate degree. The character and internal arrangements of the building, though of subordinate moment, are by no means unimportant; and every indication of wilful, irreverent neglect, in things appropriated to the most sacred uses, can hardly fail to injure those whom it does not offend. But this at least it is always possible to avoid. A high strain of eloquence can never be common; nor perhaps is it suited to most of our congregations. But earnestness and thoughtfulness, with the skill gained by experience in adapting the discourse to the capacity and circumstances of the hearers, will always enable the preacher to awaken their interest, and command their attention. And so, if our ordinary Services are found wearisome by those who do not bring with them a lively spirit of devotion, this cannot be fairly laid to the charge of the Prayer Book, where its directions are disregarded, and the services are conducted in a manner wholly at variance with the intention of its framers, and deprived of all their proper charm of variety and solemnity, by the practice which excludes all musical expression, and makes the effect to depend on the always uncertain, and often painfully defective taste and judgment of the reader.

While therefore I would readily admit that which is often urged in defence of the Ritualistic movement, that in many of our churches there is large room for improvement in the prevailing practice of our public worship, I cannot find in this fact any thing to justify, or indeed to account for the recent innovations. In the first place the resources of the Prayer Book were very far from exhausted. Experience, as far as it went, tended to show that a closer observance of its directions, and a fuller use of the means it places at our disposal, without the smallest excess over that which is perfectly legitimate and unquestionably authorized, would commonly suffice to relieve our services from that monotony which has been the subject of complaint; and which, allow me to remind you, my reverend brethren, may be felt by many of our hearers as very irksome and depressing, *Resources of the Prayer Book.*

while we who officiate are wholly unconscious of the effect we produce. And it must be added that, if there are congregations to whom even such an amount of variation from the established usage would be unwelcome, and even offensive, that is certainly a reason not for, but against, the introduction of other changes, which are generally obnoxious, not only from their novelty, but their character. And in the next place it must be observed, that these startling changes have been made, not at a time when the Church had to be roused from a state of apathy and torpor, but, on the contrary, while she was exerting herself with unprecedented activity for the removal of impediments, and the strengthening of aids to the public devotion of her children. I have already, at the beginning of my Charge, touched on the evidence visible in this Diocese, and still more in many others, of the growing attention paid to the structure and comeliness of her sacred buildings: and this care has been very largely extended to the details of her worship. *Formation of choral associations.* If any proof of this statement were needed as to ourselves, it would be found in the gratifying fact, that choral associations have been lately formed in three of our Archdeaconries, whose example will no doubt ere long be followed by the fourth. We have thus ground to hope, that the voice of melody will be more frequently heard in our churches, to inspirit the strains of praise and thanksgiving, and that the " psalms and hymns, and spiritual songs," which were meant to be the expression of pious feelings, will not always be made to serve merely as additional lessons. In the meanwhile it is by no means certain that the success, measured by increased attendance, of the new observances, has been greater than that of services which have been conducted strictly within the commonly recognised limits of the Prayer Book, and with an intelligent and judicious application of its rules. I have no statistics which would enable me to speak with confidence on this subject. But I believe that in most neighbourhoods the number of those who are attracted by the revived ritual bears a small proportion to that of those who dislike and disapprove of it, even if they are not shocked and disgusted by it. And I strongly suspect that those who take pleasure in it, do so mainly not on account of its superior sensuous attractions, but because it represents a peculiar system of opinions.

Hence it is clear that a comparison between the two forms of worship, with respect to their effectiveness or popularity, could lead to no trustworthy result, and, even if it did, could afford no safe ground for any practical decision. It is absolutely necessary to consider the movement in itself, apart from all calculations or conjectures as to its prospects of success or failure. Much also has been said which appears to me quite irrelevant, as to the personal character of those who take the lead in it. They are described, I have no doubt most truly, as men of exemplary lives, and extraordinary devotedness to their pastoral duties.* These certainly are qualities which entitle them to respect; and that devotedness may not be the less meritorious because they are avowedly engaged in a missionary and proselytizing work. But they themselves would probably be the last to question that many, if not most, Roman Catholic priests lead holy, self-denying lives, and give themselves unsparingly to the work of their calling, even when it is not of a missionary kind. It seems to me more to the purpose to observe, that they are apparently persons of great energy and no inconsiderable ability, thoroughly in earnest, believing in themselves and their mission, of resolute will and sanguine hopes; and that the strength of the party behind their backs is not to be measured by the numbers of those who happen to belong to their congregations. The adherents probably form a much larger body. It may not be too much to say, looking at their connections and alliances, that they are already a power in the Church: one strong enough at least to make it worth our while to gain as clear an idea as we can of their principles and aims.

Character of the Ritualistic leaders.

The fact which presents itself most obviously on the surface

---

* So the Report of the Committee of the Lower House of Convocation on Ritual. "None are more earnest and unwearied in delivering the truth of Christ's Gospel, none more self-denying in ministering to the wants and distresses of the poor, than very many of those who have put in use these observances." As the Committee throughout ignore the Romanizing character of the movement, it is not surprising that they should not have perceived the irrelevancy of this remark.

of the whole matter, is the change which has been made in the Administration of the Lord's Supper. The Communion Service of the Prayer Book is set, as it were, in the frame of the Roman Catholic ceremonial, with all the accompaniments of the high or chanted Mass, vestments, lights, incense, postures and gestures of the officiating clergy. It is interpolated with corresponding hymns, and supplemented by private prayers, translated from the Roman Missal. To make the resemblance more complete, several of the clearest directions of our own Rubric are disobeyed, and the Roman observance substituted for that appointed by our Church.* To the eye, hardly any thing appears to be wanting for an exact identity between the two Liturgies: and it is but rarely that any difference can be detected by the ear. I cannot help thinking that this unquestionable fact deserved some notice in the Report of the Committee of the Lower House of Convocation on Ritual, where it is passed over in silence, and could not be gathered by any one from the remarks which are there made on the particulars of the new practice. And it is not unworthy of note, as indicating the spirit of the movement, that according to an interpretation of the Rubric referring to the second year of Edward VI., which was for some time treated as indisputable, every ornament and rite of the unreformed Church, which has not been either expressly forbidden or tacitly excluded by the established order of our Service, is still authorized by the Statute law, and may and ought to be used. This doctrine was made the foundation of a remarkable work, which purports to direct the Anglican clergy in their liturgical ministrations, with a view to the restoration of the old practice, and treats the subject with a Rabbinical minuteness, quite worthy of the end proposed.† This interpretation, indeed, has since been discovered to be hardly tenable, though it will probably not the less continue to be acted upon. But it marks the precise character of the ideal which the Ritualists have set

Margin notes: Change in the administration of the Lord's Supper. The "Directorium Anglicanum."

---

* This is most amply shown in a pamphlet entitled "Utrum Horum," by "Presbyter Anglicanus," where the directions of the Prayer Book are compared with those of the "Directorium Anglicanum."

† "Directorium Anglicanum."

before themselves, as the object of their aspirations: the mediæval type of Ritual in its most florid development, and in the most glaring possible contrast to the simplicity of our present use.

This, I say, is a fact which, in my opinion, ought not to be kept out of sight in any statement which professes to give a clear and fair view of the subject, especially if it is meant to be a guide to practical conclusions. And it enables us the better to judge of the argumentative value of some topics which are often urged on behalf of the movement, and which have even been deemed worthy of a place in the Report I was just now speaking of. We cannot but sympathize with persons who are governed by "no other motive than a desire to do honour to the Most Holy and Undivided Trinity, and to render the services of the English Church more becoming in themselves and more attractive to the people." But it is not easy to perceive how these motives are specially connected with the practices in defence of which they are alleged; and I think it would startle and alarm most Churchmen to hear that, in the judgment of either House of Convocation, wherever these motives exist, they will of themselves, without any other kind of impulse, naturally lead to the closest possible assimilation of our Liturgy to the Roman Mass. In this case the ruling motives can be only matter of conjecture; all that is certain is the visible result. And this rather suggests a strong suspicion, that the motives assigned would not have taken this direction if it had not been determined by a prepossession in favour of distinctive Roman usages. It has also been laid down as a principle bearing upon the present question, that the use of peculiar vestments for the celebration of Divine Service, and especially of its most solemn act, the Holy Communion, is a dictate of instinctive piety.* Yet it may now be considered as well ascertained that for several centuries the piety of the early Christians did not lead them to make any change in their ordinary apparel, even for the celebration of their holiest mysteries, and that the liturgical vestments of later ages may all be traced to the

Value of arguments in support of the movement.

* See "A Sermon for Easter Day," by the Rev. Edward Stuart, Appendix, p. 45.

original dress of common secular life.* But even if the principle could claim that sanction of Christian antiquity which it wants, and which seems rather to belong, in respect both of shape and colour, to the much-despised surplice, † still, it would not either warrant or explain the partiality shown in the adoption, not only of the late mediæval forms, but of the precise variations of colour prescribed by the Roman Ritual.

These examples, however, convey a very imperfect idea of the extent to which that partiality is carried, and of the manifold ways in which it is displayed. The Debate on Ritual in the Lower House of Convocation drew forth some remarkable disclosures, ‡ which leave no room for doubt on this head. I confine myself, however, to that which is apparent in the mode of conducting public worship. Where we find such a close and studied approximation to the Roman Catholic system in externals, it is certainly not uncharitable to suspect that there may be a corresponding affinity in matters of faith and doctrine. This becomes still more probable when we place two facts side by side. On the one hand, the Reformers, who desired to abolish the ornaments and ceremonies now restored, had no aversion to them in themselves, were not only fully aware that in themselves they are things indifferent, but probably would have been ready to admit that they are graceful, picturesque, attractive to the senses and the imagination. But they disliked them the more on that very account, because, in their minds, they were things inseparably associated with doctrines which they abhorred, and against which they contended even to the death. On the other hand, those who

<small>Affinity to Roman Catholicism.</small>

---

* Professor Hefele's Essay on this subject in the second volume of his "Beiträge zur Kirchengeschichte, Archäologie, und Liturgik"—the more valuable as the work of a zealous as well as a very learned Roman Catholic—has been made the foundation of a very useful paper by the Rev. Professor Cheetham, in the "Contemporary Review," August, 1866.

† "The clergy," observes Mr. Hemans, in a paper on the Church in the Catacombs, "Contemporary Review," October, 1866, "till the end of this primitive period, continued to officiate attired in the classic white vestments common to Roman citizens, but distinguished by the long hair and beard of philosophers; and not till the Constantinian period did the bishops begin to wear purple; not till the ninth century was that primitive white costume (which was sometimes slightly adorned in purple or gold) laid aside by the priesthood generally."

‡ In a letter or paper read by Archdeacon Wordsworth.

are labouring for the restoration of the pre-Reformation Ritual though they do not neglect to avail themselves of such general pleas as I was just now noticing, grounded on the common instincts and cravings of human nature, when they come distinctly to enumerate "the ends to which Ritual and Ceremonial minister," specify as one end, that "they are the expressions of doctrine, and witnesses to the Sacramental system of the Catholic religion."* It is of course on this account above all that these things are valued by those who adopt them. These earnest men would indignantly reject the supposition that they are agitating the Church for any thing which serves merely to gratify a refined taste, and has not in their eyes a very deep doctrinal significance. The question, therefore, is forced upon us: Is the doctrine thus symbolized the doctrine of the Reformed Church of England, which has dropped these symbols, or that of the Church of Rome, which retains them?

Symbolism of Ritual and Ceremonial.

There may be persons to whom it may appear that this question admits but of one answer, that of the latter alternative. This, however, evidently depends on the further inquiry, Whether the doctrine is one of those on which the two Churches are at variance, or of those on which they agree with one another. Now, however it may be as to doctrine in the proper sense, I think it can hardly be denied that there is a very wide and important difference between the general view which our Church takes of her Liturgy, and the Roman view of the Mass. The difference is marked by their several names and descriptions. The one is an Office for the Administration of the Lord's Supper, or Holy Communion; the other, for the celebration of a sacrifice. The difference indicated by the titles is equally conspicuous in the contents of the two Liturgies. In the Anglican, the idea which is almost exclusively predominant is that of Communion. There is, indeed, an Offertory, and an oblation of common things for sacred and charitable uses. There is mention of a sacrifice of praise and thanksgiving,† which appears to include

Is this doctrine that of the Church of England or of Rome?

---

* " Directorium Anglicanum," Preface, p. xiv.
† "This our sacrifice of praise and thanksgiving."

the whole rite; and the communicants "offer and present themselves, their souls and bodies, as a living sacrifice." But of any other kind of sacrifice, and particularly of any sacrificial oblation of the consecrated elements, there is not a word. The Consecration is immediately followed by the Communion, which is the great business of the whole. On the other hand, the Council of Trent pronounces an anathema on those who say that there is not offered to God in the Mass a true and proper sacrifice, or that the offering consists only in Christ's being given to us for manducation; or that the sacrifice of the Mass is only one of praise and thanksgiving, or a bare commemoration of the sacrifice performed on the Cross, and not propitiatory. A more direct conflict of views, if they are supposed to relate to the same subject, or to two subjects not essentially different from one another, it would be difficult to conceive; for that which the Council so emphatically denies to be the sacrifice of the Mass, is the only thing to which our Church gives the name of *her* sacrifice. That which the Council declares to be the true and proper sacrifice of the Mass, is an offering as to which our Church is absolutely silent.

Harmony between Ritualists and Roman Catholics on the Communion Office. It might have seemed to any one who read our Communion Office, a strange and hopeless undertaking to bring it into harmony with the Mass; and I think that the Ritualists who have made the attempt, have failed to produce any thing more than a deceptive show of resemblance; but of the harmony between their own views and those of the Church of Rome in this respect, they have given the most unequivocal signs. The rite which they celebrate they describe as the Sacrifice of the Altar, or the Mass. The splendour with which they invest it is certainly more appropriate to the oblation of a sacrifice than to the reception and participation of a gift. And, feeling that this would still be insufficient for the purpose, they interpolate our Office with large extracts from the Canon of the Mass, in which the sacrifice is explicitly announced, and which the "celebrant" is directed to use as private prayers.* I must own

---

* See "Suggestions for the Due and Reverent Celebration of the Holy Eucharist," printed for the Confraternity of the Blessed Sacrament.

that there is something in this adulteration,—as I think I may not improperly term it,—of the Prayer Book out of the Missal, which to my sense has an unpleasant savour of artifice and disingenuousness. It is a proceeding of which I think both Churches have reason to complain : the one, that her mind is not only disregarded, but misrepresented ; the other, that her treasures are rifled to set off her adversary with a false semblance of likeness to herself.

But still all this does not amount to a proof that there has been any departure from the express teaching of our Church with regard to the Sacrament. And in one important particular there can be no doubt that those who carry the assimilation of ritual to the greatest length, most decidedly and sincerely repudiate the Romish doctrine. With our twenty-eighth Article,—whether for the reasons there assigned or not,— they reject the dogma of Transubstantiation. So indeed they might do, with perfect consistency, even if they used the Roman Liturgy without curtailment or alteration ; for to those who have studied the subject, it is well known that the Canon of the Mass is so far from teaching that dogma, that it positively witnesses against it, and can only be reconciled with it by the most violent artifices of interpretation.* The Canon had been fixed many centuries before the dogma was defined. And here I cannot refrain from pausing for a moment to remark, that there is perhaps no head of theological controversy in which our Church stands in more advantageous contrast with Rome, or in which we have more reason thankfully to recognize her characteristic moderation, than this. The tenet of Transubstantiation, decreed as an article of faith, combines in itself the two extremes of irreverent rationalism and presumptuous dogmatism. As a speculation of the Schools, it is essentially rationalistic ; a bold and vain attempt to pry into mysteries of faith impenetrable to human reason. As a dogma, it exhibits the spectacle of a Church so

marginal notes: Repudiation of Romish doctrine by Ritualists. Transubstantiation.

---

* The consecration is followed by the prayer : " Supra quæ propitio et sereno vultu respicere digneris, et accepta habere sicuti accepta habere dignatus es munera pueri tui justi Abel, et sacrificium Patriarchæ nostri Abrahæ, et quod tibi obtulit Summus Sacerdos tuus Melchidezech sanctum Sacrificium, immaculatam Hostiam." What a comparison, when Jesus Christ Himself is supposed to be on the altar !

forgetful of her proper functions, as to undertake to give a Divine sanction to a purely metaphysical theory, the offspring of a system of profane philosophy. This rationalistic dogmatism gives an imposing air of solidity and compactness to much in the Roman theology which, on closer inspection, proves to be utterly hollow and baseless. A conclusion is reached through a process of vicious ratiocination, composed of ambiguous terms and arbitrary assumptions. In itself it is "a fond thing vainly invented." But it is withdrawn from all inquiry, and stamped with the character of a Divine revelation, by means of the dogma of Papal or Conciliar infallibility. This however, when examined, turns out to be itself the product of a like abuse of reason. We are reminded of the Indian cosmology, in which the earth rests on the elephant, the elephant on the tortoise, and the tortoise—on empty space.

In what light regarded by the Church of England. The Church of England, on the contrary, has dealt with this subject in a spirit of true reverence as well as of prudence and charity.* She asserts the mystery inherent in the institution of the Sacrament, but abstains from all attempts to investigate or define it, and leaves the widest range open to the devotional feelings and the private meditations of her children with regard to it. And this liberty is so large, and has been so freely used, that, apart from the express admission of Transubstantiation, or of the grossly carnal notions to which it gave rise, and which, in the minds of the common people, are probably inseparable from it, I think there can hardly be any description of the Real Presence, which, in some sense or other, is universally allowed, that would not be found to be authorized by the language of eminent divines of our Church; and I am not aware, and do not believe, that our most advanced Ritualists have in fact overstepped those very ample bounds.

Eucharistic Sacrifice. But I am not so sure that it is possible to reconcile their view of the Eucharistic Sacrifice with that of the Church of England, or to distinguish it from that of the Church of Rome. The subject is one which requires the utmost precision of thought and language, to avoid either falling into or giving

* See however Appendix D.

occasion for misconception. At every step we are in danger of being misled by ambiguous terms, and of reasoning upon them in a sense different from that in which they are used by those with whom we contend. I wish very much to keep this present to my own mind and to yours in that which I am about to say.

The Council of Trent anathematizes those who affirm that the Sacrifice of the Mass is not propitiatory, or that it benefits only the receiver, or communicant; or that it ought not to be offered for quick and dead, to have remission of pain and guilt. The word *propitiatory* is one of those which admit of two senses: the one, strict and proper; the other, loose and inexact. It might be understood to mean nothing more than *acceptable to God*, as that " living sacrifice " of our bodies, spoken of by St. Paul, or as our common prayers made in the name of Christ. In this sense it might not unfitly, though imprudently, because in a way so very liable to misapprehension and abuse, be applied to that memorial of the one only real propitiation, which the Church makes in her Eucharist. This, however, is most certainly not the sense in which the Church of Rome asserts that the Sacrifice of the Mass is *propitiatory;* for she regards it, not indeed as a repetition of the offering made on the Cross, but neither as a simple commemoration of that. It is, in her view, a repetition of the Sacrifice which she holds to have been actually made, not merely signified as a thing to come, at the Last Supper, for the remission of the sins of the Apostles and of many.* There can therefore be no doubt in what sense she directs the priest, at

<small>Propitiation in the Sacrifice of the Mass.</small>

* Bellarmin, " De Missa," i. c. xii.: " Christus in ultima Cœna seipse sub specie panis et vini Deo Patri obtulit, et idipsum jussit fieri ab Apostolis et eorum successoribus usque ad mundi consummationem. Sed hoc est sacrificium vere ac proprie dictum obtulisse, et offerendum instituisse." So, in nearly the same words, Bona, " Rerum Liturgicarum," i. c. 4. Melchior Canus, " De Locis Theologicis," xii. c. 12, draws a distinction between the efficacy of the Sacrifice of the Cross and that of the Last Supper: " Alia efficientia hostiæ illius est, quam Christus palam mactavit in cruce: alia illius est quam sub speciebus definitis mystice præbuit in cœna. Illa generalis est, nec per sacrificium modo, sed per omnia sigillatim sacramenta ad effecta longe diversa applicatur. Hæc peculiaris efficientia est, et sub speciebus certis ad peculiaria quædam effecta concluditur. Obtulit ergo Christus in cœna tum pro culpa veniali, tum pro pœna quæ pro culpa etiam mortali deberetur." The Bishop of Brechin (Primary Charge, 2nd edit. p. 52) goes no farther than to say, " At that first Eucharist that Sacrifice was presented to the Father before it was made."

the close of the Mass, to pray that the sacrifice which he has offered "may be acceptable unto God, and propitiatory for himself and all for whom he has offered it." What, then, must we infer from the fact that this very prayer is one of those which are recommended for the use of our clergy in the administration of the Lord's Supper at the corresponding part of the Office?* Must we not conclude that it is in the very same sense that, in a manual of devotion accredited by the same authority, the celebration of our Liturgy is described as a "Sacrifice of praise and propitiation," in which our Lord, "through His own presence communicates the virtues of His most precious death and passion to all His faithful, living and departed?"†

<small>Identity of Ritualistic doctrine with it.</small>

I do not see how this language is to be reconciled with the doctrine of our Church, even as expounded by divines of that school which takes the highest view of the Eucharistic Sacrifice. But if we suppose that it is meant to express sound Anglican doctrine in Roman phraseology, how strong must be the leaning towards Rome which prompts the use of her language, where it is apparently most at variance with the sense which the authors intend to convey! The words which I was just now reading may have reminded you that the strongest condemnatory language to be found in our Articles is that of the Thirty-first, where "the sacrifices of Masses, in the which it was commonly said that the priest did offer Christ for the quick and the dead, to have remission of pain or guilt," are branded with the name of "blasphemous fables and dangerous deceits." In the celebrated Tract xc. it was contended, that the censure of the Article was aimed, not at the creed of the Roman Church, but at certain opinions which were no essential parts of her system; and that it "neither speaks against the Mass in itself, nor against its being an offering for the quick and the dead for the remission of sin, but against its being viewed as independent of or distinct from the Sacrifice of the Cross."‡ I am not just now concerned to inquire whether this opinion is well founded or not, or how far

<small>Contrary to the Church of England.</small>

---

* Suggestions, &c.
† The Manual of the Confraternity of the Blessed Sacrament, p. 29.
‡ See Appendix C.

the Church of Rome is irrevocably pledged to that exposition of the decrees of Trent which was given by her great apologists, and which is now generally received by all members of her communion. I would only observe that the doubt itself implies that the language of the decrees is in perfect harmony with that exposition, even if it admits of an explanation which would bring it nearer to doctrine which may be held in the Church of England. When therefore that language is used, as it is, in forms of devotion which are recommended as private accompaniments of the ritual which is studiously assimilated to that of Rome, without any qualifying explanation, it can only be understood in the sense generally received,—a sense in which even the author of Tract xc. did not profess to believe that it could be reconciled with the teaching of our Church, or with what he then held to be the truth. And again, I desire you to observe, if the language is supposed to be borrowed in a different and sounder sense, how strong must be the predilection which it indicates for every thing that has the Roman stamp upon it.

This close approximation to Roman views and practice, in connection with the predominance assigned to that sacrificial aspect of the Lord's Supper, which it is so difficult even to detect in the English Service Book, over that of the Sacrament, which there alone meets the eye, is especially conspicuous in the kind of encouragement given by clergymen of the Ritualistic school to the attendance of non-communicants during the celebration.* Services exactly corresponding to the Low Masses of the Church of Rome, are multiplied in their churches, without any design of affording additional opportunities of communicating, for congregations in which few are expected or desired to be more than listeners; most indeed not so much: for as they are provided with "manuals of devotion to be used at the celebration of the Holy Eucharist by such as do not communicate," they may be as little aware of what is said and done at the Holy Table, as if they were outside the door, and only apprised of the moment of consecration by the tinkling of a bell. The

<small>Attendance of non-communicants.</small>

See Appendix D.

practical question is one of some little difficulty. I should think it a most unwarrantable encroachment on the rights of conscience to compel any of the congregation to withdraw, if they wish to remain, though without any intention of communicating. This of course must needs be left to every one's discretion. But I should also consider it as an intrusion into the sanctuary of private devotion, absolutely and indiscriminately to condemn or discourage such attendance. I fully admit that there may be many cases in which it may tend to edification, without the slightest tinge of superstition. I expressed the same opinion in a Charge several years ago, and I see no reason for changing it now. But attendance simply with a view to edification, is one thing: attendance in the belief that the proper benefit of the ordinance may be enjoyed without reception, seems to me another and quite a different thing. This, if I am not mistaken, and not, as has been argued, a vulgar error, by which it was supposed that the Sacrifice of the Cross itself is repeated in every Mass, was the doctrine which lay at the root of the practice condemned by the Thirty-first Article.* From this doctrine naturally sprang

<small>Origin of solitary Masses.</small> the indefinite multiplication of solitary Masses, each of which was held to possess a certain inherent value, quite distinct from that of the Sacrifice of the Cross, though not independent of it, and which might be applied, according to the intention of the priest, either to the living, or, which was the more frequent occasion of that multiplication, to the departed, for the purpose of obtaining their release from Purgatory. The abuses reproved by the Council of Trent were only casual incidents of the practice, and in no way necessary consequences of the doctrine, which the Council distinctly asserted, expressly "approving of those Masses in which the priest alone communicates sacramentally," and on the ground, that "they are celebrated by the public minister of the Church, not for himself only, but for all the faithful who belong to the Body of Christ"—in other words, as our Article has it, "for the quick and the dead." When the doctrine is received among ourselves, it will be only

* See Appendix C.

the effect of outward temporary restraints, if it is not accompanied by the practice which the Article condemned, not indeed simply by itself, but along with, though not solely or mainly on account of, its incidental gross and shameless abuses, the recurrence of which, it may be hoped, we have no reason to fear.

But this ritual movement has by no means reached its term. It is still in the full vigour of its early years. It appears to be advancing both extensively, in the work of proselytism, and intensively, in doctrinal innovation, not always distinctly enunciated but clearly intimated. Its partizans seem to vie with one another in the introduction of more and more startling novelties, both of theory and practice. The adoration of the consecrated Wafer, reserved for that purpose, which is one of the most characteristic Romish rites, and a legitimate consequence of the Romish Eucharistic doctrine, is contemplated, if it has not been already adopted, in some of our churches, and the Romish Festival of the *Corpus Christi* instituted for the more conspicuous exercise of that adoration, has, it appears, actually begun to be observed by clergymen of our Church. Already public honours are paid to the Virgin Mary, and language applied to her, which can only be considered as marking the first stage of a development, to which no limit, short of the full Romish worship, can be probably assigned. *Spread of Ritualism.*

In the presence of these facts, the statement of the Committee of the Lower House of Convocation, that—" in the larger number of the practices which were brought under their notice, they could trace no proper connexion with the distinctive teaching of the Church of Rome,"—seems much better fitted to excite surprise, than to administer consolation, or inspire confidence. But it was to me still more surprising to hear from one speaking in another place, with the weight of high authority, and under very grave responsibility*—a most deliberate and solemn declaration of his belief, " that this present movement is not a movement towards Rome." And yet, paradoxical as it may seem, I will own that there is a sense in *Its Romeward tendency denied.*

---

* Chronicle of Convocation, Feb. 9, 1866, p. 165.

which I can myself believe that this movement is not a movement towards Rome. Not certainly in the sense that it has any other direction. Not in the sense that its "ultimate end and aim"—as has been said by one who appears to have had means of understanding it thoroughly—is any thing less than "to make the doctrine, practice, and worship of the Anglican Church as nearly as possible identical with the Roman."* In that sense I cannot doubt that it is a very decided and rapid movement towards Rome. But in another sense I might say, though I should not think it a happy way of expressing my meaning, that this present movement—and I should lay great stress on the word *present*—is not a movement toward Rome. I believe that many at least of those who are most actively engaged in it are not at present contemplating secession from the Church of England, and do not even desire that it should be immediately absorbed in the Church of Rome. I may say indeed that, with regard to a considerable number of them, there are clear proofs that this is not their present bent or aim. That which they have in view is quite another thing: something indeed which I can only regard as a dream and a delusion, but which as long as they cherish this delusion, will keep them in their present position. Their real object has been lately brought somewhat prominently under public notice, by some very remarkable documents, which at the same time afford the best means of forming a judgment on its prospects of success.

<small>In what sense this may be true.</small>

<small>Association for the Promotion of the Unity of Christendom.</small> From them we learn that a Society has been founded under the name of an "Association for the Promotion of the Unity of Christendom," whose common bond of union is an earnest desire for the visible reunion of all Christendom, especially of the three chief communions, the Roman Catholic, the Eastern, and the Anglican: the agency to be employed for compassing the end, being for the present simply intercessory prayer. The Society was composed chiefly of English Churchmen, clergy and laity; but as some Roman Catholics had been induced to join it, it attracted the attention of their Bishops,

* See Archdeacon Wordsworth's speech in the debate on Ritual.

who referred the matter to the supreme authority at Rome (the Congregation of the Holy Office of the Inquisition), which issued a rescript condemning the Association, and enjoining the faithful to beware of uniting themselves with it under peril of heresy. This document drew forth a letter addressed to its author, Cardinal Patrizi, Prefect of the Holy Office, and signed by 198 clergymen of the Church of England, including some of its dignitaries, in which they more distinctly explain the precise nature of their object, which they thought the Cardinal had misunderstood.* They disclaim the intention which had been imputed to them, of seeking " that the three communions in their integrity, and each persisting in its persuasion, might simultaneously combine into one;" which they admit to be " a scheme, from which no ecclesiastical unity could be hoped for." They explain that their object is confined to an intercommunion between the three Churches as distinct, independent bodies, like that which existed between East and West before the separation. They state that they have worked many years to hasten this result: that they have effected improvements beyond their hopes, where there was any thing imperfect in the faith of the flock, in divine worship, and clerical discipline, and that they have shown an amount of good will toward the venerable Church of Rome, which has " rendered them suspected in the eyes of some." This last statement will, I think, both receive and reflect light, if it is compared with the fact which we had just now before us.

Condemned by Rome.

Object of the Society.

It seems surprising that any one moderately acquainted with the history and character of the Papacy, should have thought it possible that such a proposal should ever be entertained at Rome. And perhaps, but for the interference of the Roman Catholic Bishops, it might have been long before the desires of the Association were embodied in one, so as to call forth the judgment of Rome upon it. The reply of Cardinal Patrizi, energetically enforced by the highest Roman

Hopelessness of the scheme.

---

* The whole correspondence may be found at the end of Archbishop Manning's " Reunion of Christendom, a Pastoral Letter to Clergy," &c.

Catholic authority in this country, must, I think, have convinced the most sanguine of the utter hopelessness of the attempt under present circumstances, or indeed without such a change in the spirit and the principles of the Church of Rome as would almost supersede the necessity of any formal reconciliation.* But whether those who have been thus rejected and rebuked will patiently acquiesce in their failure and disappointment—whether, when they find that all their advances towards Rome in a growing conformity of faith, worship, and discipline have not brought them one step nearer to the attainment of their object; when they observe that the differences which separate them from the great mass of the members of their own communion are enormously greater than those which lie between them and Rome, and which are constantly decreasing,—while they know and are frequently reminded that an act of dutiful submission to that "venerable Church" will at once place them not in a mere intercommunion but in the enjoyment of full communion with her—whether, I say, under such circumstances it will be possible for them long to maintain their present ambiguous, intermediate position, and not, however reluctantly, to be carried down, as by an eddy: this it remains for the future to disclose. If we were to listen to the experience of the past, we could hardly feel a doubt as to the final result.

Views of another section of the Church on unity. But I find that in other quarters among us persons entitled to the highest respect, and of unquestionable attachment to our Church, are strongly persuaded that the signs of our times are peculiarly favourable to the prospect of a restoration of unity in Christendom, though there appears to be a very wide difference among them as to the means by which the end is to be compassed. Some ground their hopes on the fact that, as in Italy political unity has been accompanied by religious liberty, a door has been thrown open for the doctrines of the Reformation, which perhaps were never entirely stamped out

---

* It does not, however, prevent the English Church Union from regarding "Ritualism as a means of promoting ultimately the intercommunion of the whole Catholic Church." Report of the President and Council of the English Church Union on the Report of the Lower House of Convocation on Ritual.

there, to be re-admitted and have free course. The general alienation of the people from the Court of Rome and the temporal claims of the Papacy, has been thought likely to win favour for the foundation of an independent national Church on the platform of primitive doctrine, worship, and government, not unlike, and in full communion with, our own. That such a prospect should attract and should awaken a lively interest in the minds of earnest and pious English Churchmen is perfectly natural, and we cannot but sympathize warmly with their motives and general aims. How far the means hitherto adopted are suited to the moral and religious condition of the country, now in the throes of a great political crisis, it is very difficult for a foreigner to judge. But one thing is clear. The immediate tendency of such a movement will not be to restore unity, but to multiply divisions and to foment religious discord. That may, under the gracious over-ruling of Divine Providence, be only a transition to a state of unity and concord. But it is certainly possible, and to human eyes quite as probable, that those who think they are laying the foundation of a national reformed Church, may find that they have only been planting a hotbed of sects, which as they spring up will kill one another, and leave the Church of Rome more powerful than before.*

Here, however, all is intelligible and consistent. I cannot say so much with regard to the hopes which I see are still cherished by some eminent persons of a reconciliation with the Church of Rome on the basis of a common doctrine; still less with regard to their opinion that the present juncture affords peculiar encouragement to such hopes. That the spread of unbelief should have suggested, or rather have strengthened, the wish for such re-union, I can readily understand. But how it has removed or lessened the obstacles which before stood in the way, I am at a loss to comprehend. The scheme is in the main a renewal of that which was the subject of much

Unity with Rome on the basis of a common doctrine.

---

* This was written before I had seen " a Memorandum on Church Reformation in Italy, drawn up and issued with the joint sanction of the Bishops of Gibraltar and Pennsylvania." But the perusal of it has rather confirmed than altered my opinion.

discussion and negotiation toward the end of the seventeenth century. It was then proposed under most singularly propitious political auspices, such as have never been seen since, and are not likely to recur. The Pope of that day gave it the utmost encouragement possible in his position. It was not in Italy but in France, not from an Ultramontane doctor or prelate, but from Bossuet, the champion of the Gallican liberties, that it received its death-blow, in the declaration that his Church would never recede from a single point of her doctrine, and particularly from that laid down by the Council of Trent.*

<small>Difficulties in the way of it.</small> How immensely the difficulties, which then were felt to be insurmountable, have since increased, has by no one been shown with more luminous demonstration than by the eminent theologian, who is at once the warmest supporter and the most authoritative expositor of the revived scheme of pacification and reunion. From his "Eirenicon" we learn, on the one hand, the extravagant extent to which the worship of the Virgin Mary has been already carried in the Church of Rome, and how very nearly it has superseded reliance on the mediation of Christ, who is generally regarded as the terrible Judge, whose severity can only be softened by the all-availing intercession of His more compassionate mother: and further, that this kind of devotion did not even reach its culminating point in the additional honour paid to her in the new dogma of her Immaculate Conception, but is supposed to be yet far from the last stage of its development, and is expected to yield a larger harvest of dogmatic novelties. And while we are thus led to see how deeply the Church of Rome is pledged to a doctrine and practice from which most of us recoil, as one of the grossest corruptions of Christ's religion, we learn on the other hand that, during the same period, especially during the reign of the present Pope, the claims of the Papacy have been

* See Lettres xxi. xxii. xxviii. in the Correspondence between Leibnitz and Bossuet (Œuvres de Bossuet, Tome xi.) Bossuet observes (Lettre xi.) that nothing would be gained on the Protestant side, even if the Council of Trent was deprived of all authority: "puisqu'il ne faudrait pas moins croire la Transubstantiation, le Sacrifice, la primauté du Pape de droit divin, la prière des Saints, et celles pour les morts, qui ont été définies dans les Conciles précédents." The difficulty as to the Papacy was recognized by the author of Tract xc. in his letter to Dr. Jelf.

making continual progress, and have now reached the length of despotic authority in the Church, and of a perpetual divine inspiration, ensuring his infallibility far beyond the limits of faith and morals assigned to it by the most strenuous asserters of the Papal supremacy in former ages.

To these facts I must add another, which appears to me of no slight significance in the present question—that the highest authority among the Romanists in this country has been recently committed to one who, some fourteen years ago, seceded from the Church of England. That he should take the most unfavourable view of the communion which he left, and should be inclined to exaggerate the doctrinal differences which separate it from that of his adoption, was almost a necessity of his position, to guard himself against the imputation of rashness, in quitting his old home on light grounds, and a little detracts from the weight of his new opinions among his old, if not among his new friends. But that which appears to me most significant in that selection is, that the same person is the most strenuous among the advocates of Ultramontane views of Papal authority, and would be the last to accept any overtures for reconciliation on any other terms than those of unconditional submission. On this point his published declarations have been most explicit and distinct, and it is not his fault if any person or body outside the Church of Rome expects to be received into it otherwise than as a pardoned penitent. *Increased by the attitude of the highest Romish authority in England towards our Church.*

With this history in his mind, and this state of things before his eyes, and recorded and described by himself for the instruction of others, the author of the "Eirenicon" says, as the sum of the whole matter, and speaking, no doubt, in the name of many followers: "On the terms which Bossuet we hope would have sanctioned, we long to see the Church united;"* and believing that there are individuals in the Roman Communion, who, in their hearts share that longing, he says: "To such we stretch forth our hands:" † of course, for such help as individuals can give; not, it would seem, in this case, a very solid ground of *Substance of the scheme.*

* Page 335.   † Page 334.

hope. I do not, however, presume to say that the course of events may not be shaped by Divine Providence to such a result. But I think I may venture to believe that, before this comes to pass, a revolution must have taken place in the Church of Rome, by which the Pope has been made not only to abdicate his usurped authority, but to declare many acts of his own and of his predecessors, done in the exercise of that authority, null and void. God grant that such a day may come. But even then I should not have expected that the compromise would have been quite satisfactory to divines of that school which insists on the most rigorous preciseness of dogmatical definition, but should have thought it likely to be rather more congenial to some who are reproached with the breadth of their views. And I am not sure that there would not still be danger of confusion and misunderstanding. What seems to be contemplated as the basis of the agreement is, that the Decrees of Trent should be read by Anglicans in the Anglican sense, the Thirty-nine Articles by Roman Catholics in the Roman sense. The case would be something like that of a system of imitative signs, such as are used in some parts of the East, common to several nations speaking wholly different languages. The same document, written in these characters, might be read by two persons, to whom it conveyed the same ideas, but who expressed them by sounds which made the readers mutually unintelligible, each, as the Apostle terms it, "a barbarian" unto the other. Only a bystander of superior information could know that they meant the same thing. I must not, however, omit to express my own conviction that the Articles are, not in sound only but in sense, at irreconcilable variance with the Decrees of the Council. So it has appeared both to Anglican and to Roman Catholic writers, on a careful comparison of their statements on controverted points.* And

margin note: If practicable, it would lead to confusion.

---

* Bishop Mant, who in his day passed for a High Churchman, published a little tract ("The Churches of Rome and England compared, 1836") suggested by an assertion of the late Lord Melbourne, who concurred with Dr. Pusey in thinking that "Roman Catholics in all the fundamentals of Christianity agree with Protestants," for the purpose of showing, "that as to numerous fundamental doctrines and ordinances the Roman and the Anglican Churches are so far from being in agreement with each other, that they are as diametrically opposed to each other as the east and the west ;"

though the authority of the Pope, if it was brought to bear on the Roman Catholic, would no doubt overrule his opinion, and oblige him to renounce it, it could not have the same effect on the Anglican, unless he had first admitted the Pope's infallibility, and so had virtually become a Roman Catholic.

These remarks, though they may here and there have taken a somewhat wider range than was absolutely necessary for the discussion of the Ritual question, will not, I trust, appear to any one irrelevant to it. I wished to set it before you in its principal bearings, and to place it in its true light. I believe, indeed, that on the main point I have said nothing but what is universally known; and I should not be surprised if there were many who will smile at the pains I have been taking to light a candle in the broad noonday to help them to see that which is so patent to all. I should myself have thought it a superfluous labour, if I had not observed in some quarters an appearance of a tacit agreement to treat the fact as a kind of sacred mystery, familiar indeed to the initiated but not to be divulged to the profane. I can be no party to a system of concealment which appears to me neither manly nor perfectly consistent with good faith or with a plain duty to the Church; and I regard the prevalence of such a system as one of the least honourable, and the most ominous signs of our time.

Nothing, in my judgment, can be more mischievous, as well as in more direct contradiction to notorious facts, than to deny or ignore the Romeward tendency of the movement. Its effects, indeed, on those who are not engaged in it would be the same if by them it was universally, though erroneously, viewed in that light. But it might, in that case, call for a different treatment.

Reasons for the foregoing ample discussion.

and this he endeavours to do by an arrangement in which passages from the Articles and from the Decrees and Canons of Trent are confronted with each other in parallel columns. By a like method the Rev. Mr. Estcourt, a Roman Catholic clergyman, in a Letter published by Mr. Oakeley in the Appendix to his pamphlet on the *Eirenicon*, is brought to the like conclusion; that "No one who accepts that Council as the voice of the Church and the guide of his faith could with a safe conscience subscribe to the Thirty-nine Articles:" and that "it is difficult to see any other basis for the reconciliation of Anglicans to the Catholic Church, than their renouncing the Prayer Book and Articles, and receiving the Council of Trent."

For practical purposes it is also very important that, without pretending to foresee the actual result, we should consider its natural and probable consequences. I hope that my forebodings may be too gloomy; but I think I see several serious dangers looming not very far ahead. One or two of them have been, I cannot say pointed out, but hinted at in the Report of the Committee of Convocation, with a delicacy which was no doubt thought to befit such a document, but which is not always favourable to perspicuity. The greater part and the gravest appear altogether to have escaped the Committee's observation, unless they were meant to be concealed under the statement that "in the larger number of the practices which had been brought under their notice—they do not say in all of them—they can trace no proper connexion with the distinctive teaching of the Church of Rome." As to any danger threatening the Church of England from such connexion as they were able to trace, or danger of any kind on the side of Rome, the Report is entirely silent. I wish to say a few words on this subject, and to speak a little more plainly and fully than the Committee felt it their duty to do. Though, as I have said, it appears to me highly probable that the leaders of the movement themselves have no present thought of quitting the Anglican communion, I think it almost inevitable that they should be giving occasion to more or less numerous secessions to the Church of Rome, both by fostering that general predilection for all that belongs to her, which they themselves betray, or rather exhibit, and by stimulating a craving for a gorgeous ritual, which, remaining where they are, they can never fully satisfy: even if it be possible for thoughtful and ingenuous minds long to feel quite at their ease in a form of worship which strives to engraft, not only the outward ceremonial, but the essential idea of the Roman Mass on the Anglican Communion Office, and where the officiating priest uses language in his private devotions quite incongruous with that which the Church puts into his mouth. Some I think can hardly fail to find this hybrid kind of devotion intolerable, and to be driven to exchange it for something more real and genuine, more consistent and complete. That might be found either in the Church of England or in the Church of Rome. It is unhappily too clear in which they have been trained to seek it. This is one form of the danger in its Romeward aspect. There are others still greater, though probably more remote. I have already endeavoured to point out the process by which the movement may reach its termination in the secession, not of individuals, but of a whole party. Another form which the evil might take under different circumstances, would be an open rent in the Church, which however might in the end lead to the same result.

But there is no less danger on the side opposed to Rome. And this has been in some degree recognised by the Committee, in a passage of their Report, where they remind us, "that the National Church of England has a holy work to perform toward the Nonconformists of this country: and that every instance, not only of exceeding the law, but of a want of prudence and tenderness in respect of usages within the law, can hardly fail to create fresh difficulties in the way of winning back to our Church those who have become estranged from her communion." This is indeed an allusion to a very grave and unquestionable fact, but couched in terms which seem to me singularly inappropriate, and tending to conceal both the real nature and the extent of the danger. It might lead any one to imagine that the Nonconformists with whom we have to deal, are, like the dissenters from the Russian Church, such sticklers for rigid rubrical uniformity, that they are likely to be scared away from us by any deviation from the letter of the Prayer Book. I need not observe how directly this would reverse the real state of the case, or that, if the innovations which offend many, I believe I may still say most Churchmen, are peculiarly obnoxious to the Nonconformists of this country, it is not simply as innovations, but because they present the appearance of the closest possible approximation to the Church of Rome. And the danger on this side is far greater than that which is suggested by the language of the Report. It is not merely that we may make fewer converts from the ranks of Dissent, but that we may strengthen them by large secessions, perhaps of

marginal note: And on Dissenters.

whole congregations, from our own. And the danger—if I ought not rather to say the certain and present evil—does not end there. These proceedings both tend to widen the breach between us and Dissenters, and to stimulate them to more active opposition, and furnish their leaders with an instrument which they will not fail to use for the purpose of exciting general ill will toward the Church, and weakening her position in the country.

Both influences at work simultaneously. And it must be remembered that these injuries which she may suffer on opposite sides may be going on together simultaneously. There is nothing in the one to lessen, nothing that must not aggravate the other. For every proselyte who is drawn from us to Rome, we may reckon on others who will leave us for Geneva. That this damage will be compensated by any accession of numbers from either quarter is, with regard to Dissent, in the highest degree improbable: as to Rome, it is neither pretended nor desired.

Object of the Committee of Convocation on Ritual. The object for which the Committee was appointed, was entirely practical. It was " to inquire as to such measures as might seem to them fit for clearing the doubts and allaying the anxieties" which the Lower House had represented as existing upon the subject of Ritual, and as calling for consideration. It was highly proper that, before they proceeded to perform this task, they should take a view of the state of the case on which they were to advise: and it is only to be regretted that this view was somewhat oblique and one-sided. Their practical proposals, however, though in them must be supposed to lie the whole fruit of their deliberations, and the pith and essence of the Report, while all the rest, however valuable, was only preparatory and incidental, are, with one notable exception, *How they fulfilled it.* purely negative, and inform the House what in their opinion ought not to be done. But even this rather scanty amount of information is very imperfectly and ambiguously conveyed. They deprecate a resort to judicial proceedings, as tending to promote, rather than to allay dissension. But in the sentence immediately preceding, they had expressed an earnest wish, that such a course might not be found necessary; clearly implying that it might be found necessary; but leaving the reader to guess both what kind or case of necessity they had in their minds, and whether in that event it would still in their opinion have the same evil tendency. It would, I think, have been desirable that they should have stated whether in their opinion it was to be wished, that the present obscurity and uncertainty in the state of the law should be removed, and whether they knew of any way by which this could be effected without a resort to judicial proceedings. We know from an eminent member of their own body how utterly inadequate any opinion of counsel is for such a purpose. Though deprived of the benefit of their guidance on this important point, I venture to think there are two conditions on which a moral necessity for resort to judicial proceedings would arise.* The one would be, if any clergyman should attempt to introduce the Ritual innovations in his parish church against the will of any considerable part of his congregation: and the other, if he should persist in so doing after having been admonished and dissuaded by his Bishop. I consider every such attempt as an audacious and culpable aggression on the rights of the parishioners, which I should wish to see repressed, either by judicial or even, if necessary, though I should exceedingly deplore the necessity, by legislative interference. *[marginal note: Cases in which judicial proceedings would be necessary.]*

But I am not for the present prepared to lay down any more absolute and comprehensive rule of action, though many persons —some of them worthy of all respect—call loudly for the interposition of authority in every case, to put down the excess of Ritualism, wherever it shows itself: and therefore *[marginal note: General rule of action.]*

---

* I am here assuming that the Ritual innovations are introduced by Incumbents, and not by Stipendiary Curates; a thing of which I happen never to have heard, though Sir H. Thompson, in a Speech delivered in the debate in Convocation, which he has published in a pamphlet entitled, "Ritualism, a plea for the Surplice," seems to suppose that it is a very common, if not the most common case, and on this fact grounds a charge of want of "vigour" against the bishops, on whom it is always easy and pleasant to lay the blame of every thing amiss in the Church. It would of course be easy to revoke the Licence of a "contumacious stipendiary Curate," but it does not seem to me at all clear that "such a step," by "provoking an appeal to the Primate," from whose decision there would be no further appeal, would "secure a speedy and satisfactory settlement of the question."

even where the whole of the bulk of the congregation earnestly desire it, and none take offence at it. On the same principle on which I would interfere for the protection of parishioners, on whom their minister attempts to force a novelty which they dislike, I should scruple to deprive a congregation of a form of worship which has become dear to them, though it is one of which I disapprove. And here we must be on our guard against exaggerating the importance of outward forms, and supposing that some great thing has been gained when they have been suppressed, though the opinions of which they are the visible exponents remain unchanged. Here I agree with the Committee, when they deprecate any attempt to establish a rule applicable to all places and congregations alike. I consider a uniformity which does not represent, but is the substitute for unanimity, as a very questionable blessing. I adopt the maxim of the Committee on a much higher authority. It was not in the spirit of our last Act of Uniformity, but under the guidance of one as opposite to that as light to darkness, that St. Paul wrote those ever memorable words for the perpetual rebuke of all narrow-mindedness and tyrannical encroachments on the rights of conscience and Christian liberty: "One man esteemeth one day above another: another esteemeth every day alike. Let every man be persuaded in his own mind. He that regardeth the day, regardeth it unto the Lord; and he that regardeth not the day, to the Lord he doth not regard it. He that eateth, eateth to the Lord, for he giveth God thanks; and he that eateth not, to the Lord he eateth not, and giveth God thanks."

The only remedy suggested. I observe that there was one notable exception to the generally negative character of the practical measures suggested by the Committee, and therefore I am perhaps bound to notice it. It seems that some of them shared the opinion of those who consider the paucity of Bishops as the chief root of evil in the Church; and applying this principle to the present case, they remark that "both excesses and defects in ritual observance are symptoms of a deep-seated evil, namely, the want of a more effective working of the Diocesan system." This is the gloomiest view that has yet been taken of the subject. It shows that, except for the sake of this particular disclosure, the appointment of the Committee was totally useless; and that, as the remedy of the evil depends on a contingency indefinitely remote, namely, an adequate multiplication of Bishops, the case is practically hopeless. It is therefore to myself a comfort to believe, that the remark is simply the offspring of some fervid imagination, without any foundation in fact.*

The Report concludes with a general observation, which, as such, may be true, whether applicable or not to the subject of the inquiry—" Excess of Ritualism is, in fact, the natural reaction from unseemly neglect of solemn order." *The conclusion arrived at by the Committee.* But it is clearly implied, that in the opinion of the Committee, the latest development of Ritualism is an instance of such reaction. This, as I have already intimated, I believe to be a mistake. That the movement in its origin some thirty years ago was partly the effect of a reaction, I think highly probable; but that it is so in its present phase, I find no reason whatever to suppose. And I am sorry that the Committee appear to lend their countenance to a kind of recrimination, which I often hear, but which does not seem to me either quite logical, or very becoming. When a Ritualist is reproached for his innovations by a clergyman of the opposite school, he has a favourite retort always at hand: "If you take liberties with the Prayer Book, ' by neglect,' as the Committee expresses it, ' of its plain rules and curtailment of its Offices,' have I not a right to make the Liturgy as exact a copy as I can of the Mass?" I do not say that this argument is more unsound than it would be to reply on the other side—though I am not aware that this has ever been done—"If you turn the Communion Office into a Mass, have I not a right to neglect plain rules of the Prayer Book, and to curtail its Offices?" It would be hard to say, on which side there is the more grievous lack both of sound reason and sense of duty.

* The Report has so much the look of a mosaic of compromises, cemented by a general disposition in favour of Ritualism, that it would be hardly fair to impute this particular fancy to the whole Committee.

But though the Committee's observation is so questionable as to its historical correctness, and must tend to divert attention from the real state of the case and gist of the controversy, it may very profitably remind us of another grave danger with which we are threatened by the Ritual movement; the danger, I mean, of its producing an "unseemly neglect of solemn order," which is "the natural reaction from excess of Ritualism," even when it has no special significance, much more from that which we are now witnessing. The jealousy and suspicion which it unavoidably awakens in Churchmen of a different school, must disturb the harmony which was beginning to prevail, notwithstanding the provocations to discord and ill-will, ministered by some of the Journals on both sides, and thus check a healthy and uniform progress in the Church at large. The evil spirit of party will be ever at work to magnify trifles into tests of faith, and grounds of division, and to blind men, as well to the good which is associated with that which they dislike, as to the evil which mars things which are justly dear to them. Allow me, my reverend brethren, to warn those of you who are most adverse to the Ritual movement, against this temptation, and to remind you that defect is not the proper cure of excess, and that opposite exaggerations do not counteract, but only inflame and aggravate one another. Suffer me to suggest to you, that some wholesome and precious uses may be extracted from that of which, as a whole, you may strongly disapprove. It appears to me that you may well take occasion from it to consider, both severally, and in common, whether there is anything amiss in your practice, anything which might be justly described as "neglect of plain rules of the Prayer Book, and curtailment of its Offices," and this, not merely to guard against the censure of an adversary, but to avoid giving offence to those whom you may look upon as the weaker brethren. But further, I think there is a loud call upon you, not to rest satisfied with a mere conformity to the letter of the ordinances of our Church, but to endeavour more and more to learn her mind and imbibe her spirit. You are not really faithful to her, if you neglect to avail yourselves of all the means of grace which

Danger of "unseemly neglect."

she commits to your stewardship, but having received two talents—the Word and the Sacraments—make gain of the one, but hide the other in the earth.

I would also express a hope that my younger brethren, whose opinions on many points have still to be matured and fixed, but who are open to conviction and earnestly seek the truth, may be led by our present controversies to cultivate a closer acquaintance with primitive Christian antiquity than may hitherto have entered into the course of their studies, and if possible not to rest content with the information which they may draw from secondary sources, but to go to the fountain-head, that they may in a manner listen to the voice and gaze upon the living features of the ancient Church. I venture to assure them that the pleasure which they will derive from that intercourse will more than repay any labour which it may cost them. But I recommend the study, because I am convinced that, rightly pursued and regulated, it will both enlighten and strengthen their attachment to the Church in which they have been called to minister. But for this purpose some cautions may be needed in our day, which in other times might have been superfluous. One is, that the student should not look at the primitive Church through a glass tinged with Romish or indeed any other prejudices, and that his view should be taken downward, from the standing point of antiquity to the modern Church of Rome, not upward, from her standing point to antiquity. Another, perhaps still more needful caution is, that he should approach the subject in a spirit of Christian freedom, which is perfectly consistent with the love and reverence which the image of the ancient Church is fitted to awaken in Christian minds. He will have to remember that he is not bound to adopt or to imitate every thing that was said or done by his fathers in the faith, and that when he perceives a difference of opinion or practice between the early Church and his own, it does not necessarily follow that his own Church is in the wrong; as on the other hand he may believe that she has judged and acted wisely, without absolutely condemning the maxims and usages of a former age. If, however,

Importance of a closer study of the primitive Church.

Cautions to be observed.

we were to apply these general remarks to the subject which has just been occupying our attention, we should find but little occasion for such distinctions.

We cannot read the detailed description given by Justin Martyr of the order of administering the Eucharist in his day, without joyfully recognising the closest possible resemblance, in every material point, between it and our own. We observe that there is not the slightest hint that it was regarded as a Sacrifice, other than of prayer and praise, or the presiding minister as a sacrificing priest, and not simply as the dispenser of a holy communion. The spiritual food was received by all present, and was sent to those who were unavoidably absent, but not offered for them. But along with this general resemblance, we perceive some points of difference between ancient and modern practice. Those weekly assemblies of Justin's time were never held without the celebration of the Lord's Supper. That was the one object for which the people came together every Lord's Day. In that respect there is indeed a very wide difference between their usage and ours. Here I think few will say that the advantage is on our side, though probably as few will adopt the opinion of a learned theologian who has endeavoured to prove, by arguments which it seems to be the peculiar privilege of Ritualists to understand, that weekly communion is "matter of Divine obligation," alone fulfilling the commandment of Christ, and that the clergy who omit it, "if judged by the rule of the Apostles, are false to their Lord's dying command in a particular from which He left no dispensation."* Without falling into this exaggeration we may lament the modern departure from primitive practice in that mutilation of the Communion Office which prevails in most of our churches. But we also know that this departure had its origin in an abuse which has been carried to its greatest height by the Church of Rome, in the encouragement given to the attendance of non-communicants, which some among us are so eager to restore. And their attempt is probably, through a

---

* Archdeacon Freeman in "Rites and Ritual," p. 13.

natural though deplorable reaction, one main obstacle to the general revival of the weekly Communion.

The study of primitive Christianity will also lead the thoughtful inquirer to see and feel the contrast between the Church of the Catacombs and the Church of the Vatican. In the marvellous development by which the one passed into the other, he will above all admire the mysterious dealings of Divine Providence, which, without annulling the freedom of the human will, can make even the worst of evils minister to good. *The Church of the Catacombs and the Church of the Vatican.* He will not deny whatever may be fairly implied in the identity of the two, and therefore entitled to respect; but he will not the less clearly see the accompanying growth of corruption and error. He will be enabled justly to appreciate the value of the claims set up for the modern Papacy, as the living oracle of God, the subject of a constant Divine inspiration, which constitutes every Pope the supreme and unerring arbiter in all disputes which can arise within the ever widening sphere of opinion, as distinguished from that of exact science: so that, though a like inspiration must have been vouchsafed to Linus and Cletus, it was in a degree immeasurably lower than that enjoyed by Pius IX., whose Allocutions and Encyclicals would probably to them have been simply unintelligible. Historically, the student will know how strangely such a claim would have sounded in the ears of those venerable men and of the Apostolic Fathers. And when he inquires into the ground on which this amazing pretension is based, he finds only a fresh illustration of that reasoning in a vicious circle which I have already noted as characteristic of the Romish theology. A perfectly arbitrary and precarious meaning is attached to a few texts of Scripture, to prove the alleged infallibility; and then the infallibility is used to establish the certainty of the interpretation. The supercilious arrogance which, as well as a relentless fanaticism, is naturally engendered by this delusion, should move our deepest pity; a feeling like that with which we witness the serene self-complacency visible in the features of a maniac who, confined in a narrow cell, believes himself to be the emperor of the world.

We have lately received a very solemn admonition from a person who has since been placed at the head of the English Romanists, on "the danger and the chastisement of those who," like the Church of England, "would instruct the Church of Jesus Christ."* I do not know whether any consciences have been disturbed by the sound of these words, which contain the whole pith of the writer's argument. It seems enough to observe, that the Church of England has never pretended to instruct the Church of Jesus Christ, but has always desired to receive and transmit its teaching. But certainly we do not regard it as a very rash or culpable presumption, to believe that the Church of Alexander VI., of Julius II., and Leo X., might have something to learn, and still more to unlearn. And when we are called upon to accept these new doctrines on the ground of our Lord's promise, of the abiding presence of the Spirit of Truth in His Church, we may not only rightly refuse to appropriate to a part that which was intended for the whole, but we may reasonably doubt, whether that which was secured by the promise was a perpetual preservation from error, and not rather a preservation from perpetual error, in other words, the final prevalence of truth. That we know is great and will prevail. With this belief let us comfort our hearts. To this let us firmly cling amidst the surgings of doubt and controversy, while we lift up our eyes to the Father of Lights, "with Whom" alone "is no variableness, neither shadow of turning," beseeching Him to enlighten us with His truth, according to the measure of our need, but above all to grant to us the higher grace of walking faithfully by the light we have received.

The Church of England and the Church of Rome.

---

* "The Crown in Council on the Essays and Reviews. A Letter to an Anglican Friend, by Henry Edward Manning, D.D.," p. 21.

APPENDIX.

(A.)

I subjoin a list of the places referred to at p. 92, in which a work of church building or restoration has been set on foot.

Brecknockshire.

1. Brecon Priory Church.
2. Brynmawr.
3. Cantreff.
4. Cathedine.
5. Coelbren.
6. Llanelly.
7. Llywell.
8. Vaynor.
9. Llanfihangel Abergwessin (restoration).
10.   ,,   ,, (new church).
11. Llanfechan.
12. Llanfihangel Bryn Pabuan.

Radnorshire.

13. Rhayader.
14. Abbeycwmhir.

Cardiganshire.

15. Aberystwyth.
16. Llanbadarnfawr.
17. Llangunllo.

Glamorganshire.

18. Swansea.

Carmarthenshire.

19. Carmarthen St. David's.
20.   ,,   (new church).
21. Llanelly.
22. Llandefeilog parish church.
23.   ,,   St. Anne's (new chapel).
24. Mydrim.
25. Henllan Amgoed.

Pembrokeshire.

26. Prendergast, Haverfordwest.
27. Mathry.
28. Amblestone.
29. Burton.
30. St. Bride's.
31. Pennar, Pembroke Dock.
32. Walwyn Castle.
33. St. Catherine's, Milford.
34. Llysyfran.
35. Manerbier.

I believe that some others might be added as in contemplation.

(B.)

It must be admitted that, in the Declaration or Protestation at the end of the Communion Office, the Church of England has deviated from her principles, has come down from her own vantage ground to that of her adversary, and has stated the question in the way most favourable to the doctrine of the Church of Rome; for it is made to turn on a purely metaphysical proposition as to the nature of *body:* "it being against the truth of Christ's natural body to be at one time in more places than one." This is virtually to fall into the Romish error, and to stake the truth of her doctrine on the soundness of a scholastic speculation, which, as a Church, she has no more right to deny, than the Church of Rome to affirm. The real objection to Transubstantiation is, not that it is bad philosophy, but that it is philosophy: not that it is impossible, but that it is destitute and incapable of proof. How dangerous it would be to rely on the proposition assumed in the Declaration as a ground for rejecting the dogma of Transubstantiation, may appear from the defence of it which Leibnitz sets up on the basis of his own metaphysical system. In the posthumous "*Systema Theologium*" (ed. Dr. Carl Haas) he writes: "Equidem si demonstrari posset invictis argumentis metaphysicæ necessitatis omnem corporis essentiam in extensione sive spatii determinati implemento consistere, utique cum verum vero pugnare non possit, fatendum esset unum corpus non posse esse in pluribus locis, ne per divinam quidem potentiam, non magis quam fieri potest ut diagonalis sit lateri quadrati commensurabilis. Eoque posito utique recurrendum esset ad allegoricam divini verbi sive scripti sive traditi interpretationem. Sed tantum abest ut quisquam philosophorum jactatam illam demonstrationem absolverit, ut contra potius solide ostendi posse videatur exigere quidem naturam corporis ut extensum sit, nisi a Deo obex ponatur; essentiam tamen corporis consistere in materia et forma substantiali: hoc est, in principio passionis et actionis, substantiæ enim est agere et pati posse."

He then makes a few remarks on some expressions of ecclesiastical writers apparently adverse to the doctrine, among them that of Pope Gelasius: "Gelasius Pontifex Romanus innuit panem transire in Corpus Christi, manente natura panis, hoc est qualitatibus ejus sive accidentibus (a most arbitrary and unwarranted interpretation): *neque enim tunc ad metaphysicas notiones formulæ exigebantur*." He then proceeds to expound his theory of matter, by which he is brought to the conclusion, "existentia pariter atque unio substantiæ et accidentium realium in Dei arbitrio est. Et cum natura rerum nihil aliud sit quam consuetudo Dei, ordinarie aut extraordinarie agere æque facile ipsi est, prout sapientia ejus exigit."

This great genius does not seem to have perceived that the further he dived into the depths of metaphysical speculation, the more certain it must be that what he would draw out would not be a legitimate theological dogma. It was a case for the application of his own wise remark in his answer to Pirot on the authority of the Council of Trent (Œuvres de Bossuet, XI. Lettre xxi. p. 105, ed 1778): "Nous n'avons peutêtre que trop de prétendues définitions en matière de Foi."

Lacordaire (Lettres à des jeunes gens: ed. Perreyve, p. 106) writes to a young friend who was perplexed by the metaphysical difficulty:—

"Si vous me demandez maintenant comment un corps est présent dans un si petit espace et en tous les lieux à la fois, je vous répondrais que nous n'avons pas la première idée de l'essence des corps, et qu'il n'est pas le moins du monde certain que l'étendue divisible soit essentielle aux corps. Les plus grands philosophes ont pensé le contraire, et ont cru que les corps n'étaient qu'un composé d'atomes indivisibles uni par l'affinité qui les attire réciproquement, et devenant étendus par l'espace qui se glisse entr'eux, et y cause des interstices, de sorte que plus on condense un corps, c'est à dire plus on ôte l'espace qu'il renferme en rapprochant les atomes, moins il tient de place. Voilà pour la présence dans un petit espace. Quant à la présence en tous lieux, considérez que la lumière est un corps, et qu'elle parcourt en une seconde *soixante quinze mille lieues;* considérez que l'electricité est un corps, et qu'elle parcourt en une seconde cent quinze mille lieues. Qui empêche donc qu'un corps uni à la Divinité n'ait une agilité un milliard de fois plus grande, de manière à toucher tous les points du globe au même instant?" (I must own that I do not see the force of this illustration, as there must always be an interval between the departure and the arrival; but what follows is more to the purpose.) " En outre dès que le corps peut être inétendu, il n'est plus assujetti à la loi de la localité, et il peut être présent en tous lieux, comme votre âme est présente à tous les points de votre corps, comme Dieu est indivisiblement présent à tous les points de l'univers." All excellent reasons for abstaining from such speculations in theology.

(C.)

Mr. Newman (in Tract xc.) and Dr Pusey (*Eirenicon*) agree in thinking that Article XXXI. was intended to condemn, not any doctrine which is and must be held by all members of the Church of Rome who acknowledge the authority of the Council of Trent, but only a popular error or abuse which every intelligent member of the Roman Communion would repudiate. They do not however exactly coincide with one another in their view of the error which was condemned. In the Tract, which I quote from Dr. Pusey's reprint, the argument is thus summed up:—

" On the whole, it is conceived that the Article before us neither speaks against the Mass in itself nor against its being [an offering, though commemorative,] for the quick and the dead for the remission of sin, [(especially since the decree of Trent says, that ' the fruits of the Bloody Oblation are through this most abundantly obtained: so far is the latter from detracting in any way from the former);'] but against its being viewed, on the one hand, as independent of or distinct from the Sacrifice on the Cross, which is blasphemy ; and, on the other, its being directed to the emolument of those to whom it pertains to celebrate it, which is imposture in addition." (The words in brackets were added in the second edition.)

Dr. Pusey writes (*Eirenicon*, p. 25):—

",The very strength of the expressions used ' of the sacrifices of Masses,' that they ' were blasphemous fables and dangerous deceits,' the use of the plural, and the clause, ' in the which it was commonly said ' show that what the Article speaks of is, not ' the Sacrifice of the Mass,' but the habit (which, as one hears from time to time, still remains) of trusting to the purchase of Masses when dying, to the neglect of a holy life, or repentance, and the grace of God and His mercy in Christ Jesus, while in health."

The view taken of the Article in Tract xc. is adopted by Mr. Medd in his essay on the Eucharistic Sacrifice, in "The Church and the World," in a few passing words, p. 343, where, after quoting the words of the Article, "Sacrifices of Masses, in the which it was commonly said that the priest did offer Christ," he adds the interpretation (i. e. by way of re-enacting the Sacrifice of Calvary by an actual mactation afresh); and by Mr. Stuart, in his "Plea for Low Masses," in an elaborate argument, in the course of which he says, p. 35: "In order to understand rightly the meaning of the Thirty-first Article, we must remember that this Article is not directed against the Eucharist Sacrifice or the Sacrifice of the Mass, nor indeed against any formal authoritative doctrine on this subject whatever, but against a certain popular *misapprehension* of this doctrine which had prevailed, and which manifestly impugned the sole sufficiency of the Sacrifice of the death of Christ." The nature of this misapprehension he had just before explained in the words: "To think of the offering of Christ in the Holy Eucharist as an offering made independently of His death,—to suppose that such an offering could have been made, for instance, if He had never died," &c. And p. 37: "As there is but one real Sacrifice, which is Christ, once only sacrificed, i. e. upon the Cross, it would be blasphemy to speak of sacrifices in the plural,—the Sacrifices of Masses, for instance,—since in all the Masses or Eucharists ever yet celebrated there has been but one real Sacrifice, which is Christ Himself."

There is a general objection, which seems to me to stand in the way of both these modes of interpretation. It appears to me very improbable that the framers of the Article should have levelled it, not against any doctrine held by the Church of Rome, but against either an error or an abuse which had crept in among the people. This might have been ground for charging the rulers of the Church of Rome with culpable neglect or connivance, but would have been out of place in an Article. If this had been the meaning, I can hardly conceive that it would have been so expressed. For then the only hint of that which was the object of such very severe condemnation, would be contained in the single letter *s*, the sign of the plural number. From this the reader would be expected to infer that what the authors really had in their minds was this: "The Sacrifice of the Mass, in which the priest offers Christ for the quick and the dead to have remission of pain or guilt; this we admit to be consistent with sound doctrine, but this doctrine has been corrupted and perverted to bad ends, through a popular misapprehension as to the nature of the offering, which is irreconcilable with the fulness and sufficiency of the Sacrifice of the Cross. Such Masses we stigmatize as blasphemous fables and dangerous deceits." But how does this paraphrase, when we have it, either explain or justify the language of the Article? The Mass itself remained the same rite, however multiplied. It could not be affected by any erroneous view that might be entertained of it, still less by any unholy purpose to which it might be abused. How then could it be consistent either with justice or common sense to speak of the Masses themselves in terms which were only applicable, and only meant to be applied, to the error and the abuse? It might as well be said that the administration of the Holy Communion becomes a blasphemous fable and a dangerous deceit as often as it is received by an unworthy communicant. The abstinence from any further allusion to the real scope of the Article would be the more singular, because the writer, if he had had the thought now attributed to him in his mind, would so naturally and almost unavoidably have said, instead of "the priest did offer Christ," "the priest did sacrifice Christ afresh." On Dr. Pusey's supposition that the thing condemned was "the habit of trusting to the purchase of Masses;" beside that this would be so clearly matter of discipline, not of doctrine, the obscurity and impropriety of the language would be still greater, and as it appears to me, absolutely incredible. On the other hand, if the writer of the Article believed that the Sacrifice of the Mass was in itself inconsistent with the doctrine of "the one oblation of Christ finished upon the Cross," I see no difficulty in the form of expression. He would naturally be thinking, not only of the doctrinal error, but of the enormous practical abuses which had sprung from it: and this would, I think, sufficiently account both for the use of the plural, the reference to the common way of speaking, and the extreme severity of the censure.

The Rev. Mr. Estcourt (quoted by Mr. Oakeley in his pamphlet on the "Eirenicon," p. 73) utterly rejects Dr. Pusey's construction of the Article. His own comment on it is:—

"False and impious: nor can it be defended on the ground of the phrase 'Sacrifices of Masses,' being in the plural number, because the term 'Sacrificia Missarum' is equally correct, and has the same meaning with 'Sacrificium Missæ.' Thus, in the *Missa pro Defunctis*, 'anima famuli tui bis sacrificiis purgata, et a peccatis expedita.' This Article is, therefore, nothing else than a charge of blasphemy and imposture on the most holy Sacrifice of the Eucharist." Some persons may attach the greater weight to this judgment as coming from a Roman Catholic priest. Candour, however, obliges me to own that I do not set any higher value on it on that account, and that I think Dr. Pusey's explanation of the plural number more probable than Mr. Estcourt's. But it certainly shows how little it was to be expected that the Article should be understood in the sense assigned to it by Dr. Pusey. In support of his opinion, Dr.

Pusey reproduces a passage cited by Gieseler from a work of an Ultramontanist Bishop of the fourteenth century, in which the multiplication of Masses for unholy ends is deplored and condemned. Dr. Pusey's object seems to be to show that the abuse to which alone he supposes the Article to refer was, so far from being a doctrine of the Church of Rome, that long before the Reformation it had been censured in the strongest terms by one who was an Ultramontanist Bishop, and even a Penitentiary of Pope John XXII. But to me this fact appears not at all to strengthen Dr. Pusey's argument, but to lead to the opposite conclusion, as it makes it the more improbable that the Article was meant simply to condemn an abuse which was acknowledged, lamented, and reprobated within the Church of Rome itself. But I must further observe that this extract foom Alvarus Pelagius, *de Planctu Ecclesiæ*, has another bearing on the meaning of our Article, which Dr. Pusey seems to have overlooked, at all events has not noticed. It contains an allusion to a remarkable fact, which the writer explains so as to suit his purpose. "Whence also St. Francis willed that the brothers everywhere should be content with one Mass, foreseeing that the brothers would wish to justify themselves by Masses, and reduce them to a matter of gain, as we see done at this day." The words of St. Francis himself deserve to be quoted, both on their own account, and that their import may be better understood. They occur in Epistola XII. (Francisci Assisiatis opera omnia : ed. von der Burg).

"Moneo præterea et exhortor in Domino, ut in locis in quibus morantur fratres, una tantum celebretur Missa in die secundum formam sanctæ Romanæ Ecclesiæ. Si vero in loco plures fuerint sacerdotes, sic sit per amorem charitatis alter contentus audita celebratione sacerdotis alterius, quia absentes et præsentes replet, qui eo digni sunt, Dominus Noster Jesus Christus. Qui licet in pluribus locis reperiatur, tamen indivisibilis manet et aliqua detrimenta non novit, sed unus verus, sicut ei placet, operatur, cum Domino Deo Patre et Spiritu Paracleto in sæcula sæculorum."

On the ground of this passage, as we learn from Cardinal Bona (Rer. Lit. i. c. 14, p. 387), the authority of St. Francis was pleaded against the private Mass : "En, inquiunt (Sectarii), vir Dei unam duntaxat in die Missam admittit, idque secundum formam Romanæ Ecclesiæ. Porro Catholici vim hujus objectionis variis modis declinare nituntur." He then enumerates several of these methods, all more or less strained and improbable. Others had, on this ground alone, pronounced the letter a forgery. Bona himself is quite satisfied as to its genuineness, and offers his own solution of the difficulty. "Ego admissa epistola tanquam vera et legitima, sumptam ex ea objectionem nullo negotio dilui posse existimo, si dixerimus Seraphicum Patrem, qua humilitate a Sacerdotii susceptione ipse abstinuit, eadem hortari suos ne quotidie celebrent."

And as to the words " secundum formam Romanæ Ecclesiæ," which had been misunderstood to apply to the single daily celebration, he observes : " Optime noverat plures in die fieri celebrationes : sed sicut in regula præcepit, ut fratres officium recitarent secundum morem Romanæ Ecclesiæ, ita hic monet ut secundum formam ejusdem Ecclesiæ agantur Missæ : tum humilitatis causa, et ne Sacerdotes ex frequenti celebratione tepidiores fierent hortatur ut unica celebratione, cui omnes interessent, contenti, reliquis abstinerent."

Bona, we see, entirely differs from Alvarus Pelagius, and does not suppose that St. Francis either saw or foresaw any abuse of the private Mass. The private Mass itself was never admitted by any Roman authority to be an abuse, and it received the express approbation of the Council of Trent. "Nec Missas illas in quibus solus Sacerdos sacramentaliter communicat, ut privatas et illicitas damnat, sed probat atque adeo commendat" [here the plural *Missæ* is certainly equivalent to the singular]. If, therefore, the Thirty-first Article only condemns flagrant abuses, and is supposed to allow that which it does not condemn, we are brought to the rather startling conclusion that it tacitly sanctions, not only the sacrifice of the Mass, but private Masses, which, by the Rubric at the end of the Communion Office, the Church of England (as Mr. Stuart reluctantly admits, "Thoughts on Low Masses," p. 46) has expressly forbidden.

Turning from this to the explanation of the Article given in Tract xc., and lately repeated by Mr. Medd and Mr. Stuart, by the former in somewhat different terms, according to which the Article was pointed at a popular misapprehension as to the nature of the Sacrifice, I think that the common prevalence of such an error, especially as it is described by Mr. Medd, has been too hastily assumed without proof, which perhaps it would be difficult to produce. But it is more important to observe that Mr. Newman, when he had spoken of the Mass " being viewed as independent of or distinct from the Sacrifice on the Cross," appears to treat these two expressions, " independent of " and " distinct from," as synonymous, and as conveying a meaning which he calls " blasphemy." But there is a very wide difference between the two things. To view the Mass as independent of the Sacrifice on the Cross, would indeed be a very gross error; but until I see some proof, I shall continue utterly to disbelieve that it is one into which any worshipper at the Mass, even in the darkest ages, ever fell. But though not independent of, it might be viewed as distinct from, the Sacrifice on the Cross ; and so it is viewed, not by the ignorant and vulgar only, but by the Church of Rome.

The distinction between the two things, which the language of Tract xc. appears to confound with one another, may be illustrated by reference to another point of doctrine. Roman Catholic Apologists defend the use of direct prayer to the Virgin Mary, by the explanation that nothing more is meant than the effect of her all-powerful intercession. I may observe, by the way, that this assumption is altogether arbitrary, and that it is not very easy to reconcile it with language such as I find in a Sequence in the Arbuthnott Missal, p. 439.

> "Supplicamus, nos emenda,
> Emendatos nos commenda
> Tuo Nato, ad habenda
> Sempiterna gaudia."

Hitherto, however, the Virgin Mary has not been elevated by any formal definition above the rank of a creature. And so Mr. Oakeley ("Leading Topics of Dr. Pusey's recent work") can still say (p. 35), "Every well-instructed Catholic (alas! if they do not form the majority!) knows that the Blessed Virgin possesses no power to grant petitions, except such as she derives from God ; but he also knows that her influence with her Divine Son, in virtue of her maternal relation (!) and of her transcendent sanctity, must needs be such, that her will to grant is tantamount to the fact of granting, since her will is so entirely in harmony with the will of God, that her petitions are all in the order of His Providence. If we knew that an earthly sovereign had an almoner, to whom he had given the office of distributing his bounty, we should address ourselves to that almoner as the source from which the bounty emanates, though conscious all the while that he was merely the instrument of its bestowal."

Such a view of the case no doubt excludes the notion that the Blessed Virgin possesses any power of granting petitions independent of God. But it as clearly invests her with a power "distinct from" His, and must always tend to make her in practice the object of exclusive reliance and supreme devotion. Even if the "almoner" is supposed to have no discretion in the distribution of the Royal bounty; the "influence of the mother" is something perfectly distinct from the power of the Son. And so the Sacrifice of the Mass might not the less practically supersede that of the Cross, if conceived as "distinct from," though not "independent of" this. And it is so conceived, not by the vulgar only, but by the Church of Rome, speaking through her most accredited doctors, and in her most sacred formularies. Let us hear the prayer in the Mass which accompanies the offering of the bread :— " Suscipe, Sancte Pater Omnipotens, æterne Deus, hanc immaculatam hostiam (strange language before the Consecration, but explained by reference to that which the bread was to become), quam ego indignus famulus tuus offero tibi Deo meo vivo et vero, pro innumerabilibus peccatis et offensionibus et negligentiis meis, et pro omnibus circumstantibus; sed et pro omnibus fidelibus Christianis vivis atque defunctis, ut mihi et illis proficiat ad salutem in vitam æternam." Our Reformers, from their point of view, might well consider such an oblation as inconsistent with the oneness of that "finished upon the Cross;" and as, like the Invocation of the Virgin, on the one hand, a mere human invention, the fruit of bold, unlicensed speculation and unbridled fancy, and, on the other hand, the parent of manifold mischievous superstitions; and loathing it under both aspects alike might describe it in terms which we would not willingly now use, while we fully adhere to the view which suggested them, as a "blasphemous fable" and a "dangerous deceit."

This subject is so closely connected with that of Mr. Stuart's "Thoughts on Low Masses," that I am induced to add a few remarks on the proposal contained in that pamphlet. Mr. Stuart laments that at the Reformation, the Low Masses, which had drawn crowds of worshippers to our churches, on week-days as well as Sundays, were swept away, and an order for daily Morning Prayer, which experience has proved to be far less attractive, indeed to offer no attraction at all, substituted for them. He has observed the crowds which attend the early Masses in the Continental churches, and he thinks that ours might be as well filled by an adaptation of our Liturgy to the like purpose. He would have it curtailed, and the Rubrics, which say that there shall be no celebration of the Sacrament unless there be a certain number of communicants, removed, so that there may be nothing to prevent the congregation from consisting, as in the Continental churches, of spectators only, who come to join with the priest in the Eucharistic Sacrifice.

Notwithstanding the title of the pamphlet, by which some may have been alarmed and offended, it seems clear that, as to the positive doctrine of the Thirty-first Article, Mr. Stuart's orthodoxy is irreproachable. He takes great pains to explain that "there is but one real victim, which is Christ, and but one real act of Sacrifice, which was finished upon the Cross, and therefore to speak of Sacrifices, 'Sacrificia Missarum,' in the plural number would be a blasphemous fable and a dangerous deceit" (p. 38). He then proceeds to expound his theory of the Eucharistic Sacrifice: "In the Eucharistic Sacrifice, or the Sacrifice of the Mass (for they are but different names for the same thing), Christ is offered, but not sacrificed—offered in memory of His death, not put to death again. There is a real and propitiatory sacrifice, i. e. victim, in the Eucharist, but there is no real act of propitiation; the priest's offering of Christ in the Eucharist is not an act of propitiation or atonement, but only a memorial made before God of that propitiation and atonement which was effected upon the Cross;—by continually offering the very victim Himself who was slain, we continually plead before God the merits of His death" (p. 39). I must observe that however correct Mr. Stuart may be in his view of what the Eucharistic Sacrifice should be, to avoid direct collision with the Thirty-first Article, he is certainly mistaken if, when he says "there is a real and propitiatory sacrifice, i. e.

victim, in the Eucharist, but there is no real act of propitiation," he conceives himself (as the whole context appears to show) to be expounding and not directly contradicting the Roman doctrine of the Mass. For when, in Canon I. De Sacrificio Missæ, the Council of Trent declares, "Si quis dixerit in Missa non offerri Deo verum et proprium sacrificium, aut quod offerri non sit aliud quam nobis Christum ad manducandum dari: anathema sit," it is certain that *sacrificium* does not mean the *victim*, but the *act*—the same act which in Canon III. is declared to be an "act of propitiation." "Si quis dixerit, Missæ Sacrificium tantum esse laudis et gratiarum actionis, aut nudam commemorationem sacrificii in Cruce peracti (only a memorial) non autem propitiatorium, anathema sit." Can Mr. Stuart have a right to say that the Eucharistic Sacrifice and the Sacrifice of the Mass "are but different names for the same thing," when there is such a radical disagreement between his description of the one and the Council's description of the other? But putting the Mass out of the question and confining myself to Mr. Stuart's view of the Eucharistic Sacrifice, I must observe that it is open to one capital objection. It is indeed only the One Sacrifice which is to be pleaded, but it is to be pleaded in a special manner: namely, by the offering of the consecrated Bread and Wine in the Lord's Supper. And the question is —first, whether such a mode of pleading does not require the sanction of a Divine appointment, and, if it was a mere human invention, would not be presumptuous and profane—the more so for being engrafted on Christ's most solemn ordinance—and next, whether any such sanction is to be found in the records of the original institution unless what has been imported into them by most violent and arbitrary interpretation. Mr. Stuart would probably answer the first part of this question in the affirmative. But as to the other, he may be one of those who are easily satisfied with proofs of that which it seems to them desirable to have proved, and he may be content to interpret the words, " Do this in remembrance of me," as at once the institution of a Sacrifice and the ordination of the Apostles to the Sacerdotal Office. He has the fullest right to this opinion if he is able to hold it. Only he should not assume that it is commonly received among Churchmen and scholars, on whom it has not been forced by the anathema of an infallible Council. Even, however, if it were allowable to waive this grave objection to the theory in consideration of the general desirableness of the object, as to which I give Mr. Stuart full credit for the very best intentions, there would remain another which seems to me very serious, with regard to practice. Before he could reasonably expect that worshippers will be attracted to his Low Masses, as in the churches of France or Belgium, two things appear to be needed, neither of which can be admitted to be clearly practicable or desirable. One is, that the English congregation should come with the same notions of the nature and efficacy of the Eucharistic Sacrifice which

Roman Catholics bring to the Mass. The other is, that the Anglican Office should be adapted to these notions. Otherwise, even if all Mr. Stuart's suggestions were carried into effect by the abridgment of the Liturgy and the omission of the "obstructive" rubrics, the result would be a most unsatisfactory state of things. The congregation would be thinking of one thing, the minister would be speaking to them of another. They come to be spectators of a Sacrifice, he tells them of nothing but a Communion, of which he invites them to partake, though he neither expects nor seriously desires that any of them should do so. So far would it be from an advantage to "those who are near to the altar" (p. 49), to "hear the words themselves which accompany that offering" (an offering which is not expressed by a single word in the service) that the best thing possible for all present would be that the whole should pass off—as is indeed so very nearly the case in most Low Masses—in perfectly dumb show, so that the people, with the aid of appropriate manuals of devotion, might follow their train of thought, the priest his form of words, in parallel lines, without connexion or convergency indeed, but also without conflict or disturbance.

Apart from all theological objections, I cannot think this a happy plan, though I fully admit the want which it is intended to supply, and that our Order of Morning Prayer is not in its present state adapted to the purpose of an early service which common people, even of devout habits, could be expected to attend. It labours under the twofold disadvantage of inconvenient length, especially in the Lessons and Psalms, and of monotony in the recitation. Its failure does not prove that a shorter service, interspersed with melody, might not succeed, at least as well as Mr. Stuart's experiment, and might not be at least as easily introduced.

(D.)

A few passages in the Consultation of Archbishop Herman of Cologne may be read with interest, as bearing on some of the questions discussed in the Charge. I extract them from the English translation of 1548, but have modernized the spelling.

"Before all things the pastors must labour to take out of men's minds that false and wicked opinion whereby men think commonly that the priest in masses offereth up Christ our Lord to God the Father, after that sort, that with his intention and prayer he causeth Christ to become a new and acceptable sacrifice to the Father for the salvation of men, applieth and communicateth the merit of the passion of Christ and of the saving sacrifice, whereby the Lord Himself offered Himself to the Father, a sacrifice on the Cross, to them that receive the same with their own faith."

"For to make men partakers in the Supper of the Lord of the sacrifice and merits of our Lord Jesus Christ, the minister can help no more than that first he exhibit and minister the Holy Supper, as the Lord instituted, and then faithfully declare and celebrate religiously the mystery of it; namely, the redemption and cominution (*sic*) of our Lord Jesus Christ, and furthermore dispense the sacraments (the Bread and Wine) whereby he may stir up and confirm in them that be present true faith in Christ, by which faith every man may himself apprehend and receive the merit and sacrifice of Christ as given unto him."

"But it is plain that men are everywhere in this error, that they believe if they be present when the priest sayeth mass and take part of the mass only with their presence, that this very work and sacrifice of the priest, whereby he offereth the Son to the Father for their sins, that is to say, setteth Him before the Father with his intention and prayer, is of such efficacy that it turneth all evil from them and bringeth them all felicity of body and soul, though they continue in all manner of sins against God and their conscience, and neither perceive nor receive the sacraments out of the mass, but only behold the outward action as a spectacle, and honour it with bowing of knees and other gestures and signs of veneration."

"And whereas the holy fathers call the ministration of this sacrament a sacrifice and oblation, and write sometimes that the priest in the administering the Supper offereth Christ, let the preachers know and teach other, when need shall be, that the holy fathers by the name of a sacrifice understood not application, which was devised a great while after the fathers, and prevailed with other abuses, but a solemn remembrance of the sacrifice of Christ, as Augustine expoundeth it. For while the Supper of the Lord is administered as the Lord instituted it, the sacrifice of Christ is celebrated and exhibited therein through the preaching of His death and distribution of the sacraments, that all they which rightly use the Holy Supper may receive the fruit of this sacrifice."

"As the pastors must diligently teach and dissuade them which with the rest of the congregation cannot communicate because they stick in open sins, that they be not present at the Holy Supper, and testify unto them that if they stand at the Supper with such a mind they do spite unto Christ, and that it shall be damnation unto them. So they must also diligently warn and exhort them which with a good conscience be present at the Supper, that is to say which truly believe in Christ the Lord, that they receive the sacraments with other members of Christ."

"But forasmuch as this institution of the Lord that all they which be present at the same Supper of the Lord should communicate of one bread and cup, His Body and Blood, is too much out of use, and covered a great while since through common ignorance, it shall be needful to call men back again treatably and gently to the observation of this tradition of the Lord, and the preachers must beware that the minds of the simple, which nevertheless be the true disciples of the Lord, and are entangled in no mischievous and wicked acts, for the which they should be restrained from the Lord's Board, be not stricken and troubled with sore rebukes or untimely thrusting unto the receiving of the sacrament. For there be not a few which, though they cannot thoroughly understand this mystery and the perfect use of sacraments, yet have such faith in Christ, that they can pray with the congregation and be somewhat edified in faith through holy doctrine and exhortations that be wont to be used about the Holy Supper and the ministration thereof, yea and they may be taught and moved by little and little to a perfecter knowledge of this mystery, and an oftener use of the sacraments, even by this that they be present at the Holy Supper, which abstain not from the Lord's Supper of any contempt of the sacraments which they acknowledge in themselves, but of a certain weakness of men and preposterous reverence of the sacrament."

It will be seen that the first paragraph in these extracts speaks of "a false opinion" as to what is done by the priest in *masses*, and therefore according to the principle of interpretation which has been applied to our Thirty-first Article, might be thought not to be directed against the mass itself. But in the margin we read, "The false opinion concerning the oblation of the priest in the mass must be taken away." And the statements which follow leave no doubt as to the Archbishop's meaning. The work appears to have been a joint production of Bucer, Melancthon, and other Reformers (Gieseler, Lehrbuch der K. G. 111. 1. p. 322). Luther, as appears from a letter in De Wette's Collection, v. p. 708, was dissatisfied with the chapter on the Lord's Supper, as not sufficiently explicit with regard to the "substance." And Gieseler observes that it passes over the real presence of the Body. Yet the pastors are enjoined to "warn the people that they doubt nothing but the Lord Himself is present in the midst of them, and giveth them His very Body and Blood, that they ever may more fully live in Him, and He in them."

X.

A CHARGE

DELIVERED OCTOBER AND NOVEMBER, 1869.

DISESTABLISHMENT OF THE IRISH CHURCH.—RITUALISM.—THE EUCHARISTIC CONTROVERSY.—THE VATICAN COUNCIL.

MY REVEREND BRETHREN,

IF it had been customary to prefix a text of Scripture to a Visitation Charge, that which would most readily have occurred to me, as appropriate to the circumstances in which we now meet, would have been the words of the Psalmist: "If the foundations be destroyed, what can the righteous (the righteous man) do?"* Not, thank God, that the period in which we are living is one of revolutionary convulsion, in which the institutions on which social order reposes have been violently upturned. But it may be said, without exaggeration, that it is one in which change follows change with unexampled rapidity, each apparently fraught with more and more momentous consequences, reaching down to fundamental principles of thought, belief, and action, laying them bare to the most searching investigation, and threatening whatever they are found too weak to sustain, however hallowed and endeared by traditional associations, with collapse or overthrow. It is therefore a time for the question, "If the foundations be destroyed, what can the righteous man do?" or, what ought he to do? What is the frame of mind and the course of action which befits one who desires to live as in the Divine presence, and to shape his conduct by the rule of duty toward God and his neighbour?

* Ps. xi. 3.

Such a one will surely not forget, but rather will be led to bear in mind more earnestly than ever, that the changes which startle us by their apparent suddenness, are indeed but the outcome of a long, silent, and unseen preparation, working through a variety of unsuspected agencies toward an inevitable result. One advantage of this view is, that it lifts the mind out of the turbid atmosphere of personal prejudice and passion, as it shows how little individuals or parties really have to do with either the good or the evil of which they are the instruments. It lifts the mind, I say, out of this unwholesome atmosphere into a region of serene contemplation, in which it may find calmness, consolation, and assurance. For we firmly believe that the course of events is guided, not by a blind chance or a mechanical necessity, but by the mind and will of a wise and Fatherly Providence, Whose designs are never fully known to man, are often wrapt in utter darkness, or present an aspect which we are unable to reconcile with supreme wisdom and goodness; but which will, we doubt not, be fully justified by the final issue, and which even now become more and more discernible as we extend our survey over a larger field of history, and observe the working of the Divine Government on a greater scale, so as in some measure to see how abiding and general good is evolved out of apparent partial and temporary evil.

[Sidenote: The course of events guided by God's Providence.]

Such a habit of thought will best secure the peace of our souls when the foundations seem to rock under our feet. But for the righteous man peace and comfort are not the only or the highest aim. He would not consent, even if it was in his power, to remain an inactive and unconcerned spectator of events which deeply affect the weal or woe of his fellow-men. And the Psalmist's question is not, how may he be free from care and trouble, how may he enjoy uninterrupted ease and quiet? but, on the contrary, "What can he do?" And this must mean, not for himself only, but for others. The peculiar character of an extraordinary time is not only a trial of faith, but a call to action, for every one, according to his sphere and capacity. It is true, opportunities of action, which can,

[Sidenote: Aim of the righteous.]

[Sidenote: The time of trial the time for action.]

in any sensible degree, affect the course of events, must be very rare and confined to a few. But the conduct of all is swayed by their opinions and beliefs, and may exercise a powerful influence on others. And thus the formation of a right judgment may become an important part of practical duty. Such a judgment is indeed a gift, for which the Church teaches us to pray, as not to be obtained without the operation of the Holy Spirit; and this implies that it will not be vouchsafed to minds clouded by wilful prejudice, or selfish aims, or evil passions. But neither is it to be looked for in such as remain in a state of sluggish passiveness; which shrink from the labour of obeying the Apostolic precept: "Prove all things: hold fast that which is good;" which are content with simply echoing the dictates of some human authority, are too careless about truth to take the trouble of thinking for themselves, and of making the opinion, on which nevertheless they do not scruple to act on very important occasions, a personal conviction of their own breasts. But in persons who have dedicated themselves to the office of spiritual Teachers and Guides, such inertness and indifference, manifesting itself in a thoughtless repetition of the utterances of other minds, amounts to nothing less than an abdication of their most sacred function, at the very season when its exercise is most urgently required.

And no one may claim exemption from this duty on the plea that as a minister of religion he ought, or is at liberty, to keep aloof from political contention. That would be perfectly true, if it is meant to apply to contests which concern only personal or temporary interests. But it would be a lamentable error if it was extended to questions which involve the welfare of the State. Undoubtedly the Church of Christ has the first claim on our affections and our energies. But they would be misplaced and misdirected, if we were to regard the State as a region foreign to our sympathies; one in which we have no proper home, to which we are bound by no tie but such as springs out of the wants of our lower nature, and which therefore, in proportion as we are devoted to the work of our sacred calling, ought to occupy a narrower and lower place in our thoughts. *Ministers of religion not exempt from this duty.*

This is indeed, if we trace it to its root, an upgrowth of the old Manichæan error, which leavened the early Church, and was never entirely purged out; which wasted so many lives in a selfish barren asceticism; treating the body as essentially unholy because the creature of a Being opposed to the Father of Spirits, and as incapable of administering to the good of the soul, otherwise than by its own suffering and degradation. Such a view, though once extensively prevalent, now shocks us as a wild and monstrous delusion. But it is closely akin to that which regards the State as simply secular and profane, as a necessity to which we reluctantly submit, while we strive as much as possible to avoid all active contact with it. It was of a Pagan and a persecuting State that the Apostle declared, "The powers that be are ordained of God." This would suffice to show that the end of the State, or civil society, in itself is holy and just and good, though it is only through the Church that this end is ever fully attained, or rather the nearest practicable approach made towards the attainment of it.

Relations between Church and State. The questions which arise out of the relations between Church and State, are among the most difficult with which the human mind has to deal. And the difficulty is greatly increased by the imperfection and ambiguity of language; which so easily leads us to forget that *Church* and *State* are both abstract terms; that the concrete reality which underlies each, is an aggregate of persons knit together by an ideal bond; that in the happiest state of things, that in which each best fulfils the purpose of its institution, the very same persons who, in one view, constitute the State, in another view, constitute the Church; and that, as the head is not the body, so the ruler, or governing power, is not the State, but the representative and organ of its mind and will; and the Clergy, or ministering agency, is not the Church. These questions are forced upon us with peculiar urgency by the events of our own day; and it is on them above all that it behoves us to endeavour to stay our minds on clear notions and solid principles.

You are all aware of the subject—long uppermost in the

thoughts of all of us—which has suggested these reflections. Even if I had no special reasons for desiring to draw your attention to this subject, its intrinsic importance would have entitled it to the foremost place in this address. It is true it has been the occasion of an excitement often quite alien to the tone of feeling befitting the place in which we are now assembled. But this appears to me a reason, not for avoiding the subject, but on the contrary for dwelling upon it in a different spirit, and weighing it, not in the scales of selfish interests and party passions, but, as far as we can, in the balance of the Sanctuary.

Here, as usual, it is only by the light of the past that we can hope to gain any clear view of the present, or any true insight into the future. *Retrospect of Irish history.* The retrospect is indeed one of the most saddening to be found in the annals of history; but we may not shrink from pondering its lessons and its warnings. It presents a Land abounding in the sources of national wealth, in all that can stimulate and reward industry, and by its natural features exercising a peculiar charm on the affections of its inhabitants; a People richly gifted with many noble qualities of mind and heart; singularly deficient indeed in the faculty and the spirit of political and ecclesiastical organization, neither comprehending its conditions, nor appreciating its advantages, but naturally disposed to yield to the guidance of a friendly and beneficent authority, and for many centuries closely connected with a more powerful nation, endowed in an eminent degree with the qualities which the weaker most lacked. Here, then, it might have been thought, were the elements of prosperity and happiness for both. And yet in the whole course of Irish history there is not one bright spot; not a single period on which memory can dwell without finding matter chiefly for shame, sorrow, and regret. I cannot even except that to which many look back as to a golden age, the time when Ireland won the name of the Isle of Saints. That description does not prove it to have been a land of holiness. The seventh century, an age in which the Church was sunk in the grossest darkness and corruption, was called the Age of Saints; and we cannot doubt that, while the Irish monasteries were seats of piety and learning, and sent forth many illustrious missionaries to spread the Gospel in foreign lands, their own country was in the same state of anarchy and barbarism in which we find it as soon as we become acquainted with its internal condition.

I am not going to relate its history; but there are in that history some prominent epochs to which I must invite your attention, because they have a most important bearing on the subject now before us.

Union with England, how effected. The most momentous epoch in the history of both countries was that which first yoked them together under a common rule. This event, big with such a vast train of consequences, was ominously marked with the character of unprovoked aggression and violent conquest. It is true this wrong was sanctioned by the Papal oracle, then generally acknowledged throughout Western Christendom as supreme in all questions of faith and morals, in perfect accordance with the ancient maxims of the See of Rome, always ready—as in the cases of Phocas, of Clovis, and of Pepin—to countenance any injustice which tended to promote its own aggrandizement. And if the end could have sanctified the means, the invasion might have been justified by the prospect of the advantages which might have been expected to ensue from the comprehension of the two islands under one sceptre. But the effect was only to divide the less powerful into two hostile camps, and to make it a theatre of incessant, wasting, and demoralising warfare. The policy of the English Government was one of physical force, rendered the more insupportable to the native population by the studied display of hatred and contempt on the part of the conquerors. It may be said that this was the policy of a rude, wild, lawless age. But its effect was not the less irritating, and did not the less call for reparation and atonement which were never made. The influence of the Roman Catholic religion did not restrain the most outrageous excesses of this unchristian spirit. The power of the Pope, who claimed to be sovereign lord, was uniformly exerted on the side of the strongest. The victims of English tyranny appealed to him in vain.

But the stroke of retribution fell when England received the greatest of all blessings, that to which she owes her place among the nations. It then appeared that she had deprived herself of the power of imparting this blessing to the people whom she had treated as a race of abject serfs, below the level, and outside the pale of humanity, who might be killed with impunity, and without remorse, as beasts of the field.* She had associated it in their minds with the idea of violence and oppression, of insolence and cruelty. She made it the object of their bitterest hatred. She united them in the closest alliance with the Continental Powers who were leagued together for the destruction of the Reformed faith, especially in this land. So the breach was widened by that which should have healed it. The animosity of race was envenomed by religious rancour, and the influence of a purer creed failed to inspire the dominant nation with milder sentiments towards its subjects. It would indeed be unfair to overlook the provocations which roused its resentment, and the peril which compelled it to resort to rigorous measures in self-defence. But neither may we forget that this necessity was the effect of centuries of misrule. And if it be admitted that the penal legislation was excusable in the heat of a great crisis, can this plea avail for the tenacious maintenance of that atrocious code, when it could serve no purpose but that of nourishing the evil passions of those who regarded the affliction and degradation of their countrymen as the only sound basis of Protestant ascendancy?

<small>Retribution.</small>

It was not until a very late period that better thoughts, if not more humane and Christian sentiments, began to stir in the minds of English statesmen, roused indeed it is to be feared by a sense of the folly rather than of the wickedness of the system by which the country had been so long misgoverned, to the detriment alike of the sufferer and the oppressor. This apathy with regard to the first principles of justice and humanity admits indeed of one most unhappy palliation. Even in those whose sacred calling should have quickened their perceptions of

<small>Improvement in English administration.</small>

---

* Wordsworth's "History of the Church of Ireland," p. 152.

right and wrong, we not only miss any protest against the iniquity of the penal legislation, any attempt to assume the part of mediators and intercessors, but we find the most strenuous resistance to every proposal made to mitigate its rigour. It may be said that the clergy could not reasonably be expected to be in advance of their age; that it was natural their attention and sympathy should be absorbed by the interests of their own Church. That may be true, and certainly none would have been selected for high office in the Church who were suspected of any sympathy with Irish wrongs. But we have here nothing to do with the allotment of individual responsibility, but only with the impression left on the mind of the people. The introduction of the Reformation into Ireland was an object in which the power and safety of the kingdom was deeply concerned, and all the authority of the State was exerted to bring it about. But when it appeared that the only benefit to be derived from it was the spiritual welfare of the Roman Catholic population, it ceased to occupy the thoughts either of statesmen or of Churchmen, and a proselytizing movement would have been viewed in high quarters with displeasure.

<small>The Union effected against the wish of the majority.</small> Finally, the union of the two countries, indispensably necessary as it was for the security of the British Empire, was notoriously brought about against the will of the great majority of the Irish people, by means morally indefensible, and alike discreditable to both parties, the bribers and the bribed.* It might, nevertheless, have opened a new era of peace and concord, if it had been accompanied by the measures which entered into the original design of its author, followed up by others conceived in the same spirit of conciliation. But as, unhappily, this was prevented by causes too well known to need mention, it not only contributed nothing to cement a real union of minds and hearts, but rather embittered the previous animosity of those who saw their national existence merged in that of a foreign power, and their country, according to the Roman phrase, reduced into the form of a province, without any compensation to console them for the loss of an, at least nominal and

---

* See note C, in the Appendix.

formal, independence. The Union had all the legal force of an Act of Parliament, and even of a solemn treaty. But morally it was a mere name, a fiction, a piece of parchment, utterly inoperative for its professed purpose. It neither expressed a fact, nor tended to realize the supposition which it assumed. The cry for its repeal never ceased to awaken an echo in the Irish bosom; and the most important boons lost all their conciliatory value, because they appeared to be not free offerings of our good-will or of our justice, but concessions wrung from our fears.

So the great problem has been handed down to us, still awaiting a solution, which has become more and more necessary, but more and more difficult. The only cheering and hopeful sign is that now, for the first time in the course of that doleful history which we have been reviewing, it has been taken up with a sincere desire and firm intention to redress every real wrong, and remove every reasonable ground of complaint. Let it not be supposed that, when I say this, I am thinking of individuals or of parties. That which appears to me hopeful in the present aspect of things, is entirely independent of all particular views and feelings. It is that the general voice of the country has declared its resolution to reverse the old blind and iniquitous policy, to abolish the anomalies and wrongs to which it gave birth; and, if possible, to establish a rule of righteousness and peace. *Reversal of England's old policy.*

But the difficulty of carrying this intention into effect is greatly increased by the variety of objects which demand attention and contend for precedence. Whether that which has been selected as the first subject of legislation might have been safely and advantageously postponed, is a question which, from the moment that the selection was actually made, ceased to be of any practical importance, and is totally unfit for discussion in this place. But undoubtedly, if there was in the Irish Church Establishment no offensive anomaly which required correction, no sensible grievance which called for redress, no palpable contrast between that which had been imposed upon Ireland, and that which, if it had been an independent nation, Ireland would have chosen for itself, then it must be admitted that the abolition of the *Irish Church Establishment.*

Irish Establishment was a wanton innovation, for which hardly any of the terms of reprobation which have been applied to it were too strong. But it is on that supposition that they *have* been applied to it. They have assumed that this view of the case is so evidently the right one, as not to admit of any candid doubt; and yet nothing is more certain as a matter of fact, than that, whether rightly or wrongly, the opposite opinion has been very generally held, both at home and abroad; and in particular that among intelligent foreigners, even the most friendly, and the warmest admirers of our institutions, the Irish Church Establishment has been universally regarded as the most glaring of all anomalies, the grossest of all abuses, that which, above all others, tests the sincerity of those who profess to aim at a just policy in the government of Ireland. It has been said that the opinion of foreigners on our domestic concerns is entitled to no weight. That is not quite in accordance with a familiar proverb on the advantage of a bystander's position. But however worthless such an opinion may be in itself, it seems hard to believe that what to strangers appears an intolerable wrong, should be viewed in a totally different light by those who are subject to it, even when they assure us of the contrary; and it would seem as if the prevalence of the opinion, whether well founded or not, must itself tend to engender and nourish the feeling.

<small>Opinion of foreigners on its abolition.</small>

The religious theory of the Irish Church Establishment rests upon the assumption, that it is a right and a duty of a Christian State to exert all its power and influence for the maintenance and propagation of true religion. This, of course, involves the farther assumption that the State, as represented by its rulers, is capable of ascertaining which is the true religion, and this not only as between Christians and adherents of other creeds, but as between various forms of Christian faith. As long however as the society, in its religious aspect, is homogeneous, this question will not arise, unless as matter of otiose speculation for thinkers in their closets. But the case is manifestly changed, when the unity of Christian belief has been broken up into a number of conflicting sects. The application of the general

<small>Theory of the Irish Establishment.</small>

principle to such a state of things is beset with very grave difficulties, both of theory and practice. If we attempt to vindicate the Irish Church Establishment on the ground of that principle, it seems as if our argument must take some such form as this:— "Three centuries ago we renounced the old errors to which you still blindly cling. We offered you the pure doctrine of our Reformed Church. It was your fault if you rejected it with abhorrence. But we do not force you to profess what you do not believe. We even permit you openly to celebrate the rites of your religion, much as they shock our feelings, and to support its ministers, strongly as we dislike them. It is true we reserve all the provision made for religious instruction, and all the privileges and distinctions annexed to the pastoral office, to the clergy of a small minority, whom you regard as teachers of deadly heresy. But if from your point of view this appears to you unjust, because you think that a large portion, at least, of the funds so employed rightfully belongs to you, and because you consider your own clergy as, at least, equally entitled to public acknowledgment, you must remember that, by virtue of the Union—which, though it was forced upon you by the right of the strongest, is still legally valid—you were fused into one nation with us: and thus, what had been a minority became a majority, entitled to all the advantage of superior members."

The argument stated.

Whether this is in itself sound reasoning or not, I think that, if we place ourselves for a moment in the position of an Irish Roman Catholic, and imagine his feelings, we should see that the effect on his mind could be only to strengthen his repugnance to the Union, and to inflame his hatred of those who use it for such a purpose. For the argument implies a claim to a kind of superiority, which is just the last that men can be brought to admit. It assumes that those whom we so address have no right to judge for themselves in matters which lie between God and their conscience. We know to what Church these maxims and pretensions properly belong. They spring naturally out of the doctrine of infallibility. But they are out of place in a Church which exists only by the right of protest against

Its tendency to strengthen repugnance to the Union.

a usurped authority; one in which conscience is supreme, and cannot suffer its decisions to be overruled by any judgment which it does not freely adopt as its own.

<small>No express guidance in Scripture on Church Establishments.</small> Religious Establishments have been both defended and impugned by good and pious men, who have naturally been anxious to claim the authority of Scripture in favour of their views. But when we find the same texts adduced in support of contradictory propositions,* we are forced to despair of obtaining any direct Scriptural guidance in the controversy, and to resign ourselves to the conviction, that the utmost we can expect to find is some broad general statement of principles which we are left to apply by the light of our own reason and conscience. And it is observable that those who maintain the duty of providing for a public profession of religion to be incumbent on the Christian magistrate, commonly build their theory on the hypothesis of an ideal ruler in an ideal State: a ruler invested with absolute power, and governing a people united by the same religious profession. In such a case it is not difficult to show that it is the duty of the ruler to exert his power for the protection of the interests of that religion which he and his subjects profess.

<small>Despotic government favoured by the Church of Rome.</small> It is on this account that the Church of Rome has always favoured despotic forms of government when administered by adherents of her own faith. The sovereigns who, like Philip II. and Louis XIV., wielded their absolute power for the extirpation of heresy, realized her ideal of the perfect State.† And this, I think, may serve to allay any regret which we might otherwise feel, when we reflect that such a state of

---

* As John xviii. 36, by Archbishop Whately ("The Kingdom of Christ," Essay i. § 9) on the one hand, and by Mr. Birks ("Church and State," chap. iii.) on the other.

† "The modern civil constitutions, and the efforts for self-government, and the limitation of arbitrary royal power, are in the strongest contradiction to Ultramontanism, the very kernel and ruling principle of which is the consolidation of absolutism in the Church. But State and Church are intimately connected: they act and react on one another, and it is inevitable that the political views and tendencies of a nation should sooner or later influence it in Church matters also. Hence the profound hatred, at the bottom of the soul of every genuine Ultramontane, of free institutions and the whole constitutional system."—"The Pope and the Council," by Janus, p. 21. An excellent translation of a most valuable work.

things is visibly and rapidly passing away; that it only lingers in the imperfectly civilized parts of Europe, while in those which represent its highest intelligence and culture it belongs to the irrevocable past. Both as men and as Christians, we have reason to rejoice in this change. But it has evidently intro- *Its decline has complicated the question of Church Establishments.* duced new conditions into the question of Church Establishments, which render it much more complicated and difficult, and deprive much of the reasoning which was grounded on that imaginary basis of all force and relevancy. And it may be safely said that there is no country in the world where the difficulty is so great, the problem so complicated, as it is in our own: the seat of a vast empire, extended over a great variety of races and religions, and itself inhabited by a population divided by endless diversities of opinion and belief, and subject to a monarchy so tempered by constitutional restraints, that no small sagacity is required to determine where the centre of power is to be found, and it is only certain that it depends on the concurrence of many subordinate agencies. It is clear that rules of action which under a system of personal government might be binding on the conscience of the ruler, would become utterly inapplicable to a Legislative Body, representing widely divergent religious sentiments, and of masses too large and powerful to be ignored or neglected. The practical neutrality or impartiality which in the one case would have been a fault or a sin, becomes, under altered circumstances, a necessity and an obligation. The zeal which was a duty, becomes an error and a weakness.

And here I would interpose a more general reflection. That many good and thinking men should be distressed and alarmed by the changes which are passing on the condition of society, *Reflections on the condition of Society.* and which make it impossible for the State to maintain the profession of a national religion in the same sense as while the Church and the nation were numerically identical; that they should regard with anxious forebodings the preponderance recently acquired by the democratical element in the Constitution; —this is a feeling which we can well understand, and with which we must all sympathize. But I must return once more to the

Psalmist's question; and remind you that it is not, "How will the righteous man feel?" but "What can he do?" and the first thing, as it seems to me, which he has to do, and which is quite in his power, is to satisfy himself whether this change is a mere momentary fluctuation, which may be expected soon to subside, or is a mighty stream of tendency, which no human power can arrest or control. If it is unmistakably marked with the character of a natural, social development, then, however much we may see in it to deplore and to dread, still, as believers in a superintending Providence, we cannot look upon it as merely evil; and instead of mourning over it, and keeping aloof from it in a gloomy passiveness, or wasting our strength in a vain attempt to stem the tide which is carrying all before it upon earth, and can only be overruled by Him Who "sitteth above the waterflood," we shall hold it our duty to deal with it in a loving and hopeful spirit, to recognize all that is good or capable of good in it; and, approaching it in such a spirit, we shall probably find much more than we looked for; and to apply all our diligence to mitigate the evil, and to foster the good.

State countenance of religious Establishments. The adversaries of religious Establishments often appeal to the history of the Church in the first three Centuries, as a proof that Christianity flourished most when it was not only unestablished, but persecuted by the State, and that its alliance with the Empire was attended by a sensible decline in its purity and fervour. They are met by the reply, that religion did not, and could not, fully manifest its power of leavening the whole mass of society, and of hallowing all social relations, until it had entered into union with the State, and that its corruption was owing to causes independent of that union, which in itself was highly beneficial. It may, however, be imagined as a possible case, that, after the conversion of Constantine, the countenance of the State might have been withdrawn from Paganism, but not transferred to Christianity, and that the Christian faith might not have been publicly recognized by any official authority. Its influence on all classes would have continued the same; only the Law would have remained neutral, and would not have dispensed either rewards or punishments in its favour. But when we consider how utterly foreign such motives are to religion, it seems difficult to contend that it would have suffered any loss from their absence. Rather we may clearly trace some of the worst evils which afflicted the Church to the Imperial patronage. The head of a family, the citizen, the magistrate, may also be a member of a religious society, and if he is earnest and sincere, his conduct in his private and civil capacity will be shaped by his religious convictions; but the two characters are not the less distinct from one another. And so the Christian State may regulate its acts by Christian principles, though it is wholly severed from the Church. The State does not necessarily become heathen or infidel, because it confines itself to its own sphere, and does not intermeddle with that of the Church. And it seems hardly to be questioned that the reign of Christ upon earth was more fully, more heartily, and more practically recognized by the primitive Church, in her poverty, her weakness, her political nullity, than in the subsequent period, when kings became her nursing fathers, and their queens her nursing mothers, shielding her indeed from outward violence, but often injuring her by mistaken kindness.

The conclusion which seems to me to follow from these premisses, is one, I am aware, alike unacceptable to both parties: to that which condemns religious Establishments as unlawful, because injurious to the sovereignty of Christ, and to that which holds them to be essential to the full assertion of that sovereignty. I regard both these extremes of opinion as untenable. The very fact of their conflict, and that they are espoused by persons equally entitled to respect, appears to me a sure indication that the truth lies somewhere between them, that neither is the one constitution forbidden, nor the other prescribed by any Divine authority; that neither is absolutely good or bad; that it must always depend on the circumstances of each case which is preferable to the other; and that the decision must ultimately rest with the supreme power in every State, not as exempt from error, but because there is under heaven no other of higher jurisdiction, or of fuller competency; none that possesses any better right to

Establishments neither absolutely good nor bad.

decree, or any clearer light to guide its judgment. This is, of course, only a Protestant view of the question. But those who insist on the necessity of choosing between the two extremes, are really, though unconsciously, taking ground which can be consistently maintained only by those who acknowledge an infallible earthly oracle, which is empowered to speak in the name of Christ, and entitled to claim implicit submission to its responses.

<small>Power of the State to sever its connexion with the Church.</small> If, however, the State is, and in a Protestant community must be, at liberty to exercise its discretion on the question of contracting an alliance with the Church, it seems to follow that it may exercise the same discretion on the question of dissolving an alliance contracted in time past; as no one doubts that the Church may sever the ties which connect it with the State, if they seem inconsistent with the end of its institution. But though in the abstract the one liberty may seem to carry the other, there is an immense difference between the two things, in the difficulty, the danger, and the responsibility incurred. It is as the difference between the omitting to plant a tree, and the uprooting of one which has weathered the storms of centuries, and has afforded shelter and nourishment to many generations. And this image does but very imperfectly illustrate the magnitude and peril of such an undertaking. For the soil in which a long established Church has struck its roots, is no other than that of man's higher nature, the seat of his loftiest aspirations, his deepest cravings, his holiest affections; all liable to suffer grievous hurt in their most delicate fibres from the operation. And this is no doubt a motive for entering upon it, if it is believed to be necessary, with the utmost caution, and for conducting it with the greatest possible tenderness. But it is another question, whether we can say that it is in itself absolutely unjustifiable, and a breach of the Divine Law. And here I think it is not irrelevant to recollect the testimony of one who lately passed from us amidst the highest tributes of affectionate veneration from the Church which he had adorned by his life as well as by his writings,—the Author of the "Christian Year." It was on the disestablishment of the Irish Church that he expressed his

opinion by the question, "Is it not just?"* Whether we consider his scrupulous conscientiousness, his piety, or his ecclesiastical prepossessions, it does not seem to be laying undue weight on his authority, to say that it is not inferior to that of any who have condemned the measure as a repudiation of Christianity.

But the question becomes much more complicated and difficult, when the separation is accompanied by the alienation of property which the Church had enjoyed during the union, either as a gift of the State or under the sanction of its laws, giving to the will of private donors a validity which of itself it could not have claimed. By some every such alienation is regarded as sacrilegious, on the ground that whatever has been so dedicated to a sacred use has become "the property of God." To you, my Reverend Brethren, I need only remark in a single word that whenever we speak of the sacredness of any material offering made to the Most High, it must always be with the reservation—tacit, if not express—of the fundamental truth, that such an offering can never be acceptable to God in itself, or as supplying any want of the Divine nature; but only as a sign of that devotion of the heart, which he has declared to be pleasing to Him, and by virtue of which it is at the same time in the highest degree beneficial to the offerer: so that the benefit to man is a measure of the degree in which it is acceptable to God. But when the offering is of a permanent kind, as an ecclesiastical endowment, a large experience has abundantly shown that the sign may remain after the thing signified has passed away; that it may become a form without the substance, a letter without the spirit: unmeaning as a sign; powerless as an instrument; worthless alike to God and man. In such a case, unless the sacredness of the original destination is held to impress it with an indelible character, independent of all vicissitudes of public affairs, and all changes in social relations, the State would be not only exercising a right, but discharging a duty, in applying it to other uses. This may be admitted or denied. Here are two opinions between which we are at liberty to choose, but we *must* make our choice between the

Alienation of Church property.

* Memoir of Keble, by Sir John Coleridge, p. 518.

two. We are not at liberty to adopt both, and to use this for one purpose, and that for another. We may lay down the principle that every alienation—or, as it is called, secularization—of Church property is sacrilege, and, as such, absolutely forbidden by God's Law; that whatever has been once so consecrated to a pious use, has become in such a sense the property of God, as to be for ever withdrawn from the disposal of the State; that no failure of the original intention, no abuse or perversion, however gross, of the instrument designed to promote the glory of God and the welfare of man, to purposes most directly adverse to both, can divest it of its sacred character. That is a proposition which, if we follow it out into its consequences, it may seem to need some hardihood to maintain, when we think of the enormous wealth which flowed into the Church in the tenth century, through the prevailing expectation that the end of the world was at hand; and of the way in which those endowments were employed before the Reformation in our own and other lands. It would even raise the question, whether, according to this description, sacrilege must not be oftener a duty than a sin. But still the position is intelligible and self-consistent. It is held by the Church of Rome, which, identifying the Church with the clergy, and the interests of the clergy with the interests of God, regards every alienation of ecclesiastical property, though acquired through ignorant credulity, or, as so large a part of her temporal dominion, by fraud and forgery, as a robbery of God. But if we commit ourselves to this position, we must abide by it. We may not say of the same act, it is one which cannot be justified by any reasons, because it is sacrilege; and it is sacrilege because no sufficient reason can be assigned for it. The charge of sacrilege must occupy the foremost place, to the exclusion of every other argument, or there is no room for it at all. If we once let in the consideration of reasons, which may or may not justify the act, the charge can serve no purpose but that of fastening an ugly name on an opinion from which we dissent. But unless the view I have taken of the history and peculiar features of the Irish Church question is altogether erroneous, it is hard to conceive one which can present

In what sense it becomes sacrilege.

greater difficulties, both of theory and of practice, or in which more room is open for honest difference of opinion, and in which, therefore, an imputation of evil motives, or of moral blindness, is less justified by the state of the case.

But though I cannot share the opinion of those who consider the subject as by its very nature withdrawn from the legitimate range of statesmanly deliberation, I deeply lament the way in which it has appeared necessary to deal with it. I believe that the modification proposed in the Upper House of Parliament in the disposal of the surplus, would have been more generally beneficial, more in accordance with the professed object of the measure, more conciliatory to Irish feelings. It would have spared that which might have been usefully retained, while it gave that which, so given, would have witnessed, more clearly than in any other form, to the sincerity of our good-will. I can see no force in any of the objections which have been made to it, on the ground of principle. I think it is through misapprehension, or by a rhetorical artifice, that it has been represented as an endowment of error, in the only sense in which the phrase expresses something inconsistent and reprehensible. It could be only by a most violent and arbitrary misconstruction that a slight addition to the comfort of the Roman Catholic clergy, and a relative elevation in their social position, could be interpreted as indicating any acknowledgment of the truth of their distinguishing tenets. I had occasion to express my views on this point in a Charge delivered nearly twenty-five years ago, with reference to the Grant to the College of Maynooth. That opinion remains unaltered; but in the present case it would not be necessary to take such broad ground; and one who disapproved of the Grant to Maynooth, might consistently consent to such an appropriation of Irish funds as was proposed.

Proposition in the House of Lords respecting the Irish Church surplus.

At the same time I am bound to admit, that what seemed to me most desirable appears to have been for the present impracticable, and so opposed to the general mind and will of the country, that it would have been beyond the power of any government to have carried it into effect. This of course does not

Public opinion on the subject.

in the least affect the merits of the view which the voice of the country has condemned, but it is decisive on the practical conclusion. Public opinion, as well as that of each individual who helps to compose it, may be unenlightened and misguided, but when it has been freely formed and lawfully expressed, there is no higher tribunal on earth that can overrule its decisions. Language has been used of late tending to depreciate the significance of majorities in the determination of political questions.* Certainly they can have no weight whatever as a measure of truth; otherwise all the Churches of the Reformation must give way to Rome, and Christianity to Buddhism. But until some one shall have devised a more satisfactory mode of deciding the course of political action, it seems useless to murmur against that which has been sanctioned by the universal experience of mankind in all countries and in all ages. It may be a very clumsy expedient, but the only alternative hitherto discovered is either anarchy, or stagnation of public affairs.

<small>Justice of the Irish Church disestablishment.</small> The claims of Justice are absolute and inflexible. She cannot waive them. They are entitled to precedence over all calculations of expediency, and no such calculations can lead to any result more certain than the maxim that, in the affairs of nations as of individuals, justice is in the long run the best policy. It is indeed perplexing to find that a measure which to such a mind as Keble's appeared so manifestly just, is denounced by other excellent men as a monstrous wrong, and we can only suppose that those who judge of it so oppositely, consider it from widely different points of view: the one party perhaps from the English the other from the Irish side. But this is a case in which the consideration of consequences cannot be wholly excluded from the view of justice itself: as it is impossible to separate the question of right and wrong from that of good and evil. Speculation on the political effects of this great change would here be out of place. I will only remark that its most sanguine advocates have never represented it as a panacea for the evils of Ireland, or denied that its success, as a measure of paci-

* Birks u. s. chap. vii. On Parliamentary and Local Majorities.

fication, will turn upon that of other remedies which remain to be tried. The final result must depend on the combination of a general diffusion of material well-being, with a general sense of just government. As long as either of these is wanting, there must be discontent and disaffection. When we look back at the past, we may easily be inclined to despair of ever undoing the work of so many centuries, during which there has been a constant accumulation of the elements of discord and hatred. But a government can have no right to despair, until it has exhausted all the resources at its command for the attainment of an object so essential to the welfare and safety of the empire. But our interest in this matter is, if not wholly absorbed, at least for the present chiefly occupied by the consequences which it seems to portend to the Church in Ireland and at home. And on these you may naturally expect that I should say a few words.

It is not surprising that the suddenness of the blow which has fallen on the Irish Church, should have inclined those who feel the deepest interest in her cause, to take a gloomy view of her prospects, to exaggerate the difficulties and dangers of her future career, and to overlook the more cheering aspects of the case. No doubt there is cause sufficient for painful anxiety; but I firmly believe that there are still stronger grounds for hope and confidence. The new Church will remain united as closely as ever to the Church of England by a spiritual bond, which will not be the less strong, rather all the more so, because it is perfectly free. Subject to this voluntary union, it will enjoy the fullest liberty of self-government. There are, as we all know, not a few among our own brethren who consider this liberty as so desirable, that in their opinion it outweighs all the advantages of an Establishment, which without it are in their eyes but gilded fetters, the price of a degrading bondage. I entirely dissent from this opinion. I have no sympathy with the motives of those who hold it. I believe that the kind of liberty which they desire would be a grinding tyranny, and the worst calamity that could befall the Church. But I do not on that account doubt that the liberty which the unestablished Irish Church will enjoy, subject as it will

Effects of the disestablishment.

be to that condition of union with the Church of England, and regulated, as I trust it will be, by a prudent caution, will be a very great advantage. Henceforward the Church will possess synodical assemblies, constituted, it may be confidently hoped, on a much broader and firmer basis than our own. And these assemblies will meet, not merely for discussion, but for deliberation. They will need no precarious licence, either to enter upon their conferences or to carry their resolutions into effect. They will even lend a new value and importance to the debates of the English Convocations. We shall no longer be saddened by the thought, that so much learning and eloquence, so much laborious research, so many instructive Reports, so many valuable suggestions as are stored in their records, are condemned to lie barren, for want of power to turn them to a practical account. There will be, on the other side of the Channel, a Body able to profit by whatever it may find useful in them.

Capacity of the Irish Church to maintain its ground against Romanism. And most certainly the witness which this Church will continue to bear to the truth will be at least as earnest, as weighty, as powerful as ever. Is there then reason to fear, that it will notwithstanding be so crippled by the failure of material resources, as to be unable to hold its ground against Romanism? That superior organization of the Romish hierarchy, on which so much stress has been laid, as rendering the contest hopelessly unequal, little as it is to be envied by any Christian Church, and fearful as is the price paid for it, may be a very formidable engine, but it is not one with which the Irish Reformed Church will have to cope for the first time; and its own organization most probably will, and certainly may be, better fitted for the contest than it ever was before. Then, when I consider the wealth of its members, and that their liberality will be stimulated by the share they will have in the management of its affairs, and when I remember the munificence lately displayed by one of them in a great work of piety, I think I see reasonable ground of hope, though I am fully aware that the financial prosperity of an unestablished Church depends much more on the contributions of the many than of the few. Again, when I think of the outburst of Protestant zeal which was evoked by the recent measure, it seems to me that I am hardly at liberty to imagine that it will evaporate in clamour and invective, and leave the cause for which it professes such ardent devotion, without substantial support. Least of all do I think it likely that there will be any abatement of the Church's missionary activity, which some years ago was attended with remarkable success, among the Roman Catholics. There appears to be rather more ground for the apprehension which has been expressed, that the proselytizing movement may be carried on with increased energy, but with some lack of discretion. On the whole, the future of the Irish Church is, under Providence, in her own hands. There appears to be nothing in the nature of things to prevent her from enjoying a degree of prosperity, at least as great as in any former period of her history.

Our sympathy with the fortunes of the Irish Church cannot be wholly disinterested, or unaccompanied by grave reflections on the mode in which our own Church may be affected by that which has come to pass. I cannot agree with those who consider it as paving the way for the destruction of our own Establishment, and I am surprised that friends of our Church should have taken pains to show that the event which they anticipate, is a natural and logical sequel of that which they deplore. Candour does not seem to me to require that, in estimating our own position, we should dwell exclusively on the points most favourable to our adversaries, and overlook those which make for our own interests. Those who have been so anxious to show an analogy between the cases of the two Churches seem to have forgotten that if they succeeded in their attempt, the result would be, not in the least to strengthen the security of the Church which they wished to defend, but only to involve the other in its ruin, by supplying its assailants with the most powerful engines for its overthrow. The whole argument proceeds on an erroneous assumption. It supposes that a certain abstract principle, previously laid down, had been applied to the Irish Church, and that this principle, being also in some degree applic-

Its disestablishment viewed in relation to our own Church.

able to the Church of England, would therefore be sure to be applied to it. This supposition is quite unwarranted by the facts of the case, and at variance with the whole tenour of our experience. The truth is, that the peculiar features of the Irish Establishment had presented to the minds of statesmen what, whether rightly or wrongly, was commonly regarded as a monstrous anomaly and a great practical evil. In the reformation of this abuse, the principle of religious equality was called into action in a somewhat rough, unscientific way indeed, and, as I think, in an unhappy form of common destitution. But, as has often been remarked, especially by foreigners, nothing is more alien from the character of the English mind, than a consistent embodying of general principles in political institutions, or in legislation. There is nothing which, as a people, we value less, or rather which we regard with more of positive suspicion and dislike, than that carrying out of a precedent into its logical consequences, on which some other nations pride themselves. We rather glory in the absence of theoretical symmetry, as a sign of the historical growth, and as a cause of the happy working, of our Constitution.

No resemblance between the English and Irish Establishments. It can be only when all the special features of the case are overlooked or ignored, that a comparison between the English and the Irish Establishments can seem to show resemblance, and not an almost complete contrast. And this is true, not only in general, but with regard to that part of the Church in which our own lot has been cast, though it has sometimes been represented as exhibiting a close parallel. To make one, it would be necessary in the first place to create or revive—and only for the purpose of immediately destroying it—an institution entirely unknown to our law, a Church of Wales, having, like that of Ireland, a history distinct from that of the Church of England. It would further be necessary to separate the Principality from England by a physical partition like the Irish Channel, and also to increase its population sevenfold. And the analogy in this respect would still not be complete, unless there existed in the Principality a wide-spread desire for a political severance from England. But above all it would be necessary that there should be an inward spiritual partition, separating one sect of the population from the rest; as in Ireland, above all other countries, Protestants are separated from Roman Catholics. I need hardly remind you, my Reverend Brethren, how wide is the difference between the two cases in this last particular, which is the most important of all. You are aware of the comparatively recent origin of Welsh Nonconformity, that it arose for the most part within the Church itself, through the exertions of clergymen, intended by them not to create a schism, but to infuse new life into the ministrations of the Church, and thus to increase its usefulness and to strengthen its foundations; and at how late a period the separatist congregations which they founded, felt themselves at liberty to receive the Sacrament of Holy Communion from any other hands than those of episcopally ordained ministers. I need not dwell on the painful recollection of the fatal blindness through which the breach was widened and became seemingly irreparable.

Origin of Welsh Nonconformity.

But still, after all, what even now is that breach, compared with that which parts Protestant from Roman Catholic Ireland? It is as a crevice caused by the summer heat, to a chasm opened into the depths of the rocks by an earthquake. It has been urged as an argument, and I believe it to be perfectly true as a fact, that the Irish Protestant clergy enjoy the respect and goodwill of their Roman Catholic neighbours, especially of the poorer class, who willingly avail themselves of their kindness, and entrust them with the management of their temporal concerns. But it is equally certain that, notwithstanding this confidence and esteem, there is not one of those who gladly receive these benefits, who would not deem it a mortal sin to accept the ghostly counsel, and still more to attend the public ministrations, of their legal pastors. I need not say how impossible it would be for a Romish priest to join in the devotions of a Protestant place of worship.

Relation of Protestant to Roman Catholic Ireland.

And of Nonconformists to Churchmen.

How does that correspond with the state of things which we have before our eyes? to the crowds of Nonconformists who flock to our churches when the pulpit is to be filled by a popular preacher? to that which is in the experience of several now present? I have ordained not a few Nonconformist ministers, who, sometimes at a considerable sacrifice of emoluments, sought admission into the ministry of our Church. But in no instance have I found that they regarded themselves as having renounced religious convictions which had before satisfied their own souls, and had been the ground of their teaching. It was not another Gospel which they meant to preach in the new pulpit, or which their new congregation desired to hear. It was just on this account that they felt at liberty, and even bound in conscience, to lay aside a show of dissent which betokened no substantial difference, and to become Churchmen in profession, as they had long been at heart. Let it not be thought that I regard the questions on which those who are called orthodox Nonconformists, are really at variance with us as unimportant. But their importance is of a quite secondary order, and they mostly excite much greater interest in the clergy than in the laity; and whatever their importance may be, it vanishes in comparison not only with those which are at issue between the Churches of England and of Rome, but with those which separate members of the Church of England who regard the Reformation as a blessing, from those who speak of it as "an act of Divine vengeance."*

Tendency of public opinion towards our own Church.
But though I cannot view the disestablishment of the Irish Church in the light of a cause operating to subvert that of our own country, I do think that as a sign of the times, as an indication of the direction in which public opinion is moving, it may well inspire the friends of our Church with uneasy forebodings. The facts which I have stated do indeed in my opinion sufficiently account for the strength of the adverse sentiment to which the Irish Establishment succumbed. But the

* As the Rev. Dr. Littledale, Priest of the Church of England. There is too much reason to fear, that in this view he may not stand alone; but it may be hoped that the amenities which accompanied the expression of this opinion, which, though not new to those who ever heard an Italian Capuchin rail against Luther and Calvin, sounded a little strange in the mouth of an English clergyman and gentleman, are peculiar to the Rev. Dr. Littledale, Priest of the Church of England.

manner in which its abolition was effected, the rejection of every proposal which, however consistent with the principle of religious equality, seemed to preserve a remnant or shadow of Establishment, attest the prevalence of a feeling, which was not confined to the one object assailed, and which will not be content with the victory it has won. It shows that we must not only be prepared for a like assault, but that we must make up our minds to expect an equally rigorous application of the principle which governed the treatment of the Irish Church, to our own. I might point to some other omens of less moment, but not devoid of grave significance, which look the same way. Until very lately it was new to us to see the views of the Liberation Society adopted by clergymen who still minister in our Church. We know indeed for what ends they advocate separation between Church and State; why it is they are impatient of their present position, and desire to exchange it for a congregational independence which will enable them to advance as far as they will toward the goal which they have in view. This may deprive their opinion of all weight with any but those who concur in their aims; but it deserves nevertheless to be taken into account as one of the corrosive and disintegrating elements which threaten the stability of the edifice.

Advocates of disestablishment among the clergy of different schools.

And as a sign of the times it does not stand alone. Voices are heard, proceeding from an entirely different, if not directly opposite school, not indeed calling so loudly for a dissolution of the union between Church and State, but not less clearly showing that it is a contingency to which the speakers look forward, not only without fear, but with complacency and hopefulness. And to these must be added a third and very considerable party of persons, clergy and laymen, who, while professing their desire for the continuance of the Establishment, are constantly expressing, in the strongest language, their vehement dissatisfaction with its present condition; though they hardly affect to believe that, as long as the Union lasts, the changes which they represent as essential to the welfare of the Church, if not to the legitimacy of its title to that name, though by others they are deprecated as fraught with mischief, will ever be brought about.

These things are signs and symptoms; but they are more than that: they tend to produce the effect to which they point. I have no commission to prophesy, nor any desire to speak smooth things. But as far as I can see by such light as has been given me, it does not appear to me that our Church is actually in danger from without, certainly not as the effect of that which has befallen the Irish Church. But I think that she is threatened with very serious danger from within. The safety of her temporal state must, so far as earthly agencies are concerned, depend ultimately on public opinion; and it seems to me beyond a doubt, that what has been going on within our pale, especially during the last ten years, has acted with great force on public opinion, and has tended more and more to turn it against her. And the danger is not confined to the loss of her temporal position. If that was all, though I should think it an evil not likely to be counterbalanced by any advantage which it is reasonable to expect, still I should not contemplate it with despondency. I should be ready to hope that it may be overruled, so as in the end to work for our good. But I cannot look forward with the same equanimity to the ulterior consequences of the event, which present themselves to my mind as inevitable. For it seems to me hardly possible to doubt that the final result would be the disruption of the Church into two or three sects, one of which would probably, sooner or later, be merged in the Church of Rome. There would be diverse Anglican Churches, but no longer a Church of England. Who could pretend to forecast the effects of such a dismemberment on the Colonial Churches, or our foreign missions? It is enough to say that it is the state to which our chief adversary, whom nothing can satisfy but our destruction, most eagerly desires, and is most actively labouring to see us reduced.

A Church may perish through decay of its vital forces, may shrivel up into a mere form, from which the spirit has fled, and for which nothing can be more desirable than that it should be swept away to make room for a living reality. But the spectacle of a Church going to wreck through the opposite cause, through an exuberance of vigour wasted in internal conflicts, is even more painful to contemplate. But as long as it is not a mere possibility, but a real and actually imminent danger, it is right that we should keep it steadily in view, because *Necessity for keeping the danger in view.* it has a most important bearing on practical questions, which are constantly coming before us, and calling for decision. I trust I hardly need say that I do not mean to suggest any unmanly suppression of opinion, still less any compromise of truth. But I think there is a special call upon us, "seriously to lay to heart the great dangers we are in by our unhappy divisions;" not to do any thing which it would not be our duty to do at all times; but to do it under a more solemn sense of personal, individual responsibility; to be more than ever careful that we do not in our several spheres of action needlessly increase those dangers by the manner in which we give effect or expression to our opinions; that we do not set stumbling-blocks in the way of our brethren; that we abstain from all that can only serve to provoke passion and kindle strife; that we take pains to discriminate between things essential and things indifferent, and make sure never to sacrifice peace to any thing less sacred than Divine truth.

The length at which I have been led to dwell on these topics will not, I hope, have appeared disproportioned to their interest and importance. But the remark I have just made, naturally turns our thoughts to the causes of that inward ferment and distraction which has assumed so threatening an aspect. I dealt with this subject so largely in my last Charge, that it will be sufficient for me now to touch briefly on some of *Recent phases of Ritualism.* the recent phases through which it has passed. So much has been said and written of late, which tends to a confusion of ideas on the state of the question, that it may be useful to recall it distinctly to our minds.

It has been observed with much truth, though with little relevancy, that the Ritualistic movement corresponds to a general tendency of the age in which we live, toward a larger application of the Fine Arts to public and private purposes.* It was impossible, it is said, that the effect of this newly-awakened craving for the satisfaction of a more refined and intelligent taste, should not manifest itself in all material objects connected with the public exercise of religion. May it not be considered as a duty virtually implied in the precept, "Let all things be done decently and in order?"† So the condition, outward and inward, of our sacred buildings, and even of our schoolrooms, which satisfied former generations, is in our day felt to be no longer tolerable. Why then, it is asked, should it be thought less natural and fitting that the influence of this feeling should be extended to the public services of the Church? that a craving should arise for a larger amount of ornament in the furniture of the sanctuary and in the vesture of the clergy? And if outward splendour was divinely enjoined in the Temple worship, must it not be at least permitted in that of the Christian Church?‡

<small>Ritualism the application of the Fine Arts to religion.</small>

---

* "A Plain View of Ritualism." By Francis T. Palgrave, late Fellow of Exeter College, Oxford, in "Macmillan's Magazine," September, 1867.

† "Let all Things be Done Decently and in Order:" a Homily by the Rev. J. M. Rodwell, M.A.

‡ "The Law of Ritual." By the late Bishop Hopkins, of Vermont. This work has been warmly greeted by persons with whom, as to the root of the matter, the author certainly felt any thing rather than sympathy, and who, on that very account, have actively circulated the book, as if it had been the admission of a reluctant witness in favour of their views. The Bishop's position is, that the Ceremonial Law was not abrogated, but continues in force, except as to the Gentiles, and as to the Jews in points—such as the limitation of the priesthood and animal sacrifices—in which it would have been inconsistent with the Christian Revelation. He grounds this opinion partly on the absence of a formal express abrogation, partly on the fact that the Apostles taught daily in the Temple, and used the synagogues for the like purpose; but mainly on the two concessions made by St. Paul to Jewish feelings, in the circumcising of Timothy (Acts xvi. 3), and in his own association with the persons under a vow (Acts xxi. 26). As to the last, it may be observed that it was a voluntary act, not involving any doctrinal principle. As to the former, the narrative itself shows that St. Paul did not take the step because it was prescribed in the Law, but "because of the Jews." If a clergyman who had made a disciple of a Quaker, was to baptize him, *because of his brother clergy or of parishioners*, he could not believe Baptism to be a Sacrament of Christ. But it must also be remembered that though we may hardly possess sufficient data for judging St. Paul's conduct, we have no surer guarantee of his infallibility in a matter of discipline than he himself had of St. Peter's (Gal. ii. 11). By this process Bishop Hopkins is led to a somewhat startling conclusion. "If," he says, p. 30, "in the Providence of God, a Church should again arise, consisting of converted Jews, or if individual Jews should be added from time to time, as members of a

The justice of these remarks is unquestionable, as long as they are confined to the abstract, and kept clear of all direct bearing on the practical question. We thankfully rejoice in the happy change which has renovated the face of the Church with goodly buildings, and has in many respects brought the mode of conducting Divine Service to a closer observance of the Apostolic precept. No greater injury can be done to the cause of Protestant truth, than to represent it as inconsistent with either cheerfulness or solemnity in public worship, and as compelling those who desire to worship in the beauty of holiness, to seek it elsewhere than in the Church of England. We may go farther, and concede that the gorgeousness of the Temple worship is not in itself absolutely unlawful, or excluded by any Divine command from the Christian sanctuary, however questionable may be the propriety of introducing it with regard to the use of edifying; though we cannot admit that the pattern of the Temple ought to regulate the worship of the Church. The idea of such an imitation arose after the love of the Church had begun to wax cold, and it was more and more developed as the primitive purity of faith and practice declined. But it is idle to discuss these points when the real question is, Whether our Communion Office is to be transformed into the closest possible resemblance to the Romish Mass? We shall not find our way the more easily to any conclusion on that question, by means of

How far the craving for church ornament is beneficial.

The real question.

Church which belongs to Gentiles, I do not see by what warrant we could forbid those Jews to imitate the course of the Apostles, or count it an error in them to circumcise their children, and 'walk orderly, and keep the Law.'" Circumcision would not indeed, in those cases, be more generally necessary to salvation than Baptism; but, according to this theory, it would be no less so; and a clergyman who admitted a Jewish convert into the Church, would not only have no right to "count it an error in him to circumcise his children," but be bound to exhort him to do so. As the excellent author himself is no longer able to develop his theory into the necessary practical details, it remains for the admirers of his work to solve a number of curious questions as to the two ordinances, when cumulative; as whether the elder is equally a means of grace with the other, and consequently confers a benefit of which the children of Gentiles are deprived; and, then, why they should be deprived of it? One corollary of this theory is, that the whole Christian world has, from the beginning, been guilty of a gross breach of the Divine Law in omitting the observance of the seventh day, which was never expressly abrogated. There is nothing else in the Bishop's work sufficiently new or important to call for notice.

any general statements either on the employment of the Fine Arts for religious purposes, or on the propriety of grafting the Jewish ritual on the New Dispensation. The most strenuous advocates of the movement themselves indignantly repudiate the supposition, that their object is simply to make the service more attractive. In their eyes the whole value of ceremonial consists in its significance as a visible symbol of doctrine;* and the question is as to the right of individual clergymen to introduce innovations of such a character. This right was claimed on the ground of the language of the Church in the Rubrics of the Prayer Book. But this language was so far from clear, that lawyers of the highest eminence took opposite views of its meaning.

Still there can be no doubt that every clergyman, however wanting in familiarity with legal reasoning, however destitute of learning, and of all qualifications that could give the slightest weight to his opinion, is at full liberty to form one for himself, and to hold it with the firmest conviction. But if, not content with this, he attempts to impose his private judgment upon the Church, and makes his public ministrations a vehicle for publishing them in her name, and as with her authority, he is abusing the privilege of his position, and usurping a licence irreconcilable with law and order. And the door thus thrown open for the wildest play of individual caprice, is indefinitely widened when each clergyman takes upon him to interpret the Rubric according to his private idea of something which he calls Catholic usage. And from this we may see the futility of the plea which is often urged in defence of these proceedings, that they are at least more harmless than unsound doctrine, which clergymen sometimes utter with impunity through the press and the pulpit. This would be something to the point, if those clergymen altered the language of the Prayer Book, to make it express their opinions. That is an abuse of which I have

The right of forming an individual opinion on the Rubrics.

---

* See the evidence of Mr. Bennett before the Ritual Commission: "2606. Is any doctrine involved in your using the chasuble? I think there is.—2607. What is that doctrine? The doctrine of the sacrifice.—2608. Do you consider yourself a sacrificing priest? Distinctly so.—2611. Then you think you offer a propitiatory sacrifice? Yes, I think I do offer a propitiatory sacrifice.

not yet heard; but for which, if it occurred, a legal remedy is provided.

It seems clear that a law so ambiguous and obscure as to lend itself to the most widely divergent interpretations, cannot serve the purpose of a rule to guide any one's conduct. Practically, it is no more a law than if it were written in an unknown tongue. One who professes to be governed by it, in the sense which he chooses to adopt, is really making a law for himself; and when he does so in contravention of the general long-received usage of the Church, he is sacrificing peace and charity to a selfish spirit and a lawless will. Even a judicial decision can never impart more than a temporary and insecure authority to any one of the conflicting interpretations. It can only indicate that, to the mind of the Court, the weight of argument appeared to turn the scale on this side. It is no doubt binding in practice, as long as it remains unreversed, on all alike, whether they assent to it or not. But it can have no greater intrinsic value than that of the arguments on which it rests. Yet the Rubric commonly called the Ornaments Rubric— on which so many volumes have been written, proving nothing more clearly than the hopelessness of arriving at any satisfactory conclusion on its legal force—has been taken as the groundwork of the Ritualistic practices, with a confidence as strong as if it left no room for the slightest doubt. It appeared to some—and among others to our late lamented Primate*—that this was a case for which provision had been made in the Preface of the Prayer Book, where it is directed that, " for the resolution of all doubts concerning the manner how to understand, do, and execute the things contained in this Book, the parties that so doubt or diversely take any thing, shall alway resort to the Bishop of the Diocese, who by his discretion shall take order for the quieting and appeasing of the same, so that the same order be not contrary to any thing contained in this Book." It has, however, been ruled by the highest authority, the Supreme Court of Appeal, that the Bishop can have no jurisdiction to modify or

_{An ambiguous law practically useless.}

_{Ornaments Rubric the groundwork of Ritualistic practices.}

---

* In his posthumous Charge, p. 16.

dispense with any thing expressly ordered or prohibited in a Rubric; and it appears to be now well understood, that the direction in the Preface applies only to cases where, through the absence of such express order or prohibition, latitude is given for diversity of opinion, and for the exercise of discretion; but that it was not intended to give the Bishop jurisdiction in his domestic forum, to decide whether a thing is ordered or prohibited by a Rubric. But if this is beyond the power of a Bishop, can it be within the discretion of a Presbyter? Can he be allowed to plead the steadfastness of his reliance on his own private judgment, as a proof that no "doubt has arisen" in the matter? The direction in the Preface does not empower the Bishop to solve the legal doubt. But the spirit of the direction, taken as a rule of charity, of humility, of modesty, seems eminently applicable to this case. It is hard to conceive one in which it would more become a clergyman to consult his Bishop, before he took a step which, whether legally justifiable or not, was so sure to give offence to many, and to open a fresh breach in the Church; and this is equally true whether the matter in dispute be accounted of great or of little importance. To most persons this whole question of vestments appears to be in itself something exceedingly small and petty. And one of the leading Ritualists admits, that " in trivial and immaterial things it would be natural to follow the Bishop's advice." But in his eyes the vestments are "important things," and therefore as to them " the Bishop has no authority." They are too important to be submitted to the judgment of the Bishop, but not too important to be determined by that of any clergyman in his diocese, and that not even professedly according to the directions of the Prayer Book, but according to the " rules of the Catholic Church," of which he claims to be a fully competent interpreter.*

Marginal note: Bishops have no power to modify or dispense with any thing in a Rubric.

It was generally felt that the peace and the honour of the Church required that an end should be put to this state of confusion and anarchy; and a Royal Commission was appointed with that

---

* See Mr. Bennett's examination before the Ritual Commission, p. 83, 3024. 3030. 3031. 3033.

view. But, in the meanwhile, proceedings were instituted to try the legality of the recent practices; and the result has been that, on every point hitherto contested in the Ecclesiastical Courts—points, it must be remembered, on which the innovators assumed the law to be so clearly on their side, as not even to admit of any doubt or diversity of opinion—on every one of these points their departure from the long-received usage, has, by the Supreme Court of Appeal, been pronounced illegal. *Appointment of a Royal Commission on Ritualism.*

The questions mooted were the elevation of the paten and cup during the Prayer of Consecration, kneeling and prostration before the consecrated elements, the lighting of candles on the Communion Table during the celebration, the using of incense, and the mixing of water with the wine used in the administration of the Holy Communion. There was no doubt as to the antiquity of all these ceremonies, nor that some were things indifferent, and not at variance with any principle of the Reformed Church. And in favour of the use of lights it was urged—and successfully before the learned Judge of the Court of Arches—that they symbolized Christ as the light of the World.* It seems to have been overlooked that, when placed on the Communion Table during the celebration of the Holy Communion, though not on the pulpit at the Sermon, they must be supposed to have some more peculiar significance, and that this could be no other than that to which the Incense, the Elevation, the Kneeling and Prostration also pointed. But the ground on which they were condemned was not their significance, but simply that they had not been adopted by the Church of England. And after having laid down the broad principle of their decision, the Court makes a remark which seems to me pregnant with larger conclusions:— *Questions mooted in the legal proceedings.*

"Their Lordships have not referred to the usage as to lights during the last 300 years; but they are of opinion that the very general disuse of lights after the Reformation *Opinion of the Court upon lights.*

---

* Mr. Rodwell, in the above-cited Homily, p. 16, gives a different interpretation, founded on the number of the lights, and treats it as a well-known fact: "Of course, you know that the candles lighted on the altar signify the light of faith revealed to Jews and Gentiles—the two natures of Christ, the Divine and human, united in His sacred person." Why not the two sacraments?

(whatever exceptional cases to the contrary might be produced) contrasted with their normal and prescribed use previously, affords a very strong contemporaneous and continuous exposition of the law upon the subject."

<small>Construction of the Rubric before the Prayer of Consecration.</small>

I need hardly point out the bearing of this remark on the question of the Vestments. But I must observe that there is a passage in the Judgment which has been diversely interpreted, and which threatens to disturb that uniformity of practice which it was its general object to promote. Speaking of the Rubric before the Prayer of Consecration, the Committee say, "Their Lordships entertain no doubt on the construction of this Rubric, that the priest is intended to continue in one posture during the prayer, and not to change from standing to kneeling, or *vice versâ;* and it appears to them equally certain that the priest is intended to stand, and not to kneel. They think that the words 'standing before the Table' apply to the whole sentence; and they think that this is made more apparent by the consideration that acts are to be done by the priest before the people as the prayer proceeds (such as the taking the paten and chalice into his hands, breaking the bread, and laying his hands on the various vessels) which could only be done in the attitude of standing." This has been construed as ruling that the priest is to remain standing in front of the Table throughout the Prayer of Consecration. But it must be observed that the Court was not called upon to decide any question as to the position of the minister, but only as to his posture; and that the context seems clearly to show that it was this alone they had in view. The whole relates to the alternative of standing or kneeling; and the reason assigned for the attitude of standing applies equally, if not with greater force, in favour of the usual position. I think, therefore, that a clergyman would be ill-advised who, until this question shall have been judicially decided, should turn his back to the people during the Prayer of Consecration. No doubt, if it was clear that this was the meaning of the Judgment, it ought to be obeyed. But I think that the best way of so doing would be for the minister to stand before the table with his face to the congregation, which I believe to have been the primitive usage, as well as the only one which fully carries out the direction of breaking bread *before the people.*

It was to be expected that a judgment which not only forbade practices to which the Ritualists were strongly attached, but convicted them of rash presumption in acting with such confidence on a private opinion which turned out to be erroneous, should provoke loud complaints and be vehemently assailed. I may be allowed to believe that, in a question of law, the learned persons who delivered that judgment under such grave responsibility were, at least, as competent to form a sound opinion as any of the theologians by whom it has been impugned. Still every one is, of course, at liberty to think as he will for himself, and to believe that he is in possession of the truth which had eluded their investigation. But it could hardly have been expected that clergymen should have been found to set the judgment at defiance, and to persist in the practices which it has unequivocally condemned. Some however, it seems, have done so in professed obedience to a higher law of the Catholic Church, which overrules the decisions of every secular tribunal. And it must be observed that when they appeal to that higher law, what they really mean is nothing more than their own interpretation of it. In other words, it is their own private judgment which they set up as the Supreme Court of Appeal and measure of truth. *The Judgment distasteful to the Ritualists.*

The Vestment question still awaits a judicial decision, which may or may not be conformable to the general principle laid down in the passage I have cited from the Judgment of the Judicial Committee. In the meanwhile the discussion it has undergone has, I think, placed it in so clear a light as to leave no room for doubt in any impartial mind on the most important practical points. That the Church, which has the right to restore purity of doctrine, has full authority to regulate the official dress of her ministers, can hardly be denied, except by those who would exalt the outward above the inward. But it is our happiness also to know that the almost universal feeling which discarded the gaudy pre-Reformation vestments, and retained the *Further proceedings on the Vestment question.*

surplice as the most fitting garb for the celebration of the Lord's Supper, as well as of every other part of Divine service, is in perfect accordance with that of primitive Christianity, which subsisted until the Church, through the sinister influence of Rome, began to be corrupted and disfigured by an imitation of the Temple worship.

<small>Vestments of the Primitive Church.</small> In the earlier ages a Christian who read in the Apocalypse the description of the woman "arrayed in purple and scarlet colour, and decked with gold, and precious stones, and pearls," could not recognize an image of the Church of Christ: he could only view her apparel as proper to the "mother of abominations."* It was not through poverty that the Church abstained from such ornaments. We have the fullest evidence that vestments of brilliant colours were regarded by Christians as heathenish, unmanly, and meretricious, fit only for the stage, or for the rites of Pagan superstition, in which they were worn by the sacrificing priests. On the other hand, white raiment satisfied all their wants of appropriate symbolism, and appeared to them most truly beautiful. The thing which would probably have amazed them most of all would have been to hear that the ornaments which in their minds were associated with all that was most profane, effeminate, and impure, were the best fitted for the celebration of their holiest mysteries. Yet these ornaments are often described as essential parts of "Catholic" Ritual, as if during the first four centuries the Church was not Catholic. Their absence is said to make our worship cold, bare, and naked. Let us console ourselves with the reflection that, if it is less fervent than that of the Church of the Martyrs, it is not because either our sacred buildings, or the persons of our ministers, are less richly adorned; and that the outward splendour was never in any age a help toward reviving declining fervour of devotion, but only a very poor substitute for it. We may also infer with great confidence from all we know, that the need or propriety of a peculiar vestment for solemnizing the Lord's Supper—which is now insisted on almost as an axiom—never

* Rev. xvii. 4, 5.

entered the minds of those early Christians; though, if it had, the vestments adopted by the Ritualists after the Romish fashion, are the last they would have chosen for the purpose. If these are expressive of any doctrine, it must be one which either was not held by the early Church, and therefore is not Catholic, or which the Church did not think it right so to express.*

The doctrine which is now propounded under the name of the Real Objective Presence is, as I believe, no less foreign to the faith of the primitive Church than the modern symbolism to its practice. In the sense—if it may be so called—attached to it by its leading advocates, it appears to me to have no warrant either in Scripture or in genuine ancient tradition. Nevertheless, I think it much to be lamented that any statement of this doctrine, purporting to be in accordance with the mind of the Church of England, should be made the subject of penal prosecution. It still appears to me—as I expressed myself on a similar occasion in my Charge of 1857—that, "to sustain a charge of unsound doctrine, involving penal consequences, nothing ought to suffice but the most direct unequivocal statements, asserting that which the Church denies, or denying that which she asserts." Since I last addressed you, the question has been publicly raised by a Memorial on the Doctrine of the Eucharist, which was presented to our late Primate. It was signed by twenty-one clergymen, all more or less distinguished members of the Ritualistic party, though not all adopting the Ritualistic practices, and including one eminently learned theologian. But its importance does not depend upon these signatures; for it is clearly to be considered as the manifesto of a great party in the Church; and, viewing it in that light, I think I am hardly at liberty to pass it over in silence.

The real Objective Presence.

Memorial on the Doctrine of the Eucharist.

It divides itself into three heads: the Doctrine of the Real Objective Presence, of the Eucharistic Sacrifice, and of the Adoration of Christ in the Blessed Sacrament; and under each, states first the opinion which the memorialists repudiate, and then the doctrine which they hold. Under the first head they repudiate

* See Marriott, " Vestiarium Christianum," chaps. iii. iv.

the opinion of a "Corporal Presence of Christ's natural Flesh and Blood;" that is to say, of the Presence of His Body and Blood as They "are in heaven;" and the conception of the Mode of His Presence, which implies the physical change of the natural substances of the Bread and Wine, commonly called "Transubstantiation." They believe that in the Holy Eucharist, by virtue of the Consecration, through the power of the Holy Ghost, the Body and Blood of our Saviour Christ, "the inward part or Thing signified," are Present, really and truly, but spiritually and ineffably, under "the outward visible part or sign," or "form of Bread and Wine."

<small>Its language as to the Corporal Presence.</small>

It must be observed that, although at the outset one of the Doctrines to be maintained is described as that of the Real Objective Presence, the word *objective* does not appear in any of the subsequent statements; so that it would seem as if—in the opinion of those who framed the document—it would have added nothing to that which is signified by the adverbs *really* and *truly*. But we are thus led to ask, whether these terms themselves add any thing to that which is signified by the word *present?* For whatever is present any where at all, must be really and truly present. But the sense which would most readily suggest itself, when these words are used with reference to the Presence of the Body and Blood of Christ, is that they are present as they really and truly are, that is, as real Flesh and Blood. But as this sense is expressly repudiated, unless they are merely superfluous adjuncts, they must have some other meaning which is not explained in the context, and is not very easy to find. There are two senses in which we may speak intelligibly of the presence of a material object: the one literal, the other figurative. Literally, a body is present in the space which it fills; figuratively, it may be present as a thought to the mind. And in this last sense it might be properly said to be *spiritually* present to the thinking subject. But that could not be the meaning of those who describe that which they speak of as an Objective Presence. They seem to have used the word "spiritually" as opposed to *corporally* or *physically*. We are therefore left to search for some

<small>Exclusion of the word "objective."</small>

kind of Presence which is neither literal nor figurative. But in what region of nature or of thought is such a Presence to be found? If our absolute incapacity to conceive it is not a proof that it has no existence, at least it makes it impossible to frame any proposition concerning it, of which we could say that it is either true or false. The only term really appropriate by which it is described in the Memorial, is *ineffable*. And thus it turns out that the statement which purports to be positive, is, in fact, merely negative. It denies that the Presence is one of which any thing can be predicated. The addition of the words, under "the outward visible part or sign," or "form of Bread and Wine," as it only expresses what is literally present, can throw no light on a Presence of a totally different kind. This negative truth may be of no great value, but it is at least inoffensive. It might even afford a basis of general agreement, if it had not been so worded as to hold out the appearance of an affirmation which, on closer inspection, proves fallacious. The Objective character of the Presence was probably supposed to be marked by the description given of it, as affected by virtue of the Consecration, through the power of the Holy Ghost. But if the change wrought in the elements by Consecration was purely relative, and if we hold with Hooker that "the Real Presence of Christ's most blessed Body and Blood is not to be sought for in the Sacrament, but in the worthy receiver of the Sacrament," still the Presence would not be the less Objective. It would not be the work of the receiver, but would be brought about "through the power of the Holy Ghost," imparting to believing souls the benefits signified by the communion of Christ's Body and Blood.

Its statement on the Presence not positive, but negative.

The next thing repudiated is the notion of any fresh sacrifice, or any view of the Eucharistic sacrificial offering, as of something apart from the One All-sufficient Sacrifice and Oblation on the Cross, which alone is that perfect Redemption, Propitiation, and Satisfaction for all the sins of the whole world, both original and actual, and which alone is "meritorious." To this is opposed the belief that, "as in heaven Christ our great High Priest ever offers Himself before the

Repudiation of innovations on the Eucharistic Sacrifice.

Eternal Father, pleading by His Presence His sacrifice of Himself once offered on the Cross, so on earth in the Holy Eucharist, that same Body, once for all sacrificed for us, and that same Blood once for all shed for us, Sacramentally present, are offered and pleaded before the Father by the Priest, as our Lord ordained to be done in remembrance of Himself, when He instituted the Blessed Sacrament of His Body and Blood."

<small>Differences in the mode of celebrating the Eucharist ignored.</small> In this last statement there is a remarkable omission, doubtless not unintentional, and a little perplexing. While it speaks of the Holy Eucharist, it takes no notice of any difference between one mode of celebrating the Eucharist and another. The whole description is perfectly applicable to the Roman Mass. But it seems rather too much to assume that whatever is true of the Mass, also holds with respect to our "Order of the Administration of the Lord's Supper, or Holy Communion." Yet the motive assigned for publishing the Memorial was the desire to repel imputations of disloyalty to the Church of England, which are said to be current, to the discredit of those who inculcate and defend the doctrines set forth in it. For this purpose an expression of belief in the doctrine of the Mass would seem, to say the least, irrelevant, and some farther definition of the Eucharist, as administered in the Liturgy of the Church of England, almost indispensable. We must at least assume that our Liturgy was not meant to be excluded from the scope of the statement, and it is with this alone that we, as ministers or members of the Church of England, have any concern.

<small>Comparison between the Mass and the Communion Service.</small> The comparison itself seems to lie open to the objection, that it inverts the rule dictated by common sense, and instead of illustrating that which is obscure by that which is clear, affects to illustrate that which is clear by that which is most profoundly and impenetrably obscure. The nature of the heavenly intercession is a mystery transcending all our powers of thought and imagination, and which human speech is utterly incompetent to express. How then can it shed any light, if that were needed, on the work of the priest in the celebration of the Eucharist? And if it was intended as an

argument to the effect that, because Christ offers Himself in heaven, therefore it is the object of the Eucharist to make the same offering on earth, the argument would be as illogical as the comparison is misapplied. But when, waiving this objection, we proceed to test the justice of the comparison by reference to our Eucharist, as administered in our own Communion Office, we find that there is not a word to suggest it to any mind not previously imbued with the opinion, and which did not import it into the words against their plain and natural meaning. It is not to any transaction which is taking place in the heavenly sanctuary that the Church turns our thoughts in the Prayer of Consecration, but to that which took place in the guest-chamber at Jerusalem at the institution of the Lord's Supper. By what interpretation she is made to speak a different language, we shall see presently.

But the faultiness of a comparison need not affect the truth of the proposition which it is designed to illustrate or confirm. If in this case there had been no comparison, it would have been equally true, or equally false, that "on earth in the Holy Eucharist that same Body once for all sacrificed for us, and that same Blood once for all shed for us, Sacramentally Present, are offered and pleaded before the Father by the priest." Is then this statement true or false? or rather, Is it, or is it not, consistent with the doctrine of our Church? I can only say that when I analyze the statement, and examine the several propositions involved in it, I can find none that any Churchman, however he might prefer to express himself in different terms, is bound to reject. None, I think, would deny that the Sacrifice pleaded by the Church, as well in her Communion Office as whenever she prays through, or in the name, or for the sake of Jesus Christ, is the Sacrifice of the same Body which suffered on the Cross. And as to the Presence, the expression "sacramentally present" appears to be most happily adapted to comprehend every possible shade of opinion, as some kind of Presence is admitted by all, and none question that it is one according, and not contrary, to the nature of a Sacrament. An

Are the statements respecting the Eucharist consistent with the doctrine of our Church

agreement depending on the ambiguity of language cannot indeed be perfectly satisfactory; but it may be the best that the nature of the question permits.

As the statement begins with a comparison which was not essential, so it ends with a remark which may be separated from it without altering its character. It is, "as our Lord ordained, to be done in remembrance of Himself, when He instituted the Blessed Sacrament of his Body and Blood." That what Words of Institution. is done in our Order of the Administration of the Lord's Supper is done according to His holy institution, is of course the belief of our whole Church: so that to a person not conversant with the controversies of the day, the remark might have seemed superfluous. But, in fact, it is so far from expressing any thing on which all are agreed, that I believe the opinion to which it alludes is that of a very small minority. It is that the words of Institution, recorded by St. Luke, and recited in our Prayer of Consecration, have been mistranslated and generally misunderstood; that the Greek word rendered *do* properly means *sacrifice*, and that the word rendered *remembrance* also signifies a sacrificial *memorial*.* I believe this to be altogether a mistake, and that the argument as to the word rendered *do* moves in a vicious circle, and assumes the thing to be proved. It is true that the Greek verb in the Septuagint often has the sense of *sacrifice* or *offer*; but only when the noun which it governs signifies that which is a *victim* or *offering*, and thus determines the sense of the verb. But in the words of Institution, that which we render *this* has no such sense, except on the hypothesis which is to be demonstrated. Equally arbitrary is the sense attached to the word *remembrance* as implying sacrifice; which must always depend on the context. The view which our Church takes of this point, seems sufficiently evident from the words which she uses in the delivery of the consecrated elements. She nowhere indicates any other. But I need hardly say that no clergyman is bound to acknowledge the correctness of the authorized version of Scripture, even in passages where important doctrines are supposed to depend upon it.

* See the late Bishop Hamilton's Charge of 1867, p. 52.

Under the third head, in the statement of that which is repudiated, the Memorial follows the Declaration on Kneeling at the end of the Communion Office. "We repudiate," say the signers, "all 'adoration' of 'the Sacramental Bread and Wine,' which would be 'idolatry;' regarding them with the reverence due to them because of their sacramental relation to the Body and Blood of our Lord. We repudiate also all adoration of 'a corporal Presence of Christ's natural Flesh and Blood,' that is to say, of the Presence of His Body and Blood as they are in heaven." The doctrine asserted is thus expressed: "We believe that Christ Himself, really and truly, but spiritually and ineffably, present in the Sacrament, is therein to be adored." *[margin: Adoration of the Sacramental Bread and Wine.]*

Here are two points: the Presence of Christ in the Sacrament, and the adoration due to it. Enough has been said already as to the effect of the words *really, truly, spiritually,* and *ineffably,* in explaining or qualifying the nature of the Presence. Perhaps it would have been better if the writer had substituted for them the single word *sacramentally,* which covers every thing; not indeed conveying any distinct thought to the mind, but leaving unbounded room for every devout feeling of the heart. But a difficulty arises with regard to the description of the Presence, as "*in* the Sacrament," and "*therein* to be adored." Taken in their common sense, these expressions would suggest the idea of a Presence circumscribed by the dimensions of the visible elements, and thus would seem to assert what is most offensive in the Roman view of the Sacrament. But from other statements, proceeding partly from the same quarter, and which must be regarded as equally authentic expositions of the doctrine, it seems that we are not to consider the words *in* and *therein* as signifying a *local* inwardness, which is indignantly repudiated as equivalent to a material or natural Presence.* On the *[margin: Difficulties involved in the terms of repudiation.]*

---

* See "The Real Presence: the Worship due." Correspondence between the Archdeacon of Taunton and the Archdeacon of Exeter.

Archdeacon Denison (p. 14) says, "I contend for the Real Presence of the Body and the Blood of Christ in the Holy Eucharist: for the Real Presence, not for the local presence." I share Archdeacon Freeman's perplexity about his correspondent's meaning, and am sorry that Archdeacon Denison insisted on his right of withholding any further explanation, though he may have had good reason for despairing of other hand I find expressions which I can only understand as implying that the inwardness *is* local; for what else can be meant when it is said, "The true oblation in the Eucharist is not the Bread and Wine—that is only as the vessel which contains, or the garment which veils it;"* local therefore, but yet not after the manner in which a body fills space; not material nor natural, but incorporeal and supernatural? Still such an inwardness may not the less properly be termed local, because divested of all the grossness of a material presence. The comparison of the *vessel* and the *garment* is equally familiar to us when applied to the body as the receptacle or clothing of the soul. And I doubt much that any one who is offended by the expression would be reconciled to it by this explanation. On the whole, we cannot lay too much stress on the qualification *ineffably*, as extending to the locality, and taking it altogether out of the reach of language and thought.

<small>Local Presence.</small>

Then there remains only the question of adoration, disentangled from that of local or extra-local inwardness, on which there is nothing to be said. And this question at once reduces itself to the single point, whether there is any real and substantial difference between that which is here said to be due to Christ, and that which is claimed for Him by the Church in the Declaration on Kneeling. The Kneeling of the Communicants, when they receive the Lord's Supper, which is ordained by our Office, is there explained and defended as "a signification of our humble and grateful acknowledgment of the benefits of Christ therein given to all worthy Receivers." But this acknowledg-

<small>Declaration on Kneeling</small>

---

making himself intelligible. He complains (p. 3) of having been charged with holding the tenet, that one purpose of the Holy Eucharist is to *provide the Church with an object of Divine Worship actually enshrined in the elements, namely, our Lord Jesus Christ*. Of course he is not answerable for the language or the doctrine of Mr. Keble. But still, it is puzzling to find such an apparent contradiction between two such eminent doctors of the same school, that, while the one does not scruple to speak of the Bread and Wine as "the vessel which contains, or the garment which *veils*, the true oblation in the Eucharist," the other rejects the expression, "enshrined in the elements," as a calumnious imputation. Bishop Hamilton also (Charge, p. 50) says of the Bread and Wine, that "by consecration it has been made the *veil* and channel of an ineffable mystery."

* Keble, "Eucharistic Adoration," p. 70.

ment must be made to the Divine Author of these benefits, and then how can we distinguish such humble and grateful acknowledgment from adoration? Who among us would not be willing to adopt the language of Keble?* "Religious adoration is of the heart, and not of the lips only; it is practised in praise and thanksgiving, as well as in prayer; we adore as often as we approach God in any act of Divine faith, hope, or love, with or without any verbal or bodily expression." I cannot indeed agree with that excellent person in his opinion, that there is a little uncertainty as to the meaning of the Declaration, when it speaks of the benefits of Christ therein given to all worthy Receivers.† I conceive that the use of the plural, *benefits*, precludes the construction that not they, but Christ Himself, is said to be given. But it is not the less true that the result of a worthy reception is described in our Office itself to be, that "then we dwell in Christ, and Christ in us." Surely *adoration* is not too strong a word to express the feeling suited to such an occasion. And but for the unhappy dispute about the Real Presence, it would probably never have appeared so to any one.

I am conscious, my Reverend Brethren, that I may seem to owe you an apology for having detained you so long with a discussion which to many of you may have appeared to turn on subtle and unprofitable points of metaphysical theology. But there are others who speak of this Real Presence as a "great fundamental matter," and a "vital doctrine of the Gospel."‡ Such an estimate of its importance will no doubt seem strangely exaggerated to those who have been used to take a different view of the foundation truths of Christianity, and who have sought in vain for any allusion to this doctrine in Holy Writ. But every one knows best what belief is vital to himself, that is, necessary for the support of his own spiritual life. And this is a subject in which, above all others, I should wish the largest room to be left for private feeling and speculation. If any one, having been assured by the Church that the consecrated Bread

Importance attached to the doctrine of the Real Presence.

---

* Keble. "Eucharistic Adoration," p. 117. † Ibid. p. 129.
‡ Ibid. pp. 96, 128, 161.

and Wine become in a certain sense the Body and Blood of Christ, finds comfort and edification in the thought, that along with the Sacramental Body and Blood, he in a certain sense receives the whole Person of Christ, God and man, I think he has full right to such edification and comfort. It is a region of mystical contemplation and feeling, an inner chamber of the heart, into which no stranger may intrude. I go farther. If he cannot resist the temptation of speculating on this subject; if he tries to conceive and to reason upon the mode of this Presence, I should think that he was acting unwisely, that he was overstepping the legitimate bounds of human thought, indulging a vain and hardly reverent curiosity; but I could not deny that he was exercising an unquestionable right, qualified only by his moral responsibility. If he should argue in this way: inasmuch as the natural Body and Blood are inseparable from the whole Divine Person of Christ, so that wherever they are that is, therefore the same holds with regard to the Sacramental Body and Blood, so that it also, by virtue of the Hypostatic Union, is Christ himself;*—this to me appears a sad abuse of words, a playing with the forms of reasoning by the arbitrary substitution of a totally different sense in the terms of the same proposition. Nor to my view does this doctrine in the least exalt the dignity, or enhance the value of the Sacrament as a means of grace, but, on the contrary, tends to degrade it into the semblance of a magical rite, and to divert the attention of the communicant from the main ends of Holy Communion, to bewildering and unprofitable questions.

But I do not pretend to set up my judgment or feeling as a standard to which others are bound to conform. If they believe that they see a logical connexion which is entirely hidden from me, I may wish that they should explain it, and may think that, if that is impossible, it would have been better that they should have kept it to themselves. But I have no right—unless perhaps in the name of charity—to call for such expla-

<small>Liberty of thought and speech.</small>

---

* Such is Bishop Hamilton's statement, Charge, p. 50: "The inward part of the Sacrament of the Lord's Supper is Christ's precious Body and Blood, and so, by virtue of the Hypostatic Union, Christ Himself."

nation; and probably no two among those who hold the opinion would agree in giving account of it. But while I would earnestly maintain their liberty of thought and speech on this point, I would most strenuously resist every attempt to impose their private sentiment or speculation on the Church, as her doctrine. I could not consent to make our Church answerable for a dogma, differing from Transubstantiation by a hardly perceptible shade of meaning or phraseology,* and equally committing those who hold it to the belief that, in the institution of the Supper, that which our Lord held in His hand and gave to His disciples, was nothing less than His own Person, Body, Soul, and Godhead. There was a time when to show of any proposition that it involved such a consequence, would among us have been accounted a sufficient *reductio ad absurdum*. Now I am afraid a spirit is abroad, to which there can be no greater recommendation of any doctrine than that it shocks the common sense of mankind. This creates a strong prepossession in its favour, and affords an opportunity, which is eagerly seized, of eliciting the power of language to conceal the absence of thought, from the speaker or writer, no less than from the hearer or reader. It may be said that this doctrine of the Real Presence is not more inscrutable than many mysteries of our faith, or indeed many things which are not mysteries of faith. But it must be remembered that in the present case the objection to the alleged mystery is, not that it is inscrutable, but that it is factitious, a creature of human speculation, the

marginalia: The Church not answerable for private sentiment or speculation.

marginalia: Doctrine repulsive to common sense readily received.

---

* It is however high time for every one to ask himself what he means by Transubstantiation. According to the view maintained with great ability by Mr. Cobb, in the "Kiss of Peace," and "Sequel," "the common notions of Roman doctrine" on this head are "utterly false," though not confined to the vulgar, but shared by "many in positions of authority and influence, Archbishops and Bishops, Deans and Archdeacons," who, "sad to think," "now, when at last our Church is beginning to teach her members the doctrine of the Real Objective Presence" (I suppose through divines of the school to which Mr. Cobb belongs, though I did not know that they already constitute the Church), are "hindering the advance of truth," by a "cruel" and "unjust" misrepresentation of the teaching of the Church of Rome, which, as Mr. Cobb contends, is on this Article absolutely identical with that of the Church of England. I believe that it is Mr. Cobb himself who is under a mistake with regard to the doctrine of Transubstantiation taught by the Church of Rome, and I shall endeavour to show this in a note, which I must reserve for the Appendix.

product of an arbitrary and fanciful exegesis, disguised by an accumulation of unmeaning or mutually contradictory terms. To accept such a doctrine, is not humility, but self-will.

Nature of inquiries of the Royal Commission on Ritual. Although the occasion for the appointment of the Royal Commission on Ritual, arose out of a few questions connected with the administration of the Holy Communion, which created an extraordinary agitation in the Church, and possibly, but for that temporary excitement, or if the judicial decision on the greater part of those questions had been previously given, the Commission might not have been deemed necessary, the range of inquiry assigned to it comprehended a very much larger field, including the whole of the Rubrics and the Lectionary. Few, I believe, who have applied any serious attention to the subject, and know how many important and difficult questions it involves, in matters which have been the subject of long and earnest controversy, will be surprised that the labours of the Commission, though now in the third year of its sittings, have not yet been brought to a close. It is not to be expected that the final result should give universal satisfaction, even if there were not persons who are opposed to all change in the matter, as hardly any can be made which does not touch some debatable point. Nevertheless I hope that the greater part will be generally accepted as desirable.

Popular Education. The great question of Popular Education still awaits a solution, which all admit to be beset with difficulties, and which some do not believe to be necessary, thinking that nothing more is required than a development of the present system, and that it could not be advantageously exchanged for any other. Little fault indeed appears to be found with the present system, except that there are large masses of our population which it does not reach. The complaint that it forces the poor man to accept as a succour of private charity, that which he might rightfully claim as his due from the State, expresses what I believe to be perfectly true in the abstract, but not, I think, any thing that is commonly felt as a grievance by the poor. It remains however to be seen, whether the object can be attained without powers of compulsion, which, however justifiable in theory, are foreign to our national habits and modes of thinking, and can at present only be regarded as a doubtful and hazardous experiment. A well-considered scheme for supplying the inevitable shortcomings of the present system, while leaving it in the main untouched, would probably be generally hailed as a boon. But a revolutionary measure, which would sacrifice what is by most persons accounted most important in the quality of education, to the extension of its area, would, I believe, be fraught with manifold danger. And it is to be feared that it would not even be attended with the advantage of that tranquillity which results from uniformity, but that it would have the effect of dividing the education of the country between Church Schools and State Schools, and thus opening a perennial spring of discord and strife.

But while I should deprecate any such sweeping change, I think that the friends of Education ought not to rest satisfied, as long as a large part of the children of the State are left destitute of the elements of useful knowledge. The truth on this head appears to me to have suffered from various fallacies and exaggerations, which in the end must damage the cause they are intended to serve. *Its low state.*

None would deny that moral and religious training—where it is successful—is infinitely more valuable than the mere development of the intellect, and that the intellectual development affords no guarantee whatever for the formation of moral or religious habits. But it is no less certain that intellectual vacuity, ignorance and stolidity, are no safeguard against vice or crime. Unless they are so, every child has, as it seems to me, as much right to such instruction as lifts him above this brutish condition, and enables him to cultivate his natural faculties, as he has to his daily bread. Nor do I find any reason for believing that this instruction, though quite powerless to lay any effectual restraint on the impulses of the animal instincts, or to counteract the influence of bad example, is ever in itself other than wholesome, if it be only as filling time which would be *Importance of moral and religious training.*

wasted in baneful idleness, and occupying the mind during a part of the day, with thoughts which afford it at least harmless exercise. And I have yet to learn that this instruction is answerable for any of the offences which are rife among the lower classes. The crimes which could not be perpetrated without the abuse of some advantages of education, are those of persons moving on a higher social level, most of whom have enjoyed not only intellectual, but moral and religious training. It is not by the knowledge of reading, writing, or arithmetic, that the boy who falls into bad company is enabled to become an expert thief, though without that knowledge a clerk in a banking-house could not commit a forgery.

Does merely secular education prevent crime? I see a question asked, in a way which seems to imply that it is considered as a powerful argument, bearing on our own educational controversies: " Does the Common School System prevent crime?"* The Common Schools to which it refers are those of the United States. Statistics and authorities are produced to show that the working of the Common Schools in America is very unsatisfactory, in fact, "a disastrous failure," and that pious and good Americans are painfully sensible of the evils which arise from the neglect of religious teaching. But if we are to apply these facts to our own case, it would seem that we ought also to ask, Does the Denominational System prevent crime? Or, if the question in this form should seem too exacting, it might be: Does it prevent the increase of crime, or sensibly lessen the number of youthful criminals? A judicious friend of the system would probably say that this was more than could be reasonably expected; that it is enough if its general tendency is favourable to morality. But perhaps the same may be true of the American Common School system; and it remains to be proved that it is responsible for the absence of religious instruction, or that this might not be associated with it; and that the fault, if there is one, rests with the State, which offers the benefit of secular instruction to all, and not with parents and pastors who neglect the religious training of the young.

* Title of a pamphlet reprinted and published by the National Society.

I also venture to think that the line commonly drawn between secular and religious instruction is too sharp and trenchant. I do not think that a school in which instruction is confined to secular subjects is therefore necessarily irreligious. I believe that it may be a school of morals as well as of learning, acting upon the habits and character, by discipline, precept, and example, and thus opening the way, and disposing the heart, for an intelligent reception of religious truth. I attach much greater importance to the tone, to the moral atmosphere of a school, than to the nature of the things taught in it.* I also believe that enormous exaggeration prevails as to the capacity of children, especially of the poor, for the reception of theology; and that clergymen are very apt to deceive themselves as to the impression made on the mind of a child, by incidental allusions to points of doctrine, which they may find opportunity of dropping in the course of lessons not expressly doctrinal or religious. It is only, as far as I know, in schools for the poor, that this was ever considered as an important part of religious education. It seems to imply a catechetical talent which probably few clergymen possess, and fewer still have leisure to cultivate and exercise. Much less, of course, is it to be expected in the schoolmaster, so that the cases in which a school suffers any loss from the absence of such opportunities, must be exceedingly rare and exceptional. As a ground for any general school regulations, this consideration may safely be left out of the account, and it is to be hoped will not continue much longer to be urged as an objection to the Conscience Clause, which, at least in its principle and spirit, may now be considered as universally received.

I find my view of this subject confirmed by the experience of her Majesty's Inspector of Schools in Mid Wales, in his Report

Secular and religious instruction.

---

* Canon Norris ("The Education of the People") observes (p. 187). "Knowledge, even of the most sacred subjects, may be given to a child without any real training of that child's character. The effect—religious or irreligious—of the school lessons on a child's character, depends far more on the spirit in which they are given than on the quantity of the directly religious instruction included in them. I have been sometimes pained and shocked to find a school passing a really admirable examination in what we call religious knowledge, when morally and religiously the school was in an unsatisfactory state."

for 1868, which deserves very serious attention. His opinion indeed is grounded on a state of things peculiar to Wales, but it involves principles of much larger application. In my last Charge I had occasion to observe, that I found no less than 120 parishes in which it did not appear that any provision had been made for the education of the poor through the instrumentality of the Church. Mr. Pryce reports 92 parishes in the counties of Cardigan, Carmarthen, Pembroke, and Radnor, with a population over 400, "containing no schools of any description recognized by Government." He remarks that very many of these are in remote and inaccessible places; and thinks it most desirable that proper Government schools should be established in some of the most central of these neglected parishes. But this could only be effected by a union which at present is prevented by religious rivalry. Nothing indeed can be more saddening than this rivalry,* whether we consider the waste of means, the continual jealousy and heart-burning provoked by the competition, or its effect on the instruction and discipline of the contending schools. Yet so far as the scholars are concerned, they are founded for precisely the same objects. The theological differences which are the pretext for the separation, in themselves little more than technical and professional, are to them absolutely unintelligible. The chief outcome of the religious teaching appears to be the fuel it ministers to self-conceit and evil tempers.

sidenotes: Report of Inspector for Mid Wales. Provision for education in Wales.

---

* The whole passage is worth transcribing. Speaking of two parishes in Cardiganshire (p. 16), he says, "No sooner did one party determine upon having a school, than the other party felt bound to start an opposition one; and thus, while many parishes in my district are without a school of any description, there are in these villages too many schools. The natural consequence is, that such schools are small and inferior. The two schools, the National and the British, work against each other, and not against ignorance and indifference. In towns and parishes where there is a fair population, this opposition and rivalry work beneficially, for there is always plenty of raw material to act upon; but in villages and parishes, where the number of children who can possibly attend school within a radius of three miles does not exceed 60 or 80, an increase in one school merely means a decrease in the other, one can only flourish at the expense of the other; the object in such places is not to get half a dozen poor children from the streets to attend some school, but to entice half a dozen children from the National to the British School, and *vice versâ*. I need not point out what a bad effect all this has upon the discipline and instruction in both schools."

Casting about for a remedy to this state of things, Mr. Pryce is led to the conclusion, that it is only to be found in the establishment of secular schools in the strictest sense of the word for these small parishes. He believes that all cause of religious jealousy having thus been removed, the clergyman would be allowed to retain the government of the school and the appointment of the Master. He has no fear that "the cause of religion or of the Established Church will suffer from" that complete severance which he proposes to make between secular and religious instruction. Indeed, under the circumstances which he describes, it is scarcely possible that it should. For in his district, the clergy, as he believes, have universally adopted the principles of the Conscience Clause, so far even as often to exclude doctrinal teaching from their schools altogether. But this *doctrinal teaching* is apparently that which he elsewhere terms *distinctive religious teaching*, relating to controverted points of doctrine. He questions much—I think with good reason—that the children derive much spiritual profit from the religious instruction which they receive as part of the school work from the acting teacher, an apprentice, or a monitor, even when the character of the instruction reaches up to "good" and "fairly good." If the purpose of such teaching is to make them better Christians or better Churchmen, he thinks that it utterly fails; while there is reason to fear that it leads the clergyman to neglect his own share in the work, which, but for this false semblance, he would have felt it his duty to take entirely upon himself.

Establishment of secular schools proposed.

Whether this suggestion will be adopted by those who have the power of carrying it into effect, I have no means of knowing. But the practical result which concerns ourselves, and depends entirely on our own will, seems very clear. Whether it be desirable or not that religious instruction should cease to form part even nominally of the prescribed business of the day school, I think there can be no doubt that you, my Reverend Brethren, are bound to act as if no such instruction was given; as if it still rested wholly with yourselves, whether the children of your parishes shall or shall not receive a

Duties of Clergymen toward schools.

teaching, which with God's blessing will not fail to turn to their spiritual profit, and to make them better Churchmen, but, above all, better Christians. With regard to every one of them who is committed to your care, from the moment that he is of age to receive a lesson, if you take an interest in his welfare, you will have a definite and simple object in view, towards which you will direct all your efforts; that is, to prepare him for admission into the full privileges of the Church through the rite of Confirmation. This preparation comprehends the whole body of Christian doctrine, so far as it is within the grasp of the child, the boy, the youth, in the successive stages of his mental growth. This is a part—it should be not the least interesting part—of your pastoral work, with which no one has a right to interfere, and which you should jealously reserve to yourselves, as you are alone responsible for it. And where it happens that many of the lambs of your flock have been drawn into other folds, as the labour of feeding those which remain is proportionably lightened, the stronger is their claim to the fullest measure of your care and diligence.

Church Restoration in the Diocese. I will take this occasion to say a word on another subject of special interest to the Diocese. I am glad to be able to report that the work of Church Restoration is proceeding with unabated activity. In the Appendix to my last Charge I enumerated thirty-five Churches which were in various stages of progress. Of these twenty-three have since then been completed, and fifteen have been added to the list; most of them very nearly ready for consecration or opening. Among those which have been partially completed, three are objects of peculiar interest: the Priory Church, Brecon; the venerable Parish Church of Llanbadarn Fawr (Aberystwyth), and the Cathedral of the Diocese.

The Cathedral. It is to the Cathedral that I would now draw your special attention. When we met last I was able to congratulate you on the completion of the most important —that is, immediately necessary—part of the work, the restoration of the Tower. Since then, the most beautiful and architecturally interesting portion of the building, the eastern arm with its aisles and other adjuncts, and a part of the nave, has been very nearly finished. But the work which remains to be done includes by far the greater part of the nave and its aisles; that is, the part designed for the great mass of the congregation, which, until this has been repaired, can derive no benefit from that which has been already done. And we must remember that the Cathedral is both the parish church and the only place of worship for members of the Church of England within the parish. Considered in this light it has at least as strong a claim as any other parish church. But it is also pronounced by Mr. Scott "the most historical, the most nationally typical, the most beautiful, and in every way the most valuable (of course in the architectural point of view) ecclesiastical building in the Principality." And, in fact, it has on this ground received contributions from strangers, not all even members of our Church.

I am not surprised that its unfinished condition should appear to Mr. Scott "a discredit to the Diocese and to Wales." *Its condition a discredit to the Diocese and to Wales.* I am well aware indeed of the circumstances, connected with the absolutely unique peculiarity of its position, which renders the fact far less surprising than it is deplorable, and which, as they have not arisen from any fault of ours, enable us to witness the magnificent restoration of Llandaff Cathedral with a pleasure, I will not say quite free from envy of advantages which we do not possess, but unalloyed by any feeling of shame or self-reproach for the past. On the other hand, the present state of the work is, I think, in every point of view, a motive which should urge us to a fresh and more vigorous effort for the completion of the undertaking.

I may here add that after careful inquiry and consultation with the Archdeacons, I found that the scheme of a Diocesan Church Building Society did not commend itself to the judgment of the great body of the clergy.

The meeting of Bishops of the Anglican Communion from all parts of the world, assembled by our late Primate at Lambeth, ought not perhaps to be allowed to pass *The Pan-Anglican Synod.* wholly unnoticed. It left many agreeable recollections, but not any monument of its presence which can be viewed with unmixed satisfaction, or, I think, any general wish for its return. The best effect it produced, was perhaps the strengthening of a brotherly feeling between the Churches of England and America. Even if the assembled Bishops had really represented their several Dioceses, so as to be able to express more than their individual views and wishes, the wide differences in their conditions, with regard to their relations to the State, would, I believe, have prevented the possibility of any practical result. Some, however, of the Resolutions adopted by the Committees appointed by the Meeting, may possibly germinate in measures useful to the Colonial Churches. But they included a scheme for "the constitution of a voluntary spiritual tribunal, to which questions of doctrine may be carried by appeal from each province of the Colonial Church," which, if not important, is at least significant. It lays down the principle that, "as it is a Tribunal for decisions in matters of faith, Archbishops and Bishops only should be judges." This tacit condemnation of our present Court of Appeal, no doubt expresses the views of an active party in the Church. But unless those views should become predominant, the principle would not, I believe, be generally accepted under any circumstances in which our Church will ever be placed.

Proposition for a voluntary spiritual tribunal.

I pass to another topic, and one of immeasurably great importance.

The convocation of a Council of the whole Roman Catholic episcopate, and styled Œcumenical, to be held at Rome under the presidency of the Pope himself, is an event which we could hardly under any circumstances view with indifference, or with no feeling stronger than mere curiosity, as wholly foreign to our own concerns. A movement which affects the condition of the largest part of Christendom, can never be absolutely without influence on our own. But the present state of our Church affords some special motives, which oblige us to watch the progress and results of this movement with lively interest and earnest attention. It is not only the manifestation of a leaning to Romanism, which we have been witnessing of late years

Convocation of a so-called (Ecumenical Council at Rome.

among members of our own communion, nor even the desire of reunion with Rome, which has been expressed by some whom we cannot doubt to be still sincerely attached to the principles of the Reformation; but it is that voices have been heard among us, claiming our sympathy for the coming Council, and treating it as matter of surprise and regret, that no overtures have been made on the part of the Anglican episcopate, for some kind of participation in its proceedings. *

No doubt the most rigid severity of Protestant principles would not prevent us from earnestly desiring that the deliberations of the Council may be overruled for a good end. And until lately it was possible for an eager partisan of reunion to maintain that we had been churlishly disregarding a kind and courteous invitation. That delusion has been dispelled by the highest authority.† The Church of Rome has never recognised the existence of a true episcopate in the Anglican Church, and therefore the Pope could not include its Bishops in his general invitation, and could only comprehend them under the description of Protestants. ‡ And all that he addressed to them in that

_{The Anglican Episcopate not recognised by Rome.}

---

* "A Few Words on Reunion and the Coming Council at Rome." By Gerard F. Cobb, M.A., Fellow of Trinity College, Cambridge. An antidote to this pamphlet, sufficient, I believe, for every mind still open to conviction, and not incapable of discerning truth, will be found in Janus.

† Though the Pope's letter to Archbishop Manning, the original of which is to be found in the *Times* of October 5, was designed as a reply to Dr. Cumming's inquiry, it could not have been more to the purpose, if it had been written to undeceive Mr. Cobb and his readers. Mr. Cobb assured them (p. 25), as of something "quite certain," that "the Roman authorities are ready to make very large concessions to the separated bodies." The Pope—who should, at least, be one of those authorities—thinks that a little consideration would have enabled Dr. Cumming at once to "perceive that no room can be given at the Council for the defence of errors which have already been condemned, and that we could not have invited non-Catholics to a discussion, but have only urged them to avail themselves of the opportunity afforded by this Council,"—for what? for "returning to the Father, from whom they have long unhappily gone astray." This is perfectly candid and outspoken, but it is not Mr. Cobb's programme.

‡ "The Apostolic See charges those who call themselves the Archbishops and Bishops of the Church established in England and Ireland with being intruders, by favour of the civil power, into the Sees of these realms: inasmuch as they and their predecessors took possession thereof in spite and to the detriment of the patriarchal rights of that See, which from the canons and immemorial usage had been exercised in the nomination or approbation of all Metropolitans and Bishops." Dr. Wiseman (afterwards Cardinal) in Palmer's "Jurisdiction of the British Epis-

character, was an exhortation to submission. I am not saying this in the way of complaint or reproach. We have rather reason to be thankful that he acknowledges our right to the name of Christians, which is so often denied us in Roman Catholic countries by persons not wholly uneducated.* But it is desirable that every one should clearly understand the terms on which alone any overture on our part could be received. And the language of the exhortation itself shows that we are considered at Rome, not only as heretics, but as very obstinate and perverse heretics, sin-_{Regarded as heretics.} ning against light and knowledge, denying truths *which do not admit of dispute*, such as the Pope's Divine right to the government of the Universal Church.† It was not to be expected that the Pope should be conversant with the writings of our Divines. But how broad an intellectual gulf is disclosed by this language, between a person capable of making such a mistake, and those who know the real state of the case. But at the same time the Pope very clearly stated the point which he most truly calls the hinge ‡ upon which the whole question between Roman Catholics and all who dissent from them turns. It is that "the _{The primacy of St. Peter.} primacy, both of honour and jurisdiction, conferred upon Peter and his successors by the Founder of the Church, is placed beyond the hazard of disputation."§ This indeed makes it very difficult to understand the position of persons, who, still

copacy Vindicated." Mr. Cobb indeed (p. 21) has a correspondent, whom he describes as "an eminent Roman Catholic theologian," who wrote to him, "If your Bishops believe themselves to be Bishops, they ought to go to the Council; if they do not go, it will be tantamount to an implicit acknowledgment on their part that they are *not* Bishops at all." If this is a fair sample of the intelligence or the candour of Mr. Cobb's Roman Catholic friends, we cannot receive their statements with too much mistrust.

* I speak in part from personal recollection. (See my Charge of 1866, p. 39, note.) In the Report of the Anglo-Continental Society for 1866, p. 8, a clergyman writes from Boulogne: "Not so very long ago, while some children were playing close by one of our churches here, one asked the other what building it was. Imagine the reply, 'C'est le temple des païens.'" The spring of this general ignorance (illustrated by Mr. Cobb, p. 67) is wilful misrepresentation.

† "Diximus extra disputationis aleam constitutum esse primatum, non honoris tantum sed et jurisdictionis, Petro ejusque successoribus ab Ecclesiæ institutore collatum.

‡ "In hoc nimirum cardine tota quæstio versatur inter Catholicos et dissentientes quoscunque."

§ Compare Acts xix. 35, 36.

remaining in the visible communion of our Church, nevertheless not only avowedly hold all Roman doctrine, but acknowledge the infallibility of the Church which one of our Articles declares to have "erred in matters of faith," while others expose the particular errors into which she has fallen. They profess to believe that the two Churches are kept apart, not by any essential differences, but only by a misunderstanding, which might be cleared up by friendly explanations.* Those who use such language seem to overlook both their own position and that of the person with whom they would have to deal in any attempt at reunion. The difficulty is not only that the party or school to which they belong, neither has nor is likely ever to have authority to represent the Church of England; but it is that the Pope cannot admit that there has ever been any error or misunderstanding on his part, either as to his own doctrine or ours, though he may readily admit that there has been such on our part as to both.

An opinion has been expressed by a dignitary of our Church, that in this question of reunion a great deal depends upon the personal character and inclination of the Pope.† This appears to me a sheer mistake. It is true that in the administration of the laws of his Church, in the exercise of his prerogative of dispensation, in the enforcing or relaxation of discipline, his power is almost unlimited, and in the course of this century has been carried to a length beyond all previous precedent.‡ But with regard to doctrine, he is not so much a person as an institution and a system. His personal character and ability may enable him to carry out the system with which he is identified into fresh developments. But he is utterly powerless to introduce any change which would involve an admission of the smallest dogmatical error; though indeed where infallibility is

<small>Reunion not dependent on the inclination of the Pope.</small>

---

* Mr. Cobb, p. 6, and passim.

† A letter to his Holiness Pius IX. from William Selwyn, Canon of Ely Cathedral. At p. 16 we read, "Holy Father, . . . upon you, more than on any other human being, rests at this moment the hope of peace and unity for the family of Christ on earth."

‡ I allude to the dealing of Pius VII. with the Gallican Episcopate.

concerned, there can be no distinction between *great* and *small*.* The smallest is just as fatal to the claim as the greatest.

What strikes me as most surprising is, that the assembling of the Council should have appeared to any one in the light of an opportunity for an approach toward reconciliation. The Pope indeed is consistent enough from his own point of view. He considers the great number of Bishops whom he is able to bring together, as a proof of the "close unity and invincible vitality" of his Church, which he hopes will make a deep impression on Protestant minds.† And undoubtedly it does prove the compact organization of the Papal Church, though it is not so evident that such unity is a surer sign of vitality in a religious body than in a Byzantine despotism. But, at least, the action of the Council will be a more convincing sign of vitality than its mere coming together. But for all friends of union who have not made up their minds beforehand to accept whatever the Council may decree, it would seem that the plainest dictates of common prudence require that they should defer their adhesion, until it is known how its proceedings affect the condition of the Roman Catholic Church, and consequently our position with regard to it.

<small>Vitality of the Papal Church.</small>

But though I do not look on the convocation of the Roman Council as an opportunity of action for those who are outside the Church of Rome, I think it is an occasion which may most fitly be allowed to lead our thoughts to dwell on the history of that

---

* Nor, it may be added (with reference to language of Canon Selwyn, reported by Mr. Cobb, p. 42), between *far* and *near* in an approach to unity which fails to reach it.

† So the Council of Trent (Sessio xii. caput v.) assigns, as one of the reasons for the celebration of the Festival of Corpus Christi, the effect it must produce on the minds of heretics : " Sic quidem oportuit victricem veritatem de mendacio et hæresi triumphum agere; ut ejus adversarii in conspectu tanti splendoris (of so many lights and of so much brocade) et in tanta universæ Ecclesiæ lætitia positi, vel debilitati et fracti tabescant, vel pudore affecti et confusi aliquando resipiscant." It was thought that, however they might be proof against all the arguments of the theologians, the spectacle of a magnificent procession must be irresistible. The avowal is one of singular *naïveté*, but the calculation is well grounded in the weak side of human nature. The attraction of a sensuous worship is always strong in proportion to the decay of spiritual life and the absence of rational conviction.

Church in the period subsequent to the Reformation, and especially on the transactions of its last general Council. It was the Council of Trent that made the Church of Rome what it is. Such as it then became, it has remained ever since; with great changes indeed in its outward condition, but with few affecting its inward character. I know of no subject of study which I would more earnestly recommend to all who wish to form a well grounded opinion on those prospects of union which are now held out to us, than the acts and the history of the Council of Trent. Not the acts alone; though I venture to think there are few minds in which a comparison of the Canons of Trent with our Articles, could leave a doubt as to the futility of every attempt to reconcile them with one another; not the acts alone, but also the history, which shows how they were brought about,—by what worldly intrigues and unholy motives. This study would enable every one to judge of its claim, I will not say to infallibility, but to confidence and respect;* to satisfy himself whether there is any appear-

<small>The Council an incentive to the study of the history of the Romish Church.</small>

<small>Lessons derivable from it.</small>

---

* The history of the Council of Trent is, in one sense, very well known, in another very little known. There is no portion of modern history for the study of which there is a greater abundance of trustworthy evidence; but it is very little studied and actually known. In our language I am not aware that there is any good or tolerably readable History of the Council. It is much to be desired that some one would translate Bungener's "Histoire du Concile de Trente," 2me ed. 1854. The nimbus which, in the course of three centuries, with the help of Jesuitical manipulation of history, has gathered round the Council, would have surprised contemporaries who saw behind the scenes. It was a Cardinal (Gieseler, *Lehrbuch der neueren K. G.* p. 505) who wrote of it—

> " Namque inter istos ut fatear patres
> Unum notari posse vel alterum
> Quem conferas illis beati
> Tempora quos aluere secli,
> Totius at pars concilii quota est,
> Quæ recta spectet."

Vargas (a member of the Imperial Embassy at the Council) wrote, "Les paroles et les remontrances sont fort inutiles ici. Je crois qu'elles ne le sont pas moins à Rome. Ce sont des aveugles. Ils ont pris une ferme résolution de ne penser qu'aux intérêts de la chair et du monde. Le Concile ne peut rien faire de lui-même. Le Légat est le maître, il tient tout dans sa main. Après cela on ne doit plus s'étonner de rien." Ibid. p. 522. "Isidore Chiari, Bishop of Foligno, who had opportunities at Trent of becoming thoroughly acquainted with his Episcopal colleagues, says, that in Italy, among 250 Bishops, one could scarcely find four who even deserved the name of spiritual shepherds, and really exercised their pastoral office." Janus, p. 356.

ance to render it credible, that the spirit by which its counsels were guided, was one of truth, or of holiness, or of charity, and not one of an opposite nature. By this we should learn rightly to appreciate the merit and the value of the reforms which are represented by Roman Catholic writers, and now by some of our own,* as having removed all reasonable ground of offence, and as having deprived us of the right of claiming the title of a Reformed Church, in contradistinction to the Church of Rome. We should see how many of those which were extorted from the Court of Rome by the cry of the nations still acknowledging its rule, were reforms only on paper; how far any of them was from touching any profitable abuse or superstition; how many served only to extend the Papal prerogative, by opening a new field for the exercise of the dispensing power. It would not be necessary for the purpose of this inquiry to enter into the labyrinth of disputed details. The broad facts which stand out in the clearest light, furnish sufficient ground for a certain conclusion. And there are two which are patent and conspicuous above all others; on the one hand, the steady resistance to every demand which tended either to limit the plenitude of Papal authority, or to close any source of revenue to the Court of Rome; on the other hand, the consistent endeavour to widen the doctrinal breach between Rome and the German Protestants, and to engage the Roman Catholic princes in a crusade against them. This is not indeed an excuse for its doctrinal innovations; but it is the only explanation by which many of them can be defended from the charge of being merely wanton and capricious. In no part of its proceedings is this more clearly apparent than in its treatment of Holy Scripture; not merely in the disciplinary regulations which were intended to keep it a sealed book, but in the parity of rank assigned to tradition, and in the assertion of the Canonicity of the Apocryphal books, and of the authenticity of the Vulgate. I advert to these examples for the sake of a more general remark.

Two prominent facts.

I observed that in matters of doctrine the Head of the Roman Church is not a free agent. Nothing depends on his individual

* Mr. Cobb, u. s. p. 68.

will and pleasure. He cannot make the smallest concession. He cannot reopen the discussion of a question which has been determined by the vote of the majority in a General Council. That is the fatal unhappiness of his position. But there is on the other side a counter-impossibility with regard to matters of fact. In such questions nothing depends upon the will. Men cannot change their convictions in these matters, unless constrained by the force of evidence, and it must be remembered that facts of history and of grammar are susceptible of as complete certainty as facts of astronomy or arithmetic. No effort of Galileo's will could have enabled him to disbelieve the motion of the earth. The power of the Inquisition might have prevented him from learning the truth; it did force him to deny it; but it could not alter his inward conviction of the fact. As little could the authority of a Council, though composed not merely, as at Trent, of two or three score,* but of a thousand bishops, enable a scholar to accept that which he knows to be a mistranslation as a true rendering. Yet this is what is required of him, when he is called upon to recognise the Vulgate as authentic Scripture. † Still less can it do that which exceeds the power of

<small>Matters of fact not dependent on the will.</small>

---

* Lainez, the General of the Jesuits, urged the fact, that under Paul III., articles of the first importance (principalissimi articoli) concerning the Canonical Books, interpretation of Scripture, parity of Tradition and Scripture, had been defined by less than fifty voices—as a proof that the authority of these decrees was derived entirely from the Pope, as a Council is General only because the Pope gives it that title, which he may do, however small its number. (Siccome un numero di Prelati dal Pontefice congregati per far Concilio Generale sia quanto picciolo si vuole, non d' altronde ha il nome e l'efficazia d' esser generale, se non perchè il Papa gliela dà, così anche non ha d' altrove l'authorità.) Sarpi, vii. 20.

† Some later apologists of the Council have endeavoured to restrict the sense of the word "authentic," so as only to exclude any error affecting faith or morals. But this is an interpretation not warranted either by the terms of the Decree, or by the discussion of it in the Council. The most liberal construction there put upon the word (that of Vega, Sarpi, ii. 51) only admitted the possibility of such departure from the sense of the original, as is inevitable in a translation. Pallavicino himself (vi. 17) knows only of two discordant opinions on the subject: one, that of the theologians who maintained the perfect exactness of the Vulgate; the other, that of those who interpret the Decree less rigidly, but hold that the translation is free, not only from errors pertaining to faith and morals, but also from even the slightest patent unconformity with the original text (aperta difformità ne pur minima dal testo). One of the more sensible speakers thought that the translation should have been examined before its correctness was guaranteed. Others argued that, although the translator was not inspired, since the Council was, its approval

Omnipotence itself; abolish a historical fact, undo the past, make it not to have been. Yet this is what was attempted by the Council of Trent, when it decreed the canonicity of the Apocrypha, not merely inserting them for the first time in the canon—which would only have been a scandalous abuse—but declaring that they had always formed part of it, which was notoriously untrue. When men not ignorant of history are invited to believe this as a fact of the past, they too must plead, *non possumus*. It is in vain for them that a Council stakes its infallibility on a proposition which they know to be false, with as full assurance as they have of their own existence. A thousand echoes cannot change falsehood into truth. When two such impossibilities come into conflict with one another, compromise and conciliation may well seem hopeless. There is however this difference between the two cases. The one impossibility is a fact in the divinely ordered constitution of the human mind; the other has no basis in the real nature of things, and is indeed nothing more than an arbitrary inference from most doubtful premisses, grasped with a tenacity proportioned to its intrinsic weakness. This last is indeed the only part of the case which seems to me to open a door for a single ray of rational hope.

How far the Papal Church has improved since the Council of Trent. But discouraging, with regard to the prospect of reunion, as is the aspect presented by the Papal Church, when it emerges from the Council of Trent, with its new Canons, Creed, and Catechism, and its old maxims of exterminating persecution sharpened for new excesses, we must not forget that three centuries have elapsed since the close of that Council, and that in the course of this period some of the most momentous changes recorded in the history of mankind have passed on the face of European society, and on the inner current of thought and feeling. It was probable, *a priori*, that the Church

and anathema against all who do not receive the translation, would have the effect of making it free from error (quando sara approvata la volgata edizione, e fulminato l'anathema contra chi non la riceve, quella sara senza errori, non per spirito di chi la scrisse, ma dello Sinodo che per tale l' ha ricevuta. Sarpi, u. s.). This to us sounds ludicrous, but does not seem to have been thought absurd in the Council. It is perhaps only a somewhat strong example of that disregard of historical truth which pervades Romish controversial theology.

of Rome should feel the influence of these changes. It was impossible that it should not be more or less beneficially affected by the vicinity of Protestant populations, wherever the two communions were found side by side. Let us not deny that, through the concurrence of these causes, considerable improvements have taken place in the state of the Church of Rome. There has been a notable amendment in the general character of the persons who have filled the Papal Chair. The last who created any very grave scandal, was the Pope who assembled the Council, and directed its earlier proceedings!* Since then their lives have mostly been at least decorous and respectable. In France, and in the parts of Europe which were swept by the torrent of the French Revolution, the clergy was to some extent purified and strengthened by suffering. The post-Tridentine monastic institutions were distinguished from those of the Middle Ages by a character of practical usefulness, and by works of mercy, with which Protestants can fully sympathize, and which should inspire them with a holy emulation; though they may well be content to do the same things in a more simple and unostentatious way. {*Amendment in the character of Popes.*}

But the question which we have now before us is, whether whatever movement has been called forth during this period in the Church of Rome, has tended to narrow or to widen the breach between us, to make reunion more or less hopeful? It might have happened that, without any formal abandonment of its outward position, a new spirit might have begun to breathe through the Church of Rome, affording some encouragement to those who yearn for the restoration of unity. Unhappily it is impossible to mistake the direction which the movement has really taken, the spirit by which it has been impelled, and not to see that it has parted the two communions more widely than ever asunder. The reign of the Pope {*Has the prospect of reunion become more or less hopeful?*}

---

* Paul III., while professing his desire for the reformation of the Church, raised two boys, one of 16, the other of 14, children of his illegitimate offspring, to the dignity of Cardinals. Sarpi observes (1. c. 52) that this immediately dispelled the fear which some of the Cardinals had conceived, of a reform in their own body.

who is now exhorting us to throw ourselves at his feet, has been marked by a series of measures, perhaps more repugnant to our deepest convictions than those of any of his predecessors since the Reformation. He appears to have kept three objects steadily in view : the exaltation of the Papal supremacy, and more complete concentration of the Church in his own person ;* the accumulation of new honours, as they are supposed to be, on the Virgin Mary ; and lastly, the subjugation of the whole domain of human thought under his control, and the establishment of a theocracy, in which the most extravagant pretensions of Boniface VIII. should pass into a Law of the Church and an Article of Faith. In the memorable Definition of the Immaculate Conception, he may be said virtually to have combined all these objects.

<small>Definition of the Immaculate Conception.</small>

The utterly unpractical, frivolous character of the scholastic subtlety thus exalted into a dogma, has very generally diverted attention from much that it involves, besides its unsound, anti-scriptural theology. It is also perhaps the most violent strain of papal prerogative, and the most audacious perversion of historical truth, to be found in history. For the Church of Rome disclaims the power of decreeing any new Article of Faith, and thus is compelled to assert that whatever it defines was from the beginning the doctrine of the Church.† But this assertion subjects the dogma to the test, not only of reason or of Scripture, but of history. It thus becomes one of those questions of fact, in which, when the evidence is sufficiently clear, men have not the power of rejecting it. For all who have any sense of historical truth, this dogma alone would constitute an insurmountable barrier, which, as long as it lasts—and it cannot be removed without an admission of error—must prevent them from acknowledging an authority which lays such a burden on their consciences.

It would perhaps be unjust to charge the present Pope with a more determined hostility to religious liberty, toleration,

---

* It is the application of the famous word of Louis XIV. to the Church—L'Église, c'est moi.

† Bishop Dupanloup, "Lettre sur le Futur Concile Œcuménique," p. 12. "On ne fait pas le dogme dans les Conciles, mais on le constate."

freedom of conscience in thought and speech, in a word, to all the principles and institutions which are regarded, not by Protestants only, but by some of the most devout members of his own communion and even of his clergy, as the most precious fruits of social progress, than has been uniformly manifested by his predecessors. But it is certain that none of them ever gave more decided and emphatic utterance to those views. And it was therefore not unreasonably believed by those who are most deeply concerned in the event, that he would not be satisfied with having stamped them with the sanction of his personal authority, but that one of the main ends for which he convoked the Council was to transform his political doctrines into religious dogmas and terms of salvation, so as to place some of the noblest spirits of the age, who are at the same time among the most faithful adherents of his Church, under the cruel necessity of choosing between their spiritual allegiance and principles dearer to them than their lives. It is while men like Montalembert are looking forward to the Council with grief and dismay, that we are exhorted by members and ministers of our own Church, to hail it with joy and hope. Hostility of the Pope to religious liberty, toleration, &c.

I can find but one excuse for this, as it seems to me, prodigious obliquity of spiritual vision. The Pope has described the supreme object of the Council as twofold: to remedy evils and avert dangers which threaten the foundations of religion on the one hand, and of civil society on the other. We cannot deny the existence of such evils and dangers; and at such a juncture we would not raise the question how far the Papal Church is answerable for them.* The object is one with which, as Christians and as men, we must heartily sympathize. But our approval of the end cannot make us indifferent to the means by Object of the Council.

---

* Father Hyacinthe however does not hesitate to express "his most profound conviction, that if France in particular, and the Latin races in general, are given up to social, moral, and religious anarchy, the chief cause lies, not indeed in Catholicism itself, but in the manner in which Catholicism has been long understood and practised." "Ma conviction la plus profonde est que, si la France en particulier et les races latines en général sont livrées à l'anarchie sociale, morale et religieuse, la cause principale en est, non pas, sans doute, dans le Catholicisme lui-même, mais dans la manière dont le Catholicisme est depuis longtemps compris et pratiqué."

which it is to be reached. It cannot relieve us from the duty of inquiring whether they are legitimate in themselves, and whether they are well adapted to the attainment of the object. I waive the preliminary doubt, whether the persons to be assembled at Rome—however otherwise respectable—are likely to be the best qualified, by their education and habits of thought, for the treatment either of philosophical questions, or of subjects which fall within the province of a Congress of Social Science. But we are able to judge whether any of the measures hitherto announced as designed to occupy their deliberations, warrant an expectation that they will lead to the desired result, and not much more probably to one of an exactly opposite kind. That a time so pregnant, in the view of the Pope himself, with changes affecting the very basis of religion and society, when social problems of the most awful moment are weighing upon all earnest minds, should have been selected as the right season for pledging the Church to a fable extracted from the legendary history of the Virgin Mary, might have seemed incredible, if it had not been in sad accordance with the past, and especially with the history and character of the present Pope. It will probably disgust not a few intelligent Roman Catholics, as well as Protestants who are not pledged to accept all the decrees of the Council. Feelings of still deeper indignation have been excited by the pretensions which, if admitted, would establish a theocracy in every Roman Catholic State. The Governments whose rights are threatened, look on, some with anxiety, others with contempt, all with the firm resolution to resist this invasion. It remains to be seen whether the influence of religion or the security of social order will be promoted by the struggle which it will provoke, or by the new element of chronic discord which it will introduce into every European State.

Marginal note: How far it will be carried out.

Verily the Seven Hills are not those to which we can lift up our eyes in the belief that from them cometh our help.

The proceedings of the unhappy Council of Trent were fitly closed by a series of acclamations, which have been duly recorded for perpetual memory with the rest of its acts. The last, pronounced by the sanguinary Cardinal of Lorraine, was "Anathema to all heretics;" and the final response of the assembled prelates echoed and re-echoed the word, "Anathema, Anathema." Its meaning was expounded a few years later by the Massacres of St. Bartholomew, hailed at Rome with transports of joy and solemn thanksgiving to the Almighty.* To renew such scenes is no doubt out of the power, and, I would fain hope, not even in the will of Pope or Council, however they may anathematize toleration in theory. But that there has been any abandonment of the principle of persecution, as a religious duty, wherever it appears to be expedient, or the slightest mitigation of the feeling which it has been the policy, as well as the instinct of Rome, to associate with the name of heretic, we have no reason to suppose. On the contrary, one of the doctrines proclaimed indirectly in the Syllabus, by the condemnation of the opposite opinion, and which is expected to be defined by the Council, is the external coercive jurisdiction of the Church to inflict temporal penalties on dissentients. And these penalties have been authoritatively explained as including fines, imprisonment, and scourging, without prejudice to the Church's right to take stronger measures if they should appear necessary. †

The policy of the Romish Church unaltered since the Council of Trent.

* In the interval, S. Pius V.—the only Pope hitherto canonized since the Reformation—had enjoined his general to give no quarter to heretics (an order not issued against the Turks at Lepanto). It may be asked, why revive these painful memories? It is because they are only to a very small extent things of the past. The form only is changed, the spirit remains the same. In the words of the Genevese pastors, speaking of the Pope's address to Protestants, "La forme de cet écrit, modérée, charitable, ne rappelle pas les anathèmes dont Rome nous a tant de fois chargés. Malheureusement, les anathèmes subsistent. Ils n'ont jamais été révoqués. Ils servent de texte à ce qu'on enseigne aux populations Catholiques sur les Réformateurs, la Réforme et les Réformés: ils inspirent les lois et les mesures dont nos frères sont l'objet partout où l'Eglise Romaine impose aux gouvernements ses volontés." And therefore the truth is needed as a balance to misrepresentations now industriously circulated among us in the interest of Rome.

† "They are greatly mistaken who suppose that the Biblical and old Christian spirit has prevailed in the Church over the mediæval notion of her being an institution with coercive power to imprison, hang, and burn. On the contrary, these doctrines are to receive fresh sanction from a General Council, and that pet theory of the Popes—that they could force kings and magistrates, by excommunication and its consequences, to carry out their sentences of confiscation, imprisonment, and death—is now to become an infallible dogma. It follows that not only is the old institution of the Inquisition justified, but it is recommended as an urgent

Under that anathema we must be content to live, until it is moved by an authority equal to that which laid it on us. Our consolation is that we can say, "Though they curse, yet bless Thou;" and with the fullest conviction that the Divine Blessing on the cause of Truth and Righteousness will not be intercepted by the fiercest cursings of fallible, presumptuous, unrighteous judges.

<small>Our consolation under Anathema.</small>

I have dwelt on this topic longer than I had intended, but not, I venture to think, without a cause. I hasten to conclude; and I am reminded of the question with which I began: "What can the righteous man do?" None of us, my brethren, it is to be hoped, could hear these words with any such thought as that of applying them to himself as a description of his own character, and nothing could be more foreign to my purpose in all that I have been just now saying, than that our Church should take up an attitude of Pharisaical self-complacency over against the Church of Rome. The deepest humility and the largest charity are perfectly consistent with the clearest perception of the breadth and depth of the gulf which separates the two Churches from one another. We ought not to think that the errors into which the Papal Church has fallen, entirely neutralize the benefit of the truths which it has preserved. The latter half of the creed of Pius IV. contains a series of erroneous novelties, which it is impossible for us to accept, even without the monstrous addition since made to them. But it also includes the Nicene Creed; and this is not the less a bond of spiritual union, because the new articles appended to it are a bar to visible unity. The Church of Rome ministers the bread of life, adulterated indeed by many heterogeneous and unwholesome ingredients; but they are not sufficient to deprive it of all its nutritive virtue. Still the fullest acknowledgment of this truth, to the utmost extent of its application, need not and ought not in the slightest degree to weaken our assurance of the strength of our position, in all the

<small>The spirit in which we should contemplate the Papal Church.</small>

<small>necessity of the present age. The *Civiltà* has long since described it as 'a sublime spectacle of social perfection;' and the two recent canonizations and beatifications of inquisitors, following in rapid succession, gain in this connexion a new and remarkable significance." Janus, p. 12.</small>

points on which we are at variance with Rome, or our conviction that so far our cause is the cause of truth and righteousness.

The question then recurs: having this consciousness, What can we do? I quite agree with those who hold, though from a different point of view, that we have a duty to discharge toward the approaching council. It would clearly be wrong to look on it with contemptuous indifference. It is indeed the height of rashness and presumption to interpret any promise made by our Lord to His Church, as a guarantee which excludes the temporary prevalence either of error in doctrine or of viciousness in life.* But there is nothing in the experience which refutes that interpretation, to forbid the hope or the prayer, that the Church of Rome may yet come to her right mind, or that the proceedings which betoken a disposition to perpetuate and aggravate the evil, may be overruled into an instrument which

The duty of Churchmen respecting the Council.

---

* Mr. Cobb (p. 54) reproduces the old Romish sophism, apparently without any misgiving. He thinks that "no more terrible defeat from the gates of hell could be imagined than is involved" in the failure of our Lord's promise (Matt. xvi. 18) interpreted in the Romish sense. "Conceive," he says, "the total shipwreck of all faith among the one hundred and sixty millions in communion with the Holy See which would ensue, were a Council of Reunited Christendom to decree that even one single doctrine which they and their forefathers for thirteen generations of men have (on the strength of Roman Decrees) held to be part of the infallible Word of God, was after all a mere human invention." It must be observed, that the promise could not, by the mere force of the word *prevail*, preclude a temporary prevalence of the Gates of Hell, as Amalek *prevailed* against Israel, though finally discomfited. Again, the Gates of Hell were certainly *prevailing* against the Church, when the Papal Chair was filled by men of evil and scandalous lives. They were *prevailing* in the enormities of the Avignon Papacy, and in the Great Schism. And the moral damage they then inflicted was irreparable, whereas an error in doctrine may be corrected, and may do little harm to any one while it lasts. If the Decree of the Immaculate Conception was to be rescinded by a Council of Reunited Christendom, the "millions in communion with Rome" would, it is to be hoped, be brought into the state of those who now both reject that Decree, and believe that the mooting of such a question, no more concerning the Church than a theory of the moon, was a sin which proved the ascendancy of the Power of Darkness. But it is rather too much to expect those who take this view of the subject, to admit that it involves a "total shipwreck of all faith." On the contrary, they believe that its universal reception would be an unspeakable blessing to the Church. The handling of the text adopted by Mr. Cobb, is characteristic of the license with which Romish theologians, but especially the Popes, as if it was a privilege of their office, habitually wrest Scripture to their own purposes. The interpretation is so purely arbitrary and subjective, that, to serve as an argument, it needs the assumption of the thing it is designed to prove. Belief in the infallibility of the Pope, will always turn out to be at bottom nothing but the believer's faith in his own.

may hasten its removal. I will not say whether our Church, so far as it was represented at the Lambeth conference, has sufficiently discharged its duty in this respect, by the clause in its "Address to the faithful in Christ Jesus," which refers to "the pretension to universal sovereignty over God's heritage asserted for the See of Rome." It may be that the occasion may call for some more distinct protest against the Papal usurpation, and the authority of the Council which is to give it further sanction and larger extent.

<small>Recognition of the Papal authority deprecated.</small> But the greatest breach of charity which either the Church or any of its members could commit, would be any kind of overture which might be construed into acquiescence in that usurpation, and recognition of that authority. It would, I believe, so far make us accomplices in a conspiracy against the most sacred rights of mankind.* And we shall but very imperfectly appreciate the importance of the issue, and the fearfulness of the danger with which Christendom is threatened, unless we bear in mind that the question is not simply, where this power, so little short of omnipotence, is to be lodged, but by whom it is to be wielded. Nominally it will be by the Pope, but really by those who have his ear. And who will they be but the hereditary sworn ministers and advisers of the Holy See? The <small>Real meaning of Papal infallibility.</small> infallibility of the Pope means the sovereignty of the Jesuits. The Pope—however ignorant and imbecile—will reign; the Jesuits will govern. And the question, most deeply interesting indeed to every sincere Roman Catholic, but very far from a matter of indifference to us, is whether for the future the Jesuits are to be absolute lords of the Church of Rome, and to have all its machinery and resources at their disposal. But among those who are engaged in this undertaking, there is no one who seems to me entitled to larger allowance, than the personage

---

* I might use much stronger language without coming up to the force of Father Hyacinthe's protest: "Contre ces doctrines, et ces pratiques qui se nomment romaines, mais ne sont pas chrétiennes, et qui dans leurs envahissements toujours plus audacieux et plus funestes, tendent à changer la constitution de l'Église—contre le divorce impie autant qu'insensé, qu'on s'efforce d'accomplir entre l'Église et la société du dix-neuvième siècle—contre cette opposition plus radicale et plus effrayante encore avec la nature humaine atteinte et révoltée par ces faux docteurs dans ses aspirations les plus indestructibles et les plus saintes."

in whose name it is carried on. When we consider the claims which he inherits from his predecessors—all, in his eyes, " beyond the hazard of disputation"—the collision into which he has been brought, as a temporal prince, with the spirit of the age, and the counsellors by whom he is surrounded,* we may well trust that he has been governed by better motives than vanity or ambition, and that he sincerely believes his universal sovereignty to be the condition of all hope for the future of mankind. And this belief is, no doubt, very generally shared by his clergy, most of whom have been led by the insecurity of their relations to the State, to look to him as their only permanent support. A far graver responsibility seems to me to rest on the allies whom he has found within our own pale. There may however be a certain kind of consistency in the conduct of those who being avowedly at one with him in mind, heart, and soul, only stand aloof in visible profession, on some nice point of honour or etiquette. † The cry for reunion

---

* It seems to be universally admitted as a notorious fact, that the Pope is in the hands of a party. Father Hyacinthe, in his celebrated letter to his Superior, speaks of "the intrigues of a party all-powerful at Rome." But it is questioned who they are. They are commonly supposed to be the Jesuits. What is certain is, that the Jesuits, from the first institution of their order, have been distinguished by their zeal in the prosecution of the two objects which Pius IX. seems to have most at heart: the extension of Mariolatry, and the absolute monarchy of the Pope. As to the first, they did all in their power to popularize the doctrine of the Immaculate Conception (see in Gieseler, iii. c. iii. sec. 60, note 19, the persecution which they kindled against the Dominicans); as to the second object, we have seen in a previous note the doctrine of Lainez. It was that of the Society.

"We owe it to Bellarmine and other Jesuits, that in some documents the Pope is expressly designated Vice-God."—Janus, p. 39.

Mr. Cobb (p. 27) thinks "that if the Pope be in the hands of the Jesuits it is a very good thing for us; he might be in plenty worse." Perhaps he should know. But the reason he assigns is not very reassuring; for it amounts only to that which no one who knows their history can doubt: that their conduct will be governed by their view of expediency. The sons of Loyola were never supposed to be deficient in the wisdom of the serpent. One of the worst features in Mr. Cobb's pamphlet is his attempt to gain credit to the Jesuits for *moderation*, as if an object was the better for the craft and dissimulation with which it is attained. The Pope would, no doubt, be delighted to see the Inquisition, described by his organ, " *La Civiltà* " (see Janus, p. 12), as " a sublime spectacle of social perfection," planted in England; but it is not a Jesuit who would advise him immediately to issue a Bull for that purpose.

† This appears to be the most appropriate description for the " grievances of the most advanced among us," enumerated by Mr. Cobb (p. 36). Compared with the importance of the subject, and the danger to which the Pope alludes in his letter to Archbishop Manning, they seem indeed very paltry and pitiful.

with Rome comes naturally from those who are doing all in their power to break up the unity of the Church of England. But for all others I can conceive no line of conduct at once more inconsistent and more cruel, than to offer demonstrations of sympathy which can only serve to foster what, as members of a Reformed Church, we believe to be a spirit of error, and a calamitous delusion.

I am well aware, my Reverend Brethren, how far you are from the slightest tendency toward this kind of unfaithfulness to the principles of your own Church, and that to many of you it may seem something strange and almost incredible. Let me then remind you that its existence is an additional reason why you should not be content with a merely negative loyalty. At such a juncture as the present, whether we look abroad or at home, we must feel that our Church has a right to some positive proofs of our allegiance and affection. You repudiate the jurisdiction claimed by the Bishop of Rome, not only because the claim rests on no more solid ground than a fanciful interpretation of Scripture and a corruption of primitive tradition, but because you believe him to be in spiritual things, not merely a fallible, but a blind and actually erring guide. I rejoice to know that such is your conviction, and I am sure that the farther you inquire into the position of our Church in this controversy, the more fully you will be assured of its essential agreement with primitive faith and order. Certainly you cannot prize this privilege too highly, or watch over it too jealously. But that which concerns us most is, not that we go to no other, but that we *do* go to Him Who alone hath the words of eternal life. It is that we strive to live and labour, as under His immediate eye; that we search the Scriptures more and more diligently, not for that which ministers to doubtful disputations, but for that which will nourish our own souls and those committed to our charge. It is that, while we neglect no light which the Church supplies, or to which she directs us for our guidance, we endeavour to lay open our hearts and minds to that heavenly teaching, which is at the same time the unfailing source of all holy comfort. Whether our appointed sphere of duty be large or

Incentive to loyalty to the Church.

narrow, conspicuous or obscure, each may try to fill it, as if the welfare of the whole body depended on his individual exertions, and as if the view taken of the Church from without, would be entirely governed by the character of his life and ministry. More than this cannot be required by the Church, or by her Divine Head. Does he require less? I leave the answer to your private meditations.

APPENDIX.

(A.)

List of Churches newly built or under restoration since the last Visitation.

Archdeaconry of Carmarthen.

Merthyr (entirely rebuilt).
Pendine.
Llangain.
Llanllwch.
Loughor.

Archdeaconry of St. David's.

The Cathedral (half finished).
Lambston.
Lamphey.
Rhoscrowther.
St. Florence.

Archdeaconry of Cardigan.

Elerch (new).
Lampeter (new).

Archdeaconry of Brecon.

Llandrindod (new).
Vaynor (new).
Crickhowell.
Gladestry.
Nantmel (Parish Church and new School Chapel).
Taffechan.

(B.)

What is Transubstantiation?

Mr. Cobb ("Kiss of Peace," p. 100 foll.) has endeavoured to show that it is only through a vulgar error, that persons unacquainted with scholastic language, have supposed that the Roman doctrine of Transubstantiation is at variance with that of the Church of England. The same opinion is intimated in the Declaration, commonly known as Archdeacon Denison's, on the Real Objective Presence, by the words *commonly called* "Transubstantiation." The mistake, Mr. Cobb thinks, has been, that Transubstantiation, properly so called, that is, the conversion of the substance of the consecrated elements, has been confused with what he has happily termed *Transaccidentation*, that is, a change in their sensible properties, or accidents, which both Churches deny, while the Transubstantiation which is really taught by the Church of Rome, is not denied, but virtually held by the Church of England. The Twenty-eighth Article Mr. Cobb supposes to have been aimed, not at the Roman doctrine, but at that which had been mistaken for it. It may seem surprising that there should be any room for doubt as to the meaning of Transubstantiation in the Roman sense, when it has been defined by the Council of Trent, in a Chapter (Sess. xiii. cap. iv.) headed *De Transubstantiatione*. We there read, "Sancta hæc Synodus declarat per consecrationem panis et vini, conversionem fieri totius substantiæ panis in substantiam Corporis Christi Domini nostri, et totius substantiæ vini in substantiam Sanguinis ejus. Quæ conversio convenienter et proprie a sancta Catholica Ecclesia Transubstantiatio est appellata." But as *substance* is the name given to a thing utterly unknown, and to our present faculties absolutely inconceivable, this definition is in fact merely verbal, and tells us no more than that x takes the place of y. We must look elsewhere for some explanation of the nature of the change, which may enable us to form a judgment on Mr. Cobb's proposition. He himself relies on chap. i. and chap. iii. In chap. i., on the words, "Nec enim hæc inter se pugnant, ut ipse Salvator noster semper ad dexteram Patris in cœlis assideat, juxta modum existendi naturalem, et ut multis nihilominus aliis in locis sacramentaliter præsens sua substantia nobis adsit, eâ existendi ratione quam, etsi verbis exprimere vix possumus, possibilem tamen esse Deo, cogitatione per fidem illustratâ, assequi possumus, et constantissime credere debemus." Having cited this passage, Mr. Cobb asks, "Can any thing be plainer than that the Church of Rome here distinguishes between the 'natural' and the 'spiritual,' or, as she calls it, the 'sacramental' mode of Christ's presence, and maintains with us that Christ's natural Body is in Heaven, *and not here*" (this is an interpolation of Mr. Cobb's), " it being against the truth of Christ's natural Body to be at one time in more places than one, whereas she holds that this *is* possible with the 'spiritual' body, although we cannot express the mode of its existence, that is, the laws to which it conforms?"

What to me is made plain by this remark, is that Mr. Cobb is not a competent expounder of Roman doctrine. It is clear that he has confounded two things, between which Roman Divines most carefully distinguish, viz. the natural *body* and the natural *mode* of its existence. The Council does not deny the presence of the *natural body* in the Sacrament, but only that it is there according to its natural *mode* of existence. In this very chapter it repeatedly urges the literal interpretation of our Lord's words, in proof of the reality of His Flesh and Blood in the Sacrament, without any qualifying expression (" post panis vinique benedictionem se suum ipsius Corpus illis præbere, ac suum Sanguinem, disertis ac perspicuis verbis testatus est "), and it inveighs against those who distort them " ad fictitios et imaginarios tropos, quibus veritas "— not *substantia*—" Carnis et Sanguinis Christi negatur." Mr. Cobb also asserts, that the Church of Rome maintains with us (in the Declaration on Kneeling) that " Christ's natural Body is in Heaven, and not here, it being against the truth of Christ's natural Body to be in more places than one ;" but he offers no proof of this assertion, and if he had sought would have been unable to find one. In the Appendix to my last Charge I cited two passages, one from the posthumous *Systema Theologicum* of Leibnitz, the other from Lacordaire, both assuming that, according to the doctrine of the Church of Rome, Christ's natural Body is in many places at once, and endeavouring to show that it is possible. The dispute between the Franciscans and the Dominicans at the Council of Trent— one party contending that the Body of Christ was translated from Heaven into the Sacrament ; the other, that it was created by each consecration —proceeded on this assumption. Nor without this would there have been any such stupendous miracle as to render it necessary to insist upon the text (Luke i. 37). *With God nothing shall be impossible* (Catechismus Romanus, Pars ii. cap. iv. Quæst. xxxv).

Mr. Cobb also cites chapter iii. of the same Session, where the Council teaches as " the faith ever held in the Church of God, that instantly after consecration, the true Body of our Lord and His true Blood are there (existere), together with His Soul and Godhead, under the form of Bread and Wine ; but with the distinction, that the presence of the Body under the form of bread, and of the Blood under the form of wine, is due to the words of consecration (ex vi verborum) ; while, by virtue of the natural connexion and concomitance, whereby the parts of the risen Lord are knit together, the Body is there under the form of wine, and the Blood under the form of bread, and the Soul under both.

Moreover, the Godhead is there, in consequence of the admirable hypostatic union between it and the Body and Soul. Wherefore it is most true that as much (tantumdem) is contained under either form as under both; for Christ whole and entire is there under the form of bread, and under every part of that form; also whole Christ under the form of wine, and under its parts." ("Ipsum Corpus sub specie vini, et Sanguinem sub specie panis, animamque sub utraque, vi naturalis illius connexionis et concomitantiæ, qua partes Christi Domini, qui jam ex mortuis resurrexit non amplius moriturus, inter se copulantur, Divinitatem porro propter admirabilem illam ejus cum corpore et anima hypostaticam unionem. Quapropter verissimum est tantumdem sub alterutra specie atque sub utraque contineri. Totus enim et integer Christus sub panis specie et sub quavis ipsius speciei parte, totus item sub vini specie, et sub ejus partibus existit.")

Upon this, Mr. Cobb exclaims, "Now have we, I ask, in the whole range of our Liturgy, Articles, and Catechism, any more emphatic declaration of a wholly supernatural, transcendental, celestial Presence, or any more emphatic disclaimer of a natural sensible corporeal Presence, than this?" And he then breaks out into a strain of rapturous admiration on this "exalted, majestic, glorious belief," and of indignation at the "persons of authority and influence in our Church, who have imputed the teaching of a 'carnal' view to the Church of Rome." But there is a question which must be allowed to take precedence of Mr. Cobb's; and it is, whether in this quotation there is any such "declaration," or any such "disclaimer," as he describes; and whether that which he finds in it has not been imported into it by himself, without any warrant or any attempt at proof, through the confusion already noticed in his ideas, between a *presence* and the *mode* of a presence. That this is really the case, I believe I can prove beyond a doubt, by the evidence of the Roman Catechism, the most authentic exposition of the doctrine of the Council, and of Bellarmine, whose authority on such a point will not be questioned.

In the Catechism (P. ii. cap. iv. Quæst. xvii.) it is stated, "Since we observe that bread and wine are every day changed by the force of nature into human flesh and blood, we may be the more easily led, by this similitude, to believe that the substance of bread and wine are converted into the true Flesh of Christ and His true Blood, by heavenly benediction." ("Cum panem et vinum in humanam carnem et sanguinem quotidie vi naturæ immutari animadvertimus, facilius adduci possumus hac similitudine, ut credamus, panis et vini substantiam in veram Christi Carnem, verumque ejus Sanguinem, cœlesti benedictione converti.") Under the twenty second *Quæstio*, we find an enumeration of three "most admirable effects wrought by consecration in the Sacrament." The first is, "that the true Body of the Lord Christ, that same which, born of the Virgin, is seated in heaven at the right hand of the Father, is contained in this Sacrament." ("Primum est, verum Christi Domini Corpus, illud idem, quod, natum ex Virgine, in cœlis sedat ad dexteram Patris, hoc Sacramento contineri.") And this is still more distinctly explained in *Quæstio* xxxiv., "The Body is truly conjoined with the Godhead : the Body born of the holy Virgin ; not that the very Body which was taken up, comes down from heaven (the opinion of the Franciscans), but that the bread itself and the wine are transmuted into the Body and Blood of Christ." ("Corpus secundum veritatem conjunctum est Divinitati : corpus ex sancta Virgine ; non quod ipsum corpus assumptum de cœlo descendat, sed quod ipse panis et vinum in Corpus et Sanguinem Christi transmutentur.") I may observe, by the way, that in the title of this *Quæstio*, the Catechism has, by anticipation, refuted Mr. Cobb's remark (" Kiss of Peace," p. 112) on the use of the plural *substances* in the "Declaration on Kneeling," which—though with a creditable misgiving—he considers as an indication of inaccuracy. For the title runs, " Quomodo fit tam admiranda *substantiarum* conversio," viz. " ut tota panis substantia divina virtute in totam Corporis Christi substantiam, totaque vini substantia in totam sanguinis Christi substantiam, sine ulla Domini nostri mutatione convertatur." Mr. Cobb has no less reason for misgiving about his criticism on the words " very " and " natural," as epithets of " substances." It is grounded on his purely arbitrary assertion (p. 111) that " substance " is not " natural," but " supernatural," for which he has no reason to give, but that its nature is not known to us. He may be at liberty to define what he means by " nature," so as to confine it to that which is known to man ; but he can have no right to make this private definition the ground of an argument which is to convince others.

If the extracts already given do not speak plainly enough, all reasonable doubt must, I think, be removed by the twenty-seventh *Quæstio*, which is entitled, "An ossa, nervi, et quæcunque ad hominis perfectionem pertinent, una cum Divinitate, hic vere adsint ? " " Are bones, nerves, and whatsoever things pertain to the perfection of man, really present here together with the Godhead ? " The answer is meant to show that this not only is, but must be so. " Here, too, it must be explained that not only the true Body of Christ, *and whatsoever pertains to the true nature of a body, as bones and nerves*, but also whole Christ is contained in this Sacrament. For the pastor must teach that Christ is the name of God and man, that is, of one person, in whom the Divine and human nature are united together ; wherefore it includes each substance, *and the things which belong to each substance*, the Godhead and the whole human nature, which consists of the soul and *of all parts of the body*, and also the blood, all which must be believed to be in the Sacrament. For since in heaven the whole manhood is united to the Godhead in one person and hypostasis, it may not be suspected that the body, which is in the Sacrament, is separated from the same Godhead." ("Hoc loco etiam explicandum est, non solum verum Christi Corpus, *et quicquid ad veram corporis rationem pertinet, reluti ossa et nervos*, sed etiam totum Christum in hoc Sacramento contineri. Docere autem oportet, Christum, nomen esse Dei et hominis, unius scilicet personæ, in qua divina et humana natura conjuncta sit : quare utramque substantiam, *et quæ utrique substantiæ consequentia sunt*, Divinitatem et totam humanam naturam, quæ ex anima et omnibus corporis partibus, et sanguine etiam constat, complectitur, quæ omnia in Sacramento esse credendum est. Nam cum in cœlo tota humanitas Divinitati in una persona et hypostasi conjuncta sit, nefas est suspicari, Corpus, quod in Sacramento inest, ab eadem Divinitate sejunctum esse.") It seems impossible to state more clearly that the substance which after consecration takes the place of the substances of the bread and wine, does not, and cannot exist apart from its *consequentia*, which include all things pertaining to the completeness of human nature, as bones and nerves ; in other words, the natural body in its full integrity.

But for a fuller explanation of the *mode* of the Presence, and of the language in which it may be correctly described, we must turn to Bellarmine. In the second chapter of the first book of his treatise, "De Sacramento Eucharistiæ," he first comments at length on the terms, *vere, realiter*, and *substantialiter*, in which the mode of the Presence is described at the beginning of cap. i., sess. 13, of the Council of Trent, and then proceeds to lay down certain rules for speaking correctly on the subject. We must bear in mind that Mr. Cobb believes that " nothing can be plainer " than that in this very chapter the Church of Rome distinguishes between the " natural " and the spiritual, or, as she calls it, the Sacramental mode of Christ's Presence, and maintains with us that " Christ's natural Body is in Heaven, *and not here :* " while in cap. iii. of the same Session he finds " a most emphatic declaration of a wholly supernatural, transcendental, celestial Presence," and " a most emphatic disclaimer of a *natural, sensible, corporeal* Presence." Bellarmine, in his second rule, contradicts these assertions almost as if he had foreseen them. He says, " Dicemus quidem Corpus Christi, ut est in Eucharistia, esse verum, reale, *naturale*, animatum, quantum, coloratum, &c., et Carnem illam dicemus esse *corporalem non spiritualem*, nisi nomen *spirituale* sumatur sicut 1 Cor. xv., *Seminatur corpus animale, surget spirituale*, id est obediens spiritui in omnibus. At non dicemus Corpus Christi in Eucharistia esse *sensibile*, visibile, tangibile, extensum, licet tale sit in cœlo." In his third rule about adverbs, he observes, " Dicemus Christum esse in Eucharistia vere, realiter, substantialiter, ut Concilium recte loquitur, sed non dicemus corporaliter, id est eo modo quo suapte natura existunt corpora, nec sensibiliter, mobiliter," &c., and he would recommend great caution in the use of such language as St. Bernard's, who affirmed, "In Sacramento exhiberi nobis veram carnis substantiam, sed spiritualiter non carnaliter." The negative he thinks would be dangerous: "Periculum esset, ne traheretur ab adversariis non tam ad modum quam ad ipsam naturam significandam." The reader will observe that the misconstruction which Bellarmine apprehends from adversaries, is the very misconception into which Mr. Cobb, though so far from an adversary, has actually fallen. He has confounded the *natura* with the *modus existendi*, and, with the most friendly intentions, has misrepresented the doctrine of the Church of Rome, making her deny what she asserts, and assert what she denies. Bellarmine will call the Body in the Eucharist, not only *true* and *real*, but *natural*. He will attribute to it *life*, *bulk*, *colour*, &c., i. e. all things belonging to the perfection of the natural body, and he will call the Flesh *corporeal*, *not* spiritual, unless the word *spiritual* be taken in a sense consistent with the nature of body. But he will not call the Body *sensible*, as if that epithet was equivalent, as Mr. Cobb supposes it to be, to *natural* and *corporeal*.

Mr. Cobb's mistake is not surprising, nor, I think, discreditable to him. Independently of his affection for the Church of Rome, he might well be loth to attribute to her such a doctrine as that which Bellarmine expounds. It supposes a twofold miracle: one, by which the Presence is produced; the other, still more stupendous, by which the first is concealed; and both depend upon a third, of perhaps a still higher order. For whereas it has not been questioned that the two former are possible to God, this appears to belong to a class which is generally admitted to exceed the power of Omnipotence itself. If a substance and its accidents are correlatives, it can be no more possible for the accidents to exist without their substance than the parts without their whole.

This doctrine of Transubstantiation is clearly not that which excites Mr. Cobb's enthusiastic admiration, but it is, I believe, that of the Church of Rome, and nothing short of this would satisfy a devout Roman Catholic. When in a Roman Catholic city, the Host is brought forth in a gorgeous procession, surrounded by all that splendour to which the Council of Trent (Sess. xiii. cap. v.) attributes so much efficacy—amidst a blaze of lights, clouds of incense, showers of roses—what do the people understand to be the object of their adoration? Certainly not a metaphysical entity, an incorporeal substance; but Christ Himself, perfect God and perfect man: in the full integrity of His manhood, not a bone, not a nerve, not a hair wanting; in His full, proper, natural dimensions, —but all unseen, hidden under a veil. "The faithful," says the Catechism (u. s. Quæst. xxvi.), "can never sufficiently admire the perfection of Holy Church and her height of glory, seeing that between that and the heavenly blessedness there is only one degree of difference. For this we have in common with the dwellers in heaven, that both have Christ, God and man, present. The only difference is, that they enjoy the beatific vision of His presence, we adore Him, present, but *withdrawn from the sense of the eyes, concealing Himself under the admirable covering of the sacred mysteries*, by a firm and steadfast faith." ("Ac profecto satis mirari fideles nunquam poterunt sanctæ Ecclesiæ perfectionem, ejusque gloriæ altitudinem; cum inter eam et cœlestem beatitudinem, unus tantum gradus interesse videatur. Hoc enim nobis cum cœlitibus commune est, ut utrique Christum, Deum et hominem, præsentem habeamus: sed (quo uno gradu ab iis distamus) illi præsentis beata visione perfruuntur; nos præsentem et tamen *ab oculorum sensu remotum, sacrorum mysteriorum admirabili integumento se occultantem*, firma et constanti fide veneramur.") It would, to say the least, be a very singular way of speaking, to say that a thing, invisible in itself, like *substance*, is *hidden by a covering*, and *withdrawn from the sense of the eyes*, to which it never was, or could be subject. But according to my view of the doctrine, all is clear and consistent.

I do not wonder indeed that such a belief should appear too extravagant to have been ever admitted into a sane mind. But according to the view of the Church of Rome, this apparent extravagance is the very thing which constitutes the merit of the belief. "Credo quia impossible est." This is one of the reasons assigned by the Roman Catechism (Quæst. xxxviii.) for which it was Christ's pleasure to give His Body and Blood under the form of bread and wine. "It would have been shocking to human nature to feed on human flesh, and to drink human blood." It would also have exposed Christians to calumny from unbelievers, if they had been seen to eat the Lord under His own form. Another advantage is, that when we receive the Lord's Body and Blood, in such a way, *that what is really done* cannot be perceived by the senses, this serves much to increase faith in our minds, faith being considered as a grace which is strengthened by exercise (" dum Corpus et Sanguinem Domini ita sumimus ut tamen *quod rere fit, sensibus percipi non possit*, hoc ad fidem in animis nostris augendam plurimum valet, quæ quidem ibi non habet *meritum*, ubi humana ratio præbet experimentum "). That which is received is the very natural Body and Blood, but hidden from sense by the elements. I cannot see how the language and the whole argument of the passage admit of any other interpretation. And I have no doubt that it was in the literal sense that Aquinas meant to be understood, when he sang,

> " Verbum Caro panem verum
> Verbo carnem efficit :—
> Fitque Sanguis Christi merum ;
> Et, si sensus deficit,
> Ad firmandum cor sincerum
> Sola fides sufficit."

The translation in "Hymns Ancient and Modern," "which whoso

taketh, must from carnal thoughts be free," gives a turn to the thought which I believe to be quite foreign to the author's meaning.

I will only add one remark. Whether it is Mr. Cobb or myself that is in error on this question, what are we to think of the teaching of a Church which expresses herself on such an article of faith so as to leave room for such a difference of opinion as to her meaning? one, it must be observed, not at all arising out of the obscurity of the subject itself, but entirely out of the manner in which she has treated it. It was not without good cause that Pius IV., in the Bull of Confirmation of the Council, forbade the publishing of any commentaries, or any kind of interpretation of its decrees, without his authority (" ne quis sine auctoritate nostra audeat ullos commentarios, glossas, annotationes, scholia, ullumve omnino interpretationis genus super ipsius Concilii decretis quocunque modo edere "). Should any one find any thing obscure in them, and needing interpretation or decision, let him go up to the Apostolical See (" ei cui vero in eis aliquid obscurius dictum et statutum fuisse, eamque ob causam interpretatione aut decisione aliqua egere, visum fuerit, ascendat ad locum quem Dominus elegit, ad Sedem videlicet Apostolicam. Deut. xvii. 8 ").

It would have been better if the Council had spared him and the faithful this trouble, by a little greater perspicuity.

(C.)

After the Charge had been delivered at three out of the four places of my Visitation, I learnt, by a private letter from a gentleman who had seen some account of it in a London paper, that the statement, that "the Union was brought about against the will of the great majority of the Irish people," is disputed: and I was courteously invited to refer my correspondent to " the sources from which I had drawn this conclusion." I am aware that the subject is one on which it is impossible, especially after an interval of seventy years, to speak with certainty, and that no authority can be absolutely conclusive. But I think that so strong a presumption is raised in favour of the statement, by the whole course of previous and subsequent history, as to throw the burden of proof on those who deny it, and that this presumption is confirmed by the nature of the means which the Government had to employ to carry the measure through the Irish Parliament. I will, however, refer the reader to Massey's " History of England," and to Goldwin Smith's " Irish History and Irish Character." Mr. Massey writes (Vol. iv. p. 334), "However conclusive the argument in favour of Union may appear to Englishmen, it was difficult for an Irishman to regard the Union in any other view than as a measure to deprive his country of her independent constitution, and to extinguish her national existence." It seems to me clear, that when this was the general feeling, real consent to the Union must have been the exception, hostility the rule. So Mr. Massey observes (p. 347), " There was one mode of carrying the Union, and one mode only. Bribery of every kind must be employed, without hesitation and without stint." I cannot take into the account on the side of the Union, either votes so purchased, or support obtained by delusive promises. " The consent of the Catholic clergy," observes Mr. Goldwin Smith (p. 178), " so far as that body did consent, must be held to have been vitiated, since hopes of an arrangement in their favour were held out to them, and not fulfilled." And as he says, p. 186, " Of the absurdity and iniquity of a Union, which excluded three-fourths of the people of one nation, on the ground of their religion, from the common legislature, there is now no need to dwell." Were these " three-fourths," " the great majority of the Irish people," absolutely insensible to this " absurdity and iniquity ? "

Mr. Massey is impartial, and all Mr. Goldwin Smith's leaning is in favour of the Union. I know how cautiously the views and judgments of such a violent partisan as Mr. Mitchel are to be received. Yet I do not believe that he wilfully misstates facts, and therefore I think I may refer to his " History of Ireland," vol. ii. chap. iii. and foll., in confirmation of my conclusion.

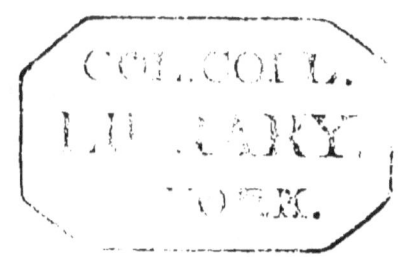

XI.

A CHARGE

DELIVERED OCTOBER AND NOVEMBER, 1872.

THE VATICAN COUNCIL.—DISSENSIONS IN THE CHURCH OF ENGLAND.—THE ATHANASIAN CREED.—THE EDUCATION ACT OF 1870.

MY REVEREND BRETHREN,

I CANNOT meet you on this occasion without a personal reflection, which, if I was able, I should not think it right to suppress. The temporary disability by which I was compelled, two years ago, to seek assistance for my last Confirmation, called forth marks of sympathy and kindness which I can never forget. But it also admonished me that the time could not be very far distant when my strength would no longer suffice even for the ordinary work of the Diocese, to say nothing of new calls which might be expected to arise out of the shifting circumstances of the Church. And I now address you with the solemnity of a deep conviction that this is the last time my voice will be heard from this chair. But speaking under this feeling, I do not know how I could better avail myself of the present opportunity than according to my practice in past years, when I have been used to take a broad survey of our condition and prospects, and to express my opinion on the main topics which had arisen in the intervals of successive Visitations to occupy the minds of Churchmen, and affect the interests of the Church. In the course of an episcopate protracted far beyond the average length, these topics have been constantly growing in number and magnitude, and have often rendered it difficult to avoid exceeding the ordinary measure of a

Visitation Charge. On the present occasion I believe I shall be in least danger of trespassing unduly on your patience, if I first look out on that which lies farthest on our horizon, and then pass to matters in which we are, if not more deeply, yet, as it may seem, more immediately concerned.

The most important event that has taken place since our last meeting—one, I venture to say, far more important than the great change in the balance of power which we have witnessed during the same interval—is the promulgation of the new dogma decreed by the Council of the Vatican, on the 18th of July, 1870, by which the decisions of the Pope in all questions of faith and morals were declared to be irreformable, that is, absolutely exempt from possibility of error, as Divine Revelation, irrespectively of any previous or subsequent assent of the Church, whether diffused throughout Christendom, or represented in a General Council. I cannot expect that all my hearers should fully appreciate the importance of this event. Many may have wanted leisure or means of studying its character and bearings, and may see in it nothing more than a fresh display of arrogant pretensions, which illustrate the character of the Papacy, but make no alteration in the state of things, so far, at least, as we are concerned. I am very sure that it can be so regarded only by those who do not comprehend its nature; and I believe there is no subject of deeper practical interest to every one of us, or on which a portion of our time can be more profitably employed. *Infallibility of the Pope.*

Though the number of Bishops brought together in the Vatican Council appears to have exceeded that of every previous Synod, its right to the title of an Œcumenical or General Council has been questioned. And, no doubt, if it is tried by the standard of Anglican orthodoxy, it will be found wanting in one particular. It is laid down in our Twenty-first Article that "General Councils may not be gathered together without the commandment and will of Princes." But the Vatican Council was convoked by the mere will and pleasure of the Pope, not only without regard to any secular authority, *The Vatican Council not Œcumenical.*

but so as expressly to exclude all reference to any such authority,* and with a studied display of independence, which was treated by the advocates of the Papacy as matter of boastful exultation. It was, no doubt, a very significant innovation on the practice of former ages. But I do not find that any scruple was felt by Roman Catholics of any school with regard to the Œcumenicity of the Council on this account; and considering the circumstances of the time, I cannot attribute much weight to this objection. It is at least conceivable that such a gathering might be urgently needed for the interests of the Church, and yet that the state of public affairs might make it impossible to obtain the express concurrence of the Powers whose consent was required. In such a case their passive acquiescence might perhaps be deemed equivalent to an expression of their will. Very remarkable, no doubt, is the contrast between the circumstances under which the Council of the Vatican was convoked, and those of the Council of Trent, in this, as indeed in almost every other respect. The Council of the sixteenth century was forced by the Emperor on a reluctant Pope, who dreaded nothing so much as that Reformation of the Church in Head and Members which it was the Emperor's main object to bring about; † and the place at which it was held was selected for the convenience of access to the Princes who appeared by their envoys at the Council.‡ That of the Vatican was viewed with apprehension and distrust by all the Roman Catholic Sovereigns, who knew that they had nothing but evil to expect from it, and the more because it was to be held at Rome, where it would be completely subject to the power and influence of the Pope. This contrast may suggest some instructive reflections on the course of that development which has reached its culminating point in the new dogma. But it seems to me that it would be

Convoked under different circumstances from the Council of Trent.

---

* For the negotiation on this subject see Quirinus, "Römische Briefe vom Concil," p. 24.

† Paleotto, "Acta Concilii Tridentini," ed. Mendham, p. 10, admits the prevailing belief, though holding it to be sufficiently refuted by the convocation of the Council.

‡ Paleotto, u. s., p. 11, " ut facilius Christiani principes possent convenire." Cf. Quirinus, u. s., p. 11.

going too far to say that no change of circumstances could justify such a variation in the mode of proceeding.

There is another point of view in which the Council of the Vatican fails altogether to satisfy our notion of a General Council, inasmuch as it is not, and does not even claim to be, commensurate with the whole extent of the Christian World. It confessedly excluded a very large part of Christendom; only, however, it must be observed, those who, according to the Roman view, were disqualified from taking part in its deliberations by heresy or schism, and who rejected the invitations by which they were summoned to entitle themselves to its privileges by repentance and submission. To the Churches of the East, proud of their antiquity and their immaculate orthodoxy, and to the Churches of the Reformation, united in opposition to the corruptions of Rome, such invitations could hardly sound otherwise than as an insult unworthy of serious notice. But we cannot be surprised that from the Roman point of view they should seem to justify the assumption of a title which else would have stood in glaring contrast to the real character of the assembly. So far therefore the question of Œcumenicity is only a branch of the general controversy between Rome and the Churches which reject her authority.
Excluded a large part of the Christian world.

Neither of these objections appears to me to touch the main point. According to ideas which are not peculiar to the Church of Rome, a purely clerical assembly, in which no layman had either vote or consultative voice, might be fully competent to deal with questions of doctrine which affected nothing but religious convictions, especially if, like the dogma of the Immaculate Conception, they were totally destitute of practical interest, and utterly unworthy of notice, except for the audacity of their invention. But that which the Council of the Vatican undertook to decide, was not only the fundamental doctrine of the Christian faith, that on which all others must ultimately rest, but a question most deeply affecting the whole framework and the very foundation of civil society, the institu-
Object of its convocation.

tions of every State,* the peace of every household. The work for which it was assembled was not simply a new ecclesiastical constitution, but, through and under cover of this, a complete political and social revolution. It is only when this is clearly understood, that we can duly appreciate the audacity by which the laity were excluded from all share in deliberation on matters so nearly concerning all that was most precious to them, and were expected to receive the decrees of their spiritual guides with passive submission. And fully to estimate the boldness of this attempt, we must recollect the vast strides which the human mind has taken in the last three centuries, and the consequent growing impatience of clerical dominion and dictation.

To members of the Roman communion who admit the Pope's authority to convoke a General Council, and the formal Œcumenicity of the Vatican Synod, there remain only two questions of any moment; one, whether the Council was free, the other, whether the dogma it decreed is a truth of Divine Revelation. Indeed, since every Roman Catholic is bound to admit the infallibility of a General Council, the two questions resolve themselves into one, and the whole turns on the single issue of freedom, which is agreed on all hands to be indispensable to the validity of the proceedings of every deliberative assembly, and above all of a General Council.† The truth of the dogma indeed cannot depend on the freedom of the Council. If true, it would have been equally so though the Council had never met: as the Council itself does not profess to make, but only to find and declare, the truth.‡ But the obligation of the faithful to accept its decrees, depends not on their truth, but on its authority, of which freedom is an essential condition. And when we are considering how the issue is likely to

Freedom indispensable to deliberative assemblies.

---

* On the political aspect and consequences of the Dogma, see the petition drawn up by Cardinal Rauscher in Friedrich's " Documenta " ii., p. 388.

† " Libertas illa, quam oportuit esse in omnibus consultationibus, maxime vero de rebus sacris." (Jewell, Epist. De Concilio Tridentino.) But I do not see that the Bishops of the Vatican Council were bound by their oath of obedience to the Pope, to accept any definition proposed to them, even with his express sanction.

‡ " Ecclesia in suis definitionibus semper est Testis, et judicium nonnisi testando efformat." (Archbishop Kenrick in Friedrich, " Documenta " i., p. 210.)

affect the interests of the Church and of society, this becomes the most important point in the whole inquiry.

The facts which bear upon it lie within a comparatively narrow compass. The most notorious of all is that down to the eve of the day on which the dogma was proclaimed, the want of necessary freedom was the subject of incessant, though unheeded, complaint, petition, and remonstrance, on the part of the Minority in the Council itself.* The defect was radically inherent in its composition. Virtually and practically it was an Italian Council: Italy alone having more voices than all the Roman Catholic countries of Europe together. This preponderance of the Italian vote was further strengthened by a host of titular prelates, many of them created for the occasion, without churches or flocks, absolutely depending on the Pope for their daily bread, and by chiefs of the monastic Orders entirely devoted to him. On the other side was a Minority representing a population of ninety millions, and of the most civilized nations of the world. But the vote of each titular prelate counted for as much as that of the occupant of the greatest see, and his testimony to the tradition of the Church was received as of equal value. *The Council not free.*

The order of proceeding was so regulated as to make the result depend on the will of the Pope, just as if the question of his plenary authority had been already decided. The public deliberations were so mere a mockery, that they were carried on in a room where no speaker could be heard by more than two-thirds of those present; and none were allowed to print their speeches, even for the sole use of their colleagues.† Neither within nor without the Council Hall was there the possibility *Order of proceeding.*

---

* "Notre faiblesse vient de notre défaut de liberté, qui est radical. La majorité n'est pas libre. A notre arrivée tout était fait sans nous. Mais voici ce qui achève d'opprimer notre liberté ; elle est écrasée de tout le poids du respect que nous portons à notre chef. Nous avons trouvé une majorité toute faite, très-compacte," &c. (Quirinus, Anhang, p. 656 ff. Cf. Friedrich, "Doc." i., pp. 138, 168. "Pio IX. préjuge solennellement la question soumise au Concile." Ibid., p. 183.)

† "In prima congregatione generali, inter oratores, quorum aliqui fortissima pollebant voce, ne unus quidem erat, quem omnes exaudire possent Patres, et etiam postquam aula in arctius reducta est, magna congregatorum pars cunctis, quæ dicta sunt, percipiendis impar est." (Friedrich i., p. 247. V. Schulte, "Das Unfehlbarkeits-Decret.," p. 11.)

of a free interchange of ideas among the members.* The Council was practically represented by a select committee nominated by the Pope, either directly or through the Majority, composed, as we have seen, so as to consist entirely of devoted partisans.

Pressure exercised by the Pope. But the gravest of all obstacles to the freedom of discussion, was the pressure exercised by the Pope, who neglected no opportunity, public or private, of making known that the question was one in which he took the deepest personal interest, and of denouncing the opponents of the dogma as a faction hostile to himself and to the Church. It is difficult for us adequately to conceive, but impossible to exaggerate, the weight thus thrown into the scale among persons used to receive every expression of the Papal mind and will with religious veneration and awe.

Precipitation of the Decree. This series of oppressive interferences with the liberty of the Council was fitly crowned by the scandalous precipitation with which the measure, taken out of its place in the prescribed order of the proceedings, was finally hurried through: haste, which would have been indecent, even if the matter had been one of slight moment, or which called for little study and research, instead of being, as it was, the gravest of all questions that could occupy the attention of the Christian world, reaching more nearly to the foundation of the faith, and involving a wider range of inquiry than any other. The Decree was ultimately carried by a numerical majority, against all precedent, which in such a case, above all, required moral unanimity; in the absence indeed of the dissentients, but after they had declared to the last that their opinion remained unchanged.

Protest of the minority. A minority of more than a hundred protested, in the strongest terms consistent with respect for the Pope, against the restraints imposed on the freedom of discussion, and against the dogma itself. These protests they never withdrew, and the facts on which their remonstrances were grounded could not be changed by their subsequent submission, however it might affect their character for courage or sincerity. Thoughtful lay-

† Friedrich, "Tagebuch," pp. 33 and 47.

men of their own communion, who had watched their proceedings with deep sympathy, and had been convinced by their arguments, could not abandon their convictions, because their teachers had become silent. It was not enough, as one of them remarked, for such things to be retracted, unless they were also refuted. It had gone forth to the world that the Vatican Council was one long intrigue, carried through by fraud and violence.* *Character of the Council.* No subsequent act of theirs could alter its character, or do more than contribute a little to the temporary success of triumphant iniquity. It remained not the less true that, since the Robber Synod of Ephesus, no assembly claiming the title of a General Council had been disgraced by more shameless breaches of freedom and justice. If at Ephesus there was more of brutal violence, there was at Rome an equally unscrupulous exertion of arbitrary power, and a far greater depth of cunning.

To us however the most important question, indeed the only one in which we can feel any immediate interest, is the *Truth of infallibility considered.* truth of the dogma. And in this case truth means—at least had until now been believed to mean—antiquity. We must remember that the Council did not affect to proclaim any new doctrine, or to invest the Papacy with any new dignity or jurisdiction. The only purpose for which the Bishops were supposed to be brought together was to attest the doctrine handed down by tradition in their respective dioceses. How the titular prelates who had no diocese could be qualified to bear such witness, we are happily not concerned to explain. But the proposition which the Council makes binding on the conscience of everyone who acknowledges its authority, under penalty of eternal perdition, is that the personal infallibility of the Pope was revealed from the beginning, and has been held ever since by the Church. With our recollections of the New Testament, we find it difficult to conceive how so astounding a paradox could have been seriously asserted. Independently however of scriptural testimony, it was thought, not unreasonably, that a doctrine of such a nature, of such constant application to cases which must

* Lord Acton, "Sendschreiben an einen Deutschen Bischof," p. 18.

have been continually arising, could never have been forgotten or questioned in the Church; and therefore that it is disproved by the very fact that it has been found necessary, at the end of eighteen centuries, to affirm it for the first time in a General Council. And, waiving this objection, we may remark that if Ecclesiastical History can show a single well-attested instance in which a Pope has fallen into heresy, that would confessedly be fatal to the dogma. No less conclusive to the same effect would be a case in which a Pope had retracted a solemn judgment on an article of faith. We are familiar with the error of Pope Honorius, venial indeed in itself, but one which was accounted deadly heresy, and repeatedly condemned both by Councils and his successors. Attempts have been made to clear him from this charge, but it appears to have been overlooked, that on the theory of personal infallibility the charge could never have been brought against him. The same remark applies to the waverings and retractations of Liberius and Vigilius. On the modern theory, they were not only impossible, but could never have been imputed to a Pope. As little could cases have occurred in which the most solemn dogmatical decrees of an infallible Pope were subjected to examination and revision before they were adopted by a Council. Yet this was not only a common case, but the constant rule of proceeding.

Illustration of the dogma. One illustration of the novelty and strangeness of the dogma is so remarkable in itself, and so nearly concerns us, as to deserve special notice. The belief which prevailed among Protestants in this country, that the dogma which has been now proclaimed was indeed an article of faith in the Church of Rome, was the main obstacle to the admission of Roman Catholics to an equal share of civil rights. This obstacle was only removed by the solemn assurances given by Roman Catholic Bishops and eminent theologians that this doctrine formed no part of the Roman Catholic faith.* The Irish members of the Vatican Council, who retained a lively recollection of these events, found

---

* See the Speech of Archbishop Kenrick in Friedrich, "Doc." i., p. 213, and Appendix.

themselves called upon to take part in a proceeding hardly consistent, as far as they were concerned, with common honesty. That which, when a political object was to be gained, they had represented as a calumnious invention, they were now required to affirm to be, and to have ever been, the simple truth. "Who," one of them asked, "shall persuade Protestants that Catholics are not acting contrary to honour and good faith, if, when civil rights were in question, they professed that the Pope's infallibility did not form a part of the Catholic faith, but when they had obtained their end, retract this public profession, and affirm the contrary?"*

We had been used to suppose that the question belonged to the domain of Ecclesiastical History, and that persons were competent to form a judgment upon it in proportion to their familiarity with that field of literature. The value of the Italian vote in the Council was thought to be greatly impaired by the notorious fact that the Italian Bishops were on this point almost universally the dupes of the forgeries which had imposed on Thomas Aquinas. Hundreds of such votes would be outweighed by that of a single theologian who could speak with the authority of a Hefele or a Döllinger. But since the meeting of the Council it has been discovered that all this is a mistake, that Ecclesiastical History has nothing to do with the matter, that learning is quite superfluous for the solution of this question, and that the very object of the Council is to dispense with the need of scientific historical research. According to the view of the most ardent advocate of the dogma, the history of the Church can only be learnt from the witness she bears to herself,†

Viewed in relation to Ecclesiastical History.

---

* Bishop Clifford, in Friedrich, *ib.* ii., p. 258.

† Friedrich, "Tagebuch," p. 85, gives an extract from an Italian pamphlet of Archbishop Manning, published at Naples, 1869:— " È ormai tempo che le pretensioni della 'scienza istorica' e di certi 'scienziati storici,' riducansi ai limiti della propria sfera. E ciò farà il Concilio, non con dispute ed altercazioni, ma con le sole parole, ' E piacuto allo Spirito Santo ed a noi."—" La chiesa è la prova di sè stessa, anteriore alla sua istoria, e independente da essa. La sua istoria non può che da essa impararsi." (It is now time that the pretensions of "historical science" and of certain "scientific historians" should be reduced to the limits of their proper sphere. And this the Council will do, not by disputes and altercations, but by the simple words, "It has seemed good to the Holy Ghost and to us." The Church is the proof

which is now gathered up in the single oracle of the infallible Pope, whose assertion of his own infallibility needs no corroboration from any other testimony; and according to the same authority, this infallibility is a personal charisma, known by inward experience to the person who has been favoured with it, and to him alone. With him alone rests the exercise which he may think fit to make of his gift. It can never be subject to any external limitation. That which he declares to have taken place in the past, in all matters affecting religion—such as the Assumption of the Virgin Mary—becomes historical fact. That which he teaches on points touching faith and morals becomes theological truth. No one has a right to try either the fact or the truth by any other standard. It is to be accepted as the voice of the Holy Ghost, just as if he was incarnate in the person of the Pope.

<small>The history of the Romish Church only to be learnt from herself.</small>

Bearing this in mind, we may see how vast is the change which the promulgation of this dogma has made in the position of every Roman Catholic throughout the world, and in the relation of every civil society to the Church of Rome. As there can be no political question of the slightest moment that does not bear upon faith or morals, or both, the Papal infallibility implies a claim of absolute sovereignty over the whole range of human thought and action. As that which is true with regard to it now was equally true in all time past, the most extravagant pretensions, as they appear to us, of the mediæval popes, are now revived, re-affirmed, invested for ever with a divine authority. The one thing which is beyond the power of the Pope himself is to renounce or limit them. We may be quite sure that the authors of this ecclesiastical revolution will never cease to keep two objects steadily in view; on the one hand, to conceal its real nature and scope, so as to quiet the alarms of those who are not prepared to surrender the rights of the state to the priesthood;* on the other hand, to put the dogma in use; to make the

<small>Bearings of Papal infallibility on the world at large.</small>

of herself, anterior to her history and independent of it. Her history can only be learnt from herself.)

* The state of the case is explained by Cardinal Antonelli in a despatch to the Nuncio at Paris (inserted in an English translation in Archbishop Manning's

Papal sovereignty felt in every relation of public and private life. It is true, that whatever comfort we can derive from the assurance, that the Pope will not again assume the title of King or Lord of England, or claim the right of repealing Acts of Parliament, that we may securely enjoy. In general we may be sure that as long as he can obtain the substance of power, he will be well content to dispense with the form. But his agency will not be the less real or effectual, because it is carried on underground and in the dark. And it would be a great mistake to imagine that this danger has been rendered less formidable by the recent course of political events. The loss of the Pope's temporal dominion is likely to give a stronger impulse to the zeal of his partisans, in their endeavours to propagate his spiritual empire; and the unscrupulous arts which were employed to bring about the pro-

---

Appendix to his Pastoral Letter, 'The Vatican Council and its Definitions'), with a clearness and openness which leaves nothing to desire:—

"The Church has never intended, nor now intends, to exercise any direct and absolute power over the political rights of the State. Having received from God the lofty mission of guiding men, whether individually or as congregated in society, to a supernatural end, she has by that very fact the authority and the duty to judge concerning the morality and justice of all acts, internal and external, in relation to their conformity with the natural and divine law. And as no action, whether it be ordained by a supreme power, or be freely elicited by an individual, can be exempt from this character of morality and justice, so it happens that the judgment of the Church, though falling directly on the morality of the acts, indirectly reaches over everything with which that morality is conjoined. But this is not the same thing as to interfere directly in political affairs." One who cannot see the meaning of this, must be wilfully blind. But by way of illustration I subjoin an extract from the "Revue des Deux Mondes," December 1, 1871, p. 540 :—" Le Pape se considère en Bavière comme un prince souverain ; il y publie ses propres décrets en dépit des lois positives du pays. L'archevêque de Bamberg lui-même a publiquement avoué, le 24 mai dernier, que 'l'épiscopat bavarois ne prêtait serment que sous la réserve mentale de toutes les lois de l'Église. Quand les évêques cherchent à nier l'hostilité du Catholicisme Romain à l'égard de la société civile, le ' Syllabus' leur donne un démenti. Rome se considère comme en guerre ouverte avec les gouvernements européens. Comme preuve à l'appui, les journaux allemands ont réproduit le texte des instructions secrètes du Pape aux confesseurs du royaume d'Italie publié par l'Unita Cattolica au mois d'avril, 1871 ; on y voit que la cour du Vatican ordonnait aux confesseurs d'imposer comme un devoir de conscience aux soldats italiens de déserter dès qu'ils le pourraient faire sans péril de la vie."

Friedrich, "Tagebuch," p. 243, relates: "Manning now makes it his business to demonstrate to every one who will give him a hearing, that the infallibility relates only to matters of dogma, not to the State. But even Count Trautmannsdorff observed to him that the words were not simply *quoad fidem* but also *quoad mores.*"

mulgation of the dogma, will not be spared in the application of its logical consequences to all human concerns.

<small>Roman Catholic loyalty.</small> It has now become impossible for a Roman Catholic, consistently with the first principles of his religion, to be a loyal subject of any government which is not itself subject to the will of the Pope. Heretofore he might conscientiously profess that his submission to the decrees of his Church was consistent with his duty as a citizen. If he was pressed with the claims put forward by such Popes as Innocent III., or Boniface VIII., to temporal supremacy, he could argue with some degree of plausibility, that they only asserted an authority which was conceded to them by the consent of the age in which they lived. He could repudiate the charge of a divided allegiance, as a calumny forged for a pretext to cover the withholding of a right. But there is no longer room for such a protest. His allegiance indeed can no longer be truly said to be divided, but only because it is now exclusively due to his spiritual sovereign, whose side he is bound to take whenever the interests or the will of that sovereign come into collision with the institutions of his earthly country. No statesman can be worthy of the name, who overlooks or ignores the gravity of the change which has been effected by the new dogma, when he has to deal with proposals for a further development of Roman Catholic influence, especially in the control of education. We have received ample warning, that the adherents of the Papacy will never be satisfied until the present barriers of the constitution have been swept away, and the throne has been made accessible to a sovereign pledged far more deeply than James II. to obedience to the Pope.*

<small>Probable consequences of Papal infallibility.</small> Of the consequences which may be expected to result from this event, either abroad or at home, it would be premature to speak. If in Germany it should lead to a permanent schism, this will probably be due rather to the political

---

* Mr. Gladstone is reported to have said, in a speech delivered at King's College, on the 14th May last :—" I must own that, admitting the incapacity of my understanding to grasp fully what has occurred, the aspect of the recent decrees at Rome appears to me too much to resemble the proclamation of a perpetual war against the progress and the movement of the human mind."

than to the religious aspect of the question, though the one may react upon the other. We watch the progress of the so-called Old Catholic movement with friendly interest. The dignitaries of our own Church who attended the Congress of Cologne, though they did not appear in an official character as representatives of the Anglican Church, probably expressed a very general feeling. All our sympathy is with Döllinger and his friends, as against the revolutionary party to which they are opposed: but we cannot make their present position our own. The Council of Trent indeed becomes comparatively respectable by the side of that of the Vatican, and its proceedings a model of freedom and equity. But we are not prepared to adopt its decrees; and our rejection of the new dogma does not reconcile us to the Creed of Pius IV. As members of the Church of England, we must continue to protest not only against the Pope's personal infallibility, but against what we may call the infallibility of the Pope in Council.

Whether in our own country any such gain will accrue to the Church of Rome from the dogma by an increase of proselytes, as the Pope was led to expect by his English counsellors, still remains to be seen. Its influence on our Church. I am far from confident that it will not be attended with any such result. I believe there are minds so constituted or trained that they not only readily adopt the Jesuit maxim of the merit earned by the sacrifice of the intellect, but find it a relief to transfer the whole labour and responsibility of thought and conscience, in matters of religion, to another, and so are prepared to welcome the doctrine of an infallible teacher. But I own I should be painfully surprised and disappointed if, on the whole, the effect of this innovation among ourselves was not to widen and fix the gulph which separates us from the Church of Rome, and to unite all members of our own Communion, who have ever indeed been of us, in more decided opposition to her claims, both new and old. I am far from saying that this is a result desirable in itself, or one which any Christian mind can contemplate with unmixed complacency. But it may be the least of two evils. Speaking in the abstract, we cannot but sympathise with every "Association formed for the promotion of the Unity of Christendom." But we must not disguise from ourselves, that even so great a blessing would be purchased too dearly, or rather, that it would be completely neutralized by a compromise of truth. And if, even before the proclamation of the new dogma, it was difficult to conceive how such a reunion could be brought about otherwise than on terms of absolute submission to Rome,—such therefore as we have no right to believe that any Church will ever accept,— I need hardly observe how completely such a prospect has been shut out by the position now taken up by the Church of Rome. The hopelessness of the event indeed is no reason why it should cease to be the object of our wishes and of our prayers. But it may well be questioned, whether persons who, without any Divine commission, undertake to co-operate in the working of such a stupendous miracle, must not either be labouring under some strange delusion as to the relation of means to the end they have in view, or be using language which does not exactly convey their real meaning and intention.

Unity of Christendom may be purchased too dearly.

I now pass to subjects more specially affecting the Church at home.

State and prospects of the Church. When we met last, the prospects of the Church, as to its temporal position, were regarded by many of its friends with much anxiety. Its adversaries were assailing it with growing confidence, and with the machinery of a more compact organization. The recent example of Ireland had awakened hopes on the one side and fears on the other, which experience alone could prove to be groundless. A sensible change has passed upon this state of things. It is not that the uneasiness has been succeeded by a sense of absolute security. Never was there a time when it was less possible to count upon the duration of any human institution, or to be sure that the forces which not long ago astonished Europe by the outbreak of their destructive energy, and by the full revelation of their direct antagonism to the first principles of religion, morality, and social order, may not regain their ascendancy, or at least be enabled to renew the struggle in which their wildest excessess found apologists and advocates in educated men among ourselves. But as to any danger specially threatening the Church, her position appears to have become relatively stronger, by the more decided failure of every fresh assault. It is at least evident that for the present our chief, if not our only, danger is that which threatens us from within. It is not Disestablishment or Disendowment, but Disruption, Disorganization, and Disintegration, that we have immediately to dread; with the certainty that the evil which is incomparably the greater in itself, would, if unchecked, sooner or later draw the other after it. It is fit that we should look it calmly in the face, that we may neither underrate nor unduly magnify its importance. But no one who is not blind to the signs of the times can question that it affords matter for serious apprehension.

If we would trace it to its origin, we see at once that it is not the effect of any alteration in the doctrinal formularies which had long been received as a sufficient bond of union. *Origin of the Disorganization.* Nor is it that now, for the first time in our history, the Church has been divided into parties or schools, which have taken different views of those formularies. There had never been a period when one party, whose leaning was toward the Church of Rome, and which held that the Reformation had been carried too far, was not confronted by another which inclined towards the views of the Continental Reformers, and thought that our Reformation had not been carried far enough. But the great sacrifice made to uniformity two centuries ago, though it did not efface the old division of parties, was followed by a long period of tranquillity—the tranquillity indeed of stagnation, which we have little reason to look back upon with regret—interrupted only by occasional controversies of no general or permanent interest; useful perhaps, as preventing the diffusion of a deeper lethargy. It has been within a very recent period that the breach between the two parties has been so widened as to make it doubtful whether they can continue to find room within the same Church. *The breach widened.* It is a mistake, we have been informed, to regard them as "merely differing aspects of the same religion," and not as logically "two distinct religions—two great camps, Catholic and Protestant—quite as diverse from each other as Judaism from Islam."* And we learn from another high authority of the same school, that "the vast majority of our countrymen belong exclusively to no party, but are simply Protestant, with no other bond of union than a common dislike of Popery."†

This hostility might have been the result of a development by which either party had brought out its latent tendencies, so as to provoke more active antagonism; but in fact I do not find that there has been any such development on more than one side. On that of the Protestant or Evangelical party there has been, so far as I am aware, no deliberate systematic innovation, either in doctrine or practice, on the usage of centuries; rather perhaps signs of a growing disposition to make concessions in things indifferent. But on the other side the development which has been proceeding before our eyes during the last ten years, has culminated in an approximation to Romish doctrine and ritual so close as to render the remaining interval hardly perceptible to common observers. Whether those who lead the van in this movement regard the position which they have taken up as one in which they could finally rest, or as a step toward an ulterior object, it would be useless to inquire. But they do not profess to be satisfied with the present amount of innovation, or to regard it as anything more than a beginning and an instalment. They make no secret of their desire and intention, so far as lies in their power, to bring about a complete transformation of the Church of England into the likeness of the Church of Rome in every particular short of immediate submission to the Pope.‡

The result of increased activity on one side.

Designs of Ritualists.

It is necessary to bear this in mind, that we may form a correct estimate of the course taken by the opposite parties. We cannot but respect the courage and openness with which the leaders of the Ritualist movement avow their designs,

---

* "The Two Religions: a Lecture by Richard F. Littledale, LL.D.," p. 2.
† "Secular Judgments in Spiritual Matters." By Rev. Orby Shipley, M.A., p. 9.
‡ See Mr. Orby Shipley, "Cardinal Virtues," p. 247.

and disclose their plan of operation. They inform us that their party is engaged in a "crusade against Protestantism,"* and aims at nothing less than "re-Catholicizing the Church of England;† and that with a view to this ultimate object, they are agitating for Disestablishment."‡ After this it must be our own fault if we are not on our guard. But when the same persons put in "a plea for Toleration," I do not know how to illustrate the character of such a proposal more aptly than by the image suggested by one of themselves, in the words I was just now quoting, of "two great camps." It is as if one of these camps should send to the other some such message as this: "We are on our march to take possession of your camp, and to make you our prisoners: but all we desire is that you should let us alone, and should not attempt to put any hindrance in our way."

It could hardly be supposed that such a transformation could be accomplished in the name of the law without raising legal questions which must lead to litigation; and the result has been that extraordinary frequency of judicial proceedings in cases of doctrine and ritual which we have recently witnessed. All such litigation is to be most deeply deplored, as it issues from a root of bitterness and inevitably aggravates the bitterness from which it springs. But without assuming the truth to lie exclusively on either side, and only giving both parties equal credit for sincerity and earnestness, we must see that the persons who instituted these proceedings, though to their adversaries they might appear as persecutors, could not but look upon themselves as simply acting on the defensive, in resistance to an unprovoked and unlawful aggression, and for the purpose of averting what to them seemed a tremendous evil. They could not attach less importance to that which they regarded as error, than their adversaries, who held it to be the truth. If the matter

margin: Litigation a necessary result.

---

* See Mr. Orby Shipley, "Cardinal Virtues," p. 174.

† Ibid., p. 220: "Consider how much has to be done ere we stabilitate our conquests over Protestantism, or still more, ere we re-Catholicize the Church of England."

‡ Ibid., p. 194: "The Catholic party in the Church are now agitating for disestablishment."

was too slight to justify the resort to prosecution, it could hardly be weighty enough to be worth the risk of such consequences.

<small>Claim of Ritualists to be descendants of Tractarians.</small> The Ritualists claim to be spiritually the lineal descendants and consistent followers of those who in the last generation set on foot the Oxford movement. But the old Tractarians confined themselves to the inculcation of their doctrines through the pulpit and the press, and attempted no innovation in the forms of worship. When Ritualism first made its appearance, the old Tractarians did not view it with favour. They thought it premature, unseasonable, inexpedient, more likely to check than to forward the progress of their movement. The Ritualist thinks he has reason to complain of the neglect and discouragement with which he has been treated by his spiritual parents and national allies.* But there was a very plain and <small>Difference between the Old and New Tractarians.</small> broad line of separation between the Old and the New Tractarians. The authors of the Oxford movement said many things which at that time were thought strange and startling. But they were content to bear the responsibility of their own opinions, and did not attempt to impose them upon the Church. The later Ritual innovations made the clergyman's public ministrations an instrument for investing his private opinion with the sanction and authority of the Church. It was, as I think, most justly observed by the final Court of Appeal in a recent case: "If the minister be allowed to introduce at his own will variations in the rites and ceremonies that seem to him to interpret the doctrine of the service in a particular direction, the service ceases to be what it was meant to be, common ground on which all Church people may meet, though they differ about some doctrines."† This was the abuse which the law was invoked to

---

* "The summons to make a stand against secular judgments in spiritual matters at last has been sounded by the remains of the old Oxford Tractarian party, which had refused, oftentimes bitterly refused, to be associated with, to support, or even to follow, and still less to be enlisted into the ranks of the Ritual forces in the Catholic Revival. Verily, we have had a sweet and ample revenge!"—Rev. Orby Shipley, u. s., p. 12.

† Judgment in Shepherd v. Bennett. The Court had just before laid down the principle: "In the public or common prayers and devotional offices of the Church all her members are expected and entitled to join; it is necessary, therefore, that such forms of worship as are prescribed by authority for general use should embody

repress. Viewing it in this light, I cannot assent to the claim which has been laid on behalf of the Ritualists to superior forbearance and moderation, on the ground that they have instituted no prosecutions for the numberless offences against obsolete Canons and Rubrics, which might have afforded opportunity of retaliating on their opponents.* This claim could only be admitted if it could be shown that in the prosecutions instituted against them no principle was involved, and no end sought but the infliction of personal annoyance. It can hardly be considered sound reasoning to argue that if one clergyman is left at liberty to neglect an old Rubric, another must have an equal right to introduce a new doctrine as the mind of the Church.†

The successive judgments of the final Court of Appeal which have decided all the main questions that had arisen with regard to public worship, appear to me to have been on the whole strictly conservative, and, while repressing innovations which had given general offence, as violating the principle to which I was just now referring, to have left us large a liberty of teaching and practice as could be reasonably desired. But it cannot be denied that the immediate effect has been to heighten and extend the dissatisfaction which had been long felt by many with the constitution of the Court, and thus to create a common ground on which the most advanced Ritualist may join hands with the most moderate of the old Tractarian School, and even with many who belong to neither. For few probably would be found prepared to contend that this constitution is perfect and not liable to some grave objections. It might seem as if such unanimity opened a prospect

Effects of the judgments of the Court of Appeal.

those beliefs only which are assumed to be generally held by members of the Church."

* In a Memorial to Convocation on the present aspect of the Ritual question, it is observed: "The so-called Ritualists have never moved in the prosecution of any nonconforming clergyman; they do not consider uniformity in strict accordance with the very letter of the law, after long disuse and neglect, either practicable or expedient; rather they believe that any attempt to enforce it would inevitably involve a destruction of the peace of the Church—perhaps even a disruption of the Church itself; they only ask for *justice*, and that a small portion of the *liberty* so largely extended to others may, more especially in consideration of the recent judgments given in the cases above alluded to, be allowed to themselves."

† The fallacy is ably and fully exposed in Mr. Shaw's Essay, "Ritualism and Uniformity," in "Principles at Stake."

of speedy and peaceful solution of the difficulty, in a reconstruction of the tribunal, which should remedy all acknowledged defects. Unhappily we know that a great, perhaps the greater, part of those who call most loudly for such a change, would be content with none but a purely clerical tribunal, possibly including a civilian or two as assessors, to aid the Court with their advice on any merely legal questions that might incidentally arise.* All their arguments would be just as conclusive against the admission of a single lay member, as against a Court composed entirely of laymen. A Court so constituted might perhaps work well enough in a very small narrow sect. In a Church established in this country it would be utterly impracticable. And seeing this, those who are most eager for the change look forward with hope to an approaching Disestablishment, which, as they believe, will restore the liberty and privileges of the clergy, and replace them in their proper position of independence and authority over the laity. Whether the general tendency of the main current of public opinion in this country, or in any part of the civilized world, warrants such a hope, and does not rather insure bitter disappointment to those who cherish it, I need not stop to inquire. But it is saddening to think that such a feeling should have sprung up among members of our Church, especially among the clergy, and that not a few should have transferred their affection and allegiance from the Church to which they still professedly belong, to an ideal body, which never existed in time or space, which they call the Catholic Church, and which, as it is purely a creature of their own imagination, they can securely invoke, to sanction any doctrine or practice which they may desire to introduce.† And it it is still more painful to hear from one of eminent reputation and great influence, that Churchmen, who think with him, "will to a very great extent indeed find relief in co-operating with the political forces which year by year more and more steadily are working

Impracticability of a purely Clerical Court.

Advocacy of Disestablishment by Ritualists.

---

* See Rev. Orby Shipley: "Secular Judgments," and Preface to his Sermons on the Four Cardinal Virtues.

† See the Rev. Orby Shipley, "Secular Judgments in Secular Matters," for "the ten points in the Charter of Anglo-Catholic Ritual," p. 64.

toward Disestablishment;"* though, as we have been assured, this was not meant for a menace, but for the statement of a simple fact, it was a statement manifestly implying approbation of the course of proceeding which it foretold. I should be very loth to censure persons who so express themselves, and whose judgment may be clearer and their sense of duty keener than my own. But I find it difficult to enter into their feelings. If any one is convinced that it would be an advantage to the cause of religion, if our Church was broken up into two or three sects, he has no doubt a right to his opinion. But if not, when he deliberately co-operates to bring about such a result, I do not understand how he can be acquitted of a breach of charity, or of that self-will which is the essence of heresy and schism. Still less can I sympathize with those who, by word or example, instigate their brethren to set the law at open defiance, and declare their own intention of maintaining an attitude, not only of passive resistance but of "active disobedience."†

Still we may find some comfort in the not unreasonable hope, that the leaders of the so-called Catholic Revival, who are chiefly responsible for all the evil and danger of our present position, may have been deceived by the eagerness of their desires, and have mistaken their wishes for realities. It is natural that they should wish to share so grave a responsibility with as many as they can induce to take part in it. But until experience shall have proved the contrary, I shall continue to believe that the great body of the clergy of every school may be credited with a sufficient measure of charity and good sense, to prevent them from following such guidance. It

_{Disapproved by the bulk of the clergy.}

---

* Canon Liddon's Letter to the "Guardian," March 1, 1871.

† "In the place of passive obedience under useless and feeble protest, the party as a party, it is not too early to affirm, with an unanimity hitherto unknown, is prepared for active disobedience, animated by a spirit nearly akin to defiance."—"Secular Judgments," p. 14.

Mr. Orby Shipley himself, however, is under no illusion as to the prospects of the Disestablished Church. "I disbelieve," he says, "in anything but a change in the contest of the Church Militant, a change from a contest against the State without to a contest within, against Puritanism, against Latitudinarianism, against Infidelity, and against what may be termed Lay-elementarianism in the Church."—See. Judg., p. 168.

was the observation of a Churchman who was eminently qualified by station and character to speak with peculiar authority on such a subject, and the more as his general sympathies were on the side of those from whom he differed on this point: "For the clergy to join in a political crusade to accelerate their Disestablishment, would seem to me to argue such a dementation both as to the act and the object, as would indeed almost cause the most confident to despair. *Hoc Ithacus velit, et magno mercentur Atridae.*" *

<small>Judgment of the Court of Appeal on the Eucharist.</small> The most recent Judgment of the Court of Final Appeal, which has declared the legal construction of our Formularies with regard to the Eucharist, has certainly erred, if at all, on the side of freedom, in the exercise of that indulgence which, according to the maxim of English law, is due to the defendant—especially when he is unrepresented—in a penal case. It has been generally felt that in this instance the application of the maxim had been carried to its utmost length. Perhaps the strongest recommendation of the Judgment to all unprejudiced minds is the dissatisfaction with which it has been received by some extreme partisans on both sides. It was quite to be expected that the person whose language had given occasion to the proceedings should scornfully repudiate the authority of a Tribunal constituted only according to the law of the land, and not according to his own opinions and wishes. And we cannot be surprised that there should be found here and there on the other side some who regard the lenity with which he has been treated as connivance at error, or that it should have been used as a handle for attack on the Church as tolerating a plain avowal of distinctively Romish doctrine. I am thankful both for what was said and for what was left unsaid:

---

* Sir John Coleridge, Letter to Canon Liddon, p. 22. He adds—expressing I hope the sentiment of the great majority of Churchmen—" good and wise Christians have thought, that considering how far we agree, and the mysterious nature of those points as to which we differ, our unhappy differences are not such as to prevent both parties from being united in one Church." Undoubtedly the differences are not such in themselves; as is proved by the experience of centuries; but what they may be made to do by the spirit of partizanship, is unfortunately quite a different question.

for what was done, and for what was left undone. We may indeed think it matter of regret, that it should have been deemed necessary to declare that Hooker's doctrine on the Eucharist is admissible in the Church of England. But as the language of the Judge in the Court below intimated that this was a questionable point, it was highly desirable that all doubt should be removed by the distinct statement that the Church " does not by her Articles and Formularies affirm or require her ministers to accept any presence of Christ in that ordinance which is not a presence to the soul of the faithful receiver." On the other hand, it was no less desirable to show that this statement is not to be considered as so exhaustive that no other form of expression can be allowed rightly to describe the mystery, or that anyone is forbidden to speak of it in different terms, not inconsistent with the truth which he is required to affirm. No doubt this latitude, like all liberty, may be abused. And it will never be possible to prevent anyone from availing himself of the ambiguity of language, and of the mysteriousness of the subject, to come indefinitely near to the distinct avowal of Romish doctrine. But I hardly think that the success of the attempt in this case has been such as to invite anyone to repeat the experiment.

In one or two points indeed the maxim by which the defendant in a penal case is entitled to the benefit of a doubt, may seem to have been strained somewhat beyond its reasonable limits. The defendant's original statement affirmed a " visible presence of our Lord upon the altars of our churches." It seems that a more judicious friend led him to observe that this language went too far, even beyond the Romish doctrine of the Real Presence, and he was thus induced to substitute a different expression. But he took care to explain that he meant precisely the same thing by both statements. It might therefore have seemed that he wished to be understood as continuing to maintain that complete identification of our Lord's Body and Blood with the Bread and Wine which is implied in the phrase " visible presence." The Judge in the Court of Arches had no hesitation in pronouncing that the expression " visible

Views of the defendant on the visible presence.

presence of our Lord upon the altars of our churches," is in its plain meaning at variance with all the Formularies of our Church upon the subject, at variance with the language of the Service of the Holy Communion, of the Twenty-eighth Article, and of the Catechism; and that the doctrine which it expresses overthroweth the nature of a Sacrament even more than Transubstantiation." *
But the Defendant never explained how the sense in which he used the original words differed from that which the Judge considered as their plain meaning; or, if his language was susceptible of more than one construction, which it was that "passed through his mind in writing." And having expressed the same thought in two different forms of words, the one perfectly plain and simple, the other in the highest degree obscure and ambiguous, he was allowed the privilege of expounding that which was unmistakably erroneous by that which might mean anything or nothing.

<small>Charitable interpretations of the Court.</small>
It was perhaps a still more arduous achievement of charitable interpretation, and one which was not accomplished without doubts and division of opinion in the Court, to suppose that one who "adored Christ present in the Sacrament under the form of bread and wine, believing that under their veil is the sacred Body and Blood of Jesus Christ," might mean something essentially differing from the statement, that he "adored the consecrated elements believing Christ to be in them, and that His Body and Blood are under their veil;" and this notwithstanding His own assurance that the two expressions were intended by Him to convey precisely the same meaning. It is at least a distinction which it requires a very high degree of legal acumen to perceive. But I am glad that a majority of the Judicial Committee found it impossible to come to this conclusion, and were thus enabled to avoid the necessity of investing the Defendant with the halo of martyrdom. The legal condemnation could only have weakened the force of the moral

---

* Probably however it is no more than was meant by Mr. Orby Shipley, when he speaks of "God's Presence now shortly to be manifested on His Altar." "Card. Virtues," p. 71. It is perhaps to be taken as one of the points in which "Catholic" doctrine does not yet exactly coincide with that of Rome. An old Latin Hymn on the Sacrament began: *Adoro te devote latens Deitas, Quae sub his figuris vere latitas.*

sentence in which both Courts entirely concurred. The one thought that "if a private clergyman steps out of the ordinary course of parochial duty, to discharge the office of a public writer upon the most awful mystery of our holy religion, the least that our Church has a right to expect from him, is the knowledge and erudition of a theologian, and the use of the most careful and well-considered language." The other was of opinion, "that there might have been expected from a theologian dealing with this subject, if not a charitable regard for the feelings of others, at least a careful preparation and an exactness in the use of terms." No doubt in itself a very reasonable expectation; but one which has been so often disappointed, that it can hardly be indulged without some degree of presumption.

It was while the questions which have since been decided by successive judgments were still agitating the public mind, that the Royal Commission was issued for "inquiring into the differences of practice in Public Worship, with a view to secure general uniformity in such matters as might be deemed essential," by means of peaceful conference. *The Royal Commission on Public Worship.* This however was done only after a suit had already been commenced in one case, and the issuing of the Commission was not allowed to suspend the course of the legal proceedings. It was clearly desirable that the authority of Parliament should not be invoked for the settlement of any question which was within the jurisdiction of a legal tribunal; and so there is no reason to regret that the Ornaments Rubric, though it had been the chief occasion of the whole agitation which it was the object of the Commission to quiet, was left untouched. *Its results.* The fact itself seems to show that it would have been hardly possible, even if the Commissioners could have come to an agreement on this point, to bring any action of the Legislature to bear upon it without risk of very inconvenient consequences. But notwithstanding its failure in this respect—one which might have been anticipated from the manner in which the Commission was composed—it cannot be said to have proved abortive. It was indeed always viewed with dislike and suspicion by that section of Churchmen which is jealous of all intervention of the Laity in ecclesiastical matters, except as ministering to the Clergy; and it was to be expected that its work would be severely criticised. But I hope it will be found not to have laboured in vain, and that its recommendations, both as to the Rubrics and the Lectionary, when carried into effect, will prove a great gain to the Church. I have little doubt that the new Table of Lessons will make its way to almost universal acceptance long before the term allowed for retaining the old one has expired.

<small>Committee on the revision of the Bible.</small> A still greater benefit will, I believe, have accrued to the Church, whenever the Committee appointed by the Southern Convocation for the revision of the Authorized Version of the Bible shall have completed its task. The preliminary objections raised to the undertaking had been met by anticipation, when a like work was undertaken by St. Jerome.* In a time when minds were less heated by controversy, it would have been hardly possible to question the desirableness of enabling the English reader to reap the benefit of the progress which has been made in the course of the last two centuries in the interpretation of Scripture. The most important step for ensuring the ultimate success of the work was taken when it was placed on a broad Catholic basis, by the resolution, "that the members of the Committee of Revision should be at liberty to invite the cooperation of any eminent for scholarship, to whatever nation or religious body they may belong;" and by a subsequent declaration unanimously adopted by the Upper House, that "this House does <small>Its guiding principle.</small> not intend to give the slightest sanction or countenance to the opinion, that the members of the Revision Companies ought to be guided by any other principle than the desire to bring the translation as near as they can to the sense of the original texts; but, on the contrary, regards it as their duty to keep themselves as much as possible on their guard against any bias of preconceived opinions, or theological tenets, in the work of revision." That both Companies will faithfully adhere to this principle, I feel fully assured by the opportunities I have enjoyed of observing the spirit in which they have addressed themselves to their work. I

* See Professor Lightfoot, "On a fresh Revision of the English New Testament."

am also able to testify, so far as my own experience has reached, to the groundlessness of the apprehensions which have been expressed, either of needless alteration, or of the introduction of modern phraseology, not in harmony with the style of the Authorized Version. If in this respect there be any room for question, it is whether the Revisers may not sometimes have carried their scruples on the conservative side to an excess. It is no doubt to be lamented that they have been deprived of the aid of some eminent scholars, through causes which would have rendered such an undertaking impossible at any time. But I do not believe that the Revised Version will be found behind its age, or that anyone will seek in it in vain for the ripest fruit of modern Biblical scholarship. The Revisers would not be worthy of their office if they did not court the utmost severity of candid criticism, and their work will have to make its way by its own merits. There is no fear of its being imposed by authority, any more than this was the case with the preceding revisions of St. Jerome and the Authorized Version itself. Whenever it takes the place of that now in use it will be simply on the ground of its intrinsic superiority.

The work of the Ritual Commissioners unavoidably drew their attention to the Rubric of the Athanasian Creed, and various opinions were expressed, and proposals discussed, with regard to it. It is important to keep this fact in mind, because it has apparently been forgotten or ignored by some who have spoken as if they believed that the attempts which have been made to procure some alteration in the manner of dealing with it had been prompted by a desire to banish its doctrine from the faith of the Church.* How such a design could have entered any sane

The Athanasian Creed.

* Archdeacon Denison, in a letter to "The Times" of August 28th, has unveiled a "plot, in which Broad Church and Low Church—the last in its despair—have joined hands to fight against the Creeds." He has discovered that "the astute contrivers of the plot," as "it would not have answered their purpose to go straight to their work," "thought they saw a convenient by-way through the Fourth Report of the Royal Commission." The superiority of the clerical over the lay intellect in the detection of deep-laid plots, is placed in strong relief by a letter to the same journal of Sept. 18, from Lord Redesdale, in which his Lordship, speaking of the secessions which have been threatened in the event of the use of the Athanasian Creed being declared optional, is simple enough to say, that " so long as the first four sentences of

mind as long as the Nicene Creed, the Te Deum, and suffrages of the Litany, form part of our weekly service, and the collect for Trinity Sunday retains its place, it is not easy to conceive. But it is at least certain that the character of the persons who have expressed a desire for the alteration ought to have secured them from suspicion of such a design. The dispute was not between advocates and impugners of the doctrine, but between those who did and those who did not think the Creed suited for recitation in public worship. To fasten on an opponent an opinion which he disavows, in order to turn it into an argument against him, is a controversial artifice which in my judgment no eminence of station, no depth of learning, no power of eloquence, can make allowable. In the present case it has been freely practised, and I believe with the effect of misleading or intimidating many of the Clergy, who have been led to fear either that they might be unwittingly contributing to the success of an attempt most repugnant to their deepest convictions, or might incur the suspicion and obloquy of favouring it in their hearts.

The practical question. The practical question was entirely independent of the age and authorship of the Creed, and of the soundness of its doctrine. That could no more prove its suitableness for recitation in public worship, than that of the Thirty-nine Articles.* But questions have arisen out of the discussion far more important than that out of which they arose, because deeply affecting the rights of Churches, the liberty of individual consciences, and fundamental truths of morality. It is on this account that I feel myself constrained to dwell upon it at somewhat greater length than I should otherwise have thought necessary.

I hold that every National Church has a right to regulate its forms of public worship, and to make any change which it may deem expedient even in its most ancient usages. Whether

the Litany are used as at present in every Church on every Sunday, it is absurd to consider that doctrine would be abandoned by such permission, and wrong to act in a manner which may induce others to believe that it would do so." It must be presumed that his Lordship had not seen the Archdeacon's revelation.

* This was written before I had seen Canon Perowne's Sermon on the Athanasian Creed, in which (p. 27) he makes the same remark.

a document which has been variously described as a Creed, as an Exposition, as a Hymn, as a Homily,* and as a Pandect,† shall be publicly recited, and how often in the year, is a point on which the Church must be as competent to judge as on any of her Rubrics. Assertions, however *Right of Churches to regulate their forms of worship.* peremptory, that its omission from public worship implies rejection of any truth contained in it, as they are incapable of proof, are sufficiently refuted by a simple contradiction. The Article which affirms that it "may be proved by most certain warrant of Holy Scripture," leaves the use which may be made of it perfectly open to the decision of the Church. It is a simple question of Christian prudence and charity. Nor can the Article be fairly held to preclude any interpretation which may commend itself to anyone's mind, either on historical or on internal evidence, such as the opinion held by several eminent persons, that the damnatory clauses are the setting of the exposition, and no part of the exposition itself. The Article is unfairly treated when it is construed as if it was a trap laid for tender and timorous consciences, excluding all discrimination between different portions of the Creed in their relation to Scripture.‡ It cannot pledge anyone who subscribes it to any higher estimate of the Creed than was formed by Jeremy Taylor. Views widely differing from one another in this respect may be held with perfect consistency by persons who, with him, accept its contents as consonant with Scripture, that is, as capable

---

* "The Admonitory Clauses of the Church's Homiletical Creed." A letter to the Rev. C. J. Vaughan by Archdeacon Freeman.

† Bishop Ellicott's New Translation of the Athanasian Creed. By Rev. R. C. Malan.

‡ Dr. Pusey, in a letter to "The Times," dated Mayence, Aug. 10, has promulged a new Canon of discipline for the Clergy. He writes: "Clergymen have no plea to demand a change, for of their own free will and choice they received Holy Orders in a Church which recites the Athanasian Creed in her service." According to Dr. Pusey therefore no one has a right to enter into Holy Orders in the Church of England if he believes that any Rubric of the Prayer-Book is capable of improvement, still less to join in any attempt to bring about such improvement. It is a comfort to be sure that there is no immediate danger of such a degrading and pernicious yoke of bondage being laid upon the Clergy. But it is instructive to learn that there is a party which wants, not the will, but only the power to impose it, and that it is the same which in the meanwhile is putting forth "Pleas for Toleration." This is one of the glories reserved for the Disestablished Church of the Future, as it is pictured by some imaginations.

of being proved, or at least incapable of being disproved by Scriptural testimony.

<small>History of the Creed.</small> Every genuine feeling of attachment to the Creed, grounded on habit and early associations, is entitled to our sympathy and respect, but it cannot require that we should shut our eyes to historical facts. The veneration with which we might naturally regard a document which has come down to us from a very remote antiquity must be a little tempered by the reflection that, according to the earliest date that can with any probability be assigned to its authorship, it was the product of a very evil and unhappy time. The interval between the first and the fourth General Council—especially as it drew near to its close—was a period to which it is impossible for any thoughtful Christian to look back without sorrow and shame. It was no doubt a period of great intellectual activity, and adorned by several illustrious names. But it was also marked by a rapid decline of spiritual life in the Church. The leading minds of the age were absorbed in barren speculation on inscrutable mysteries, unrestrained by any misgivings as to the capacity of the human understanding. The misguided policy of the Imperial government, swayed by motives partly secular, partly religious, was bent on fixing a hard fast line of orthodoxy, as well in the interest of public tranquillity, as for the satisfaction of personal prejudices cherished by the rulers. Thus all the power of the State was exerted to fan the flame of theological controversy, to exasperate and envenom the spirit of discord by the distribution of temporal rewards and penalties, and to animate the combatants by the hope of Imperial favour, and the dread of Imperial displeasure, when that favour meant wealth, dignity, and power; that displeasure, degradation, exile, imprisonment, and lingering death. An ill-chosen phrase in a sermon, interpreted by an unscrupulous adversary, was enough to convulse society. The most solemn assemblies of the Church were desecrated by scenes of disgraceful tumult and brutal violence. It was then possible for such a man as Cyril of Alexandria, the type of a thoroughly worldly, ambitious, remorseless, unprincipled Churchman, to earn the title of a Saint. This

was the period in which the invention of the unfortunate expression Θεοτόκος gave the strongest impulse to that Mariolatry which has culminated in the dogma of the Immaculate Conception. To this period belongs the upgrowth of that monastic system which disfigured the Eastern Church with the wildest fanaticism, and the most degrading superstition. This was the age in which what little more than half a century before was the Church of the Martyrs, began to shed the blood of heretics. From it we have inherited much of that phraseology which has ever since inflamed the fierceness of theological hatred, by the confusion of error with moral delinquency.

I cannot but consider that freer use of unscriptural metaphysical terms, which distinguishes the Athanasian from the earlier Creeds, as another sign of progressive deterioration. <small>Causes of its deterioration.</small>

"The Nicene Creed itself," observes a very learned ecclesiastical historian,* "had many opponents in the East, partly because some believed that they found Sabellianism in the expression ὁμοούσιος, partly because it was thought wrong to lay down as Church doctrine such more precise definitions of that which until then had been undefined." Athanasius endeavoured to meet the objections which had been raised to the Nicene Creed on this ground by an elaborate apology, but only on the plea of absolute necessity.† The introduction of such terms was evidently in his view a blemish, though as he thought inevitable. Such was the feeling of the Nicene Fathers themselves. "It is evident," writes another historian who had devoted special study to this period, "how unwillingly they had recourse to the decreeing of a formula which was not contained literally in Scripture, and that it was only under the constraint of the extremest necessity that they set forth a formula at all." ‡ But the sufficiency of the Nicene Creed was frequently and strenuously asserted by Athanasius,§ to whom, nevertheless, it would appear that some persons still ascribe the authorship of that which bears his name.

Until the liberties of the Clergy have been straitened in a way which I hope I may not live to witness, no clergyman need scruple

---

* Gieseler, i., p. 373. † See Appendix, note A.
‡ Möhler, Athanasius der Grosse, p. 210. § See note B, in the Appendix.

to adopt the language in which Jeremy Taylor pithily stated what so many feel as the twofold objection to the public use of the Creed, the rigour of the damnatory clauses, and the metaphysical character of its distinguishing propositions.* But every one has an equal right to take a different view of the subject, and it would not be surprising if some new light had been thrown on each branch of the question by the active discussion it has lately undergone. The desire which has been shown to veil or mitigate the harshness of the Damnatory Clauses, and to exchange that epithet for one less jarring on the ear, would have been hailed with greater satisfaction by those who dislike them, if it had not turned out that the thing was to be retained in its utmost rigour under a milder name, or with some explanation which would leave it just as it was. What is gained by the substitution of the term *monitory*, or *warning*, I have never been able to understand. It seems to me only to perplex the question, without affording the slightest relief to those who are offended by the thing. None, I believe, ever doubted that the condemnation is general, and not applied to any particular case. The question has not been who are the offenders, but what is the offence which incurs the sentence of everlasting perdition. These clauses have been defended on various grounds, which seem to imply a wide divergency of views among those who maintain them. By some they are simply taken in their natural and obvious sense, and are thought to be sufficiently justified by our Lord's words at the close of S. Mark's Gospel: the difference of the conditions recorded by the Evangelist from those under which the threat is denounced in the Creed—the miraculous confirmation of the Apostolical message, and the Divine co-operation, "the Lord working with them," being overlooked or ignored, as if they were of no importance, and did not at all affect the responsibility of the hearers.

According to another view, the everlasting perdition is simply

<small>*Its objectionable clauses.*</small>

<small>*One view of them.*</small>

---

* Lib. of Proph., vol. vii., p. 491, ed. Heber: "Nothing there but damnation and perishing everlastingly, unless the article of the Trinity be believed, as it is there with curiosity and minute particularities explained."

the inevitable consequence of the abuse of human freewill. We are informed indeed that the damnatory clauses "cannot possibly apply to any but such as wilfully deprave the Faith, since the conscious consent of the will is essential to any act of sin."* But, together with this most certain and precious truth,† we are required to accept the paradox, that " it is as reprehensible to reject any part of the contents of Revelation as it is to break any part of the moral law." ‡ No doubt the reception of spiritual truth is often impeded by prejudices arising out of the perverse bias of a depraved will. But to maintain that this is always the case, that there is no such thing as honest, disinterested unbelief, is an arbitrary assumption, incapable of proof, and apparently contradicted by large experience. Yet it is only on this assumption that it seems possible to justify the assertion which has been advanced by some eminent Divines in the course of the present controversy, without any qualification, that unbelief is in itself sin. To me this doctrine appears to be subversive of the first principles of religion and morality. I can conceive no greater dishonour cast on the Divine character than is implied in the supposition that any one is responsible in the sight of God for intellectual any more than for physical infirmity. And I can hardly doubt that the persons who, in the heat of controversy, have been led to affirm this revolting paradox, unconsciously qualified it by a tacit reservation which implied some act of the will as the cause of the unbelief.§

Another view.

Considered in relation to unbelief.

---

* The "Damnatory Clauses" of the Athanasian Creed rationally explained in a letter to the Right Hon. W. E. Gladstone, M.P., by the Rev. Malcolm MacColl, p. 80. Some statements of this work will be found examined in the Appendix, notes B and C.

† It was more briefly, and not less forcibly expressed by Jeremy Taylor, sup. p. 466: "No man is a heretic against his will."

‡ Ibid., p. 88, and p. 163 : " I shall continue, till better informed, to believe that he who deliberately rejects an article of faith, transgresses God's commandments as really, and opposes His will as effectually, as the man who breaks the moral law." The quiet assumption, necessary to reconcile this assertion with morality and common sense, as well as with the writer's previous statement at p. 80, that the person who rejects the article of faith, does so, knowing or believing it to be divinely revealed, will not escape the attention of the intelligent reader.

§ Our Lord's complaint against the Jews was, " Ye *will* not come to me, that ye might have life."—John v. 40. οὐ θέλετε ἐλθεῖν.

The exception which has been made to the operation of the Damnatory Clauses by some other learned persons,* in favour of "those who by involuntary ignorance or invincible prejudice are hindered from accepting the faith declared in the Creed," does not seem to differ essentially from that which was proposed by the Ritual Commission: "that the condemnations are to be understood as a solemn warning of the peril of those who wilfully reject the Catholic Faith." In what sense anyone can be properly said wilfully to reject the truth is hard to understand. He may wilfully refuse to acknowledge what he believes to be true, but he cannot inwardly reject it. He may be unfaithful to his convictions, but he cannot alter them at his pleasure. The exception manifestly proceeds on the arbitrary assumption that the fault rests not in the intellect but in the will. And it does not seem to help us much if the proposition is modified by the statement, that men "are responsible for not believing wherever sufficient evidence of Divine Truth is furnished to them." † If the sufficiency relates to anyone else than the person to whom the evidence is offered, since that which is sufficient for one may not be sufficient for another, the statement is clearly irrelevant. But if that which is furnished is sufficient for the person himself, then it is out of his power inwardly to reject it. The inward acceptance is the test and the only possible test of the sufficiency. There can be neither sin nor merit in the withholding our assent from that which we do not believe to be true, as it is impossible for anyone to act otherwise. Whether

marginal note: And to involuntary ignorance and invincible prejudice.

---

* The Oxford Professors of Divinity.

† Dean Goulburn's Second Discourse on the Athanasian Creed. The whole passage, p. 32, runs: "Like the clauses in the Creed, the warnings of these two passages (John viii. 24, and iii. 36) are directed, not against wrong conduct, but against unbelief, showing clearly that unbelief is a sin, and that men are responsible for not believing, wherever sufficient evidence of Divine Truth is furnished to them." It is to be regretted that the Dean did not explain how the sin for which men are responsible can be committed without *wrong conduct*. To me the passages which he cites from S. John seem quite irrelevant. In John viii. 24, the ἁμαρτίαι are evidently quite distinct from the ἀπιστία, the effect of which is only that the sinner will be left to die in his unrepented sins. In the other passage, as Meyer observes, the μένει implies that the wrath of God was not the consequence of the unbelief, but had been previously incurred. A most lucid exposure of the fallacy will be found in the Charge of the Bishop of Peterborough, pp. 59—65.

unbelief is sinful must depend, not on the nature or importance of the doctrine propounded, but on the state of the unbelieving soul. That state is only transitory. All Christians would agree that eyes which are closed against the truth by an honest doubt will be opened to it in the light of the last Judgment. The only difference is, that some find it agreeable to their conceptions of the Divine Justice to believe that this final disclosure will be accompanied with a sentence of eternal perdition, while others shrink with horror from the thought of such a decree. But the more obscure, speculative, and mysterious the doctrine, and the less immediately it is connected with practice, the less reason is there for imputing the rejection of it to any sinful motive. Strangely as it may sound to those who have been used to hear heresy described as the most atrocious of crimes, there is no fair pretence for doubting that the errors of Arius and Apollinaris, of Nestorius and Eutyches, whatever may have been the weakness and faultiness of their characters in other respects, were purely intellectual, and that they were only misled by their zeal for the glory of God and the honour of Christ into taking one part or side of the truth for the whole.

What constitutes the sinfulness of unbelief.

The Athanasian Creed has the advantage of embodying the substance of the earlier Creeds; and the Nicene, which had so long appeared a sufficient exposition of the Christian faith, must be considered as the most valuable part of the later one. That which is most peculiar to it is described by Jeremy Taylor as "explaining the Article of the Trinity with curiosity and minute particularities." And it had been generally thought that its metaphysical terminology was ill-adapted to the intellectual capacity of the great bulk of our ordinary congregations. I cannot help retaining that opinion. We have been informed indeed from the highest authority, that the savages of New Zealand—an intelligent race, though still in a low stage of civilization—find little or no difficulty in those clauses of the Creed which, to the minds of many among ourselves, including some eminent Divines, appear very abstruse and obscure.* I do not question the fact,

Characteristics of the Creed.

---

* Speech of the Bishop of Lichfield, reported in the "Guardian" of 8th May.

even if it ultimately rests on the testimony of the New Zealanders themselves; for I think I have observed that the persons who are least apt to stumble at any passage of a difficult work are not always those who are most capable of understanding it. But among those who are not satisfied with Jeremy Taylor's description, there is a notable variety of language. Some are content to regard the things which he calls " minute particularities " as a safeguard, a fence, and a bulwark, of the main doctrine, while others speak of them as " the most central truths of the Faith." * I will only observe that, if they are indeed such, the great body of the Clergy must have grievously neglected a most important part of their duty as preachers of the Gospel. For they have acted almost universally—if indeed there be any exception—as if they thought that the subject belonged more properly to the lecture rooms of Professors of Ecclesiastical History than to the pulpit. I more than suspect that this has been the case with those whom I am now addressing. But if it be so, I am not prepared to say that they have withheld from their hearers any saving truth; and I doubt whether, if they were to dwell more frequently on the errors of the old heresiarchs, whose names have probably hitherto been heard by few in their congregations, and to show how the statements of the Athanasian Creed were pointed against them, this revival of long defunct controversies, however it might raise their reputation for learning, would be likely to interest or edify their people more than the topics on which they are now used to enlarge. How far it might usefully find a place in missionary work among some heathen races is another matter, but wholly irrelevant to the present question.†

marginal note: Various estimates of it.

---

* See a Memorial to Convocation of the English Church Union.

† A passage from a Charge of the lamented Bishop Cotton has become almost classical, as an argument in favour of the continued public recitation of the Athanasian Creed. It was cited at length in the Debate in the Upper House of Convocation on the 3rd of May, and is inserted by Mr. MacColl in his Appendix. Yet it could never have been quoted as in the remotest degree bearing upon the question, if it had not been arbitrarily assumed that the transfer of the Creed to a different part of the Prayer-Book—though much less than that would satisfy most objectors—was the same thing as " expunging it from the records of our Church." Equally irrelevant is the story of missionary experience related by Bishop Macdougal. Whether the missionary teaching of a Protestant Church is best drawn from any other source

Other advocates of the Damnatory Clauses have taken a line of apology different from that which we were just now considering, contending, though not all from the same point of view, that they have been entirely misunderstood. One thinks that the case to which they refer is not that of unbelievers, but of persons who have accepted the orthodox faith, and are charitably exhorted to hold it fast, and warned against the danger of apostasy.* Whether this is really consistent with the language of the Creed, may be questioned; but it clearly proceeds on the same supposition, that dissent from the doctrine can only be the effect of moral depravity. Another learned and able writer,† whose moral sense was shocked by the supposition that "assent to a speculative doctrine could be made the indispensable pre-requisite of eternal happiness," persuaded himself that the words only meant, "the Catholic Faith is a necessary preliminary for a saving communion with the Church, and the keeping that faith to the end in a corresponding life is the necessary condition of everlasting salvation."‡ The proposition so worded would probably have given no offence to any. But it is now many years since this discovery was published, and we are witnessing how little it has been generally accepted as a solution of the difficulty; and I see no sign that any of the

The Damnatory Clauses misunderstood.

Explanations not generally accepted.

than Scripture, is another question. But the use of the Creed for elucidation of doctrine, would be exactly the same in whatever part of the Prayer-Book it is found.

* See Mr. Vogan in the "Guardian," of 22nd May, and compare, "Canones Concil. Toletani," iv., 1.

† Dr. Donaldson, "Christian Orthodoxy," p. 473.

‡ Dr. Donaldson (u. s., p. 465) observes that Hilary of Arles, having before his eyes the contrast lamented by Salvian, between the licentiousness of the Catholics and the pure lives of the Arian Visigoths, "could not but feel that Christianity required something more than a precise form of sound doctrine; and he has left to the Church a Symbol or Creed, not less distinguished from other documents of the same class by the logical accuracy of its theological statements than by the earnestness with which it insists on the necessity of a sober, righteous, and godly life." I very much doubt that the clauses to which he refers had any such origin. I strongly suspect that they had a more specific dogmatical application. They seem to have been pointed against an antinomian heresy, of which S. Augustine speaks in a passage quoted by Gieseler (I., p. 437, n.) from ep. 214. Some, he says, "sic gratiam prædicant, ut negent hominis esse liberum arbitrium, et quod est gravius, dicant, *quod in die judicii non sit redditurus Deus unicuique secundum opera ejus.*" In contradiction to this doctrine, the Creed affirms that, at Christ's coming, all men *reddituri sunt de factis propriis rationem.*

others have made a deeper impression upon public opinion in the way of reconciling it with the obnoxious clauses, even if they have not rather provoked some degree of resentment, as sophistical glosses, reflecting on the understanding of those to whom they are addressed. I cannot anticipate any happier result from the researches which have been instituted with a view to emendation in the text of the Creed. However interesting they may be to the learned, I do not expect that they will be commonly believed to have made any material change in the state of the question.

<small>Compromise suggested.</small> No issue could be less satisfactory than an appeal to a numerical majority, especially as it would probably be found that the opinion prevailing among the Clergy is opposed to the general wishes of the Laity. The case is one in which, as no principle is involved unless it be one which has been fabricated for the occasion, a compromise seems eminently desirable, and for men of good will, of no insurmountable difficulty. It has indeed been called for by the admissions of most of those who, though strenuous advocates of the Creed, have acknowledged the need of some kind of qualifying explanation. But the temper which has been displayed in the menaces of secession which some have thought it not unbecoming to brandish, and which have supplied others with their strongest argument, must prevent us from cherishing any very sanguine hope of this kind. The reasonableness and decency of such a menace can only be fully appreciated when we remember that for eight or nine centuries, the Creed was never heard in the services of the Church, and was first introduced as a part of monastic devotion in the thickest darkness of the Middle Ages. That it should have been possible for persons to whom all look up with respect, to hold out such a threat, is both a calamity in itself and one of the most saddening signs of the times.

<small>The Laity only affected by the denunciations.</small> We have however been seasonably reminded by an eminent lay churchman,* that it is not the Clergy who are affected by the recitation of the Damnatory Clauses; but the Laity, who have the remedy in their own hands, since,

* Lord Redesdale, in the above-cited letter to " The Times."

if they disapprove of the responses assigned to them they cannot be compelled to utter them. And, in fact, I believe it would be found on inquiry, that in the great majority of our parish churches, the entire responsibility of these tremendous denunciations devolves upon the Clerk, whose voice alone breaks the silence which follows the Minister's declarations of orthodox doctrine. Under these circumstances, that the difference of opinion on this question should be allowed to make a breach in the Church whatever might be its extent, would be something worse than a calamity;—it would be a perpetual shame and reproach. If this evil can only be averted by a concession on one side or the other, I must say that I should be very much more loth to accept a concession extorted by menaces such as we have heard, than to make it. When one of two fellow-travellers threatens to part company if his wishes are not complied with on a point which to an intelligent bystander appears absurdly trifling, it seems to me that the more dignified course is to let him, for once at least, have his way. We must lament that persons of high position in the Church, and of eminent ability and character, should have been betrayed by the heat of controversy into a course of proceeding, for which we can hardly find a fitter epithet than *childish;* but to imitate it would certainly not be more manly. If we think that they have shown a deplorable readiness to sacrifice the general welfare to an arbitrary caprice, it would be the less excusable in us to follow their example. I do not say that this would be a perfectly satisfactory termination of the dispute. I do not think it would be a termination at all; but it may well be preferable to any immediate settlement in which both parties did not acquiesce. If the forbearance cannot be mutual, let us be found on the side of those who exercise, and not of those who withhold it. Only let it be clearly understood that this is a sacrifice to peace, and not a surrender of principle, or a pledge to bind anyone for the future.

<small>The mode of conducting the controversy deprecated.</small>

A much larger question than any of those I have been discussing, one involving the highest interests of the future, both in

Church and State—I mean the question of elementary education—still remains unsettled, and cannot be viewed without painful anxiety by anyone who has the welfare either of the Church or of the country at heart. It is the question whether the training of the rising generation is or is not to be divorced from religious instruction: whether those who, when they have reached manhood, will find themselves entrusted with a large share of political privileges, constituting their possessors a predominant power in the State, are to grow up in the fear of God and in the faith of Christ, or to be a law to themselves. We may lament that such a question should ever have arisen, and as Churchmen we might have preferred a different solution of the problem which forced itself upon the Legislature, from that which was adopted by the Government. But we can neither deny the urgency of the need which The Elementary Education Act was framed to supply, though we may believe it to have been often grossly exaggerated; nor can we undertake to affirm that under the conditions of the case, it would have been possible to provide for it by a simple extension of the denominational system, however we may wish that the experiment had been fairly tried. A measure which is fiercely assailed by the most violent partisans of opposite extremes has a strong presumption in its favour. It may not be absolutely perfect, but there is high probability that it comes nearer than any other to the best that could have been devised.

Elementary education.

The Act of 1870 is still on its trial. Its success in the carrying out of a compulsory system against the will of parents who are indifferent to the advantage of an education which they themselves never enjoyed, and who grudge the cost because they prefer their own pleasure to their children's welfare, still remains to be ascertained. Should it prove more complete than either the character of our own people, or the experience of foreign countries, would lead us to expect, there would still be room for doubt, whether the benefit of the new system will compensate for all that it has taken away; and we may question the expediency and the justice of sacrificing the highest interests of the many, who have hitherto enjoyed a fuller measure

Education Act of 1870.

of religious education, to those of the few who had been left entirely destitute. I say this irrespectively of abuses, through which the intention of the Legislature has been partially frustrated, by the erection of new schools where ample provision had already been made for the wants of the neighbourhood. But on the supposition of the happiest result, the value of instruction which is confined to the simplest rudiments of secular knowledge, may easily be overrated. I could not indeed admit that even such instruction is not an immense gain in comparison with the utter neglect to which so many thousands of children of the poor have hitherto been abandoned. Churchmen, but especially clergymen, who deny this, and denounce secular education as if it was a positive evil, and ignore the moral influence of school discipline in contrast with habits of vagrancy and lawlessness, are I believe doing more damage to the cause of religious education than its avowed enemies. *Injurious effect of the denunciation of secular education.* But they would be still farther from the truth, and in greater danger of showing themselves unfaithful toward their most sacred duty, if they treated such instruction as sufficient, or as constituting anything that deserves the name of education, and did not feel that it only adds a new motive for the discharge of that part of their office which relates to the feeding of Christ's lambs. And if their opportunities are restricted by the conditions imposed by the new law, it must be remembered, on the other hand, that those who are brought within the reach of their ministry, come with a better intellectual, and even moral preparation, than they might otherwise have received.

Hitherto the working of the Act has been generally favourable to the cause of religious education. We are not grieved to hear, though it is a complaint of our adversaries against the Act, that in the six months' grace which it allowed, grants were asked for 2,852 Church Schools, and that these applications were met in the most generous and even lavish spirit.* Nor is it painful to us to learn from the same authority that "there are now thousands of parishes amply provided with *Operation of the Act on religious education.*

---

* General Conference of Nonconformists held in Manchester, January, 1872, p. 185.

school accommodation entirely in the hands of the Church." * We do not consider it either as a calamity or as a reproach to the Act, that it "has enabled the denominationalists to cover districts with schools which will render School Boards unnecessary, except for the exercise of the compulsory power to fill those denominational schools." † We are glad to receive such witness to the fact that the Church has not been insensible to the gravity of the crisis, or unmindful of the duty which it laid upon her; and we rejoice that the public mind is not yet prepared to accept the secularist ideal. It might indeed have been expected that on the general question ministers of religion of all denominations would have been agreed: and it is saddening to find that so many have been induced by their hostility to the Church to enter into an unnatural alliance with persons from whose principles they must recoil with abhorrence, and to join the secularist party in its endeavours to exclude all religious teaching from schools aided by the State. I do not question their sincerity, when they declare that "it is the intense earnestness of their piety which makes them secularists in this matter of State education." ‡ But they seem to me to be playing with words when they cast all the care of religious education on an abstraction which they call *voluntary effort*,§ as if this phrase represented anything which was known to exist, and not something which has hitherto been wanting and has still to be evoked. One of them who holds that "there can be no perfect education without religion," and that "education properly considered must include religious teaching," is at the same time "bold to say that the Nonconformist Churches have not done their part sufficiently in the past in reference to this great matter." ‖ Happily, it would require something more than boldness for any one to say this of the Church of England, as compared with any other religious body. The so-called religious difficulty, which never existed outside the minds of persons whom it furnished with the only

<small>Nonconformist support of secular education.</small>

---

* General Conference of Nonconformists held in Manchester, January, 1872, p. 186.
† Ibid., p. 195.   ‡ Ibid., p. 152.   § Ibid., p. 256.   ‖ Ibid., p. 258.

plausible basis for their argument, may continue to serve as a convenient topic for platform declamation. But when we remember on the one hand the extreme slightness of the doctrinal differences which separate the great mass of Nonconformists from the Church, and on the other hand the difficulty with which the simplest spiritual truths are instilled into the minds of children, at the age at which they commonly leave school, the fear lest they should be imbued with a prejudice in favour of some particular shade of theological opinion, extrinsic to that which the Church holds in common with almost all Christian societies, can hardly be considered as serious.

I feel that I should be offering something like an indignity to my reverend brethren, if I was to exhort them carefully to avoid even the faintest appearance of exercising a proselytising influence on the Dissenting children who attend their schools. I am very sure that any such exhortation would be totally superfluous. I read with pleasure, as an illustration of what I believe to be a notorious fact, the testimony of Mr. Pryce, Her Majesty's Inspector of Church of England Schools for Mid Wales, who in his Report for 1870 observes : " I feel bound to say that, though I have made careful inquiries, I know of no single instance, under the present system, in my extensive district, where the National School children are compelled to attend church, or to learn any creed or formulary to which their parents object, or where any undue influence is brought to bear upon the parents or children for this purpose." Mr. Pryce proceeds to show that the real danger lies entirely in an opposite direction : of neglected, or imperfect, and superficial religious instruction.

Proselytising Dissenting children.

It is however satisfactory to know that there are some in whom the Christian has been too strong for the Nonconformist. Last May several of the most eminent Nonconformist Ministers and Laymen subscribed a Protest* against " the exclusion of the

---

* Published in " The Times " of May 7. It runs : " As strenuous efforts are being made to exclude the Bible by Law from Public Elementary Schools, we the undersigned (not connected with any established Church) believing that such exclusion would be a great national evil, feel it to be our duty publicly to record our disapproval thereof."

Bible by Law from Public Elementary Schools" as "a great national evil." We sympathize with the feeling which prompted this Declaration, and honour the courage which it manifested in its opposition to a strong current of opinion among their co-religionists. But we must remember that the important question is not as to the admission or exclusion of the Bible, but as to the use which is to be made of it. I would not deny that the simple reading of carefully-selected passages may be very useful for the more advanced scholars. But to employ it indiscriminately for a mere reading exercise must in general be something much worse than useless. There will be great danger of its being degraded in the eyes of the child, and associated with disagreeable recollections of a mechanical drudgery. But, on the other hand, where it is allowed to be not only read but freely explained, it may afford a sufficient basis for all that religious instruction which it falls within the province of the schoolmaster to give. It must be remembered that the Bible contains two parts of the Catechism, the Ten Commandments and the Lord's Prayer, on which the chief truths of Christian Faith and practice may be easily grafted. Let us be careful to bear in mind the important distinction between the proper function of the Schoolmaster and the Clergyman in this respect, and to beware of confounding them under the common description of religious teaching. A well-trained schoolmaster may be fully competent to supply all that religious instruction which stores the child's memory with historical or even doctrinal truths. He may often be better qualified for such teaching by his special training than the clergyman. But the duty of bringing those truths home, not only to the understanding, but to the heart and conscience of the young, is one which no pastor has a right to delegate to any one to whose office it does not properly belong. This is the proper work of your Confirmation classes. I hardly need observe that the present circumstances of the Church add in an incalculable degree to the importance of those classes, and to that of the work of our Sunday schools. But I hope that none will be induced by this consideration to make that work laborious and irksome, by a too severe and prolonged strain upon the child's faculties and attention. Unless it be made not only easy, but interesting and attractive, it will be likely to end in something worse than failure.

In proportion to the importance of educating the child is that of training the master. It is no exaggeration to say that the whole success of the work depends upon the character of our Training Colleges. Our own has had to contend with great financial difficulties, through the exhaustion of the funds of the Welsh Education Committee, from which, down to last year, it had received a considerable part of its income. The deficiency has been but partially supplied by an appeal to Churchmen of the two South Wales Dioceses; and our future is not yet so secure as to relieve us from all anxiety on this head. But it concerns us still more nearly to preserve the religious character of the College, and to prevent it from lapsing into a school of mere secular instruction. On secularist principles the teacher best qualified for the work of education in a secular school is one who, being himself destitute of religious knowledge and belief, is unable to impart any to his scholars.* Membership of any religious body, if not an absolute disqualification, is at least a disadvantage, and one who is free from all sectarian tendencies would be clearly entitled to preference. Hence a secular system will not be complete without the exclusion of all religious instruction from Training Colleges. Even this might not suffice to counteract the prejudices of a religious education in the students. The only perfectly effectual security would be a systematic infusion of anti-religious principles. This has not yet been proposed, and may have been seen to be a consequence which will follow of itself when the system shall have been fully carried out. Let it not be thought that I mean to impute any such design to Nonconformists who are contending for

Importance of Training Colleges.

---

* I find myself repeating a remark which I made in my Charge of 1848, p. 122. "If during the whole of the time for which the school is left under the care of the ordinary teacher, all reference to religious subjects was to be rigidly excluded, it would become a question, whether a teacher who should be himself utterly destitute of religious principles, and so incapable of communicating them, would not be best fitted for the office."

secular education. I have no doubt it is one from which all would shrink with horror. I only wish to point out that it is the logical result of secularist principles fully developed. To avert so frightful a national calamity as the upgrowth of such a race of teachers, is surely an object which deserves our most earnest efforts. But it would imply strange ignorance and inexperience to suppose that all who enter our Training Colleges are animated by purely disinterested motives, and would be ready to devote a portion of their time to work which does not form a part of their engagement, and for which they expect no remuneration. Hence <small>Appointment of a Diocesan Inspector.</small> the necessity of supplying the place of that inspection which has been withdrawn by the Education Act, and of substituting other inducements in the room of those which have now ceased to operate. With the aid of the Society for Promoting Christian Knowledge we have been enabled to provide for the payment of a Diocesan Inspector for one year. But that Society does not renew its grant; and the National Society has been prevented by the extraordinary pressure of other calls on its funds from immediately taking its place. Nevertheless, through the liberality of our Inspector, to whom his work has been a labour of love, and who consented to accept a salary reduced by the amount of the Society's grant, his inspection will be continued for another year, and, it is to be hoped, until the National Society finds itself again in a condition to relieve us from a part of our burden. In this Diocese I believe no other kind of inspection will be generally and permanently efficient.

I may safely assume that there is a perfect general unanimity among us as to the main end which we have to keep in view in this matter. In conformity with the spirit of the Education Act, <small>School Boards.</small> we wish as far as possible to supersede the need of School Boards by voluntary exertion. Both Clergy and Laity have proved the earnestness of their desire by costly sacrifices. We must however be prepared for a perhaps growing frequency of cases, in which we may be unable, and can hardly even wish, to prevent the appointment of School Boards. It appears from Mr. Pryce's Report that in his district "the managers of some Church of England voluntary schools are so convinced of the necessity of compulsory attendance that it is likely that a School Board will be formed in not a few parishes in order to secure this power." We may lament the fact, but all we can do is to make the best of it. It would be quite a mistake to imagine that a School Board is necessarily hostile to religious education. That must depend on the way in which it is composed. And it is therefore of the utmost importance that Churchmen, and especially the Clergy, should not be induced by their dislike of School Boards to stand aloof from them, but should endeavour to gain a place in them, and to avail themselves as far as possible of their position in behalf of the interests of religion. An opponent who expects that School Boards will soon be spread universally over the land, believes that the majority will chiefly consist of representatives of Church of England principles. Let us be doing everything in our power to realize his anticipations.*

The Returns which I have received in answer to my visitation queries show that out of 426 parishes 54 have School Boards. But of these there are at present only 7 in which there is a Board School. On the other hand, I find that there are only 14 out of the 54 in which the Incumbent is a member of the Board. I hope, and have no doubt, that this has been chiefly the result of causes over which the Clergy have had no control. *Diocesan Returns respecting them.*

We have had reason to be thankful both for some very useful recent legislation in Church matters, and also that we have been spared from some of an opposite character with which we had been threatened.

None of us I suppose would grudge a Dissenting parishioner a place of interment in the parish churchyard, though we do not see how it could be reasonably claimed as a matter of right by one who had been exempt from all share in the burden of maintaining the inclosure. Nor should we wish to make that privilege depend on the condition that the Burial *Burials Bill.*

* Manchester Conference, p. 162.

Service should be read over his grave, against the will of the mourners. But the Burials Bill of last Session would have established the right of all Nonconformists to this privilege, without providing any sufficient safeguard against the danger which there was cause to apprehend in many neighbourhoods, that it might be made an occasion for the exhibition of political or religious animosity, wantonly offensive to the feelings of Churchmen, and tending to the desecration of the place by scenes of tumult and disorder. We have reason therefore to rejoice in the defeat of a measure so one-sided and unjust; and the more because the alleged hardship which it purported to redress is one which would be less correctly described as either real or sentimental, than as symbolical; that is to say, it consisted simply in the fact that the churchyard at present belongs to the Established Church, and is thus an incident of an institution which the supporters of the Burials Bill desire to abolish. Viewed in this light, the attempt was very generally regarded by impartial observers as at once premature and imperfect. It was thought that if it might not have been more fitly postponed until the accomplishment of the general object which it was intended to forestall, it should have gone a step further, and have thrown our churches equally open to the like promiscuous use.

Inconsistency of its supporters. No doubt this inconsistency was not overlooked by the promoters of the measure. They had previously put forward a claim to "equal rights for all citizens both to the burial-grounds and to the churches."* But it seems to have been deemed politic to begin with one of these objects, that which furnished the most plausible pretext, and the right to the church will probably not be claimed until the use of the churchyard has been won.

The mismanagement of Church property—not always arising *Ecclesiastical Dilapidations Act.* from wilful unfaithfulness in those to whom it was entrusted, oftener perhaps due to improvidence, thoughtlessness, or the pressure of adverse circumstances, but always giving occasion to deplorable waste, and sometimes to the inflic-

* Manchester Conference, p. 11.

tion of grievous wrong on the families of deceased incumbents, and on their successors—had long been seen urgently to demand a remedy. This has at length been provided by the Ecclesiastical Dilapidations Act of 1871. I have no doubt that when this Act shall have come into full operation, it will be universally admitted to have been highly beneficial to the Church. But it is not surprising that the present burden which it unavoidably imposes should be more sensible than the future benefit. And this may account for the long delay which has taken place in the introduction of a measure so urgently needed. It will tend to prevent the recurrence of abuses so gross as have heretofore been witnessed, and it may be hoped will quicken in the Clergy the sense of a sacred stewardship in the administration of the temporalities of the Church, which, if it had been sufficiently lively, would have superseded the need of compulsory legislation. But I am afraid that the object will not be fully attained without some better provision for a periodical—say quinquennial—renewal of inspection. Without this I do not see how there can be any security for the main object, the keeping of ecclesiastical buildings in repair by means of a small occasional outlay. And I do not think it wise to cast the responsibility of this inspection on the Archdeacons and Rural Deans, at the imminent risk of disturbing their friendly relations to their clerical brethren, which it is so desirable to maintain unimpaired. The intervention of the Patron for this purpose, which seems also to be contemplated by the Act, will I fear only take place in very rare and exceptional cases. But it is easier to point out a defect than to suggest a remedy.

The Act of 1871 has been supplemented in the last Session by one which enlarges the powers of the Governors of Queen Anne's Bounty for the benefit of mortgagors, and will also put an end to many irritating disputes which have arisen on the subject of fees and charges, by the substitution of a uniform table, to be binding (subject to amendment or alteration by the same authority by which it is ordained) throughout the whole of England and Wales.

A still greater benefit, and one of a higher order, has been conferred upon the Church by the Act of Uniformity Amendment Act of last Session, which has removed the restrictions which had been imposed upon her in the administration of her spiritual patrimony, the Scripture and Prayer-Book. A shortened Order for Morning or Evening Prayer may now be used on any day except Sunday, Christmas Day, Ash Wednesday, Good Friday, and Ascension Day. With the approbation of the Ordinary, there may be used a form of service drawn from Scripture and the Prayer-Book, appropriate to special occasions, such as a harvest gathering. On Sundays and Holydays, a form of service varying from any prescribed by the Book of Common Prayer, may be used at any hour, in addition to the ordinary services. The doubts which had been felt as to the lawfulness of using the Morning Prayer, Litany, and Communion Office, as separate services, have been removed by an express declaration, and the liberty of preaching a sermon preceded only by a Collect, is no longer questionable. The benefit of these enactments will be more generally felt in Dioceses containing a greater number of populous parishes than in ours. But we do not the less rejoice in the gain which they will yield to the Church.

Act of Uniformity Amendment Act.

A like remark would apply to the very useful Act of last year, enabling Clergymen, permanently incapacitated by illness, to resign their benefices with provision of pensions. It is to be lamented that in this Diocese, very few clergymen are enabled by the value of their benefices to avail themselves of this excellent Act.

Retirement of incapacitated Clergymen.

This remark suggests another which concerns the condition of our own Diocese. I had hoped that by now I should have been able to announce the completion of the work which has been for so many years in progress at the Cathedral. But it has been delayed through an unforeseen additional outlay which was required to preserve the fidelity of the restoration. I will not deny that I have felt some disappointment at the tardiness of its advance; as I had hoped that a monument of which the Principality has so much reason to be proud, would have roused a

Restoration of the Cathedral.

larger and warmer sympathy, independently of its ecclesiastical character and uses. But when I consider the peculiarities of its secluded position, and the consequent wide-spread ignorance of its very existence, and the vast number of concurrent claims of like nature, both within and without the Diocese, I am led to think that I have far stronger motives for thankfulness than for complaint. It is a matter of great satisfaction to me to know that among those who have visited the place, there is only one opinion and feeling, of the highest admiration at the beauty of the work. During the same period a like work has been going on throughout the parish churches of the Diocese. I can address no body of the Clergy of any Archdeaconry, who are not able to testify this fact from their own observation. Considered with reference to statements which are frequently heard in quarters where there is great danger of mistaking wishes for proofs, as to the alleged exhaustion of vital energy in the Church in Wales, it is indeed a remarkable fact that such magnificent and costly restorations should have been proceeding simultaneously in the four Welsh Dioceses. Never certainly was such an allegation more flagrantly ill-timed than at the present moment. Regard being had to the relative tenuity of our resources, I do not hesitate to say that there are few Dioceses with which this will not bear a not unfavourable comparison, in respect to the exertions and sacrifices both of Clergy and Laity for such purposes. But the same consideration has made me loth to multiply calls for contributions toward Diocesan objects, for the support of societies whose income must have arisen mainly out of subscriptions of the Clergy. Though in this matter I have not acted on my own judgment, without consulting that of others, it is possible that some of my reverend brethren may be of a different opinion. But they will at least I hope appreciate the motive which determined my course.

And of Parish churches.

The state of the Church in Wales has of late attracted friendly attention outside its borders. It has been the subject of a Report and a Debate in the Lower House of Convocation, and more recently of papers and a conversation at the Congress at Leeds. We must all feel grateful for these marks of interest in

State of the Church in Wales.

its welfare, and it would be hardly courteous to pass them over wholly unnoticed. But I do not think I should be warranted in occupying your time with a discussion of the opinions which have been expressed as to the causes of our weakness, or of the remedies which have been proposed for it. The subject is very large and complicated, and one of which it seems peculiarly difficult, even for persons who have had some opportunities of observation, to take a view at once comprehensive and correct. And when I find very grave mistakes committed in matters which lie—on some points exclusively—within my own experience, I cannot help feeling a little distrust as to others with which I may be less familiar, and suspecting that what for the present is most needed, is a solid basis of well-ascertained fact.

I turn once more for a few moments to the consideration of our general prospects.

While the constant renewal of a direct assault on the Established Church, carried on year after year in Parliament, excited apprehensions which the event showed to be premature, it was thought advisable to organize a system of defence, to be carried on by an Association founded for this special purpose, under the name of the Church Defence Institution. I should be sorry to say a word that might sound like disparagement of an institution formed with such an object. Nor have I any doubt that it may do good service in keeping watch over the adversary's movements, and bringing them under timely notice, in helping to counteract the effect of misrepresentations injurious to the cause of the Church, and in stimulating and combining the exertions of her friends. But I could not honestly say that I believe much will depend upon any such movement, or that it has had any appreciable share in bringing about that favourable change in the general aspect of our affairs which we have recently witnessed. The stability of the Church, so far as it rests on its connection with the State, must mainly depend on the general sense prevailing throughout the country, of the work it does, and the benefit it yields. Platform addresses, and articles in periodicals circulating almost exclusively among friends of the cause, will hardly do more

[margin: Church Defence Institution.]

than confirm opinions already formed. That they should effect any change of conviction on either side can scarcely be expected. The question is one in which abstract reasoning, however specious, will have little weight to counterbalance the force of usage, association, and personal experience. Few things I believe have contributed more to strengthen the Church than the use which has been made of our Cathedrals since they began to gather within their once empty spaces immense congregations, for whom the simple Services of the Church and the power of the Word were found to be a sufficient attraction. I am sure that the clergyman who is labouring most diligently in his appointed sphere, is the most efficient member of the Church of England Defence Institution, whether his name appear in the roll of its associates or not. I am equally sure that no one is doing the work of the Liberation Society more effectually than one who neglects his duties, lowers his ministerial character, and forfeits the affection and respect of his people.

If we might assume the continuance of the ordinary course of events, without any revolutionary interruptions, we have reason to believe that the uprooting of the Established Church will prove a much more difficult undertaking than has been supposed by the more ardent spirits of the Liberation Society. But it would not follow that it may be safely left to defy all the forces arrayed against it by its native strength. I am however inclined to think that some of our friends have overlooked the difference between our position, which is simply defensive, and that of our adversaries, which is wholly aggressive. The tactics which are suited to one of the parties so situated may not be the best fitted for the other. I see no ground for the complaint which has been made as to the "apathy" of Churchmen in this matter. I believe there are few indeed who would be content to know that the Established Church will last their time, and would not be anxious to hand it down unimpaired to future generations. But I see tokens of a deepening impression in the public mind that, if this is to be, it must be the result of some new conditions of the Church's existence. I myself feel this necessity very strongly.

Difference between Churchmen and their adversaries.

These knockings at our gates from without and from within, this co-operation of parties most hostile to one another for the common end of our destruction, may not threaten us with immediate danger. But at least they are warnings which we ought not to neglect, that it is time to think of setting our house in order, before it is left unto us desolate.

<small>Church reform.</small> Church reformers have of late become a very numerous body, comprising perhaps very nearly all who take an earnest and intelligent interest in the permanence and welfare of the Church: though with a great variety of views as to that which is practicable or desirable. I should be loth to let this occasion—which I have so much reason to expect will be the last of its kind—pass by without plainly and unreservedly, though very briefly, expressing my opinion on this subject.

<small>Subdivision of Dioceses.</small> Among the points on which a very general agreement appears to prevail, one is that the Church stands in urgent need of a further subdivision of Dioceses. That there are some in which this would be highly desirable, perhaps we may say absolutely necessary for full efficiency of administration, can hardly be denied; and for the extent to which it is really required the practical difficulty might not be very great.* But there are some who would carry the subdivision to a length at which the difficulty would be extreme and the advantage very questionable.† It would involve changes which experience forbids us to expect, and would accomplish no important object which might not be much more easily obtained in a different way which has already been partially tried with success. The main end is of course to multiply, not sees, but bishops; and we have seen that this may be effected by the appointment of suffragans, without subdivision of the existing sees. A time perhaps will come when it will be thought to deserve serious consideration whether episcopal powers may not be delegated for purposes which have hitherto been

---

* See Visitation Charge of the Bishop of Norwich, 1872, p. 40.

† See an Essay on the Increase of the Episcopate by the present Bishop of Bath and Wells, in "Principles at Stake."

commonly supposed to require the presence of a Bishop, and particularly whether Confirmation is not of that number.*

A joint Committee of the Southern Convocation on appointments to Bishoprics, appointed in 1870, recommended a partial repeal of the Statute of Præmunire, with a view to giving the Chapter a right in the event of their objecting to a recommendation from the Crown, to make a representation of the grounds of their objection. I think that a revision of the present process of appointment would be very desirable, to remove a cause of just offence. But my wish would be that the form of the election should be adapted to the reality, and not the reality to the form. The present mode of exercising the power of the Crown, the form being amended, appears to me far preferable to either capitular election or episcopal co-optation. The committee conclude their Report with the expression of an earnest desire, "that all recommendations of persons for promotion to the Episcopate may be made in a solemn sense of the responsibility of such an act." In this desire all would concur. But in the very rare cases in which appointments to the Episcopate have within our memory been made the subject of complaint, there has been, as far as I am aware, no reason to suppose that, whether judicious or not, they were made without mature deliberation and a full sense of responsibility, or without a clear view of the objections which were or might be raised against them.

Appointments to Bishoprics.

The benefit which may be expected to result from the revival of Diocesan Synods, or of periodical Conferences between Clergy and Laity, must depend in a great measure on the circumstances of each Diocese. It is possible that my successor will be able greatly to extend the application of the machinery which he will find ready to his hand in our annual meetings of Clergy and Laity. Hitherto they have been held for

Diocesan Synods, Conferences of Clergy and Laity.

---

* Among the offices entrusted to Presbyters in the Primitive Church, Bingham (II., iii., § 5) enumerates "confirmation of neophytes" and "consecration of churches." Even in Jerome's time, the power of ordination alone was reserved to Bishops in person. The additional solemnity and impressiveness imparted to the rite by the Chief Pastor of the Diocese is no doubt a consideration never to be overlooked, but which need not always be allowed to outweigh every other.

the transaction of business, in which all take a more or less lively interest, and I must own that I have always been disposed to grudge the time devoted at such meetings to the discussion of speculative questions not involving any immediately practical issue. Perhaps I might also have shrunk from the difficulty of organizing an assembly suited to such a purpose. But I am quite aware that in other more favoured Dioceses the case may be widely different. And the Diocesan Synod has the advantage of being an instrument which the Bishop has entirely at his own disposal, while other innovations on the existing order of things mostly require a sanction of the Crown or the Legislature, which cannot always be safely reckoned on. But in its bearing on the general interests of the Church, its highest value can hardly be anything more than that of a preparation for larger measures, without which it may effect some local improvements, but will not materially tend to ensure the stability of the Church. I hardly need say that I lay no claim to any peculiar insight into the future. I do not pretend to know better than anyone else how long the Church, as by Law established, will continue successfully to resist every assault that may be made on her from without and from within, without any change in her institutions, or any reform of the most generally acknowledged abuses which check her progress and impair her usefulness by the mere *vis inertiæ* or balance of parties in the State. But as far as I can see, it does not lie in the nature of things, that her present state should last for an indefinite period without some organic change, and therefore I think it is the part of wisdom to keep this contingency in view, however remote the need may appear. The question which seems to me to over-ride all others, and which, as I think, must occupy more and more of the attention of those who wish to see the Church placed on a firm basis, is the reform, or rather the reconstruction of her representative system. Since the Canon of 1603 forbade anyone, under penalty of excommunication, to deny that "the Sacred Synod of the Nation in the name of Christ and the King's authority assembled, is the true Church of England by represen-

<small>Reconstruction of the Church representative system.</small>

tation," changes have taken place which compel us to regard this declaration as true only with respect to the time at which it was made, or only in the sense that there is no other assembly which has a better claim to the title. It is indeed entirely foreign to the question which we have now before us; for that question is not whether the existing representation is in accordance with either ecclesiastical or civil law, but whether it is adequate and efficient, or, on the contrary, imperfect and incompetent for the work it has to do.

I can speak on this subject without any prejudice against Convocation as it is. I am not one of those who disparage either its character or its work. I believe that it represents a fair proportion of the learning and ability of the Clergy. It has shown itself well fitted for the task of collecting materials on points requiring elaborate research, and of submitting the information it received to intelligent and often instructive discussion. I cannot agree with those who make light of these inquiries and debates, because they have not been attended with any immediate practical results. I do not consider it either as a misfortune or a reproach to Convocation that, being what it is, it should have done no more than it has. Nothing, I conceive, could have been less desirable, or indeed a greater calamity, than that it should have been entrusted with any larger power of carrying its views into action. For it is a partial and insufficient representation even of the Clergy; the Laity are not represented in it at all; and thus it is every way disqualified for expressing the mind and will of the Church. If anyone thinks that a Church —at least that the Church of England—has no need of such an organ, he must consider the revival of Convocation as a mistake, and all attempts at reforming and remodelling it as a waste of labour. I cannot believe that many earnest minds will be found to take this view of the object, though, in presence of the difficulties which beset its attainment, some may too hastily resign themselves to the conviction of its hopelessness. The experience of the interval which has elapsed since the revival of Convocation seems to me sufficient to show that no higher benefit than it has hitherto

Convocation.

yielded is to be expected from it under its present conditions; but not at all adverse to the hope that a change may yet be brought about in its constitution, which will open a new and brighter era in its history.

Union between Clergy and Laity, and between both and the Episcopate.

The great advantage which may be reasonably looked for from the restoration of the Laity to their rightful position, in which they would have a direct voice in the government of their Church, would be a strengthening of the bond of union, now in general so slightly felt, so lightly broken, between the Clergy and the Laity, and between both and the Episcopate. Let me say a word to explain my meaning on this last point. I cannot help observing that there probably never was a time when the Bishops were more frequently the subjects of harsh judgments and bitter invectives. It may be thought that if I lament this fact, it is from a personal feeling, because it touches the honour of the order to which I belong. But on the contrary, so far as that is concerned, I have reason to be perfectly content. When I see that the gravest imputation with which Bishops, as a body, are now assailed, is not any breach or neglect of the ordinary duties of their office, but the attitude they take up in the controversies of the day, and when I observe that, as a body, they are censured with equal severity by the extreme partisans on each side, I think I have a right to conclude that the blame they incur is indeed the highest praise they could receive, and that their conduct as a body, and on the whole, has in this respect been just what it ought to have been. But with a view to the general interests of the Church, the existence of such a feeling is much to be deplored. I think the Bishops ought to be relieved from the undivided responsibility which subjects them to so much unjust obloquy while it so greatly lessens the moral weight of their decisions. This, I believe, would be one of the many good fruits which might be expected from such a reform. Without it, I do not think it possible for the Church ever to put forth her full strength, either for the purpose of self-defence or for the carrying on of her work.

No thoughtful observer can doubt that the time which lies before us will be one of extraordinary trial to the Church, and especially to her ministers. It is not given to any of us to foresee the issue. Nor is it desirable that we should attempt to anticipate it either by anxious or hopeful forebodings, which must depend more on each man's individual temperament than on any substantial ground. I am not now speaking of a *trial* in the sense of suffering; but it is certain that the coming days will test the sincerity and earnestness of everyone's attachment to his Church, if not to the eyes of men, yet in the sight of God. He will have more power over it, both for good and evil, than in ordinary times, though it is painful to reflect that the power of evil may be exercised by simple indolence and negligence, while the good can only be accomplished by some amount of exertion and sacrifice. This however is a thought which will rather animate than deter all loyal and generous spirits, who would not wish, if they could, to offer unto God of that which costs them nothing. There is a call for a more than ordinary degree of devotedness. Everyone has something to offer, and the question will not be whether it is much or little, but whether it is his best, and offered with a willing mind. There are among us diversities of gifts and of administrations, but all subservient to the same Lord, all capable of being sanctified by the same spirit. One occupies a position of authority, from which his influence commands a wide range. Another is gifted with the power of enriching the Church with the fruit of his studies and meditations; of pleading her cause against her adversaries; and of winning wanderers into her fold. The higher station and the rarer gifts may involve a more perilous responsibility; but none who have received this ministry have been left destitute of ample means and opportunities for making full proof of it in the service of God through the Church. However narrow and obscure may be the sphere of their labour, it is the same work in which they have to take part, the same faithfulness which is to be shown in that which is least as in much, the same blessing which all are invited to share. In the sense of this unity of aim and effort, which is independent of all

Prospects of the Church.

Necessity of devotedness.

Beneficial influence of unity of aim.

fluctuations of human affairs, each will find comfort and strength, stedfastness and peace. While his zeal is quickened in the care of that which is specially committed to his stewardship, his sympathy will be drawn out to all that affects the welfare of the Church at large. He will be living not in and to himself, a life which is not merely his own, but is the life of the Church in Christ, or Christ's life in the Church which is His body. We shall then indeed all the more lament the controversies which disturb the peace, and waste the strength of the Church. But we may find consolation as well as warning in the fact that our condition in this respect is not worse than the *strife and divisions* which prevailed in a primitive Church immediately subject to Apostolical guidance. We may even view it with thankfulness, as a sign of a love of truth, which, if often passionate and one-sided, is always infinitely preferable to the quiet of apathy and indifference, and to the hollow uniformity imposed by a pretended infallible authority. But we shall not the less be striving to walk by the Apostolical rule, which, if fully observed, would be a remedy for all our evils, and a safeguard against all our dangers. "Following after the things which make for peace, and things wherewith one may edify another." * "Doing nothing through strife or vain-glory; but in lowliness of mind, esteeming each better than ourselves." "Looking not every man on his own things, but every man also on the things of others." In one word, "having this mind in us which was also in Christ Jesus." †

* Rom. xiv. 19. † Phil. ii. 3, 4, 5.

APPENDIX.

Note A.

Athanasius on the Unscriptural Phraseology of the Nicene Creed.

In reply to the objection: ἔδει περὶ τοῦ Κυρίου καὶ Σωτῆρος ἡμῶν Ἰησοῦ Χριστοῦ ἐκ τῶν γραφῶν τὰ περὶ αὐτοῦ γεγραμμένα λέγεσθαι μὴ ἀγράφους ἐπεισάγεσθαι λέξεις, he says: ναὶ ἔδει φαίην ἂν καὶ ἔγωγε, ἀκριβέστερα γὰρ ἐκ τῶν γραφῶν μᾶλλον ἢ ἐξ ἑτέρων ἐστὶ τὰ τῆς ἀληθείας γνωρίσματα, ἀλλ' ἡ κακοήθεια καὶ μετὰ πανουργίας παλίμβολος ἀσέβεια τῶν περὶ Εὐσέβιον ἠνάγκασε τοὺς ἐπισκόπους λευκότερον ἐκθέσθαι τὰ τὴν ἀσέβειαν αὐτῶν ἀνατρέποντα ῥήματα. (Syn. Nicænæ contra Hær. Arian. Decreta i., p. 282.)

Note B.

Athanasius on the Sufficiency of the Nicene Creed.

ἠξίωσάν τινες ὡς ἐνδεῶς ἐχούσης τῆς κατὰ Νικαίας συνόδου, γράψαι περὶ πίστεως, καὶ ἐπεχείρησάν γε προπετῶς· ἡ δὲ ἁγία σύνοδος ἡ ἐν Σαρδικῇ συναχθεῖσα ἠγανάκτησε καὶ ὥρισε, μηδὲν ἔτι περὶ πίστεως γράφεσθαι, αλλ' ἀρκεῖσθαι τῇ ἐν Νικαίᾳ παρ' αὐτοῦ πατέρων (l. παρὰ τῶν πατέρων) ὁμολογηθείσῃ πίστει, διὰ τὸ μηδὲν αὐτῇ λείπειν, ἀλλὰ πλήρη εὐσεβείας εἶναι, καὶ ὅτι μὴ δεῖ ἐκτίθεσθαι δευτέραν πίστιν, ἵνα μὴ ἡ ἐν Νικαίᾳ γραφεῖσα ὡς ἀτελὴς οὖσα νομισθῇ, καὶ πρόφασις δοθῇ τοῖς ἐθέλουσι πολλάκις γράφειν καὶ ὁρίζειν περὶ πίστεως. (Epistola ad Antiochenses i., p. 576.)

It appears to me that this passage, where the meaning of δευτέρα πιστις admits of no doubt, ought to govern the interpretation of the ambiguous expression ἑτέρα πιστις in the decree of the Council of Ephesus, which is explained by Mr. MacColl (p. 10) and others, to mean " another *faith*," that is, doctrine repugnant to that of the Nicene Creed. That prohibition sounds superfluous. But the Fathers at Ephesus had as good right, and as much reason, to forbid that which the Fathers at Sardica had declared ought not to be done, as those of Sardica to express such a judgment;

in which Athanasius fully concurred. The fact seems to me clearly to disprove Mr. MacColl's arbitrary assertion, that the Fathers of Ephesus and Chalcedon " had as little authority as inclination to forbid the imposition of a new Creed if circumstances required it." If that had been true with regard to them, it must have been equally true with regard to those of Sardica, in whose case it is palpably false.

Note C.

Bishop Jeremy Taylor and Mr. MacColl.

As I am not acquainted with Mr. MacColl's previous writings, I do not know how far he may have earned a right to look down with contempt on the intellectual side of Jeremy Taylor's character, and to restrict his merits to "charm of diction, affluence of imagination, and devotional fervour." Perhaps I may provoke an expression of still loftier disdain, if I refer to a widely different judgment of Bishop Reginald Heber (whom Mr. MacColl would probably let down as an amiable enthusiast), who, speaking of the Liberty of Prophesying (" Life of Jeremy Taylor," p. ccx.), observes, " On a work so rich in intellect, so renowned for charity, which contending sects have rivalled each other in approving, and which was the first, perhaps, since the earliest days of Christianity, to teach those among whom differences were inevitable, the art of differing harmlessly, it would be almost impertinent to enlarge in commendation." But it suited Mr. MacColl's purpose to decry the intellectual powers of a writer, whose views differed in many points from his own; and perhaps he could hardly help feeling some degree of antipathy toward one who was distinguished by strong sense, earnest love of truth, charity, and freedom from prejudice, quite as much as by the qualities conceded to him by Mr. MacColl.

Mr. MacColl could not resist the temptation of citing a passage from a work erroneously attributed to Jeremy Taylor by Mr. Lecky (see a letter of Archdeacon Churton in the " Guardian " of July 24), though, but for the purpose of damaging Jeremy Taylor's reputation, the quotation, even if it had not been a forgery, would have been utterly irrelevant: since if Taylor's fancy had been impressed with such a picture of the future state, it must have strengthened his repugnance to the damnatory clauses, which, so far from being, as Mr. MacColl represents, " milder," involved these dreadful consequences as the penalty of error. This however is a matter in which Mr. MacColl has a right to his own opinion or taste, and with which I have nothing to do. But in the charges which he has brought against Jeremy Taylor's theology, I am so implicated as to be constrained to take this occasion of noticing them.

I am not indeed directly concerned in the first charge, which in substance involves an accusation of gross ignorance and offensive levity. But I cannot pass it over in silence, lest I should appear tacitly to admit its justice. Mr. MacColl (p. 32) describes Jeremy Taylor as "a writer who could characterize the Arian controversy contemptuously as a dispute about a vowel, and who held himself at liberty to accept or reject the Nicene Creed," and as "saying that it makes no difference whether we consider the Son as ὁμοούσιος or ὁμοιούσιος with the Father" (which indeed would be quite true as to the grammatical, though not as to the conventional value of the terms). But though, when he inserted the damaging forgery from Mr. Lecky's work, he gave the volume and page in which it was to be found, he has given no reference, nor any kind of clue to the passage on which he grounds this charge of bad taste and unsound theology. He seems to have thought that his readers were likely to be more familiar with the writings of Jeremy Taylor than with Mr. Lecky's. No doubt he also presumed that all would give himself credit for a correct report of Taylor's statements, though he does not pretend to cite a single word. I am sorry that I have not been able to discover the passage. I am thus placed in a difficult and disagreeable position. Mr. MacColl does not scruple to tax Jeremy Taylor, who is unable to defend himself, with being "as a controversialist not always very scrupulous." But I might be thought uncourteous, if I was to say that this is exactly the impression which his own work has made upon myself, and that candour is among the last qualities for which I can give him credit. It appears to me not inconceivable, that he may have trusted too much to his memory, or have misunderstood the drift of Jeremy Taylor's argument. This is a point on which I must suspend my judgment until I see Jeremy Taylor's own words.

I have however a like complaint to make on my own behalf, which heightens my distrust of Mr. MacColl's accuracy. Mr. MacColl fancied that he had convicted me of something which he calls Pyrrhonism: and he takes occasion to remark (p. 18), "I cannot help expressing my regret that the Bishop of St. David's should have been a party to the hounding of Dr. Newman out of the Church of England a quarter of a century ago." I do not know that I was ever much more astonished than by this remark. Mr. MacColl gives no reference to any publication of mine to which he alludes: and I know of two only in which I could have done what he imputes to me. They are the Charges I delivered at my first and my second Visitation. The second of these was delivered in the autumn of the same year, 1845, in which Mr. Newman went over to Rome. This therefore could have no share in urging his departure; and the only allusion to him contained in it is in a note, speaking of him in terms of the highest respect. There remains then the Primary Charge of 1842. Few no doubt recollect anything of its contents. But everyone who does, or has the means of referring to it, is aware not only that there is nothing in it to warrant Mr. MacColl's observation, but that its whole tendency is as directly as possible the reverse of that which he attributes to me; and I think I have a right to call upon him to substantiate his accusation, under a penalty to which no man of honour can be indifferent.

But when he represents Jeremy Taylor as one " who held himself at liberty to accept or reject the Nicene Creed," and " claimed the right of sitting in judgment on the Nicene Council," and thus " repudiated the authority of the Church from which he received his commission," I am obliged to say that Mr. MacColl has entirely missed the point of the question, and has misstated Jeremy Taylor's position. It is not true that Jeremy Taylor held himself at liberty to accept or reject the Nicene Creed. As far as we can judge from his words, he appears to have believed it quite as firmly as Mr. MacColl himself. It is not true that Jeremy Taylor " claimed the right of sitting in judgment on the Nicene Council." The point on which he exercised his judgment, and on which the same right is claimed by the Bishop who " backed him up," is of a totally different nature, and seems to have been entirely misunderstood by Mr. MacColl. From his remarks on this subject, and from other passages in his work, I should gather that like many clever persons, he is subject to fits of absence, in which he is apt to forget to what Church he belongs. The Nicene Fathers were responsible for the profession of faith which they promulged: and this Jeremy Taylor heartily accepts. But for the Convocation of the Council, which is the thing that he held to be questionable in point of discretion, they were in no way responsible. The responsibility of that measure rested entirely with Constantine and his ecclesiastical Privy Councillor, Hosius of Cordova. Constantine, in his simplicity, believed the dispute which had arisen at Alexandria to be no more than a trifling squabble about words, which might be soon composed by a friendly conference. His ignorance was certainly excusable, since Hosius did not undeceive him. But it was morally impossible for the Bishops to disobey his summons, and equally so, when they had met, to refuse to declare what they held to be sound doctrine. That which Jeremy Taylor considered as open to doubt, was the wisdom of the whole proceeding, which is a concern of Constantine and Hosius.

It is true, Jeremy Taylor also thought that it would have been better to have kept the very words of Scripture, and not to have introduced such a term as $\delta\mu oo\acute{v}\sigma\iota o\varsigma$. In so thinking he shared an opinion held by many at the time of the Council, and, as I have shown, by Athanasius himself, who defended it only as a necessary evil. Until it is proved that every word of the Nicene Creed was dictated by Divine inspiration, everyone now must be at liberty to share that opinion, which does not in the least affect the truth of any article of the Creed. When Mr. MacColl

(p. 34) pronounces it " subversive of the dogmatic position of the Church of England," he certainly earns the distinction of having carried intolerance to its utmost possible length, and on his own private authority introduced a new limitation in her terms of communion, which no lover of truth could accept.

Mr. MacColl has had the kindness to instruct me with regard to the conditions required for the validity of a General Council. But his remarks are almost as irrelevant to Jeremy Taylor's position and to mine, as the bulk of his work is to the question of the Athanasian Creed. Nor do they appear to me of any great value in themselves, but rather likely to mislead his readers. It is true, as he says, that a Council may fully satisfy every other condition of a General Council, and yet not be entitled to that designation, unless it be received by the Church at large. The Council of Nicæa is acknowledged by the Church of England as having been stamped with the seal of that reception. But that is not the ground on which she requires her ministers to accept the Nicene Creed. The sole ground is that stated in the eighth Article. It is because it may be proved by most certain warrant of Holy Scripture, and, as is clear from the two preceding Articles, for no other reason. (See Donaldson, 'Christian Orthodoxy,' p. 419.) It is indeed most happy for us that she has laid this sure foundation, and has not left the faith of her children to depend upon the fact of reception, which it is impossible for anyone to ascertain. The theory is that the decrees of a Council claiming Œcumenicity are examined by particular assemblies convened for that purpose in all other parts of the Christian world, and if universally adopted, become henceforth part of the faith of the Church. This sounds quite satisfactory as long as no question is asked as to the meaning of the term *reception*, or as to the conditions of a valid *reception*. It may be that something short of express assent might be held sufficient. But at least it cannot be a submission extorted by fear. It must be assumed that the Synods or Churches, by which the decrees are ratified, were at liberty to accept or reject. But how precarious, to say the least, is this assumption with regard to the Byzantine Councils! At Nicæa, Arius, and the Bishops Secundus and Theonas, who with him refused to subscribe the Creed, were immediately punished with banishment, before any inquiry had been made to ascertain whether the Council really represented the mind of the Church, and was justly entitled to the name of Œcumenical. Bishops, who had the fate of Nestorius before their eyes, and were informed by the Imperial Magistrates that they must either accept the decrees of the Council of Ephesus, or avow themselves Nestorians, were hardly in a position to exercise an impartial judgment. The prospect of ending their days in an Egyptian mine, like the Bishop Alexander of Hierapolis, could be regarded by few with perfect indifference. The *reception* of the formulary decreed by the Council of Chalcedon, under the pressure of the Imperial Commissioners, appears to have been simply tacit acquiescence, enforced on all: on ecclesiastics under penalty of degradation. The object of the Imperial policy for centuries was to stifle controversy by a compulsory uniformity. And it is evident that it never occurred to Constantine to imagine that the decrees of Nicæa needed confirmation. Ὁ τοῖς τριακοσίοις ἤρεσεν ἐπισκόποις οὐδὲν ἔστιν ἕτερον ἢ τοῦ Θεοῦ γνώμη, was his language in his letter to the Church of Alexandria. (Socrat. 1, c. ix.) And as little did the Emperor Marcian intend that any of his subjects should have a voice on the formulary of Chalcedon. The theory of this period appears to have been, that for the decrees of a Council duly constituted, when confirmed by the Emperor, silence on the part of the Church was a sufficient *reception*.

The minority at the Vatican Council justly complained of the want of freedom which vitiated all its proceedings. But what was the moral influence of the Pope, however grossly abused, compared to the power of the Byzantine despots? Resting as we do on Scriptural authority for all the Articles of our belief, we can contentedly resign ourselves to this uncertainty as to the fact of reception, which might otherwise be perplexing. It is enough for us to know that the majority in the Council came to a right decision, and therefore that, whether it was freely received or not, we are safe in adopting it.

Mr. MacColl belongs to that class of persons whom prudence would dissuade from living in glass houses. He begins his Letter to Mr. Gladstone with the remark: "The real points at issue in the controversy on the Athanasian Creed have been so overlaid with irrelevant matter that it is not easy for the public at large to understand the exact position of the question." He is apparently unconscious that his own book furnishes the most signal example of the fact hitherto witnessed, having all the look of being largely made up of extracts from a commonplace book, which, as he might well think them too good to be lost, he has taken this occasion to publish.

He charges Jeremy Taylor with a breach of allegiance to the Church, "from which he received his commission," but leaves it doubtful to what Church he himself belongs. In the course of his rambles he lights upon the doctrine of the Fall, and elucidates it by the observation (p. 130): "It is the teaching of *the Church* that, in addition to that aggregate of natural endowments which we possess in common with him (Adam), and which constitute the integrity of human nature, our First Parents possessed a gift of Supernatural Grace, sufficiently powerful to sway the will in the right direction, but not strong enough to interfere with its essential freedom." I do not dispute Mr. MacColl's right to adopt this scholastic figment, of which Bishop Heber ("Life of Jeremy Taylor," p. ccxxvi.) observes, that "it can hardly stand the test of Scripture." But to whatever Church it may belong, it is no doctrine of the Church of

England, but, as far as appears, only of the Church—whatever that may be—of Mr. MacColl.

He reproves Jeremy Taylor for " flippancy," on account of his expressing the opinion we have been considering on the proceedings of the Council of Nicæa. But he does not scruple himself to make merry with some of the most solemn passages in the Prayer-Book. He has introduced a discussion on "imperfect views of the Incarnation," and observes (p. 153) that according to the view which he condemns, "in the Holy Communion no positive gift is supposed to be imparted. The Sacrament is only a symbolical picture of the death of Christ, well calculated to bring that event vividly before us, and to stir up grateful emotions in our hearts in consequence. *But the God-Man is absent—far away beyond Sirius and the Milky Way—and we are to ascend where He is in imagination and feeling. And this is what is called the 'spiritual presence' of Christ in the Holy Communion, or rather in the heart of the worthy communicant.*"

I say nothing of Mr. MacColl's perversions of the doctrine which he assails, and which I have no doubt he is sincerely unable to understand, nor of the incapacity which he betrays to conceive spiritual distance or nearness, or any that is not measured by miles or inches. But a clergyman of the Church of England might have been expected to show a little more reverence for the language of the Collect for Ascension Day, in which the Church prays for that very "ascent in heart and mind" which he represents as an idle dream, and for the *Sursum corda* of the Communion Office, which comes equally within the scope of his ridicule.

I do not think that Mr. MacColl has succeeded in demolishing Jeremy Taylor, or that he will escape the Nemesis which awaits those who wantonly assail the illustrious dead. But I have no doubt that his arguments will satisfy all who were previously of his opinion, and especially where he wanders farthest from his subject.

INDEX.

A.

Act of Submission, i. 214; obscurity of, 215; character of, ib.; principle of, 216.
Age, spirit of the, i. 50.
Anglo-Saxon Church, i. 203, &c.
Apostolical succession, different views of, i. 38; relation to the doctrine of the Sacraments, ib.; opinion of Dr. Arnold, of Rugby, 39; doubtful use of, in controversy, 40.
Aquinas, doctrine of transubstantiation, i. 241, 249, 250.
Archdeacons, visitations of, i. 147.
Arnold, Dr., of Rugby, quoted, i. 39, 49.
Article, the Eleventh, i. 32; the Twenty-second, 44.
Articles, the Thirty-nine, a standard of orthodoxy, i. 240; their literal and grammatical sense, i. 42; framed to admit different views, 43; Dr. Newman's application of the principle, ib.; their relation to the Prayer Book, i. 113.
Athanasius, on the Nicene Creed, ii. 351.
Athanasian Creed, the, i. 394, 395; ii. 317; the practical question, ii. 318; the Church has power to regulate the use of it, 319; history of, 320; characteristics of the, 325; damnatory clauses of the, differently explained, 322, 323; said to be misunderstood, 327; explanations of them not generally accepted, ib.; compromise suggested, 328; only affect the laity, ib.; mode of conducting the controversy deprecated, 329.

B.

Babbage, Prof., on Miracles, ii. 88.
Baptism, sacrament of, i. 114, &c.; benefit conveyed by, 115; tendency of opposite views concerning, 116; teaching of St. Augustine, and of the Church of Rome, 158.
Baptism, infant, i. 155, &c.; the case of baptised infants dying in infancy, 158; remission of original sin in, 168; prevenient grace, i. 156, 157.
Baptism, Calvin's doctrine of, i. 157; singularity of Mr. Gorham's tenet respecting, 158; objection to the doctrine of baptismal grace, 159; conditional or unconditional efficacy of, i. 160; bearing of the view taken of it upon the work of Christian education, ib.; Hammond's view of, 161, 166, 169; doctrine of the Church catechism, 162; statements of Bishop Blomfield and Bishop Bethell, ib.; notion of a covenant essential to, maintained by Hooker and Hammond, 166; Bishop Wilson and Thorndike, 167.
Bellarmine, *De Eucharistia*, i. 250.
Bellarmine, doctrine of transubstantiation, ii. 285, 286.
Bennett case, the, ii. 312; charitable interpretations of the Court, 314.
Berengarius, i. 331, 341.
Bevan Charity, the, i. 313.
Bible, relation of religion to the, ii. 79; history of the, 82; what is essential in, 83.
Bilingual difficulty, the, in Wales, i. 8.
Birmingham, King Edward's School at, i. 364.
Bishops, being Privy Councillors, should be members of the Court of Appeal, i. 172; but should not be the only judges of doctrine, 173.
Bishops, conduct of, with regard to Ritualism, ii. 148, 149; at the time of the Restoration, 151.
Bishops, address of, to the clergy of both provinces, ii. 147.
Bishoprics, appointments to, ii. 345.
Bowstead, Mr., his Report on the Schools in the Principality, i. 366, &c.
Bull, Bishop, his doctrine of justification, i. 33.
Burials Bill, the, ii. 337; inconsistency of its supporters, 338.
Burial office, memorial on the, i. 391; conscientious difficulties of the clergy, 393.
Butler's, Rev. W. Archer, Letters on Development, i. 186.

C.

Canon, the twenty-ninth, i. 399.
Casaubon, his rebuke of Cardinal Baronius, ii. 150.
Catechism, the, i. 112.
Catechism, Church, how regarded by Dissenters, i. 373; proper use of, 374.
Cathedral of St. David's, restoration of the, ii. 93, 94; 258, 259; 340.
Catholic Church, appeal to the, irrelevant to a question of Anglican orthodoxy, ii. 72.
Catholic teaching, that which is so called is at variance with the mind of the Church of England, i. 266.
Choral associations, formation of, ii. 156.
Christ, character of, ii. 25; divinity of, 28; human and divine knowledge of, 76; difficulty of the question, 77; attempt of Lower House of Convocation to settle it, ib.
Church, a free, ii. 142.
Church and State, relations between, ii. 206; union of, ii. 141.
Church, aspect of, externally, ii. 2; internally, 3; evils in the, i. 4; hopes of improvement, i. 6; evils not inherent in her system, i. 7; distinction between, and a school of philosophy, ii. 52; ideal of a national, 54; divisions in the, i. 87, influence of the, ii. 153; services of the, not sufficiently attractive, 154; remedies suggested, ib.; importance of a study of the Primitive, ii. 185; Church of the Catacombs and the Church of the Vatican, 187; of England and of Rome, 188; work of the, i. 190; spirit in which it should be done, 192; power of the State to sever its connection with the, ii. 218; prospects of the, i. 229, 247.
Church Defence Institution, ii. 342.
Church doctrine, popular expositions of, i. 13.
Churches built and restored, i. 143; improved architecture of, 144; condition of, in the diocese, i. 195, 196; restoration of, ii. 341; repair of, i. 9, ii. 258.
Churches and chapels, alienation of the masses from, ii. 43; prospect of winning the irreligious class, 45.
Churches and schools, building of, in the diocese, i. 309.
Church establishments, no express guidance in Scripture on, ii. 214; condition of the question, 215; movements affecting, 216; State countenance of, ib.; neither absolutely good nor bad, 217.
Church Institution, the ii. 129.
Church in Wales, the, ii. 34.
Church of England, aspect of, i. 349; contentions in the, i. 262; present condition of the, i. 151, 152; prospects of, ii. 304; fear of disorganization in, 305; Romanizing tendencies in, i. 183; compared with Church of Rome, i. 106; the true life of, 108.
Church of Rome, secessions to, i. 184; groundless nature of them, ib.; her special advantages, i. 106, 107; has forbidden or discouraged the reading of Scripture, ii. 5; language used in the Oxford Tracts respecting, i. 46; change of feeling towards, 47; charged with idolatry, i. 77, 78; controversy with, reduced to a single point, 104; vitality of the, ii. 264; character of, 265, 266; improvement in, since the Council of Trent, 269; her policy changed since the Council of Trent, ii. 273; spirit in which she should be regarded, 274.
Church order, value of, i. 18, 19.
Church principles, danger of neglecting, i. 16.
Church property, alienation of, ii. 219.
Church rates, i. 349; Report of Committee of the House of Lords on, 350; Abolition Bill passed in the Commons, 351; defeated in the Lords, 352; fallacy of conscientious objection to, 353; abolition of, ii. 97; state of the question, ii. 96; Braintree case, i. 231; motives for resisting, 233; objection to compulsion, 234; mode of levying, ib.; argument drawn from contests about, i. 355; concessions on this head will not satisfy Nonconformists, 356; amount levied by, ib.; effects of the cessation of, ib.; Report of the Select Committee on, 358; a commutation recommended, ib.; proposal for exemption, ib.; its probable effects, 359; agitation on the subject due to the Liberation Society, 360; ulterior ends in view, 361.
Church reform, ii. 344, &c.; an organic change probable, 346; reconstruction of the representative system most important, ib.
Church societies, support of, i. 315; withdrawal of Queen's Letters, i. 316; origin of it, ib., false pretences of the Declaration by which it was obtained, 317-319.
Clergy, conduct of the, i. 109; deficient supply of, i. 146; deficiency of, i. 7; importance of frequent intercourse and concert, i. 11; relation of, to the Crown, i. 211; report on discipline of the, 221; supply of, i. 225; the parochial, ought to be adequately provided for, i. 84.
Clergy Discipline Bill, i. 109, &c.
Clergymen, liberty of, in matters of opinion, ii. 36; resignation of, ii. 340.
Clerical court, impracticability of, ii. 310.
Clerical meetings, i. 13, i. 230; peculiarity

of, in Wales, i. 14; borrowed from Dissent, 15.
Cobb, Mr., on Reunion, &c., ii. 261; Romish doctrine, 275; the Jesuits, 277; transubstantiation, 281, &c.
Colenso, Bishop, publications of, ii. 59; committee of Lower House of Convocation, 61; his official position gave currency to his work, 62; effects of his mode of publication, 63; tone of his language, ib.; its assumption, 64; relation of his book to the doctrines of the Church of England, 65; action of Convocation, 66; mode of dealing with propositions extracted from the book, 70-80; remarks on the study of the work, 80-81; trial of, a mockery, ii. 143.
Collections, weekly, i. 320.
Communion office, the English, and the Romish mass, ii. 233; compared, 244; English and Scotch compared, i. 278; principal difference between, 279; Bishop Horsley's opinion, 280; omission of prayer of invocation in the English office, 281; language of the Scotch office not free from ambiguity, 282; Romish and English contrasted, ii. 161.
Communion Service, in second book of Edward VI., i. 243; ante-communion office, 244.
Confirmation, age at which the rite should be administered, ii. 127; instruction with a view to, i. 23; opposition to, i. 236; connection of the Catechism and, ib.; title of the office of, in Edward VI.'s Prayer Book, ib.; the office may be revised with advantage, 237; early preparation for, 238.
Conscience Clause, the, ii. 104; vehement denunciation of, 105; nature of discussions on, 106; Prof. Plumptre on, ib.; ground of opposition to, 107; view taken of it by the committee of the National Society, 108; weakness of their argument, 109; principles at stake in the dispute, 110; alleged violation of compact, 111, and interference with religious instruction in Church schools, 113; charged with insinuating principles of secular education into denominational schools, 115; is a necessary safeguard, 121; perpetuation of, 121.
Convocation, revival of, i. 174, 198; has not been either national or representative, 175; dangers besetting the revival, ib.; objects contemplated by it secured already, 177; further powers aimed at, 179; not properly representative, 199; the work of, 202; history of, i. 203, &c.; first session of, 209; twofold aspect of, ib.; original character of, 212; extension of, the term, 213; parliamentary, ib.; Act of Submission, 214; facilities afforded to, 216; right of clergy to return members to, 217; rights of the Lower House of, ib.; why it meets simultaneously with parliament, 218; suspension of its deliberations, ib.; in action of, 219; duties of a revived, 220; advantages to be derived from, ib.; character of proceedings, 221; committee on the constitution of, 222; joint deliberation of the two provinces, 223; representation of the laity, ib.; limits within which its functions can be exercised, 224; jealousy of, on the part of the State, 226; present state and prospects of, ib.; capacities of, for good, 228; change of opinion respecting, 286; unable to effect needful changes, 288; expression of opinion on books, ii. 66; first judgment of, since its revival, 67; its effects, 68; its judgment on theological works should be dogmatical, 69; dealing of the committee with the first proposition in Bishop Colenso's work, 70; with the second, 72; report of Lower House on the work not sanctioned by the Upper House, 74; its dealing with the third proposition of the Bishop's book, 75; fails to touch the real point at issue, ib.; dealing with the fourth proposition concerning our Lord's divine knowledge, 76, 77; serious omissions in the report, 78; reform of, 139; vindication of, 140; does not adequately express the mind of the Church, 347.
Cosin, Bishop, "History of Transubstantiation," i. 332.
Council of Trent, i. 44, 45; the history of the, ii. 265.
Councils, general, ii. 141.
Court of Appeal, constitution of, i. 172, 173; ii. 132; substitution of a purely ecclesiastical tribunal for, 135; excellence of the present, 138; proposed to refer doctrinal questions to an ecclesiastical council, 137; effects of the judgments, ii. 309; judgment of, on the Eucharist, 312; judgment of the, upon Ritual, ii. 237, &c.; distasteful to the Ritualists, 239; i. 246, 247.

D.

Davies, Rev. Llewelyn, on Miracles, ii. 88.
Declaration of the clergy on the judgment in "Essays and Reviews," ii. 122; its ulterior object, 123.
Denison, Archdeacon, his doctrine of the Eucharist considered, i. 267, &c.; erroneous interpretation of the Catechism, 271; his propositions irreconcilable with one another, 272; uses language which is the technical expression of a Romish error, 273; his views of education examined, ii. 114-120.

Development, doctrine of, i. 59, 60; how applied to establish the tenets of the Church of Rome, ib.; Dr. Newman's essay on, i. 102, &c.
Diocesan Church Union Society, i. 10; Church Building Society, ii. 97.
Diocesan Inspector, appointment of, ii. 336.
Diocese of St. David's, condition of, i. 2, 4, 85, 86; neglect of Church order in the, i. 67; condition of churches in the, ii. 92; church building in, mainly carried on by voluntary contributions, 95; improvement in the, i. 142; poverty of livings in, 146.
Dioceses, subdivision of, ii. 344.
"Directorium Anglicanum," the, ii. 158.
Disestablishment of the Church of England, ii. 228; how viewed by the clergy of different schools, 229; sources of danger, 230; would involve disruption, ib.; advocacy of, by the Ritualists, ii. 310; disapproved by the bulk of the clergy, 311. (See Irish Church.)
Divorce, law of, i. 289, 290.
Doctrine, definition of, i. 171; questions of, in a court of law, ii. 134.

E.

Ecclesiastical Commission, aid to be expected from, i. 8.
Ecclesiastical Titles Bill, i. 180, 181.
Ecclesiastical Dilapidations Act, ii. 338.
Education, elementary, i. 310; committee of Welsh, ib.; religious instruction in the Principality, 311; absence of a uniform system, 312; suggested action of the Welsh bishops in order to secure uniformity, 312; insufficient and inefficient schools, 313; remedies proposed, ib.; personal superintendence of the clergy, 315; management clauses, 126; misunderstanding respecting them, 127; ii. 330; Act of 1870, ib.; injurious effect of denunciation of secular, 321; operation of the Act on religious, ib.; Nonconformist support of secular, 332; Nonconformist protest against the exclusion of the Bible, 334.
Education in the diocese, i. 128, &c.; reports of Commissioners, 129, effort for the promotion of, 135; special fund towards, 136; progress of, ii. 99.
Education of the poor, i. 19-24, 89, 235; efforts of the Church, 90; encouragements to the discharge of this duty, 91; necessity of personal exertion, 92; religious instruction, 93.
Education, national, i. 117; government control in, 118; separation of secular and religious instruction, 119, 120; importance of religious teaching, 121; misunderstanding between the advocates of the two systems, 122; action of the government, 124; requires higher qualifications in the schoolmasters, 125; opposition to the government scheme has arisen entirely without the Church, 126, 336, &c.; proceedings of Committee of Council, 369; parliamentary grant, 370; received by Dissenters in Church schools, 372, ii. 252; low state of, 253; moral and religious training, ib.; value of secular, in checking crime, 254; line drawn between secular and religious, 255; provision for, in Wales, 256; establishment of secular schools, 257; duties of clergymen towards schools, ib.
Education, secular and religious, ii. 114-116; of the children of Dissenters, 118, 119.
Education of the World, Essay on the, ii. 126.
Edward I. summons a Convocation of the Clergy, i. 268.
Endowments, poverty of, in Wales, i. 7.
Endowed Schools Bill, i. 363; legislative interference unnecessary, ib.; operation of, on national schools, 365.
English, teaching of, in Welsh schools, i. 133.
English Church Union, report of, on Ritual, ii. 172.
Error, not a crime, i. 74; distinction between teaching it and allowing it to be taught, 75.
Essays and Reviews, ii. 5; the work of one school, ii. 51; general tendency of, 53; attention attracted to, by the character of the authors, 7; obscurity in, 8; form and conditions of publication, ib.; relation of opinions expressed in, to the doctrines of the Church, 9; unity of the publication, 10; public history of the book, ib.; attitude of the Church towards, 11; the Bishops' censure of, 12-13; apology for, in the *Edinburgh Review*, 13; refutation demanded, 14; clerical contributors to, 16; object of the writers, 24; decision of the Judicial Committee on two of the contributors, ii. 122.
Establishments—see Church.
Eucharist, doctrine of the, in the Church of England, i. 262; in primitive times, 263; language of the Reformers respecting, ib.; alleged want of explicitness in the language of our Church, 264; mystical and spiritual tendencies concerning, 265; importance of the questions raised, ib.; alleged Catholic doctrine of, 266; ambiguity of terms used, 267; declaration of the Court at Bath, ib.; beginning of the controversies concerning, i. 329; frequency of celebrating, i. 212; non-communicating attendance, 243, ii. 167; receiving of, by the priest

alone, 244; opinions of Bishop Cosin and Bishop Overall respecting, ib.; relation of the controversy to that on Baptism, 283; spiritual presence of Christ in, admitted by Bellarmine, i. 332; Justin Martyr's account of the, ii. 186; minor differences between ancient and modern usage, ib.; memorial on the, ii. 241; repudiates a corporal presence, 242, and transubstantiation, ib.; and innovations on the Eucharistic Sacrifice, 243; ignores different modes of celebrating the Eucharist, 244; consistency of its statements with the doctrine of the Church, 245; words of institution in the, i. 246; adoration of the elements in the, ii. 247.

Evangelical party, i. 30.

Evangelical party have introduced no innovations, ii. 306.

F.

Figure, meaning of, i. 340.

Figura, opposed to *Veritas*, i. 336, 340.

Freeman, Archdeacon, his "Principles of Divine Service" reviewed, i. 329, &c.; his doctrine of the Eucharist, 345.

G.

Gorham v. the Bishop of Exeter, case of, i. 153; two questions involved, that of doctrine, and that of jurisdiction, ib.

Gorham, Mr., his view of baptism, i. 156, 158; states what baptism does not give, rather than what it does, 164; contends against the unconditional efficacy of baptism, 165.

Gorham case, interest of, ii. 135.

H.

Habits, formation of, the chief thing in education, i. 23, 123.

Haimo, i. 345.

Hammond, remarks on Preaching, i. 15.

Havelock, Sir Henry, his opinion of the Church Service, i. 354.

Heresy, clause concerning, in Clergy Discipline Bill, i. 110.

Herman, Archbishop of Cologne, doctrine of the Lord's Supper, ii. 200-202.

Hincmar supports Paschasius' view of the Eucharist, i. 315.

Holy Communion, the doctrine of the, contrasted with the Romish mass, ii. 161.

Home missions, i. 225.

Hook, Dr., Letter to the Bishop of St. David's, i. 120.

Hooker quoted, i. 47.

Horsley, Bishop, quoted, i. 33.

Hyacinthe, Father, language respecting the Papacy, ii. 276, 277.

I.

Idiology expounded, ii. 43.

Idolatry, meaning of, i. 78, 79.

Immaculate Conception, doctrine of, i. 254, &c.; progress of belief in, 258; effects of its promulgation, 259; history of the, i. 322, &c.; the Pope's Circular, 323; popular ignorance abused, 325; various opinions as to the antiquity of the festival, 326; various modes of encouraging the belief in, 327; conclusions of Archbishop Sibour respecting, ib.; definition of, ii. 270.

Infallibility of the Pope, i. 256; belief in, ii. 275; real meaning of, 276; promulgation of, 291; precipitately decreed, 296; protest against, ib.; truth of the dogma, 297; novelty of the dogma, 298; assurance given that it was no part of the Catholic faith, ib.; viewed in relation to ecclesiastical history, 299; bearing on the world at large, 300; protest against, in the Church of England, 303; makes loyalty impossible to Roman Catholics for the future, 302; likely to widen the breach between us and Rome, 303.

Inspiration, not defined by the Church, i. 294.

Inspiration, different views of, ii. 50.

Intolerance, prevalence of, i. 252, 253.

Ireland, union of, with England, ii. 208; effected against the wish of the majority, 210, 288; position of, at the Reformation, 209.

Irish Church establishment, ii. 211; opinion of foreigners on its abolition, 212; theory of, ib.; attempt to vindicate, 213; effects of, on the union, ib.; method of dealing with the surplus of the property, 221; justice of disestablishment, 222; effects of the disestablishment, 223.

Irish Church, capacity of the, to maintain its ground when disestablished, ii. 224; its disestablishment viewed in relation to the English Church, 225; essential differences between the two, 226, 227.

Irish history, retrospect of, ii. 207.

J.

Jesuits, influence of the, ii. 277.

Judicial Committee of Privy Council, sentence of, not opposed to the Nicene Creed, i. 168; decision in the Gorham case, i. 170; does not sanction heresy, ib.; wisdom of the decision, 171; its rule for dealing with charges of heresy, ii. 73.

Judicial decisions, bearing of, on theological works, ii. 15; on the character of the Church, ib.

Justification, doctrine of, i. 32, 34.

K.

Kneeling, the declaration on, ii. 248, 281.

L.

Laborde, L'Abbé, his work on the Immaculate Conception, i. 255.
Laity, co-operation of, to be secured by the clergy, i. 10; regarded the Oxford movement with alarm, i. 61; admission of, to Synods, ii. 124; recognised in the *Reformatio Legum*, 125; difficulty of securing a representation of, ib.; exclusion of, from doctrinal decisions, 133.
Lanfranc, *De Corpore et Sanguine Domini*, i. 338.
Lay co-operation, i. 225.
Lessing on the Relation of the Bible to Religion, ii. 78.
Liberation Society, the, i. 360; its objects, 361; its mode of operation, 362.
Libraries and reading societies, i. 13.
Liturgy, importance of, i. 16; revision of the, i. 65; rendered necessary by lapse of time, 66; proposed, 374; rejection of motion for a Royal Commission, 375; causes of the rejection, 376; the question at issue, 377; alteration made on the second motion, 378; attempt to ascertain whether the clergy desired a renewal of the motion, 379; declaration against revision signed by 10,000 of the clergy, 379, 389; opinion of Convocation, 381; statement respecting it erroneous, ib.; Convocation not inconsistent, 382; nor the Bishop, 384, 385; how far desirable, ib.; provision for special services, i. 383; shortening of the Morning Service, 386, 390; circumstances to be taken into account, ib.; retrenchment of repetition, 387; administration of Holy Communion, 389; occasional services, 390; memorial on the Burial Office, 391; Ordination of Priests, 393; Visitation of the Sick, 394; Athanasian Creed, ib.; real aim of proposed revision, 396; arguments for, 397; proposal for State interference, 398, and for superseding Convocation, ib.; deprecation of such measures, 399; the 29th Canon, ib.; proposed "purification" of, i. 283; pretext for, 284; if attempted, would prevent beneficial changes, 285; attempt to conform it to the Romish mass, ii. 159.
Liturgy, need of a, felt by Nonconformists, i. 242; and by German Protestants, ib.
Livings, augmentation of small, by the Bishop, i. 150.
Lord's Supper, change in the administration of the, ii. 158. (See also Eucharist.)

M.

MacColl, Mr., his reckless charges against Bishop Jeremy Taylor, and Bishop Thirlwall, ii. 352, 353.

Mass, Sacrifice of the, i. 245, ii. 193, &c., 199; service of the, i. 78; the doctrine of the, ii. 168. (See also Transubstantiation, Real Presence, Eucharist.)
Masses, origin of solitary, ii. 168.
Mariolatry, impulse given to, by the title Θεοτόκος, ii. 32.
Maynooth Grant, i. 69, &c.; inconsistency of opposition to it, i. 73, 74; an act of justice, 80; likely to do not harm, but good, ib.; a reversal of a mischievous policy, 81; its probable results, ib.
Medd, Mr., on the Eucharistic Sacrifice, ii. 193.
Ministry, practical hints for the, i. 50, 51.
Miracles, denial of, ii. 16; bearing of, upon our Lord's person, 22; accepted for the sake of the moral lesson, 31; argument from, ii. 86, &c.
Missionary work, i. 95.
Morley, Mr. S., on Church Rates, i. 360, 361.
Mortara case, the, ii. 120.
Mosaic Cosmogony, essay on the, ii. 49.
Music, vocal, importance of, in education, i. 21.

N.

Natal, Bishop of, see Colenso.
National church, theory of, in Essays and Reviews, ii. 37-40; Calvinistic opinions adverse to, 42; drift of the theory, 47.
National schools in Wales, improvement in, i. 139. (See Education.)
Neology of the day, inquiry into, ii. 4.
Newman, Dr. J. H., i. 32.
Nicene Creed, objections to the, met by Athanasius, ii. 321.
Non-communicating attendance, ii. 167.
Nonconformists, relation of, to National schools, ii. 109; protest of, against the exclusion of the Bible from elementary schools, ii. 333, 334; practice of, with regard to subscription to formularies, ii. 59; recognition by, of the need of a Liturgy, i. 242.
Nonconformity, changed aspect of, i. 5; its hostility to the Church, ib.; prevalence of, i. 2; how to be accounted for, i. 3; in many respects salutary, ib.
Norris, Canon, on Religious Education, ii. 255.
North side of the table, argument on the, ii. 149, 150.

O.

Objective, meaning of the word, ii. 242.
Offertory, i. 68.
Old Catholics, relation of, to our own Church, ii. 303.
Opinion, freedom of, in the Church, i. 49.
Ordination of Priests, i. 393.
Ornaments Rubric, ii. 158, 235.

Oxford movement, the, its alleged tendency to Romanism, i. 56.
Oxford Tracts, i. 24.

P.

Papacy, position of the, i. 348.
Papal prerogative, the, ii. 266, 276.
Parishes, wide extent of, i. 8.
Parsonage houses, the Bishop's fund for the building of, ii. 98.
Pascal, remarks on the Unity of Mankind, ii. 27.
Paschasius Radbertus, quoted, i. 250; teaches transubstantiation, i. 329, &c.
Pastoral ministrations, i. 17, 18.
Pentateuch, the Mosaic authorship of the, ii. 74; historical truth of, 75.
Physical science, ii. 6; Prince Metternich on the study of, ib.; relation to faith, 17.
Pope, the, styled Vice-God, ii. 277.
Popes, amendment in the character of the, ii. 269; hostility of, to religious liberty, 271.
Powell, Prof. Baden, Essay on Miracles, ii. 16, 26; his view of miracles, ii. 86.
Prayer for the dead, i. 45.
Prayer Book, assent to, i. 113, 114; resources of the, ii. 155; free use of, i. 224; importance of adhering to the, i. 18.
Prayer meetings, i. 17.
Præmunientes, clause of, i. 210, 213.
Presence, meaning of, ii. 242, 243.
Presence of Christ in the Eucharist, ii. 247; a local, 248.
Presence, spiritual, ii. 357.
Propitiatory, meaning of the term, ii, 165.
Protestantism, misuse of the word, i. 48.
Pusey, Dr., promulges a new canon of discipline for the clergy, ii. 319; his interpretation of the phrase "sacrifices of masses," ii. 192; his "Eirenicon," 175, 192; "The Presence of Christ in the Holy Eucharist," i. 266.
Public worship, Royal Commission on, ii. 315; changes introduced in, i. 62; revival of obsolete rites in, 63; importance of avoiding offence in, 64.

Q.

Queen Anne's Bounty, ii. 339.

R.

Ratherius of Verona supports Paschasius' view of the Eucharist, i. 345.
Ratramnus, i. 329, &c., 339, 342, 343; his doctrine of the Eucharist, the same as that of the Church of England, 344.
Real objective presence, the, ii. 241; the visible presence, 313. (See Presence.)
Real presence, meaning of the term, i. 240; Capernaite notion of, 241; Hooker's view of, 246, 248; local limitation of, 270; the phrase foreign to the Church of England, i. 275; real distinguished from natural, ib., 276; importance of acknowledging, 277; importance attached to the doctrines of the, ii. 249.
Reformation, attempts to undo the work of the, i. 57; Romish views of, 284, 285.
Reformers, the, language used respecting them, i, 46, 48.
Regeneration, whether distinct from conversion, i. 163; Hammond's use of the terms, ib.; meaning of, i. 117, 155, 160, 163. (See Baptism.)
Religion, distinction between natural and revealed, ii. 33; in what sense revealed, ii. 79.
Renan, estimate of our Lord's character, ii. 23.
Reserve in communicating religious knowledge, i. 40, 41.
Resurrection of Christ, its place in Christianity, ii. 55.
Revised Code, effects of the, ii. 100; on training colleges, 102; on the labouring classes, 103.
Revision of the Bible, ii. 316.
Ritual, the question of, ii. 145; its past history, 146; lawfulness of ritualistic observances, 147; legal opinion on, 148; how received by Ritualists, ib.; advantage accruing from, 150; debate on, in the Lower House of Convocation, 160; Committee of Convocation on, ii. 180; cases in which judicial proceedings would be necessary, 181; the only remedy suggested, 182; conclusion arrived at, 183; jealousy awakened in Churchmen of an opposite school, 184; Royal Commission on, 252.
Ritualism, missionary aspect of, ii. 153; arguments in support of, 159; symbolism of, 161; spread of, 169; Romeward tendency of, denied, 169; recent phases of, ii. 231; application of the Fine Arts to religion, 232; how far beneficial, 233; the real question at issue, ib.; appointment of a Royal Commission, 237; Romeward tendency of, ii. 177; probable consequences of, in its effect on Churchmen, 178; on Dissenters, 179; a reaction, 183.
Ritualists, extravagant licence of, ii. 149; glaringly deficient in impartiality, ib.; character of the leaders, 157; Romanizing tendencies of, 161; repudiation of Romish doctrine by, 163; vestments, use

of, ii. 151, 152, 159; designs of, ii. 306; tend necessarily to litigation, 307; claims of, to be the followers of the old Tractarians, 308; difference between the two, ib.

Roman Catholic clergy, education of, i. 76.

Romanizing tendencies, i. 188; ii. 160.

Romanism, conversions to, i. 57, 58.

Rome, Church of, has no security against change, i. 185; policy of, 189; secessions to, i. 101; influences at work, i. 106, 107.

Romish aggression, i. 180; controversy, work on, recommended to the Clergy, i. 189.

Romish doctrine, meaning of the term, i. 44; claim to teach, by ministers of the Church of England, i. 57; approximation to, i. 269.

Royal prerogative, exercise of, i. 210.

Rubric, the, i. 54; obedience to, 62, 63; observance of the, i. 67; departures from, i. 16, 17; right of forming an individual opinion upon, ii. 234; bishops cannot modify or dispense with, 236; reconciliation of, with Church practice, ii. 151.

Rural Deans, i. 12; i. 149.

Ruridecanal Conferences, i. 12; possess an advantage over Diocesan Synods, ii. 128.

S.

Sacrament, definition of the word, i. 271; difference between the sacramental symbol, and the sacramental rite, ib.; objective reality in, 277; may be robbed of its specific character, 277; Court at Bath, its exposition of the, 28th and 29th Articles not binding upon the Church, i. 274.

Sacraments, efficacy of, i. 39; doctrine of, in the Catechism, i. 112.

Sacrifice, the propitiatory, of the mass, ii. 165; identical with the doctrine of the Ritualists, 166; contrary to the Church of England, ib.

Sacrifices of masses, and the Sacrifice of the mass, attempt to distinguish between, ii. 192, &c.

Sacrilege, what constitutes, ii. 220.

Sancta Clara, Franciscus a, his interpretation of the 28th Article, i. 241.

Scepticism and credulity, combination of, i. 105.

Scepticism traced to an enlargement of geographical knowledge, ii. 48.

Schism, danger of, i. 5; schools, circulating, i. 20.

School Boards, ii. 336: diocesan return respecting, 337.

Scotch Communion office, i. 280, 281.

Schoolmaster, proper functions of the, ii. 334.

Schools, building of, i. 145; schools, national, how affected by Endowed Schools Bill, i. 365; Mr. Bowstead's report on, 366, &c.; schools, establishment of, i. 314.

Schwarz, Dr. Carl, "Predigten aus der Gegenwart," ii. 55.

Services, provision for special, i. 286, 383; revision of occasional, 390.

Scripture and tradition, i. 103; Scripture, supremacy of, i. 295; infallibility of, 296; relation of, to the Church, 302; grounds of its claim to reverence, 304.

Scripture, divine and human element in, ii. 50; free inquiry in the study of, 61; its relation to tradition, i. 34; how to be interpreted, 35; the principle of the Anglican Church, 36; appeal to antiquity for its interpretation, how to be understood, 36, 37; the sole authoritative source of the faith, 37; language of the Church of England respecting, ii. 70; arguments grounded on, inadmissible in law, 72, 73.

Simon, M. Jules, on Natural Religion, ii. 46.

Society for the Propagation of the Gospel, i. 96, 97, 319.

Spiritual wants of the people, report of Committee of Convocation on, i. 224, 225.

Spirituality, identified with the Church, ii. 133, 141.

St. David's college, Lampeter, i. 10, 94.

St. Francis of Assisi, his authority pleaded against the private mass, ii. 195.

St. Peter, primacy of, ii. 262.

Stanley, A. P., letter on Subscription, ii. 57.

State, relation of, to the Church, ii. 40; duty of the, towards different religious bodies, i. 71; duty of the, in questions of religion, i. 71; may be compelled to support error, 72.

Strauss, view of the person of Christ, ii. 44.

Stuart, Mr., "Thoughts on Low Masses," ii. 196, 198.

Subscription, Clerical, ii. 144; object of the Act, ib.; subscription to the Articles, ii. 37; subscription to formularies, ii. 57; efficacy of, 58; practice among Nonconformists, ib.; in foreign Churches, 59.

Supernatural agency, possibility of, ii. 31; Renan on the meaning of the term, 32.

Surplice, use of the, i. 68.

Syllabus, doctrines of the, ii. 273.

Synod, no means of assembling a national, ii. 136; unfitted for discussing questions of doctrine, ib.; synods, Gregory Nazianzen on, i. 176; summoned by bishops, 178; synod, the Pan-Anglican, ii. 259, 260; synods, diocesan, ii. 345; revival of, ii. 123, &c.; admission of laymen to, 125; functions of, ib.; relation of a bishop to, 126, 127; purpose for which they are adapted, 129; objects contemplated by their restoration, 130; probable influence on the case of "Essays and Reviews," 131; inefficacy if opposed to the Judicial Committee, 132.

T.

Taylor, Bishop Jeremy, objects to the damnatory clauses of the *Quicunque vult*, ii. 322; on our Lord's human nature, ii. 77; assailed by Mr. MacColl, ii. 352, &c.
Temple, Dr., essay on the Education of the World, ii. 26.
Temporal power of the Pope, probable effect of its loss, ii. 30.
Tendencies of Religious Thought in England, essay on, ii. 49.
Theology and law, ii. 134.
Tradition, its relation to Scripture, i. 34.
Training colleges, bearing of the revised code on, ii. 102; importance of, ii. 335.
Training College, the, at Carmarthen, i. 137.
Transubstantiation, i. 240, 241; two definitions of, by the Council of Trent, 249; affirmed by Paschasius Radbertus, i. 336, &c.; transubstantiation, ii. 242, 281; distinction between the natural *body* of Christ, and the natural *mode* of its existence, 282; Council of Trent on, ib., 283; what is the exact doctrine of the Church of Rome, 283; extravagance of, 287, ii. 163; in what light regarded by the Church of England, 164; metaphysical difficulty involved in, ii. 190-192.
Tract XC., i. 42; its interpretation of the Thirty-first Article, ii. 192.
Tractarian controversy, i. 24; not a subject of universal regret, 25; has called forth valuable literature, ib.; led to a wider study of theology, 26; awakened an earnest practical spirit, ib.; fears entertained respecting it, 27; the controversy not really new, ib.; origin of the Oxford movement, 28; a reaction, 29; system to which it is opposed, 29, 30; differences among those who have engaged in the movement, 31; amount of departure from the doctrines of the Church, 32.
Truth, different aspects of, i. 47.

U.

Unbelief, in what sense sinful, ii. 323-325.
Uniformity, proposed amendment of the Act, ii. 55, 56; Uniformity, Act of, Amendment of the, ii. 340.
Union, necessity of, i. 400; between clergy and laity, ii. 348.
Unity, importance of, i. 100.
Unity of Christendom may be purchased too dearly, ii. 304.
Unity of aim, ii. 349.
Unity of Christendom, Association for the Promotion of the, ii. 170; object of, 171; condemned at Rome, ib.; hopelessness of the scheme, ib.
Unity with Rome, on the basis of common doctrine, ii. 173; difficulties in the way, 174-176; unity of Christendom, ii. 172.

V.

Vatican Council, the, not Œcumenical, ii. 291; convoked under different circumstances from the Council of Trent, 292; excludes a large part of the Christian world, 293; object in convoking, ib.; not free, 294; order of proceeding, 295; pressure exercised by the Pope, 296; character of the Council, 297, ii. 260; not an opportunity for reconciliation with Rome, 264; object of the, 271, 272; Rome, reunion with, ii. 261; not dependent on the Pope, 263; prospect of, 269; duty of English churchmen with regard to the, ii. 275.
Vestments, discussion upon, ii. 239; of the Primitive Church, 240.
Virgin Mary, worship of the, 1. 78; prayer to the, ii. 197. (See Immaculate Conception.)
Visitation of the sick, absolution in the office for, i. 394.
Voluntary principle, the, i. 354.
Vulgate, the, imposed by the Church of Rome as authentic scripture, ii. 267.

W.

Wales, moral condition of, i. 132, 133.
Welsh sees, proposal to unite the sees of Bangor and St. Asaph, i. 82, 83.
Welsh language, instruction in, i. 21.
Welsh nonconformity, origin of, ii. 227.
Wilberforce, Archdeacon, on the Eucharist, i. 239; object of the treatise, 242.
William the Conqueror, his ecclesiastical policy, i. 206.
Williams, Rev. Rowland, memorial charging him with false doctrine, i. 291; reasons for not acceding to it, ib.; difficulties involved in the case, 292; distinctions to be kept in view, 293; explanation given by the author, 297; his definition of revelation, 299; doctrine of

inspiration, 300; claims the authority of the Church in his favour, 301; view of the relation of Scripture to the Church, 303, 304; of Judaism to Christianity, 305; of the work of the Holy Spirit, 306; its relation to the incarnation, 307; essay on Bunsen, ii. 30, &c.; philosophy of, 34.

Wilson, Rev. H., essay on National Churches, ii. 35, &c.; relation of the essay to that on Miracles, 48; speech before the Judicial Committee of the Privy Council, ii. 87.

Word of God, meaning of the phrase, ii. 71.

END OF VOL. II.

www.ingramcontent.com/pod-product-compliance
Lightning Source LLC
Chambersburg PA
CBHW031422230426
43668CB00007B/397